The HISTORY BUFF'S GUIDE TO WORLD WAR II

TOP TEN RANKING OF THE BEST, WORST, LARGEST, AND MOST LETHAL PEOPLE AND EVENTS OF WORLD WAR II

THOMAS R. FLAGEL

CUMBERLAND HOUSE™

Published by Cumberland House, an imprint of Sourcebooks, Inc.
P.O. Box 4410, Naperville, Illinois 60567-4410
(630) 961-3900
Fax: (630) 961-2168
www.sourcebooks.com

Library of Congress Cataloging-in-Publication Data

Flagel, Thomas R.
  The history buff's guide to World War II : top ten rankings of the best, worst, largest, and most lethal people and events of World War II / Thomas R. Flagel. — 2nd ed.
    p. cm.
  Includes bibliographical references and index.
  (pbk. : alk. paper) 1. World War, 1939-1945. 2. World War, 1939-1945—Miscellanea. I. Title.
  D743.F53 2012
  940.53—dc23

2012021088

Printed and bound in the United States of America.
VP 10 9 8 7 6 5 4

Also by Thomas R. Flagel

The History Buff's Guide to the Civil War

The History Buff's Guide to the Presidents

For Clarice Mae Doty Flagel
1932–2004

CONTENTS

———◦———

PROLOGUE

───◆───

World War II involved every inhabited continent, killed more than sixty million people, permanently maimed another seventy million, and drove one hundred million from their homes. Never before had such devastation fallen upon the earth. The conflict generated some of the noblest deeds of courage and most demonic acts of cruelty ever committed in recorded history.

From the ashes came an enduring question: how was such a horrific event possible? In search of an answer, I interviewed many who had, from various vantage points, seen the conflict firsthand. To better comprehend their viewpoints, I asked them what they called the war. Witnesses generally agreed on a surname of "War" but varied on the prefix—the Pacific, the People's, the Great, the Good, the Awful, the Second European, the Stupid, the Terrible.

Walter Joseph Bryant, an American who experienced the Pacific theater as a nose gunner in a navy reconnaissance bomber, felt he could not give a suitable answer. He simply said, "Each man has his own war." His profound response eloquently synopsized the war's general nature and how it came to exist.

There was not one war but many. What humankind experienced between 1937 and 1945 was a catastrophic convergence, an abysmal host of wars. By their simultaneous appearance, the conflicts were able to grow beyond any logical limit, overlapping and interbreeding until they appeared to be a singular beast, a proclaimed "world war."

Understandably, this inherent complexity can be muddling if not frustrating. The mountains of available print on the war frequently add to the confusion. Military histories are often drowning in minutiae. Memoirs tend to be steeped in agenda. Biographies give a single portrait but often neglect the landscape. Lost in the names and dates is the big picture.

Presented here is a concise, convenient way to make sense of this most intricate era. The format and aim of this book are in keeping with its predecessor, *The History Buff's Guide to the Civil War*. Using top-ten lists, the intent is to provide a compelling overview, employing comparison and contrast to give a different and balanced perspective on people, places, and events. Every list begins with background information and criteria for the respective topic. Some are in chronological order to illustrate progression. Others are quantitative or qualitative, placing the more prominent elements of the war in their proper context. Lists for this volume were chosen for their respective ability to illustrate the fundamental aspects of the war.

A note on text presentation: where appropriate, names and words appear in SMALL CAPS to indicate a subject appearing in another list. In stating East Asian names and cities, the book displays transliterations commonly used in the West during the war years rather than the contemporary pinyin demarcation. For Chinese and Japanese surnames, the text employs the traditional order of family name first.

Though one surname is on the cover of the book, hundreds of individuals brought this work to fruition. Particular gratitude and honors go to the following: military consultants were Thomas O'Brien Sr., Walter Bryant, William Phillips Callahan, and Wendell Fry. On social and cultural issues, many thanks go to Dr. Joan Skurnowicz, formerly of Loras College, for her boundless knowledge of Central

Europe; Kent Wasson for his fluency in the Japanese language and social history; and Jerry Mach on civilian life in Eastern and Central Europe. Todd Erickson and Joseph and Robert Ortner provided considerable assistance on war films. Bob Yaw supplied exceptional insight on the conditions of Weimar Germany and the speaking style of Adolf Hitler. John Dankert served as a sounding board on topics of military leadership. In the critical writing process, the creative consultants were Michael Bryant of the U.S. Department of Education, plus Karl Green, Patti Hoffman, Sue Nading, Ann Rushton, and Marie Sundet of Prairie Writers. In addition, Mary Elworth gave much-needed marketing help. Dan and Michele Flagel commanded all computer and data-processing work and saved the manuscript on more than one occasion. As always, countless thanks go to Ed Curtis, Ron Pitkin, and the rest of the patient and professional staff at Cumberland House. Of the many archives, museums, and libraries to which much is owed, special appreciation goes to David Muhlena of the U.S. National Czech and Slovak Museum and Library in Cedar Rapids, Iowa; the SAC Museum of Omaha, Nebraska; the Airborne Museum of Oosterbeek, Holland; and the Atlantic Wall Museum of Oostende, Belgium.

The HISTORY BUFF'S

GUIDE TO

WORLD WAR II

"THE GATHERING STORM"

WARS BEFORE THE WAR

In the fifty years preceding the Second World War, Italy fought Turkey, Romania fought Hungary, and Poland fought the Ukraine. Both Nicaragua and Ireland fell into civil war. Iran, Mexico, Panama, and Russia suffered full-scale revolutions. The empires of Europe struggled to subdue their colonial and commercial holdings in Africa, the Middle East, and China. Britain managed to retain its crown jewels of India and South Africa but failed to master the populations of Afghanistan and Iraq.

Compared to other eras, this frequency of unrest was relatively standard. What had changed by the twentieth century was the volume and tempo of armed conflicts because the "art of war" was giving way to science.

In less than a lifetime, battleships tripled in size. The largest artillery shells grew from the weight of a man to the weight of an automobile, from a maximum range of two miles to more than fifty. Aircraft evolved from puttering mobile machine guns to deafening heavy bombers. This onslaught of "progress" provoked a haunting fear that warfare was spiraling out of control.[1]

Despite efforts for peace, military events proceeded. As was feared, old antagonisms and new technologies bonded together and became highly unstable, reflected by the conflicts cited here. Following in chronological order are the ten most significant military conflicts preceding World War II, judged by their contribution to the critical mass of rivalries that spawned the global chain reaction.

1. SINO-JAPANESE WAR (1894–95)

Domestic unrest in Korea at the onset of 1894 prompted both China and Japan to send in troops. Rather than instill peace, the simultaneous arrival led to immediate escalation.

Within months a modernized Japanese army conquered most of Korea, and its superior navy controlled the Yellow Sea. Early the following spring a Japanese offensive pushed into northeast China and began a grand southwesterly sweep toward then-capital Peking (Beijing). An ultrapatriotic Japanese public, euphoric over huge gains at minimal cost, called for the conquering of all China. Yet Japanese officials feared a massive Asian power vacuum if the Qing dynasty collapsed altogether and chose instead to accept peace terms.

With 17,000 fatalities, mostly to the harsh Manchurian climate, Japan acquired Formosa (Taiwan), rights to sail the Yangzte, access to four major Chinese ports, permission to establish factories on the mainland, and payments from the Chinese government equaling millions of dollars.[2]

Before the eight-month war, Japan was a rising Asian entity, yet its military was unproven. After the war, the formerly isolated archipelago had become an international empire with nearly half its national budget going toward defense.[3]

The Japanese Empire launched its inaugural attack in the Sino-Japanese War in the same fashion it would do later in the Russo-Japanese War and the Second World War, by failing to precede the offensive with a declaration of war.

2. SPANISH-AMERICAN WAR (1898)

The Spanish monarchy subjected Cuba, its last imperial jewel, to years of widespread poverty and corruption. By 1895 the Cubans began to fight back. In the United States, farmers expressed widespread support for the agricultural islanders, and investors expressed widespread interest in Cuba's plantations, mines, and railroads.

Relentless public pressure in the United States induced otherwise isolationist President William McKinley to send the USS *Maine* into Havana Harbor, where it exploded and sank under mysterious circumstances. In short order, the United States declared war on Spain and promptly routed the unmotivated and outdated Spanish navy off the Philippines and Cuba. In defeat, Spain lost its last modest holding in a hemisphere it once dominated. So, too, the United States underwent a transformation.

The U.S. Eighth Army embarks for Cuba in 1898, marking the last days of a once-global Spanish Empire.

In the twenty years before the Spanish-American War, the United States participated in virtually no international armed conflicts nor made territorial acquisitions outside North America, except for gaining exclusive rights in 1887 to a Pacific island port called PEARL HARBOR.[4]

In the twenty years after the declaration of war with Spain, the United States conducted military operations in China, Panama, Cuba, Honduras, Nicaragua, Haiti, Mexico, the Dominican Republic, France, and Russia. It also acquired the Hawaiian Islands, Eastern Samoa, Guam,

Wake Island, and Puerto Rico; built and controlled the Panama Canal; and claimed stewardship over the seven thousand islands and seven million inhabitants of the Philippines. These forays, however profitable, would later compromise an American desire for isolation.

The Spanish-American War turned a former undersecretary of the navy into a national celebrity: First U.S. Volunteer Cavalry commander Theodore Roosevelt.

---

3. RUSSO-JAPANESE WAR (1904–5)

Second-tier world powers Russia and Japan were looking to expand their empires, but their options were limited. The Monroe Doctrine proclaimed South America as off-limits. Europe held much of Africa, Australia, South and Southeast Asia, and coastal China. The leftovers appeared to be Korea and the Chinese province of Manchuria. Both Russia and Japan had made inroads to the politically weak region, securing ports, rail lines, and one-sided commercial agreements.

In an attempt to push Russia out, Japan launched a surprise naval attack on Russian-held Port Arthur at the tip of the Liaotung Peninsula just west of Korea. Two days later the Japanese declared war.

Japan's land forces then pushed through Korea, driving northwest toward the key rail junction of Mukden and southwest to link up with its navy surrounding Port Arthur. Fighting lasted for months. The total number of troops deployed by both sides surpassed a million, and total casualties reached hundreds of thousands, but Japan's short supply lines made for faster reinforcements.

In desperation, Russia launched much of its Baltic fleet, sending it around Europe, Africa, and across the Indian Ocean. The armada sailed for nearly nine months, only to be annihilated by the waiting Japanese navy at the battle of Tsushima Straits. Of eight Russian battleships, eight cruisers, nine destroyers, and a number of smaller ships, all but three vessels were either sunk, captured, or bottled up in neutral ports.

Defeat cost Russia half of sprawling Sakhalin Island, most of southern Manchuria, and all of Korea. Worse, the disillusioned home front exploded with strikes, revolts, sabotage, and political assassinations. Severely discredited, the Romanov dynasty of three centuries would endure only twelve more years.

Japanese artillery fires on Port Arthur in the Russo-Japanese War.

In Japan, patriotism boomed. Never before had an East Asian nation defeated a European power. But the price of victory nearly exhausted the island country. Public and military officials alike developed a heightened awareness of their limited resources, and Japan expanded its Asian sphere of influence accordingly.

The Russo-Japanese conflict also offered a daunting picture of warfare in the new century. Fighting saw wide use of torpedo boats, searchlights, rockets, modern battleships, and machine guns.

The May 1905 battle of Tsushima Straits involved almost one hundred ships yet lasted less than an hour. An imperial flag aloft one of the Japanese battleships would fly again thirty-six years later—at the mast of the flagship leading the attack on Pearl Harbor.

4. THE FIRST WORLD WAR (1914–18)

By 1914 the collective body of knowledge on weaponry stood ready for a great leap forward. European engineers and industry created limited numbers of armored battleships, reliable machine guns, twin-engine bombers, antipersonnel blistering agents, diesel submarines, rudimentary tanks, and long-range artillery. Perhaps the ferocity of such devices would have remained hidden had imperial egos remained manageable. But no such sobriety reigned among the major kingdoms, and a small demonstration of ethnic unrest in Sarajevo abruptly escalated into a contest dominated by factions and factories.

Sparing the details of the four-year war, a synopsis of its aftermath reads like a doomsday primer. The Poles lost nearly two million buildings, most of their livestock, and one million military and two million civilian casualties. One million Armenians perished in a Turkish-led genocide. Monstrously powerful artillery accounted for seven of ten battlefield deaths, mangling animals and men so badly that governments destroyed much of the photographic evidence for fear of domestic backlash. Fighting obliterated whole areas of northeast France and Belgium, leveled homes, buried factories, and seeded farmlands with tons of unexploded ordnance. At least eight million European children were orphaned.[5]

It was by all measures the bloodiest war in history, ending the lives of eighteen million people as well as the empires of Russia, the

French troops prepare to go over the top. The horror of the Somme and the Marne would scar the French national psyche for decades.

Ottomans, Austria, and Germany. Its lethality also severely wounded the empires of France and Britain and shocked latecomer United States away from foreign entanglements for nearly a generation.

In the last year of the war, Spanish influenza broke out among the combatants, and modern transportation unleashed the virus globally. In eighteen months, the pestilence managed to kill more than twenty million people worldwide. More than half a million Americans perished—ten times the number lost in battle during the war.

5. RUSSIAN CIVIL WAR (1917–21)

In October 1917 the Bolshevik Party of Vladimir Lenin staged a successful coup d'état against the short-lived provisional government. Much of Lenin's success stemmed from his simple promise of "peace, land, bread." However, in negotiating peace with Germany during World War I, the Bolsheviks surrendered thousands of square miles of land, much of it rich in grain and mineral deposits. As a result, the price of bread rocketed one thousand percent in a year's time. In response, peasants, army officers, Cossacks, royalists, and factory workers turned against the Bolshevik (newly dubbed Communist) regime, sending the largest state on earth into civil war.

Fighting erupted from the Baltic to the Pacific and promptly spread to neighboring countries, including Latvia, Lithuania, Estonia, Finland, and Poland. Crisscrossing armies leveled villages, burned crops, slaughtered people and animals with equal haste, and confiscated or destroyed scarce food and shelter. The Ukrainian capital, Kiev, exchanged hands sixteen times.[6]

After more than three years of bloodshed, the poorly armed but well-organized Reds conquered a hopelessly divided opposition. Victory came at the price of an obliterated industrial base, an alienated peasantry, an exhausted army, and widespread famine, but Russia became the first nation-state ever to turn socialist. More important, the Soviet leadership vowed to export its revolution to the rest of the industrialized world.[7]

> *Russia suffered 1.7 million dead in the First World War. The following*
> *Russian civil war consumed an estimated 7 to 10 million more lives,*
> *mostly by way of starvation and disease.*

6. POLISH-SOVIET WAR (1919–21)

Partitioned into nothing during the eighteenth century by Prussia, Austria, and Russia, the country of Poland struggled to piece itself back together after the First World War. Its old borders, only partially reestablished by the TREATY OF VERSAILLES, became grounds for bitter international contention. In three years the government of Jozef Pilsudski engaged in six different border wars against Germany, Czechoslovakia, Lithuania, western Ukraine, and Soviet Russia. The fight against the last proved to be the longest, deadliest, and most successful.

While the Red Army fought for survival in the Russian civil war, Pilsudski's armies advanced eastward, aiming to incorporate areas of mixed Polish ethnicity. Their success was remarkable.

Polish troops reached as far as Kiev, three hundred miles east of Warsaw, taking much of Lithuania and Byelorussia in the process. Regrouping, the Red Army counterattacked and nearly entered the Polish capital. In fact, several German and Russian newspapers reported that Warsaw had fallen. Then a miraculous Polish attack upon the southern Soviet flank shattered and dispersed three armies, forcing the weary Reds to concede Polish independence, land, and victory. The seesaw conflict consumed 150,000 Russian and at least 50,000 Polish casualties and imbued hostilities between the two states that would endure for decades.[8]

Some Westerners credited Poland with halting a Bolshevik tide that may have communized much of politically fragile Europe. Whether such an event was possible, Soviet sentiments were not against it. On November 7, 1920, just before the Red Army conceded defeat, the Soviet daily Pravda declared, "The hour of world victory is near."[9]

> *The Red Army lost three times the number of dead during the Polish-Soviet War of 1919–21 as it lost in the Afghan War of 1980–88.*

7. MANCHURIAN INCIDENT (1931)

In 1931 the South Manchurian Railway Company of Japan owned several hundred miles of track as well as mines, hospitals, schools, administration centers, libraries, repair depots, factories, and recreational parks within Manchuria. Assigned to guard these interests was an elite and largely independent division of Japanese officers and men known as the Kwantung Army.

On the night of September 18 a small explosion ruptured a few feet of rail line just outside the regional capital of Mukden. Company officials and most of the enlisted soldiers believed the explosion to be an act of terrorism perpetrated by Chinese Nationalists seeking revenge against the growing Japanese presence.

In reality, rogue Kwantung officers staged the event to justify complete occupation of the Chinese province. Their ruse paid immediate dividends. Within twenty-four hours their troops overran Mukden and fanned out into the countryside. In a matter of months most of Manchuria fell and fighting spread as far as Shanghai. By March 1932, Kwantung officers established the puppet state of Manchukuo, incorporating nearly all of Manchuria. The moderate Japanese government did not support the Kwantung Army's actions, yet it did not intervene for fear of appearing antipatriotic. As the League of Nations maneuvered to penalize Japan, the island nation withdrew from the League.[10]

The "Manchurian Incident" launched Japan's conversion from civil to military rule, unmasked the inherent infirmity of the League of Nations, and laid the groundwork for a comprehensive war in the Far East. Years later many Asians scholars and civilians pointed to 1931 as the actual start of the Second World War.[11]

> *The Japanese-appointed ruler of Manchukuo was Henry Pu Yi, the thirteenth and last Manchu emperor of China.*

8. ABYSSINIA (1935–36)

In 1830 Europe owned only a few colonial possessions in Africa, mostly along the coasts. A century later almost every African country lived under one European banner or another. Largest among the land-holders were Britain and France, followed by Belgium, Portugal, and Spain. A latecomer to the game, Italy held most of Somalia. But Benito Mussolini desired a Second Roman Empire, and he used a minor 1934 border clash between Italian and Ethiopian troops to deploy more sol-diers to the area. In 1935 he ordered an invasion.[12]

The Ethiopians—undertrained, poorly equipped, and divided—were little match against Fascist Italy's aircraft, armored vehicles, and mustard gas. By spring 1936, the fighting was over, save for sporadic guerrilla activity. An exuberant Italian public derived much pride from their victory in the seven-month war, not from defeating the feeble armies of Haile Selassie or the oppressive heat of East Africa, but by succeeding despite edicts and sanctions from the League of Nations.[13]

Italian military expenditures decreased steadily after the war, whereas defense budgets for nearly every other major state increased. Yet Italy's aggression and the futility of League condemnation signaled a European rebirth of might making right.

> *During and briefly after the war, Italian toy stores carried sets of lead soldiers featuring Fascist Italians pitted against Royalist Abyssinians.*

9. SPANISH CIVIL WAR (1936–39)

Attempting to build a democratic republic following years of dictator-ship, the best-laid plans of progressive reformers withered and failed in 1930s Spain. Resisting all change were the traditional powers of church, landowners, and the military. Demanding radical change were destitute peasants and laborers. General strikes by the latter "Republicans" degraded into violence by 1936, including the burning of hundreds of churches and the murder of more than a thousand priests. In retribution, church and military "Nationalists" resorted to mass executions.

By late 1936, this internal struggle became an international contest of extreme ideologies. Entering on the side of Gen. Francisco Franco's Nationalists were 40,000 Italian and 20,000 German soldiers, engineers, and advisers. Assisting the fractured but larger contingency of Republicans were scores of Britons, Czechs, French, Poles, Yugoslavs, nearly 3,000 Americans, and 40,000 Soviets.

Despite inferior numbers, the Nationalists and their allies possessed superior weaponry. Spanish cities, particularly Madrid and Falset, were subjected to repeated aerial bombings. Submarines hounded merchant shipping off the Mediterranean coast. By the winter of 1938–39, civilians in Madrid were down to a few ounces of food per day, and thousands began to die of starvation and exposure.

By spring 1939, Franco had attained unconditional surrender and established Spain as a dictatorship once more. Fascist Italy and Nazi Germany gained invaluable military experience from the fighting and untold confidence from the outcome. The war killed 600,000 people.[14]

At the end of the war, Franco's Fascist Spain received immediate diplomatic recognition from the governments of France, Great Britain, and the United States.

10. THE CHINA INCIDENT (1937)

For all intents and purposes, the Second World War did not begin at an American naval base on December 7, 1941, or on the German-Polish border on September 1, 1939. The bloodiest conflict yet in human history started after a bloodless volley a few miles from Peking on July 7, 1937.

On a late summer's night, while on maneuvers near the Marco

Polo Bridge, Japanese troops received a smattering of small-arms' fire. Officers claimed the shots originated from a nearby Chinese garrison and demanded the right to search neighboring cities. Local officials refused, resulting in a series of small skirmishes.

The pattern intensified through the rest of the summer. Both sides broke truce after truce. Deployments expanded. Fighting escalated. Equipped with superior armored vehicles, bombers, fighters, and heavy artillery, Japan quickly gained the initiative, occupying most of northeast China and defeating the Nationalist Army in SHANGHAI. Negotiations became impossible in December 1937, when Japanese forces conquered the capital city of Nanking and initiated a succession of atrocities.[15]

Thereafter, Japan fully engaged China, fought several pitched battles with the Soviet Union along the Mongolian border, and started to look longingly southward toward European and American possessions for precious war resources, especially oil. Predictably, Tokyo's fragile ties with London and Washington began to fray. Inversely, alliances with Rome and Berlin grew stronger, inspiring hawks in Tokyo to believe a new world order was about to dawn.

By conservative estimates, at least two hundred thousand Chinese civilians were killed during the three-week Rape of Nanking. This is three times the number of British civilians killed during the Second World War.

ATTEMPTS AT DIPLOMACY

It is common to view the pre–World War II diplomatic era as an exercise in excessive optimism candied with unrealistic peace initiatives and sanguine appeasements. A closer view reveals a very different picture. Rather than being naive, international negotiations of the period were predominantly cynical. Instead of addressing trade, finance, or humanitarian assistance, most major summits revolved around issues of warfare, either to settle old scores or to make future engagements more "humane."

In the ultimate expression of self-preservation, diplomats and heads of state consistently rejected the creation of economic or political partnerships of any kind. Contending that rigid alliances had led to the deadliest war in history, statesmen opted for flexible arrangements of short duration. Unfortunately, the strategy of keeping everything and everyone at arm's length proved incompatible with embracing lasting change.

Listed in chronological order are the ten most prominent bilateral and international meetings that transpired between 1918 and 1938. Included are their reasons for commencement, their primary players, and their outcomes.

1. WASHINGTON NAVAL TREATIES (1921–22)

On the surface, it would seem a waste of time and perfectly good warships for Great Britain, Japan, and the United States to contemplate a three-way naval disarmament. All three were allies. Japan and Britain even had a friendship treaty at the time. No other country came close to their command of the seas. Then again, capping the size and number of battleships, large cruisers, and the recent novelty of aircraft carriers was extremely farsighted. The three navies were rebuilding at a pace that threatened to accelerate into an arms race.

In Washington, D.C., from November 1921 to February 1922, the three states, plus a host of others, including France and Italy, debated how best to find a balance. All agreed to build no large warships for ten years. The United States was to dismantle or cancel production of thirty battleships, Britain would lose twenty-three, and Japan twenty-five. No new Pacific fortifications were to be constructed, and existing ones would not be expanded. The United States and Britain would have equal amounts of capital ships, with Japan allotted a lesser ratio (the so-called 5:5:3 Agreement). A "Four Power Pact" between Britain, France, Japan, and the United States respected each other's holdings in the Pacific, and a "Nine Power Treaty" secured the territorial integrity of China. Members of President Warren G. Harding's Republican Party hailed these measures as "the greatest peace document ever drawn."[16]

Within fifteen years every treaty negotiated at the Washington conference had either been canceled or broken.

---

2. THE GENEVA PROTOCOL (1924–25)

In 1915 poison gases made a toxic debut in the trenches of northern France. The effects of chlorine, phosgene, and mustard gas were so visually and physically repulsive that there was universal consensus to forever ban the use of these agents.[17]

In June 1925 in Geneva, twenty-nine countries endorsed the "Protocol for the Prohibition of the Use in War of Asphyxiating, Poisonous, or Other Gases, and of Bacteriological Methods of Warfare," better known as the Geneva Protocol. This was one treaty that endured the Second World War—barely.

During World War II Japan experimented on prisoners, killing several thousand at the infamous Detachment 731 in Manchuria. German generals recommended using nerve gas on the eastern front. The United States contemplated using gas in Okinawa. Masks were standard equipment for all regular ground troops and draft animals. Both the Axis and Allies possessed mass quantities of agents and stored them in several forward positions. But for a few accidents, the ghastly clouds did not return to the battlefield.[18]

The United States was one of the founding signatories of the Geneva Protocol but did not ratify it until 1975.

---

3. THE LOCARNO CONFERENCE (1925)

Church bells rang and crowds gathered in Locarno to celebrate what French foreign minister Aristide Briand called "the beginning of an era of trust."[19] Germany had just signed an agreement to respect forever the existing borders of Holland, Belgium, Luxembourg, and France. Relinquishing claims to Alsace and Lorraine, Germany also agreed to keep its industrial belt of the Rhineland eternally demilitarized. In return, the Allies were to end the occupation of the Rhine Valley by 1930 (five years earlier than the Versailles Treaty stipulated) and accept Germany into the League of Nations. With bold optimism, Western Europe praised the grand "spirit of Locarno."

Unfortunately, this "spirit" meant different things to different people. To the architect of the conference, German foreign minister Gustav Stresemann, this treaty placed Germany back among the powers of Europe, with the right to renegotiate the less desirable elements of the Versailles Treaty. To many in France and Britain the agreement looked like a German plea for forgiveness and a promise to behave. To many in Czechoslovakia and Poland the treaty appeared to liberate Germany from the risk of a two-front war. Time would prove the Czechs and Poles correct.[20]

For their efforts in the Locarno Conference, foreign ministers Briand and Stresemann won the 1926 Nobel Peace Prize.

---

4. THE KELLOGG-BRIAND PACT (1928)

On April 6, 1927, to commemorate the tenth anniversary of America's entry into the First World War, French foreign minister Aristide Briand sent a note of gratitude to the people of the United States. He spoke of perpetual friendship between France and America and invited Secretary of State Frank Kellogg to join him in condemning military aggression. Kellogg overlooked Briand's invitation—until it started to receive considerable public attention. He soon realized the offer was an unintended curse.[21]

Kellogg knew that a French-American eternal alliance would insult Germany and the Soviet Union. But to decline would imply the United States was not interested in denouncing war. The secretary was trapped.

In a clever maneuver, Kellogg recommended extending the invitation to all countries in the spirit of "universal brotherhood." The move paid off handsomely. In Paris on August 27, 1928, fifteen countries—including the United States, France, Germany, Belgium, and Britain—signed the Kellogg-Briand Pact. Eventually, forty-three of the world's then existing sixty-seven independent states joined the General Treaty for the Renunciation of War as an Instrument of National Policy.

Citizens everywhere praised the accord as a milestone in human enlightenment, whereas their dignitaries knew the text had no teeth. Most of the pact's five hundred words were congratulatory. The document made no stipulations concerning arms reduction, penalties against warring states, or obligations of mutual assistance in case of attack. Kellogg himself viewed the treaty as little more than a diffused bomb.[22]

Secretary of state from 1925 to 1929, Frank Kellogg set a record in U.S. diplomatic history by signing eighty international treaties.

---

5. THE THIRD GENEVA CONVENTION (1929)

In 1864, the first Geneva Convention declared the neutrality of hospitals in wartime. A second meeting in 1906 safeguarded hospital ships and shipwrecked persons. The sheer volume and violence of World War I revealed the need for another summit to protect prisoners of war.

Held in 1929, the third convention produced a document remarkably humane for its day, outlining better treatment for wartime captives than many conventioneers afforded their own citizens. Prisoners were to be removed from battle zones. Enlisted soldiers could be asked to perform manual labor, but none of it was to be dangerous or related to military operations. Per mutual agreements of involved governments, soldiers and officers were to be paid. Prisoners could send and receive personal mail. Forbidden was any resort to reprisal or torture.

Though progressive, many of the ninety-seven articles were dangerously ambiguous, particularly concerning prisoner health. As for hydration: "Sufficient drinking water shall be supplied." Food and shelter were to be "equivalent in quantity and quality to that of the depot troops." Medical inspections were to be carried out monthly, yet there was no stipulation whether qualified doctors should conduct them.

Ominously, the forty-seven signatories did not include the Soviet Union or the Empire of Japan.

Geneva conventions tended to set standards after the fact. The 1949 convention addressed civilian safety in wartime—after the Second World War resulted in more than thirty million civilian deaths.

---

6. LONDON NAVAL CONFERENCE (1930)

Though the Washington Naval Conference of 1922 restricted battleship and aircraft carrier construction, the development of cruisers, destroyers, and submarines flourished. To subdue the growing armadas, seagoing powers convened in London to discuss possible limitations.

Owning the world's largest merchant fleets, the United States and Britain called for the complete abolishment of submarines. France and Japan, viewing submarines as vital defensive weapons, refused. On the matter of destroyers, Britain and the United States were to remain ahead of all others, with Japan permitted a fleet 70 percent as large. On cruisers, the United States and Britain would again be equal, with Japan allowed 60 percent as much tonnage and others no more than 35 percent.[23]

The conference fostered harsh debate within the House of Lords, the U.S. Senate, and the Imperial Privy Council, but all three eventually accepted ratification of the treaty in the interest of international peace. Naval officers, on the other hand, were infuriated, many of them viewing the restrictions as arbitrary and unbearable. Scores of senior officers from the U.S. Navy and His Majesty's Service openly criticized the measures as defeatist, while the reaction in Japan bordered on open rebellion. The chief of staff of the Imperial Navy resigned, another officer committed suicide, and an assassin mortally wounded Prime Minister Hamaguchi Osachi.[24]

The London Naval Conference of 1930 was the first and last treaty in history to set universal limitations on all types of warships.

---

7. GENERAL DISARMAMENT CONFERENCE (1932–34)

The League of Nations tried for years to assemble a conference for universal arms limitation. Not until February 1932 in Geneva did such a meeting take place. Despite, or perhaps because of, the participation of nearly every country on earth, the discussion devolved almost immediately into lengthy bickering.

The only serious proposals came from France, the Soviet Union, and the United States. All three suggested cutting weapons collections by half. The American delegation even proposed abolishing all bomber aircraft, assumed at the time to be the superweapon of the future. No major power appeared willing to submit to the proposals or to international inspections. Nor was there any consensus on the proper response to violators of disarmament.[25]

Contrary to the principle of the conference, one country repeatedly argued for the right to rearm. Militarily emasculated Germany insisted on weapons parity with France, a particularly sensitive issue, because the Weimar government was building prototype aircraft and submarines in direct violation of the Treaty of Versailles. Germany's requests escalated to demands after Adolf Hitler became chancellor in

January 1933. The Nazi government withdrew from the conference nine months later.[26]

In response to the growing German threat, other nations began rebuilding their own military programs. The conference dissolved in failure in May 1934.[27]

During the conference, Hitler guaranteed to only build six-ton tanks, which unfortunately were large enough to conquer Poland. The invasion involved the Panzer I, which met the weight limit.

---

8. THE WORLD MONETARY AND ECONOMIC CONFERENCE (1933)

Mired in global depression, sixty-six countries gathered in London to negotiate an end to gold hoarding, roller-coaster currencies, and tariff wars. All eyes were on the United States. As the world's largest creditor nation and the largest importer-exporter—in spite of its crippling recession—the United States was the obvious choice to take the lead.

Half the world had gone off the gold standard and wanted the dollar to act as a surrogate. Britain and France wanted their massive debts to the Americans forgiven. Nearly every delegation wanted the United States to remove its protective tariffs first.[28]

But newly inaugurated Franklin D. Roosevelt announced he was in no mood to play "Santa Claus," to bear the cost of stabilizing the world's economy while the rest reaped all the benefits. He refused to remove tariffs unilaterally or lock the dollar in artificial boundaries. He also flatly rejected Britain and France's request to forgive their debts, the bulk of which were racked up during the European fiasco of the First World War.[29]

Not surprisingly, what became known as the "Roosevelt bombshell" was not well received. Delegates accused him of being isolationist and shortsighted, of single-handedly demolishing the conference. Ultimately nothing was resolved, and countries remained economically disunited until war necessitated a change in policies.[30]

If the attending parties wanted to rid themselves of archaic thinking, they picked a strange venue. The World Monetary and Economic Conference took place in the London Museum of Natural History—a building filled with dinosaurs.

9. THE ABYSSINIAN COMPROMISE (1935)

In the spring of 1935, dictator Benito Mussolini prepared for war against ABYSSINIA, stockpiling troops and weapons to the east in Italian Somaliland. He amassed ten thousand vehicles, fifty thousand pack animals, and two hundred thousand soldiers. In the eleventh hour, Britain sent to Rome the young and charismatic Anthony Eden to try and talk il Duce down.[31]

Eden offered to arbitrate a settlement between Abyssinia and Italy whereby the Italian Somaliland would receive access to a port and a rail right-of-way in British Somaliland. In exchange, Abyssinia would relinquish an area bordering Italian Somaliland consisting mostly of arid wasteland. "I am not a collector of deserts," fumed Mussolini. "If I go to war, the name of Abyssinia will be wiped off the map."[32]

The dictator proceeded with war plans, angered not only by a personal hatred for the dapper and educated Eden but also by Britain's hypocrisy in suppressing the imperial designs of others while holding a global empire of its own. Predictably, Eden's effort failed, and Italy invaded. But this setback did not prevent Britain from trying the "land for peace" tactic in 1938 with Hitler.[33]

Il Duce had another reason to distrust London. When Nazi insurgents assassinated Austrian chancellor and Mussolini's friend Engelbert Dollfuss, Germany maneuvered to enter Vienna to "restore order." Only Italian troops mobilized to stop the coup, despite Mussolini's request to Britain and others for help.

10. THE MUNICH CONFERENCE (1938)

After this meeting, the word *Munich* became synonymous with fool-ish concessions. Especially infamous was Neville Chamberlain's pre-mature declaration of "peace in our time" after conceding western Czechoslovakia to Hitler. Less well known, the Munich Conference prevented an early outbreak of a European war.

Since 1937 Hitler intended to invade Czechoslovakia. Partially carved from Austria after the First World War, one of the most pro-ductive and prosperous states in Central Europe, and containing nearly a million German-speaking people, the country would either be a brick wall or a stepping-stone to the expansion of the Third Reich. In May 1938, using pugnacious if unoriginal language, der Führer announced to senior officers of the Wehrmacht, "It is my unshakable will that Czechoslovakia shall be wiped off the map." He set the target date as October 1, 1938.[34]

By September, unguarded communications, overt troop move-ments, and a string of unrealistic demands illustrated Hitler's intentions. At one point he gave all Czechs in the Sudetenland forty-eight hours to evacuate the region. In a frightening replay of World War I, German, French, Russian, and Czech armies started to mobilize. On September 25, France and Britain threatened Hitler to negotiate or fight.

But as with Abyssinia, Britain asked the Czechs to trade land for peace. Some suggested it would be to Prague's advantage. Although it would lose the natural and man-made defensive perimeter of its moun-tainous western border, plus the mineral resources and industry in the area, the multinational Czech land would become more "homogenous" after shedding ethnic enclaves to Germany, Poland, and Hungary.

On September 28, Hitler agreed to a meeting in Munich, where, the following day, the prime ministers of Britain, France, and Italy permitted Germany to seize areas where Germans were in the ma-jority. Czech president Edvard Benes allowed the seizure, fearing annihilation of his country if he resisted. A week later he resigned, wondering for the rest of his life if he had made the correct choice.³⁵

Six months after Munich, Hitler ordered German troops into Prague, declared a Bohemian-Moravia Protectorate (the western two-thirds of the country), and once again claimed it was the final territorial adjustment he would ever make.

CAUSES OF THE WAR

A war is not unlike a bomb. It is of human construct and requires a multitude of conditions and proceedings for detonation. World War II was in effect several bombs assembled over time in Europe and Asia. Each of them contained a host of volatile components that were ancient and new, great and small, intangible and physical.

By the 1930s, these elements of instability grew, intensified, and began to overlap, creating a global environment of hostility in which diffusion of any particular conflict became less and less possible. Franklin D. Roosevelt summarized the situation best when he lamented to Henry Stimson, "These are not normal times; people are jumpy and very ready to jump after strange gods."³⁶

Following are the abnormal times and strange gods of which FDR spoke. In roughly chronological order are the foremost seeds of insecurity leading up to the Second World War.

I. THE FIRST WORLD WAR

Of all the products of the Great War—tanks, poison gas, bombers—missing was any genuine resolution. On paper the Allies appeared to be the defeated party, hosting the majority of battles and suffering the vast majority of fatalities. Britain went from being a creditor to a debtor nation. France lost more than a million young men. Russia collapsed altogether. The Allies failed to capture a foot of German soil.

In contrast, the former Central Powers were never routed and yet were saddled with a humiliating treaty. Many citizens viewed their governments as accomplices in a traitorous plot. In Germany, pockets of ultranationalists remained active, eventually collecting around a persuasive war veteran who preached revenge.

In Asia, an old country emerged as a new power. For capturing a German fort in China and conducting brief naval patrols in the Mediterranean, Japan received from the League of Nations the Marshall, Mariana, Palau, and Caroline island groups (formerly German possessions). The Japanese economy enjoyed an unprecedented boom, thanks to overseas demand for wartime supplies. From 1913 to 1919, Japanese exports increased 300 percent. Having recently annexed Korea and defeated both Russia and China in regional wars, the empire abruptly became the political, military, and economic power of East Asia. Several militarists promoted the idea of expanding Japan's influence even further.[37]

Combat veterans of the First World War included Winston Churchill, Hermann Göring, Rudolf Hess, Heinrich Himmler, Adolf Hitler, Benito Mussolini, Harry S. Truman, and George VI of Windsor.

---

2. THE RISE OF ETHNIC NATIONALISM

Tribal discord is almost as old as humankind. But in the early twentieth century, several factors enabled old ethnic tensions to become new political contests.

Victories in the Sino-Japanese and Russo-Japanese wars created an explosion of racial pride in Japan. World War I, which began after an ethnic uprising in Bosnia, gave birth to new states based largely on ethnicity—Czechoslovakia, Estonia, Latvia, Lithuania, Poland, Yugoslavia, etc. Much of American and British foreign policy bordered on the premise that "white makes right." Fables of ethnic superiority tested well in many political climates, particularly in Italy and Germany.[38]

Increasingly, race and state became virtually synonymous, to the point where international relations turned into cultural divides. In 1924, the United States, Canada, and Australia strictly limited immigration based on ethnicity, particularly against Asians. By 1930, Japan had more than seven hundred societies based on racial nationalism. In 1933, Nazi Germany imposed its first anti-Semitic laws, and in 1938, Germany annexed Austria and the Czech Sudetenland on grounds of ethnic conglomeration.[39]

Even in the League of Nations, that hopeful experiment in international cooperation, states were unwilling to even pay lip service to brotherly love. Despite several attempts to insert one, the covenant of the League of Nations never included an endorsement of racial equality.[40]

Article 9 of the Geneva Convention on prisoners of war stipulated, "Belligerents shall as far as possible avoid bringing together in the same camp prisoners of different races or nationalities."

---

3. THE REPARATIONS WAR

The harshest punishments of the Treaty of Versailles fell upon Austria and Hungary. Both were ordered to relinquish 60 percent of their territory, effectively ending their reigns as European powers. In comparison, Germany gave up 13 percent of its territory but was allowed to keep a nucleus of one hundred thousand soldiers for defense. The crux of Prussia's punishment was to come from reparations.[41]

As to the amount, no consensus could be found. Most of war-torn France wanted Germany to be "squeezed as a lemon is squeezed." Others called reparations "a sad adventure," fearing it would bankrupt

Germany and create a power vacuum in dead-center Europe. U.S. president Woodrow Wilson, and of course the Germans, wanted no payments whatsoever. Supreme Allied commander Marshal Ferdinand Foch lamented, "This is not peace: it is an Armistice for twenty years."[42]

Seemingly endless debate altered the amounts again and again. The Weimar government actually began paying—in coal, cattle, boats, and gold—without a final amount declared. Threats and reprisals sent the German mark into repeated free fall until it was valued at one-trillionth its prewar level.[43]

Emergency grants and loans eventually gave Germany more money than it ever paid, but the damage had been done. Americans and Britons believed France was irresponsibly greedy. The French believed Germany escaped punishment. Many Germans felt cheated by democratic governments, including their own. The issue was never resolved; Germany simply stopped paying.[44]

In 1929, Germany was scheduled to make reparations payments in gold until the year 1988.

---

4. THE GREAT DEPRESSION

In 1920, only two European countries were dictatorships. By 1937, there were sixteen. The primary cause of this migration to extremism was, in the words of economist John Maynard Keynes, the "greatest economic catastrophe…of the modern world."[45]

In 1929, a combination of overproduction, reduced consumption, and grossly overoptimistic stock prices led to a commercial implosion in the United States. Had the United States been a small player in the world market, the problem might have contained itself. Unfortunately, by the 1920s, America had become one of the largest creditor and trade nations on the planet.[46]

Within a year, international investments and trade began to dry up. Work orders plummeted and joblessness soared. Unemployment reached 25 percent in the United States, Japan, and Britain; 30 percent in France; 33 percent in Germany; and almost 50 percent in Eastern Europe.[47]

Banks crumbled in Austria, Britain, Czechoslovakia, Germany, Poland, Romania, and the United States, killed off by unstable currencies and multiplying loan defaults. Grain production—the foundation of nearly every national economy—fell by a fourth. Families lost their life savings, homes and businesses, pensions, and in many cases the ability to buy food.[48]

Out of deprivation came polarization. Normally moderate sections of societies, especially the middle class, became increasingly receptive to radical solutions.[49]

This bread line was in New York, but the forlorn scene appeared throughout the Western world for several years running.

The fragile democracy of Weimar Germany survived riots, armed rebellions, foreign occupation of the Rhineland, governmental scandals, political assassinations, and a total collapse of its monetary system—but it did not survive the Great Depression.

5. THE RISE OF ECONOMIC AUTARCHY

In the 1930s, Germany and Britain received most of their iron ore from Scandinavia and France. Japan was barely self-sufficient in food and almost entirely dependent on the United States for metals and petroleum. The United States imported most of its manganese, rubber, chromium, and practically all of its tin from East Asia.[50]

Such interdependence would logically oblige states to be cooperative with their suppliers. But memories of the largest war ever, coupled with lingering global economic depression, did not exactly create an environment of trust between capitals. Rather than engage in free trade, the richest states intensified their competition for raw materials.

As early as 1929, there were talks of European union, mostly to fend off "imperialist America." In a 1932 Commonwealth trade conference held in Canada, Britain declared it would exercise "imperial preference" when buying and selling anything. To secure sources of raw materials in Asia, the United States increased its military presence in the Philippines. Benito Mussolini declared he wanted to make North Africa, of all things, a wheat basket for Italy. In 1936, Japan announced the creation of the Greater East Asia Co-Prosperity Sphere, insinuating first rights to oil and ores in the region. Outdoing the rest, Germany reoccupied the industrial Ruhr Valley in 1936 and solidified designs for acquiring Lebensraum ("living space") in the east.[51]

Fittingly, some of the most intense offensives in World War II involved targets of raw material: grain in Manchuria and Russia; oil in the Dutch East Indies, Arabia, and the Caucasus; and coal in the Ruhr of Germany.

In a 1939 poll in Fortune *magazine, 60 percent of Americans surveyed said they hoped the United States could reach a point where "it does not have to buy any products from foreign countries."*

---

6. THE "CHINA SYNDROME"

Had there been no Munich crisis, no invasion of Poland, no fall of France, there still would have been a war in Asia. In the two years preceding the collapse of "peace in our time" within Europe, Soviet weapons and ammunition flowed into China, battles in Manchuria produced casualties of six figures, and more than one million had died in a conflict that engrossed a fourth of the world's population.

Amid the chaos, China struggled in vain to find equilibrium. Its three-hundred-year-old Manchu dynasty ceased to exist in 1912. Internal fighting and economic frailty prevented the development of any stable replacement government. By 1927 a bloody rivalry began between China's Communists and Nationalists. To "establish order" in the area, rogue Japanese officers staged the MANCHURIAN INCIDENT in 1931, signaling the start of intermittent military campaigns that would last until 1945.[52]

Other countries also struggled with civil wars and foreign encroachments at the time, but other countries did not have 480 million inhabitants. The outbreak of war in Europe was essentially a fabrication, a manufacture of crises where none truly existed. The war in China was a culmination, the breaking point of a fractured relic.

The early 1900s were not particularly kind to China. Between 1911 and 1936, a series of catastrophic floods, earthquakes, droughts, civil wars, and famines claimed approximately fifteen million lives.

---

7. THE WEAKNESS OF THE LEAGUE OF NATIONS

The brainchild of idealist Woodrow Wilson, the League of Nations actually developed into a reasonably efficient and effective institution. After a few growing pains, the consortium soon included most every sovereign country in the world and became the forum of choice for international relations. Between 1924 and 1931, the globe lived relatively free of wars, a span of tranquility almost unmatched in history.

But the organization contained inherent frailties, revealed in full by Japan's invasion of Manchuria in 1931. The MANCHURIAN INCIDENT was a direct violation of League Charter Article 10—respect of integrity and independence of all member states. But there was apparently little the League was willing or capable of doing. The organization had no armed forces, no actual legal control over member states, and no United States in its assembly.

Simply ignoring mandates placed against it, Japan withdrew from the League in 1933. Soon to follow were some of the more aggressive participants in a greater disaster to come. Nazi Germany left in 1933, as did Italy in 1937, Hungary by 1939, and Romania in 1940. Rejecting the League became an expression of national pride. Remaining members lost much of their previous faith. The institution barely addressed the 1939 invasion of Poland and never held a session from 1940 to 1945.

By the time the League of Nations officially disbanded in 1946, it was down to half its original members.

8. ADOLF HITLER

French historian Maurice Baumont speaks for many when he surmises, "The origins of the war of 1939 go back essentially to the insatiable appetites of Adolf Hitler." Baumont's logic stems from the "Great Man" theory, contending that history is determined mostly by the actions of kings, generals, and presidents. While succinct, such an approach is often shortsighted. Yet in the case of the Second World War, one person deserves a fair amount of credit for initiating the European portion of the spectacle.[53]

As a leader, Hitler was pure paradox. Creative and destructive, inspiring and mortifying, in command and yet out of control. His internal contradictions go far in explaining why some viewed Hitler as a rambling hatemonger and others deemed him a calculating schemer.

On the question of whether Hitler wanted to initiate a military conflict, there is no doubt. From the moment he became chancellor he informed his generals of his intent to solve Germany's problems through military force. The idea to invade Poland was his, as were the subsequent attacks on the West and on the Soviet Union.

The argument that appeasement only fueled his ambition is fundamentally weak. Looking back, nothing significantly altered his aggression—not coercion, stalemate, appeasement, victory, or defeat. Military force was simply his tool of choice for instilling national pride, priming the economy, intimidating enemies, and attaining collaborators.

Opinions still cover the spectrum on der Führer. But whether one sees him as a mastermind or a marionette, it would be difficult if not impossible to imagine Germany going to war in 1939 if Hitler did not exist.[54]

In 1933, British ambassador to Germany Sir Horace Rumbold stated, "I have the impression that the persons directing the policy of the Hitler Government are not normal."

---

9. THE ARMS RACE

Much credence has been given to the rapid buildup of arms and armies as a primary cause of the First World War. Often overlooked is the even greater increase in military hardware just before the second go-round.

Throughout the economic boom of the 1920s and into the beginning of the Great Depression, most governments viewed military expenditures as essentially wasteful. Franklin D. Roosevelt credited large military buildups as "the real root of world disease and war."[55]

Two events soon sparked a change in attitudes about armaments. In 1935, Hitler publicly declared a rejection of the Treaty of Versailles and its constraints on German arms production. In 1936 Japanese delegates stormed out of an arms limitation summit when the United States refused to allow the empire to build additional warships. The belligerent acts set off an exponential growth in military budgets.[56]

In 1932, the U.S. Congress appropriated funds for the construction of a single warship. The 1939 budget called for nineteen new ships, and Japan budgeted for sixty. From 1932 to 1939, production of military aircraft increased fourfold in the United States and sixfold in

Japan. In a few short years Germany went from having no warplanes to possessing the largest air force in the world.[57]

Japanese and German leaders became more aggressive when it was clear they were falling farther behind. Adolf Hitler believed his armed forces would not be ready for a major war until 1942 at the soonest. Five months before PEARL HARBOR, Japan's Adm. Nagano Osumi stated, "There is at this moment a chance to win a war against the United States, but the prospects will diminish as time goes by; by the second half of the year we will hardly be a match for them any longer."[58]

Starved for orders during the Great Depression, U.S. industry responded quickly to the call for arms.

The B-17 Flying Fortress, B-24 Liberator, B-26 Marauder, and Sherman tank were coming off the production lines and the B-29 Superfortress and atomic bomb were in development before Pearl Harbor.

10. THE NAZI-SOVIET PACT

The last chance for peace in Europe ended on August 23, 1939, in an event so bizarre, many said it did not seem real. Hitler's rabid hatred of "godless bolshevism" was the foundation of his message. In turn, Communists from Paris to Leningrad viewed Hitler as public enemy number one. Suddenly the foreign ministers of Germany and the Soviet Union met in Moscow and, in the presence of Joseph Stalin, signed an agreement of neutrality.

Vyacheslav Molotov and
Joachim von Ribbentrop sign
the Nazi-Soviet Pact while
Stalin looks on.

Across Europe, people were thrown into varying states of dread,
frustration, and anger. Soviets and Germans alike were dumbfounded.
Citizens of free states envisioned a Europe divided and shared by the
two dictators. Infuriated by Hitler's sudden benevolence to their longtime adversary, Japan's entire cabinet resigned.[59]

The agreement assured "peace and the consolidation of business"
between the two mortal enemies. What the pact removed was the
threat of a two-front war for both countries. The Wehrmacht could
move on Poland as it wished—to take back land "stolen" after the
First World War—without threat of Soviet attack. Stalin was liberated
from a possible German-Japanese vise.

Poland was conspicuously doomed. Suddenly, France and Britain
could not come to Poland's assistance as promised, not without access
to Russian airfields. Officials in London and Paris also dreaded that
when Poland fell, as assuredly it would between Hitler and Stalin, they
were next.[60]

As many predicted, the pact signaled war, not in years or months,
but in days. Last-minute pleas for peace from Franklin D. Roosevelt,
Pope Pius XII, and Benito Mussolini were ignored.

The Nazi-Soviet Nonaggression Pact was set to expire in 1949.

POLITICS

FORMS OF GOVERNMENT

Stalin once asserted, "If a government is not fascist, a government is democratic." Such logic was hollow but commonplace. The Second World War was popularly viewed as black and white, good versus evil, democracy against fascism. Wars and the relationships they foster, however, are rarely as clear as Stalin suggested. A more accurate observation came from Winston Churchill, "At night, all cats are gray."[1]

Wartime political systems covered the spectrum, and no system predisposed their owners to become Axis or Allied. Neutrals held a plurality for years, and many camps switched sides. Far from a world of democracies and fascist states, the globe was foremost spangled with crowns, as the vast majority of nations were either the seat or the subject of a monarchy.

Yet dictatorships were on the rise. Significantly, the war and its ensuing peace did little to break this trend, save for Italy and western Germany. Elsewhere, authoritarian regimes became the norm in Central and South America, Southeast Asia, Africa, and Eastern Europe, many of them sponsored by the victorious powers.

Below are the ten predominant forms of government among the principle war participants. Ranking is from most to least common. Countries listed with an asterisk switched sides during the war.

1. COLONY

ALLIED: FRENCH*, BELGIAN, BRITISH, AND DUTCH HOLDINGS
AXIS: ITALIAN AND JAPANESE HOLDINGS

In the war to preserve freedom, most countries were not free to begin with. The world consisted of about sixty independent or semi-independent countries and one hundred colonies. Autonomy was extremely rare in Africa, South Asia, and the Pacific, in part because several thrones survived the imperial cauldron of the First World War. King George VI of Windsor alone presided over a fifth of the world's land area.[2]

Hardly on the fringe, colonies were often the major source of raw materials that fed war industries. Though Belgium was neutral, the Belgian Congo provided the Allies with diamonds, copper, and tungsten as well as uranium for atomic testing. British colonies provided most of the world's nickel and rubber. The Dutch East Indies held large reserves of oil.

Soldiers of the Belgian Congo prepare to defend the empire in central Africa.

Somewhat obligated, colonies also provided a cache of soldiers. When Germany invaded France, eighty thousand of France's defenders were African. Nine out of ten "British" troops in Burma were from South Asia. In Syria, the French fought themselves—Free France versus Vichy.

The war revealed empires as vulnerable or eliminated them, creating waves of independence movements even before the shooting ended. From 1945 to 1965 nearly sixty countries ceased to be colonies.[3]

Colonies hosted a fair amount of the fighting in the war—Abyssinia, Algeria, Belgian Congo, British Somaliland, Burma, Ceylon, Dutch East Indies, French Morocco, Gibraltar, Italian Somaliland, Libya, Malta, the Marshall Islands, and Singapore to name a few.

---

2. CONSTITUTIONAL MONARCHY

ALLIED: BELGIUM, BRITAIN, HOLLAND, LUXEMBOURG, NORWAY, YUGOSLAVIA*

NEUTRAL: DENMARK, EGYPT, SWEDEN

AXIS: JAPAN

A constitutional monarchy is a bit like a democracy afraid of commitment—it has an elected government with a royal sovereign acting as head of state. More often than not, the reigning monarch is a figurehead, part deity, part notary public, granting approval to the functions of elected officials.

Britain, though often viewed as stodgy, was one of the more progressive constitutional monarchies, with full protection of civil rights and partial women's suffrage. In contrast, Yugoslavia was a legitimate farce. A country fabricated from the ashes of the First World War, it consisted of Croats, Slovenes, Bosnians, and a half-dozen other ethnic groups. But the state was under a hardline Serb monarch, in the capital of Serbia, with a military run by a Serb officer class, and the official religion being Serb Orthodox. The setup tended to offend the other ethnic groups, and they later expressed this frustration by unleashing a bloody civil war.

Japan was frequently and incorrectly labeled fascist. In reality, it was a parliamentary government, with its lower house elected by male citizens. Yet Japan's constitution made for a rather fragmented decision-making process. The armed forces and cabinet were responsible to no one but the emperor, who in turn practiced limited supervision over his subjects. The system worked relatively well in the 1920s and then slowly eroded into a military oligarchy in the 1930s. During the war, the army, navy, and cabinet continued to work independently from one another. Only once did Hirohito interject in political affairs: he ordered a halt to the war when he learned the fate of Nagasaki.

From 1937 to 1945, Japan went through seven prime ministers. The most powerful was Tojo Hideki, who held the post from 1941 to 1944. He also acted as minister of war and intermittently led the ministries of munitions, commerce and industry, home affairs, foreign affairs, and education.

3. PROTECTORATE

ALLIED:　　FRENCH INDOCHINA*, FRENCH MOROCCO*, TUNISIA*

AXIS:　　　BOHEMIA, MORAVIA, SLOVAKIA

An independent government under the "protection" of another state, a protectorate is a small step above being a colony. Bohemia, Moravia, and Slovakia were previously the Republic of Czechoslovakia, one of the most progressive representative governments in the world. But the 1938 Munich Agreement allowed Hitler to legally carve away sections wherever Germans were in the ethnic majority. Six months later Hitler illegally took over the rest of the country, setting up the "Protectorate of Bohemia and Moravia" and a puppet government in Slovakia.

French Indochina (Cambodia, Laos, and parts of Vietnam) existed under monarchies that were in turn subject to a French governor. Japan forcibly entered the area in 1940 and began bleeding the area dry of rice, coal, and rubber, which eventually persuaded the United States to place an oil embargo on Japan.

French Morocco had a sultan, whereas Tunisia had a provincial governor. Both functioned under large amounts of French political and military assistance. This setup underwent a hard bout of schizophrenia during the Allied invasions of November 1942. First the governments resisted heavily, then they capitulated, and then they joined the procession eastward to rid North Africa of the Third Reich.

To "liberate" French Morocco and the colony of Algeria, the Allies lost fourteen hundred men killed in action, more than the number of sailors lost on the USS Arizona.

---

4. MILITARY DICTATORSHIP

ALLIED: CHINA, GREECE, POLAND

AXIS: HUNGARY*, ROMANIA*, VICHY FRANCE

No actual ideology, no professed mandate from heaven, just power via well-armed support groups. Military dictatorships were often the by-product of failed democratic governments, as was the case with Hungary in 1919, Poland in 1926, Greece in 1935, and Romania in 1938.

Since 1912 China had tried to establish a parliamentary system only to be torn apart repeatedly by jealous factions. In 1937 the country came together, faced with the imminent threat of Imperial Japan. Searching for an answer, warlords and the small but developing Communist Party pledged support to CHIANG KAI-SHEK, military chieftain of the dominant "Kuomintang," or Nationalist Party. But paranoia ran deep, especially in Chiang, and China fought itself almost as much as the Japanese.

The Vichy government (named after the spa town in which it was headquartered) came about with the German invasion of France. In an emergency session, the French National Assembly granted World War I hero Marshal Henri-Philippe Pétain the power to rule by decree. The parliament reasoned that a dictatorship would provide stability in a time of crisis—but stability at a price. Germany did not take over the government, allowing Pétain to govern both the occupied north and the Vichy south. Pétain became a Nazi by proxy, an ultraconservative king of denial who tried to make collaboration look patriotic. It worked for nearly two years, then Germany decided to take over all of France and rule in his stead.

From his birth in 1856 to his death in 1951, Marshal Pétain watched France undergo several governmental changes, including one monarchy, sixteen presidents, and more than one hundred different cabinets.

---

5. REPUBLIC

ALLIED: FRANCE, UNITED STATES
NEUTRAL: TURKEY
AXIS: FINLAND*

When Franklin D. Roosevelt spoke of the United States as an ARSENAL OF DEMOCRACY, the only states remotely close to the strict definition of democracy (rule directly by the people) were the federated cantons of Switzerland. Since adopting its constitution in 1787, the United States had been a republic—a government ruled by elected representatives. France joined the select club in 1870, followed by Finland and Turkey after the First World War.

The only republic to fall in the war was France. The secular state of Turkey stayed neutral nearly the whole way through, despite Churchill's fervent wishes for a powerful ally in the Balkans.

Finland became receptive to the Third Reich after being attacked by Stalin in the WINTER WAR and later joined in the invasion of the Soviet Union. Several hundred Finns also served in Nazi SS divisions. But the relationship ended in 1944 when Finland simultaneously fought off German occupation and yet another Soviet offensive, keeping the country independent at a price of more than one hundred thousand casualties.

Of the four republics in the war, only the Allied United States and the Axis Finland granted women the right to vote.

---

6. DOMINION

ALLIED: AUSTRALIA, CANADA, NEW ZEALAND,
               SOUTH AFRICA, PHILIPPINES

The Philippines under U.S. protection and British Commonwealth countries were independent in all but name. The heads of state were still the U.S. president and the Crown of England, respectively, but each country had its own president or prime minister, cabinet, elected houses, and control over domestic concerns and foreign affairs.

None of the dominions were generally enthusiastic about joining the war. Filipinos had very little choice, attacked on the same day as PEARL HARBOR. South Africa declared war against Germany but did little afterward. Its large, nonwhite, considerably repressed population was not motivated to help the monarchy.

Altogether, Australia, Canada, and New Zealand committed nearly a million troops to the war effort. Many proved to be supreme fighters. But their loyalty to the Crown took a severe beating. Britain was clearly unable to protect them from harm and was generally unappreciative of their sacrifices. In turn, the dominions grew close to a much stronger military power—the United States.

Fighting in the South Pacific, North Africa, Greece, Crete, and Italy, the servicemen of New Zealand proportionally lost 30 percent more troops than Great Britain in the war.

---

7. FASCIST DICTATORSHIP

NEUTRAL: PORTUGAL, SPAIN
AXIS: ITALY

Political scientists have attempted to define fascism, but they have limited results to show for their efforts. Most generally agree that it involved intense nationalism, militarism, single-party rule, social conformity, and the glorification of the leader. Its declared enemies were usually democracy, communism, capitalism, and humanism.[4]

In the Second World War, nearly every European state had a party or faction that fit the above criteria, including the Arrow Cross in Hungary, the Iron Guard in Romania, Action Francaise in France, and the British Union in England. Yet only three states had a fascist party ascend to power—Italy, Portugal, and Spain. And in all three cases, none were eager to join in the war.

Despite direct pressure from Nazi Germany, both Portugal and Spain refused to be drawn into any kind of commitment. Portugal's Antonio Salazar was decidedly anticommunist but had no interest in aiding the Axis when his citizens were blatantly pro-Allied. Spain's Francisco Franco had emerged victorious in a bloody and elongated civil war. The potential costs of entering an even larger contest held no appeal for his fledgling government.

Italy was still technically a constitutional monarchy under Leopold III, but Benito Mussolini was its unquestioned dictator, or il Duce. In twenty years of rule, Mussolini had outlawed all opposition parties, eliminated freedom of speech and press, openly persecuted any expressed or implied dissent, and controlled the cabinet and parliament. But his military interests had always been more imperial than ideological. By 1943 both Mussolini and the Italian public had lost all desire for war, having lost too many campaigns to count. When the Allies entered Sicily, Mussolini was arrested by order of the king. Later that year Italy declared war on Germany.

Fascism comes from the Latin "fasces," a bound set of wooden rods holding the blade of an axe. It was the Roman symbol of unity and power. From a distance it looks like a log with a beak.

---

8. ABSOLUTE MONARCHY
NEUTRAL: ABYSSINIA, IRAN, SAUDI ARABIA

The last holdouts of a fading system, absolute monarchs continually resisted becoming colonies themselves. ABYSSINIA narrowly escaped conquest from Italy in 1896, only to fall to a more mechanized army in 1936. British forces liberated the country in 1941 and restored its monarch Haile Selassie to the throne. Selassie, who had been living in exile in London, thanked his British rescuers by essentially forcing them out of his country.

In Persia (Iran), the shahs (kings) of the Pahlavi dynasty marginally tolerated joint Soviet and British occupation. Greater worries came from internal pressures. On one side were nationalists who wanted to modernize the economy and government. On the other were religious fundamentalists who desired an end to Western influence. The Shahs managed to placate the nationalists and resist the fundamentalists (at least until 1979).

The Saud family had been vying for power in the Arabian Peninsula since the 1700s. By the time of the war in Europe, they were entering just their seventh year at the helm of the kingdom of Saudi Arabia. The country remained neutral until the last weeks of the Third Reich, when the Saudis declared war on the Axis powers.

The Saudis enjoyed little international clout until 1938, when oil was first extracted from their land. Though yields were initially modest, geologists hypothesized the kingdom rested on rather promising deposits.

---

9. SOCIALIST DICTATORSHIP

ALLIED: SOVIET UNION*

One way to stay in power is to kill off the opposition. No one in human history murdered more people than Joseph Stalin. Not even in the apex of Nazi destruction did a death count approach his. Through forced collectivization and purges during the 1930s, he eliminated somewhere between twenty and thirty million people and probably exceeded forty million by the time of his death in 1953. Heading a socialist state, the only one in the world at that time, Stalin was not by any indication in the killing business for the purpose of glory or sadism. He was, in theory, truly implementing the tenets of Marxism.

According to German philosopher Karl Marx, a country reaches communism by first undergoing industrialization then by eliminating the bourgeoisie. Stalin facilitated these changes through Five-Year Plans and purges. On the transformation from proletarian state to utopia, however, Marx wasn't quite clear. The change was supposed to be a natural evolution, one that apparently had not taken place before a different German philosophy appeared at the gates of Moscow in 1941.

On paper, the Soviet Union was a free democratic republic. Its 1936 constitution guaranteed freedom of press, speech, assembly, religion, and universal suffrage. Apparently, Stalin also wanted to guarantee their right to imprisonment, starvation, and execution.

---

10. NATIONAL SOCIALIST DICTATORSHIP

AXIS: GERMANY

Hitler's regime differed too much from fascist states to be placed in the same category. Whereas most fascist parties tied themselves firmly to royal houses, National Socialists, or Nazis, had no monarchy or intention to create one. Most fascists readily identified with a conservative church, yet Hitler hoped to eventually eradicate organized religion. Fascism tended to stay rooted in the country it glorified. Nazism actively sought to "purify" societies beyond its own borders.

Often viewed as the opposite of any given government, Nazism was more like a mutant combination of theoretical extremes: the far right of militant nationalism, the far left of socialist control of industry, the racial supremacy of fascism, and the end of the individual in communism. The system stayed intact by the same method that held Stalin's together: state-directed terror. Appropriately, Hitler often credited "will" as the basis of his power. An ethereal term, it summarized perfectly a political system that was based largely on reaction rather than direction.

The name of Hitler's party exemplified the mishmash of his political thinking. Die Nationalsozialistische Deutsche Arbeiterpartei means "the National Socialist German Worker's Party."

EVENTS IN POLITICS

If the governments of the world stumbled into a global conflict, they also stumbled through it. Leaders rose and fell, enemies became friends, friends became burdens, and agendas mutated. The most consistent trait of international relations was inconsistency. Of the principle political figures in the war, only Joseph Stalin and CHIANG KAI-SHEK remained in power from beginning to end. Half the Axis states eventually joined the Allies. And the Allies did not have a common war aim until 1943.

As illustrated below, few of the war's major political events were premeditated. Most were reactions to changing military conditions, and many created more problems than they resolved. Listed in chronological order, the following acts and conferences did more than any other to change the political landscape of the war and to demonstrate the tenuous unity within alliances.

1. DESTROYERS-FOR-BASES (SEPTEMBER 2, 1940)

On May 15, 1940, just five days into office, with France collapsing under blitzkrieg by the hour, Winston Churchill sent his first telegram as Britain's prime minister to Franklin D. Roosevelt. Hardly cordial, Churchill was asking for assistance—quite a bit of assistance.

He asked for a gift of "forty or fifty of your older destroyers," several hundred of the "latest types of aircraft," plus antiaircraft guns, steel, and a U.S. military presence in neutral Ireland to dissuade

German paratroop drops. Lastly, Churchill stated, "I am looking to you to keep the Japanese quiet in the Pacific."[5]

More symbolic than functional, an archaic U S. destroyer lumbers across the Atlantic on its way to the Royal Navy as part of the destroyers-for-bases deal.

Upon receiving these hefty requests, the president was cool but conciliatory. Roosevelt said he would look into the Irish proposal. He reminded Churchill that Britain was free to purchase all the steel and weapons it could afford. As for the Japanese, Roosevelt believed the concentration of U.S. warships at PEARL HARBOR was an adequate deterrent.[6]

Giving away U.S. destroyers required congressional approval, an unlikely event considering the heavy isolationist sentiment throughout the country. Churchill repeated the request several times in the following weeks, becoming insistent after France fell and Germany suddenly acquired its submarine bases.

In desperation, Churchill offered to lease British naval and air bases in the Caribbean and Newfoundland, free of charge, for ninety-nine years. Roosevelt accepted, as the transaction did not directly violate strict U.S. neutrality laws. The deal was officially settled in September, and English ports began receiving a handful of antiquated sub hunters.

The warships made a marginal difference, but the trade was monumental. The destroyers-for-bases deal was the first measurable step the United States took against twenty years of neutrality and the first successful move by Churchill to tie British and American fates together.[7]

The destroyers Britain received were not exactly state of the art. Some of the newest ships were built in 1917.

2. TRIPARTITE PACT (SEPTEMBER 27, 1940)

It seemed like a good idea at the time. For more than a year, Hitler advocated a three-way alliance between Berlin, Rome, and Tokyo. By publicly declaring the unity of the three great military powers, promising to come to each other's aid if attacked, Hitler believed he could intimidate the United States into staying out of Europe.

The Japanese government, however, was not so confident. One cabinet held over seventy meetings on the issue with no settlement. The navy opposed joining the alliance, as did the emperor, fearing it would anger the United States into war. But when Matsuoka Yosuke became foreign minister, the pact became reality. A brash, eccentric, but charismatic figure, he proclaimed the agreement to be the one and only way to assure peace. "If you stand firm and start hitting back," he reasoned, "the American will know he is talking to a man."[8]

In response, the United States placed a scrap-metal embargo on "the man," and public opinion began to equate the empire with the Third Reich. Rather than an irresistible force, the pact became an immovable obstacle to compromise between the United States and Japan.[9]

Matsuoka Yosuke had reason to believe he understood Americans. He had lived in the United States for a decade and was a graduate of the University of Oregon.

3. LEND-LEASE (MARCH 11, 1941)

Britain was nearly bankrupt. It was also fighting Germany almost on its own. President Roosevelt struggled to think of a way to help without sending troops overseas, without loaning money, and without doing as Joseph Kennedy Sr., Charles Lindbergh, Robert E. Wood (head of Sears, Roebuck), and others were suggesting—broker a peace with Hitler.[10]

Roosevelt came up with an idea while vacationing in the Caribbean, where his destroyers-for-bases trade bore fruit. The United States would provide Britain with the weapons and material required to fight on—guns, warships, transports, tanks—and when the war was over, repayment would be made in kind. While an isolationist Congress was in recess, Roosevelt presented the concept to the American public in his ARSENAL FOR DEMOCRACY radio address, an act he equated with lending a neighbor a hose when his house was on fire. Response was overwhelmingly in favor, which helped pass the bill despite bitter congressional debates.

Over the next three years, the United States allocated more than fifty billion dollars in goods and services to forty countries (equivalent to eight hundred billion in 2005 dollars). Britain received nearly half. The Soviet Union, joining the Allies later in 1941, received a quarter of the take, amounting to about 7 percent of what the Soviets produced on their own. Third and fourth in line were Free France and Nationalist China.

U.S. fighter planes are readied for shipment. Lend-Lease provided some forty Allied nations with money and materials for war.

Though boosting American industry to new heights and arguably saving Britain from destruction, Lend-Lease became yet another seed of discontent. Recipients perpetually demanded more, especially Stalin and CHIANG KAI-SHEK. Americans worried they were enabling monarchies and dictatorships to grow even stronger. Harry Truman did little to settle the issue when he shut off the valve the very moment Japan surrendered.[11]

Reportedly, upon hearing that the U.S. Congress passed Lend-Lease, Winston Churchill actually danced.

---

4. ATLANTIC CHARTER (AUGUST 9, 1941)

On a ship off Newfoundland, in their first face-to-face meeting as heads of state, Roosevelt and Churchill negotiated a set of "common principles." With eight brief points, the document (christened "the Atlantic Charter" by the London press) promoted self-determination, free trade, labor rights, civil rights, freedom of the high seas, and international disarmament. It also condemned border changes by coercion and pledged "the final destruction of the Nazi tyranny." Issued as a press release, it was intended to be a simple statement of unity against fascism. Others interpreted it as a definitive road map for the postwar world.

Within a month Churchill was backtracking. He assured Parliament that "disarmament" meant Germany and Japan, with the British military remaining dominant far into the postwar period. On self-determination he was most adamant. An ardent imperialist, he emphasized that the provision only applied to Europe, not to British colonies. His hypocrisy was not lost on Burmese, Indians, South Africans, and others living under the Union Jack. Yet the prime minister was quite ready to defend self-determination when Stalin later insisted on maintaining Soviet control over Poland, adding that "President Roosevelt holds this view as strongly as I do."[12]

Yet neither Roosevelt nor Churchill followed the charter closely. Generally repulsed by Britain's grip on old colonies, Roosevelt was more apt to recognize Soviet dominion over the Poles, the Baltic states, and Ukraine. When asked in 1944 if self-determination no longer applied to Europe, Roosevelt replied that the Atlantic Charter was not a binding treaty but merely a press release, written on "just some scraps of paper."[13]

President Franklin D. Roosevelt and Prime Minister Winston Churchill issued the Atlantic Charter after a conference aboard USS *Augusta* at Placentia Bay, Newfoundland, on August 9, 1941.

But in 1941, the charter meant far more in one respect. It was the first publicly declared statement between a belligerent and a neutral that they held the same war aims and were committed to defeating the Third Reich.

The Atlantic Charter would live on after the war as the foundation of the charter of the United Nations.

5. GERMAN DECLARATION OF WAR ON THE UNITED STATES (DECEMBER 11, 1941)

It was not his brightest act. Days after the Japanese attack on PEARL HARBOR, Hitler declared war on the United States, greatly simplifying U.S. entry into a European war.

The declaration was brief, less than a page long, and was clearly written without Hitler's direct input. Emphasis was on high-seas law, about which he knew very little. The text stated, "Vessels of the American Navy, since early September 1941, have systematically attacked German naval forces…Germany for her part has always strictly observed the rules of international law in her dealings with the United States throughout the present war."[14]

Though Hitler underestimated the military and industrial potential of the United States and overestimated Japan's chances of keeping American forces in the Pacific, he was not eager to invite yet another enemy into the fray. For years he had privately stated his desire to keep the United States out of the war. His ideal scenario involved Japan attacking the Soviet Union, with the Americans staying neutral. Yet instead of having a two-front war against Stalin, Hitler unilaterally created one against himself.

In his speech to the Reichstag announcing Germany's declaration of war on the United States, Hitler stated, "A historical revision on a unique scale has been imposed on us by the Creator."

---

6. WANNSEE CONFERENCE (JANUARY 20, 1942)

Nazi persecution of the Jews had not been systematic up to 1942. Officials initially expelled Jews from homes, businesses, and cities in an attempt to make areas "Jew free." Emigration was also encouraged. By 1940, nearly half of Germany's 500,000 Jews had left for Britain, the United States, Palestine, and elsewhere.

When the Reich overran areas with large "non-Aryan" populations, the solution was to contain the Jews in ghettos, often denying them food. Privation began to kill hundreds, then thousands, but the method was imprecise and slow. In the invasion of the Soviet Union, the Germans initiated use of Einsatzgruppen, or "Special Groups," roaming death squads that liquidated Jews by mass shootings. By the end of 1941, at least one million Jews had died, yet no systematic plan for annihilation was yet in place.

Then Adolf Eichmann, head of Germany's Race and Resettlement Office, called an assembly of fifteen administrators to the wealthy Berlin suburb of Wannsee. Their task was to coordinate a "final solution" to the Jewish problem.

In less than two hours, the officials outlined a new program, whereby Europe's Jews would be collected and transported to special sites in the east, under the pretense that they were to be used as forced labor. Meeting minutes contained no references to killing, but the "laborers" were to include infants and the elderly. Destination points were a select few concentration camps, which were at that moment being fitted with gas chambers.[15]

Wannsee was the first instance where genocide became official Nazi policy. Documentation from the conference stands as the most damning evidence to date that the Holocaust had been directed by the highest levels of the Third Reich. By all indications, the procedure was effectively implemented. Half of all Jews killed in the Holocaust died in a handful of death camps.[16]

Among the potential "labor pools" cited in the Wannsee briefing minutes was Great Britain, with an estimated 330,000 Jews.

---

7. "UNCONDITIONAL SURRENDER": THE CASABLANCA CONFERENCE (JANUARY 14–24, 1943)

On the last day of a long summit, Roosevelt and Churchill were holding a press conference in sunny Casablanca. Stalin declined to attend the summit, wanting instead to monitor events at STALINGRAD. The president and prime minister were reviewing the high-level issues of their meetings, such as the need for a unified French resistance. A photo op captured the proud but politically dim Gen. Henri Giraud (whom Churchill and Roosevelt tolerated) shaking the hand of egomaniacal Gen. Charles de Gaulle (whom they loathed), suggesting that the French problem had been solved. It hadn't.

The rest of the conference had gone generally well. The United States agreed to join Britain in a combined bomber offensive on German targets and affirmed its "Germany First" commitment. The British tacitly agreed to a cross-channel attack sometime in 1944.

As the press conference was about to conclude, Roosevelt uttered a phrase that took Churchill and journalists by surprise. He began to speak of Civil War icon Ulysses S. Grant and his famous nickname, "and the next thing I knew," Roosevelt later recalled, "I had said it."[17]

Unconditional surrender. No peace talks. No negotiating.

At Casablanca, Roosevelt and Churchill also tried to unite French forces under Henri Giraud (far left) with Charles de Gaulle (second from right).

A popular myth emerged that the president's statement was a slip of the tongue, that he neither desired it as a war aim nor discussed the idea with others. In reality, Roosevelt's and Churchill's cabinets had already debated the issue and agreed to it. But Roosevelt gave the prime minister no warning that he was going to unveil the policy at that time.[18]

From that day forward, a full fifteen months after the United States had joined in the war, the Allies had a finite, definable, and shared goal.[19]

For unknown reasons, both Roosevelt and Churchill were extremely ill for a month after Casablanca.

8. THE TEHRAN CONFERENCE (NOVEMBER 28–DECEMBER 1, 1943)

It was the first conference of "the Big Three" and the first ever meeting between an American president and a Soviet leader. Topics were kept at a high level, with specifics to be laid out in future meetings. Stalin agreed to enter the war against Japan sometime after the war in Europe reached a favorable end. Roosevelt outlined an intent to retake Burma.

On points of contention, the odd man out was routinely Churchill. He failed to convince his associates of pulling Turkey into the war. He also argued unsuccessfully for a greater commitment to a Balkan campaign (similar to a plan he had espoused during World War I) or a renewed effort to reach Germany through Italy. On several occasions he recommended delaying the invasion of France beyond the target of mid-1944, fearing a replay of Dunkirk and DIEPPE. Roosevelt and Stalin were jointly opposed. And so went most of the meetings.[20]

At Tehran, the Big Three—Roosevelt, Churchill, and Stalin—finalized plans for a two-front assault on Germany and the Soviet Union's later commitment against Japan in the Pacific.

On his impression of Stalin, Roosevelt optimistically observed, "I believe that we are going to get along very well with him and the Russian people—very well indeed." Churchill, sensing his less-than-equal status at the conference, equated the situation with being a "poor little English donkey" stuck between a Russian bear and an American buffalo.[21]

Churchill hosted a lavish dinner on the third night of the conference, which happened to be his sixty-ninth birthday. When Stalin arrived, Churchill welcomed his guest with a warm greeting and an outstretched hand. Stalin ignored him.

9. THE YALTA CONFERENCE (FEBRUARY 4–11, 1945)

Roosevelt came to the Crimea with two goals in mind: to ensure the defeat of Japan and to create the foundation of a United Nations. Both objectives, he believed, required the Soviet Union.

Stalin again pledged to fight the Japanese Empire, committing the Red Army to attack Manchuria three months after peace in Europe. In exchange, the Soviet leader demanded the Kurile Islands and the southern half of Sakhalin Island. On the United Nations, Stalin agreed to Soviet participation, provided the Soviet Union had sixteen seats, one for each Soviet state plus the USSR as a whole. Roosevelt and Churchill talked him down to three.

All agreed that Germany and Austria would be divided, demilitarized, and de-Nazified. Stalin suggested taking cash reparations from Germany, which would be split among the Big Three. Remembering how reparations had ruined the Treaty of Versailles, Churchill rejected the idea.

Most of the conference was spent on Poland, its borders, and its government. Stalin had already installed a provisional government, one very sympathetic to Soviet interests. Yet he promised to uphold the Declaration of Liberated Europe, forged earlier at the Yalta conference, which guaranteed "the right of all peoples to choose the form of government under which they will live."[22]

Historians commonly consider the conference to be "Year Zero" of the cold war, when a visibly dying Roosevelt and a politically compromised Churchill naively gave in to a land-hungry Stalin. In reality, it was the high point of Allied cooperation, when all three participants were naive and optimistic, incapable of foreseeing how future events—namely the death of an enemy and the detonation of an atomic device—could destroy what Yalta had achieved.[23]

The Big Three met for the last time at Yalta. Roosevelt had only two months to live. In four months, Churchill was out of power.

In the interest of security, transcripts from the Yalta Conference were not made public until 1947.

10. HITLER'S SUDDEN DEPARTURE (APRIL 30, 1945)

Undoubtedly, nothing united the Allies as much as Adolf Hitler. By striking fear among his rivals, the German Führer drove together devout ideological enemies. On April 30, 1945, that unifying force ceased to exist. Trapped in his Berlin bunker with the Red Army only blocks away, Hitler decided to take his own life, stating that he "preferred death to cowardly abdication or even capitulation."[24]

As time would prove, Hitler's decision meant the end of Allied cooperation. Confirming the impact of the Führer, Germany became the epicenter of East-West hostilities for more than forty years. No other location was remotely as divisive—not Japan, not Italy, not even Poland—where a tacit gentlemen's agreement assured Soviet domination. In blasting a hole through the back of his head, Hitler arguably fired the first shot of the cold war. "Now he's done it, the bastard," said Stalin upon hearing the news of the warlord's suicide. "Too bad he could not have been taken alive."[25]

Fearing Hitler's corpse would become a rallying point for future Nazi uprisings, the Soviets took his charred remains from the Berlin Chancellery garden on May 2, 1945, and secretly transported them to Moscow. The Soviet government waited until 1968 before admitting they had taken the body.

SPEECHES

The Second World War may have been the zenith of the political speech. Never before or since had so much been at stake and the public so affixed upon the voices of their leaders. Never before had so many heard the same words simultaneously, as Hitler's propaganda minister Joseph Goebbels contended, "I hold radio to be the most modern and most important instrument of mass influence that exists anywhere." And since the advent of television, never again would sound have the same leverage as image in politics.[26]

Of the following presenters, three deserve particular attention for their skills. Franklin D. Roosevelt mastered the radio like no other. Armed with a select circle of exceptional speechwriters and a baritone intonation of absolute refinement, he exuded confidence and was equally capable in a room of a thousand faces or a single microphone. In turning words into works of art, few politicians ever matched the esteemed Winston Churchill. Almost inept at impromptu deliveries, he labored for hours to write out his dissertations, each one an elegant script. In stirring mass rallies, no one ever equaled Adolf Hitler. Followed more for the passion rather than the substance of his messages, Hitler could credit oration as the alpha and omega of his power.

Listed here in chronological order are the most significant speeches uttered by Hitler, Roosevelt, Churchill, and others during the conflict, based on the extent to which each message dictated policy and defined the war itself.

1. "THE ANNIHILATION OF THE JEWISH RACE" (HITLER—JANUARY 30, 1939)

Hitler's 1925 wandering rant of *Mein Kampf* publicized his deep-seated hatred for "international Jewry" and its supposed destructive effect on German culture. The Third Reich's anti-Jewish laws, growing in number and ferocity since 1935, also demonstrated a political willingness to let harsh rhetoric turn into punishing edicts. But in a Reichstag speech on the sixth anniversary of his ascension to the chancellorship, Hitler spoke of an answer to the "Jewish question" that went beyond repression and deportation.

The long and loud sermon contained the usual contaminants—denunciations of the VERSAILLES TREATY, warnings of the "Red plague" of communism, declarations of a desired peace. More than usual, he spoke of the West. He emphasized how Americans, Britons, Dutch, and others were unwilling to take all of Germany's Jews. He then concluded that a solution to the "problem" was forthcoming.

> In the course of my life I have very often been a prophet and have usually been ridiculed for it…If the international Jewish financiers in and outside Europe should succeed in plunging the nations once more into a world war, then the result will not be the Bolshevization of the earth, and thus the victory of Jewry, but the annihilation of the Jewish race in Europe!

No document bearing Hitler's signature has ever surfaced authorizing the extermination of Jews. But his January 30, 1939, speech was the first and most damning indication that he viewed genocide as an acceptable end, if not a justifiable means, to the conduct of war.[27]

Hitler went on to use the phrase "annihilation of the Jewish race in Europe" word-for-word in five other public speeches.

---

2. "I HAVE ALSO REARMED THEM" (HITLER—APRIL 28, 1939)

In the uneasy spring of 1940, Franklin Roosevelt sidestepped diplomatic etiquette and bluntly requested Hitler spell out Germany's foreign policy. Two weeks later der Führer delivered a sober response. Standing before an audience of Reichstag members in the Berlin Kroll Opera House, Hitler gave one of his most credible and coherent summations of his political career. It may have been his best.

The Reichstag was a venue Hitler commanded but held in low esteem. On the other hand, the attendees never failed to show their support for der Führer.

On Britain, Hitler insisted he respected the kingdom but accused it of encircling Germany with hostile alliances, as it allegedly had done in 1914. On Poland, he demanded access to the Baltic port of Danzig: "Danzig is a German city and wishes to belong to Germany." In light of these "injustices," he proceeded to cancel Germany's 1934 nonaggression pact with Poland and his 1935 treaty with Britain assuring German limitations on warship construction.

He finished this virtual war warning by speaking directly to Roosevelt, painting himself as simultaneously victim, savior, and avenger.

> I cannot feel myself responsible for the fate of the world, as this world took no interest in the pitiful fate of my own people. I have regarded myself as called upon by Providence to serve my own people alone…I have succeeded in finding useful work once more for the whole of seven million unemployed…Not only have I united the German people politically, but I have also rearmed them.

It was his last major public appearance before the war. For three and a half months he sat, waited, and watched. Poland rejected his demands outright. The United States remained isolationist. Britain and France failed to establish an alliance with Moscow. To Hitler, his speech appeared to have reaped great rewards.[28]

Though compelling, Hitler's response to Roosevelt was also one of the longest of his career, lasting over two hours.

---

3. "THEIR FINEST HOUR" (CHURCHILL—JUNE 18, 1940)

When France fell to the Germans in June 1940, Britain looked to be next. Recently defeated French Gen. Maxime Weygand predicted: "In three weeks England will have her neck wrung like a chicken." Recently elected prime minister, Churchill stood before Parliament to bolster not only Britain but all states threatened or occupied. It was to be one of the most eloquent and passionate orations of his distinguished career.[29]

> What General Weygand called the Battle of France is over. I expect that the Battle of Britain is about to begin. Upon this battle depends the survival of Christian civilization...[I]f we fail, then the whole world, including the United States, including all that we have known and cared for, will sink into the abyss of a new Dark Age made more sinister, and perhaps more protracted, by the lights of perverted science. Let us therefore brace ourselves to our duties and so bear ourselves that, if the British Empire and its Commonwealth last for a thousand years, men will still say, "This was their finest hour."

Churchill's magnum opus initially received mixed reviews. Over time it became deeply inspiring and shockingly accurate. He successfully predicted a direct battle with Germany, one to be fought almost exclusively in the air. He also foretold a poor showing from fascist Italy, joking, "There is a general curiosity...to find out whether the

Italians are up to the level they were at in the last war or whether they have fallen off at all." On his prophecies of a war dominated by "perverted science," he was all too right. That evening, as if to punctuate Churchill's warnings of battles and technology, more than a hundred German bombers stormed over England and killed nine civilians in Cambridge.[30]

Churchill delivered his speech on June 18, 1940, the 125th anniversary of the Battle of Waterloo.

---

4. "I NOW SPEAK FOR FRANCE" (DE GAULLE—JUNE 18, 1940)

On June 17, 1940, France's undersecretary of state, and until recently a tank brigadier, landed in London and was brought to No. 10 Downing Street. Churchill knew the tall and stern de Gaulle, though few others had ever heard of him. When the middle-ranking Frenchman asked for BBC airtime to broadcast a message of hope, Churchill immediately agreed, as the prime minister was also diligently crafting a speech for that very purpose. Both voices would hit the airwaves the following evening.

Hours after Churchill's fatherly announcement, the deep and determined voice of de Gaulle commanded his countrymen to keep fighting:

> For France is not alone. She is not alone! She is not alone! Behind her is a vast empire, and she can make common cause with the British Empire, which commands the seas and is continuing the struggle. Like England, she can draw unreservedly on the immense industrial resources of the United States...Tomorrow I shall broadcast again from London...I, General de Gaulle, a French soldier and military leader, realize that I now speak for France.

Pure de Gaulle. Churchill had not granted airtime for the following night. Most important, the British had made no indication of recognizing him in any official capacity, nor had the United States, nor for that matter had the French. But de Gaulle's speech was the first step on a long career of self-proclaimed greatness, and he gradually became the de facto head of France.

Though he kept a small army fighting for the Allies, de Gaulle practically asked for the world in return. Repulsed by the uncooperative giant, Churchill would later say, "The heaviest cross I bear is the Cross of Lorraine."[31]

Due to a lack of equipment, committed instead to Churchill's "Finest Hour" speech that same day, the BBC made no recording of de Gaulle's historic proclamation, which angered the Frenchman for the rest of his life.

---

5. "THE ARSENAL OF DEMOCRACY" (ROOSEVELT—DECEMBER 29, 1940)

By his own measure, Roosevelt's most significant address between his first inaugural and the declaration of war on Japan was his Arsenal of Democracy speech, delivered as his last "fireside chat" of 1940.[32]

Though most of the U.S. population was dead set on staying out of the war, much of Europe and eastern China were under the yoke of foreign occupation. Speaking from the White House to an international radio audience, Roosevelt assured his listeners that the best way to avoid sending troops overseas would be to send weapons instead.

The people of Europe who are defending themselves do not ask where to do their fighting. They ask us for the implements of war, the planes, the tanks, the guns, the freighters which will enable them to fight for their liberty and for our security. Emphatically we must get these weapons to them, get them to them in sufficient volume and quickly enough so that we and our children will be saved the agony and suffering of war which others have had to endure...We must be the great arsenal of democracy…I call upon our people with absolute confidence that our common cause will greatly succeed.

Response to the speech was overwhelming. Cables, calls, and letters poured into the White House, more than Roosevelt had ever received in his career. Nearly every correspondence expressed approval and support. Roosevelt would follow up this triumph by introducing a bill to Congress for a program called LEND-LEASE.[33]

Many Londoners who tuned in to Roosevelt's historic statement had a hard time hearing it. At the time of the broadcast, the British capital was undergoing a sizable Luftwaffe air raid.

---

6. "WE MUST WAGE A RUTHLESS FIGHT" (STALIN—JULY 3, 1941)

Quivering, stuttering Foreign Minister Vyacheslav Molotov delivered the tragic news via state radio: Nazi Germany had just invaded the Soviet Union. Molotov nervously called for action, but his words were a feeble plea made less convincing by the canned idioms he sputtered: "The government calls upon you, citizens of the Soviet Union, to rally still more closely around our glorious Bolshevist party, around our Soviet Government, around our great leader and comrade, Stalin."

Stalin ordered Molotov to deliver the speech, as he was either unwilling or unable to do so. Nearly two weeks passed before the Man of Steel brought himself to talk to his people, yet when he did, his words conveyed a new message.

We must wage a ruthless fight against all disorganizers of the rear…
All who by their panicmongering and cowardice hinder the work of defense, no matter who they are, must be immediately hauled before a military tribunal…In case of a forced retreat of Red Army units, all rolling stock must be evacuated; to the enemy must not be

left a single engine, a single railway car, not a single pound of grain
or a gallon of fuel.

Stalin was unveiling a policy of slash and burn. Nothing, including
people, would be spared in creating a sea of devastation before the
approaching Germans. Listeners were not exactly enthralled, but Stalin
softened the blow by appealing to religion, ethnicity, and czarist heroes.
It was his first use of Mother Russia imagery, a departure from years of
Communist rhetoric. Citizens found hope in the changing language,
believing victory would bring new freedoms previously unimaginable.
In reality, it was a ploy—and an effective one. Stalin immediately enforced slash-and-burn tactics and speedy executions, making the Soviet
Union deadly to invaders and citizens alike.[34]

---

*During the war, four million Germans died in the Soviet Union, mostly
military. Twenty-five million Soviets died, mostly civilian.*

---

7. "A DATE WHICH WILL LIVE IN INFAMY" (ROOSEVELT—DECEMBER 8, 1941)

"They have attacked us at PEARL HARBOR. We're all in the same boat
now." Roosevelt's words elated Churchill, who had called the White
House soon after hearing ambiguous reports of a Japanese offensive in
the Pacific. The president's mood stood in stark contrast. Incoming
reports only added to the confusion within the executive mansion.
Casualty totals were imprecise. Dispatches reported Japanese landings
on Oahu. Strikes on the American West Coast appeared possible. The
situation in the Philippines was unknown.

One certainty was Roosevelt's first move. He immediately drafted
a request for a declaration of war. Unlike most of his speeches, this
one he created almost entirely on his own. Presented to a packed
joint session of Congress and millions of radio listeners worldwide, his
statement was brief—just six minutes—and to the point.[35]

Yesterday, December 7, 1941—a date which will live in infamy—
the United States of America was suddenly and deliberately attacked
by naval and air forces of the Empire of Japan. The United States
was at peace with that nation and, at the solicitation of Japan, was
still in conversation with its Government and its Emperor looking toward the maintenance of peace in the Pacific...I ask that the
Congress declare that since the unprovoked and dastardly attack by
Japan on Sunday, December seventh, a state of war has existed between the United States and the Japanese Empire.

Up to the time of the speech, Roosevelt was not completely sure the
country or Congress would approve of going to war. The Axis had previously sunk American vessels in the Atlantic and on the China coast.
None of the incidents pulled the public away from isolationism. Yet
whatever doubts the president had were quickly dispelled. Within hours
of his address, Congress approved a declaration of war, voting unanimously in the Senate and 388-to-1 in the House of Representatives.[36]

*Upon hearing of Roosevelt's call for a declaration of war against Japan,
Hitler accused the United States of provoking the attack and called
Roosevelt "mentally insane."*

8. "TOTAL WAR" (GOEBBELS—FEBRUARY 18, 1943)

The Nazi Ministry for Propaganda and Information worked diligently
to shelter the public from the unpleasantness of war, such as rationing
and casualty lists. But after the invasion of the Soviet Union, such
protective measures were impossible to maintain. Time, money, and
resources were running out. The numbers of dead and missing were
rising. When STALINGRAD ended in utter defeat for the Germans,
Joseph Goebbels feared the sudden loss would shatter the confidence
of the home front.

In a flash of despotic brilliance, wee, wiry Goebbels decided to magnify the tragedy rather than hide it, to shock the nation into sacrificing everything for victory. Hitler, hiding in his Wolf's Lair and wallowing in defeat, hesitantly agreed to the tactic.[37]

On January 30, 1943, the Reich minister unleashed the news. Though more than ninety thousand Germans were taken alive at STALINGRAD, Goebbels insinuated that they had all died, going so far as to intercept letters from prisoners to silence their existence. To emphasize a sense of mourning, he closed businesses and played songs of bereavement on state radio for three days. He then called for a huge rally to be staged at the Berlin Sports Palace, with extensive media coverage and teeming masses of party faithful, to deliver a new message.[38]

> Total war is the demand of the hour…The danger facing us is enormous. The efforts we take to meet it must be just as enormous. The time has come to remove the gloves and use our fists…The German people are shedding their most valuable blood in this battle…[T]he danger is to us all, and we must all do our share. Those who today do not understand that will thank us tomorrow on bended knees that we courageously and firmly took on the task.

On cue, sacrifices were made. In 1943 war production increased, mostly from influxes of female and slave labor. In addition, more German civilians died in Allied bombings, more German soldiers died in combat, and more "enemies of the state" died in concentration camps than in any previous year.

When Goebbels finished his speech, the crowd at the Berlin Sports Palace gave him a thunderous standing ovation that lasted more than twenty minutes.

9. "THE TIME FOR DECISIVE BATTLE HAS ARRIVED" (TOJO—JULY 19, 1944)

Echoing the German phenomenon the previous year, Japan was about to undergo a drastic change in policy. Since the war's beginning, the Japanese hierarchy concealed their tremendous losses in the Pacific. But the devastating loss of SAIPAN and the growing number of B-29s over the Japanese mainland fractured the myth of invincibility. Peace campaigners and war hawks alike demanded immediate change.

The obvious target was Gen. Tojo Hideki, prime minister of the empire since October 1941. Attempting to keep his domineering position, Tojo tried everything, from changing his cabinet to threatening to dethrone the emperor. Nothing worked.

Realizing his once solid support had liquefied, Tojo resigned along with his entire cabinet. In his last act as prime minister, he spoke on Radio Tokyo. It would be the first time the nation of Japan would hear the true and terrible costs of the war to date. As Goebbels had done in Berlin, Tojo used the revelation to shock his people into a heightened level of resolve.

> Our Empire has entered the most difficult state in its entire history. But these developments have also provided us with the opportunity to smash the enemy and win the war. The time for decisive battle has arrived.

Thereafter, Japanese spoke of "the spirit of Saipan" and committed themselves to total war. Schools closed. Families evacuated their children to the countryside. Factory workers labored round the clock. Most significantly, military tactics became increasingly suicidal. Within months of Tojo's speech, the armed forces resorted to all-or-nothing offensives, initiated the use of kamikaze, and promoted the idea of fighting until every last American or Japanese was dead.[39]

A clique of junior officers desiring an end to the war had schemed to kill Tojo using explosives if he did not step down. The target date was July 20, the same day a bomb went off in an East Prussia bunker and failed to kill Hitler.

10. "A NEW AND MOST CRUEL BOMB" (HIROHITO— AUGUST 15, 1945)

On August 14, 1945, forty-four-year-old Emperor Hirohito entered the library of the imperial palace to record a statement. He had decided to accept the Allies' demand of UNCONDITIONAL SURRENDER. The emperor and several key advisers believed he had to make the announcement personally or risk a revolution, if not anarchy.

The recording played on national radio the following day. It was the first time the Japanese public had ever heard his voice, and the first time in its twenty-six-hundred-year history that Japan surrendered. At noon Tokyo time, trains pulled into stations and waited. Street traffic ceased. Radio sets across the empire tuned in to the subdued strains of the national anthem followed by the husky voice of Prime Minister Suzuki Kantaro introducing the emperor. After a brief silence, a high-pitched, soft, melodic, and tired voice began to speak. Using the ancient formal language of the high court, which many listeners found difficult to follow, the emperor stated:

> The war situation has developed not necessarily to Japan's advantage, while the general trends of the world have all turned against her interest. Moreover, the enemy has begun to employ a new and most cruel bomb, the power of which to do damage is, indeed, incalculable, taking the toll of many innocent lives. Should we continue to fight, it would not only result in an ultimate collapse and obliteration of the Japanese nation, but also it would lead to the total extinction of human civilization.

He thanked his subjects for their selfless sacrifice and acknowledged their considerable pain and suffering, concluding with a request for calm acceptance: "Beware most strictly of any outbursts of emotion that may engender needless complications, of any fraternal contention and strife that may create confusion, lead you astray, and cause you to lose the confidence of the world." Following his speech, a brief announcement stated that surrender was due primarily to atomic weapons.[40]

By and large, citizens went into apathetic mourning. Some went to the gates of the imperial palace and cried or prayed or cheered that the war was over. Some committed suicide. Several senior politicians and officers chose to kill themselves—a former prime minister, the minister of war, a former chief of staff, the founder of the kamikaze plan. Scores of junior officers shot themselves, committed hara-kiri, or blew themselves to pieces with grenades. Several burn and radiation victims in a Hiroshima hospital demanded revenge against their attackers. But peace ensued nonetheless.[41]

To reach remote areas that did not have radio access, the Japanese government launched flocks of balloons trailing giant banners that read: "Great Emperor Accepts Peace."

SIMILARITIES BETWEEN STALIN AND HITLER

Of the twentieth century's prominent leaders, none were more despotic than Adolf Hitler and Joseph Stalin. Unquestioned in rule, extreme in method, they expressed little respect for anyone, save themselves and each other. Wary allies in the September 1939 invasion of Poland, they became malignant enemies by June 1941 and thereafter spread virulent ruination upon nearly all of Central and Eastern Europe. In the end, their respective reigns accounted for more than half the deaths administered and received during the whole of the Second World War.

For such absolute adversaries, they shared a number of fundamental traits. Brooding and temperamental, intelligent and widely read, they were also socially unskilled and physically small. Night owls with a penchant for movies, they slept with difficulty, felt ill frequently, and avoided exercise religiously. Despite their infirmities, they were eerily charismatic. People were often awed by their direct and riveting stare—Hitler's eyes a clear and azure blue, Stalin's a demonic yellow.

Naturally there were differences. Stalin was better traveled, having toiled as a revolutionary in Krakow, St. Petersburg, Berlin, London, Stockholm, at home in the sunny Caucasus, and in exile within the Arctic Circle. In 1913 he briefly visited Vienna, where hundreds of aspiring art students lived, including a twenty-four-year-old named Hitler, who at that time had seen little of the world beyond Austria and Bavaria.

Of the two, only Hitler had served in the military, fighting nearly four years in the First World War. A messenger for a Bavarian infantry regiment stationed in the trenches of northern France, he was twice wounded and twice awarded the Iron Cross before being temporarily blinded by mustard gas in 1918.

Later in life, Hitler proved to be the better public speaker. Clear of voice, he began his orations quietly, then built himself and his message into climactic frenzy. Stalin possessed a gravely tenor sound and spoke in a manner best described as stoic:

Despite their differences, fundamental parallels pervaded amid the two most dominant figures of the European war. Here in roughly chronological order are ten major similarities between the men who sacrificed millions in an attempt to destroy each other.[42]

1. HITLER WAS NOT GERMAN, AND STALIN WAS NOT RUSSIAN

Officially, Joseph Stalin's birthday was December 21, 1879, but newly uncovered evidence indicates it was actually December 6, 1878. Biographer Edvard Radzinsky credits the discrepancy as yet another example of how Stalin habitually buried the past.[43]

Born in the Transcaucus country of Georgia, Josef Vissarionovich Dzhugashvili was the last of four children and the only one to live past infancy. As a young man, he resorted to nearly twenty different aliases, including Koba ("Indomitable") and Ivanovich ("son of Ivan"), before settling on Stalin ("Steel") in 1913. His poverty-stricken and barely literate mother doted over him and sacrificed much for his happiness. His father was a cobbler and was known to be verbally and physically abusive to his son.[44]

Ten years later, Adolfus Hitler entered the world in the tiny Austrian village of Braunau am Inn on April 20, 1889. The fourth of six children, only he and his younger sister Paula survived childhood.

Adolf's mother idolized him. His father, a former cobbler turned civil servant, was born Alois Schicklgruber. In 1876, Alois took the name of his stepfather, whose surname had various spellings—Hiedler, Hüttler, Hitler. Alois often denounced and occasionally beat Adolf, yet the son would later say of the father, "I really loved him."[45]

As he grew up, Adolf expressed increasing animosity toward his native soil, especially against multiethnic Vienna. "The longer I lived in that city," he wrote, "the stronger became my hatred for the promiscuous swarm of foreign peoples."[46] To his native Georgia, Josef Dzhugashvili was icily indifferent. He eventually viewed the country as simply another frontier for socialist expansion. In time, both men ruthlessly incorporated their homelands into larger adopted states.

Among other "adopted sons," Greece's Alexander the Great was Macedonian, Napoleon was born in Corsica, Saint Patrick was British, and the House of Windsor had German origins.

2. BOTH DESPISED SCHOOL AND INTELLECTUALS

Attending secondary school, Hitler recalled of his teachers, "Their one object was to stuff our brains and turn us into erudite apes like themselves." Young Josef Dzhugashvili, subjected to an overtly strict seminary where he learned Russian, confessed he hated "the harsh intolerance and Jesuitical discipline that crushed me so mercilessly."[47]

Both displayed above-average intelligence and superior memory, but neither cared for the structure of a scholastic environment. Both were prone to fighting—meek Hitler in the verbal arena and dwarfish Josef with his fists. Out of the classroom, both were ringleaders of playground bullies, although both were also choirboys.

Neither graduated. Despite finishing his studies at age sixteen, Hitler never secured a Leaving Certificate, for reasons unknown. Fancying himself a painter, he twice attempted and failed to gain admission into the Vienna Academy of Fine Arts. He could draft buildings with meticulous skill but had a difficult time drawing nature, especially humans. Stalin claimed to have been kicked out of seminary at age nineteen for being a Marxist. In reality, he was expelled for skipping exams.[48]

In their adulthood, Stalin and Hitler showed particular contempt for intellectuals and laureates. Among their closest advisers, only Hitler's hundred-pound propaganda minister, Joseph Goebbels, and none of Stalin's lieutenants could have been considered an intellectual. In fact, the learned elite of Europe were among the first condemned to Soviet and Nazi concentration camps. An untold number of additional scholars and artists were forced into exile. Subsequently, the years of Hitlerism and Stalinism were veritable dark ages for the humanities. Perennial epicenters of the fine arts, Germany and Russia produced virtually no paintings, writing, or theater productions of merit from 1933 to 1945.[49]

For Joseph and Adolf, their best grades in school were in history.

---

3. BOTH SERVED TIME IN PRISON

Between 1902 and 1917 Stalin was arrested seven times, usually for organizing anti-czarist meetings and demonstrations. As with most detainees of the Russian Empire, he was usually banished to work colonies. These desolate camps pockmarked the empire from the Black Sea to the Pacific Ocean, the worst among them in remote and climatically brutal Siberia. The fact that he managed to escape from these nether regions nearly every time led his enemies to hypothesize that he was a czarist agent, though this "agent" spent nearly a decade of his life in jail or exile.[50]

Altogether, Hitler spent a little over a year in prison. His first stint was a five-week detainment in 1922 for inciting a riot against the Weimar government. An incensed Hitler equated his sentence with the crucifixion of Christ.[51]

Hitler's second and last incarceration occurred as a result of his failed Munich Beerhall Putsch in 1923, in which he and nearly three thousand followers tried to overthrow the regional government of Bavaria. Sixteen of his party were killed, two more were mortally wounded. For his actions, Hitler received a sentence of five years yet would serve only thirteen months, which proved to be little more than a sabbatical. Jailed with cohorts such as Rudolf Hess, the future ruler of Germany received visits and care packages from admirers and managed to complete the first half of his autobiographical *Mein Kampf*.[52]

Hitler detested the Weimar government, which had been in power for three years. Stalin conspired against the Romanov dynasty, which had ruled for three centuries.

---

4. NEITHER HAD A STEADY JOB IN HIS LIFE

With the exception of dictator, a position Hitler held for twelve years and Stalin for twenty-five, gainful employment was a rare condition for the future demagogues of forced labor.

After leaving secondary school, Hitler spent more than five years nearly destitute in Vienna and Munich. He painted postcards, designed posters, and relied heavily on a small trust fund. Contrary to legend, he was never a professional house painter or paperhanger, but from 1910 to 1914, odd jobs were his unwelcome lot. Before he became a soldier in the Sixteenth Bavarian regiment in World War I, he was down to a single suit of clothes, living hand to mouth, and occasionally homeless.[53]

Stalin was initially a political insurgent, which brought him little pay and few benefits. To augment his activism, he worked briefly in an observatory, then as a writer for various underground newspapers including *Pravda*, but he was primarily an unpaid organizer of labor marches and strikes. On his many arrest forms, the space for "skill or profession" was usually left blank.[54]

Bouts of imprisonment did little to interrupt his calling, but unlike Hitler, who longed for attention, Josef Dzhugashvili sought anonymity.

Not until the aftermath of the First World War did each man excel at a given task, specifically agitation. Hitler's penchant for oratory and Stalin's faith in action gained considerable recognition from their peers. In the summer of 1917, Vladimir Lenin took notice of the ruthless Stalin and pulled him into the upper echelons of the small but growing Bolshevik Party. In the autumn of 1919 Anton Drexler invited the talented speaker Hitler to join the minuscule German Worker's Party.

Before attaining higher-profile jobs with Hitler, Adolf Eichmann was a traveling salesman, Joseph Goebbels was unemployed, Hermann Göring was a pilot for the Danish government, and Heinrich Himmler was a fertilizer salesman.

---

5. BOTH LOST COMPANIONS TO SUICIDE

Stalin and Hitler were not always the cold and cruel figures remembered by history. Into early adulthood, each displayed a modest capacity for charm, humor, and charity.

Such attributes faded with the accumulation of power. Foreshadowing the public at large, many of those closest to Stalin and Hitler saw them undergo a gradual transformation from charismatic leaders into static figureheads. Workloads began to consume them, and leisure time became nonexistent. Relationships thus devolved into master and servant, and interactive social circles narrowed to static cliques. Their most devout companions started to view Stalin and Hitler as inaccessible, intolerable, and pointlessly cruel.

Geli Raubal was, by some accounts, Hitler's one true love. She was twenty years his junior, pretty, a gifted singer, and his niece. Through the late 1920s they had grown close and shared considerable time together. Whether the relationship was ever physical is unknown. Yet Hitler was exceedingly protective, often preventing her from interacting with other people, especially men. In 1931, after falling into deep depression over her secluded life, she hid in Hitler's Munich apartment and shot herself.[55]

During the great Russian famine of 1932, brought on by Stalin's attempt to collectivize all Soviet farmland, his wife Nadia chastised him in front of party officials for the terrible suffering he had caused. After a torrid verbal exchange between the dictator and his much younger bride, she departed alone. Hours later Nadia entered her room at the Kremlin and shot herself.

Altogether, the two men eventually lost at least a score of relatives, friends, and companions to suicide, some by the insistence of the dictators themselves.

As Hitler's new bride, Eva Braun committed suicide on April 30, 1945. As Hitler's mistress, she had attempted suicide twice before—in 1932 and 1934.

6. BOTH FABRICATED CONSPIRACIES TO CONSOLIDATE POWER

By January 1933, Adolf Hitler had become chancellor of Germany, but his duties were limited by the Weimar Constitution, and the National Socialists were just one of four large political parties in Germany. The following month, a fire destroyed the Reichstag building. In an emergency session, the government immediately suspended civil liberties and weeks later established Hitler as dictator of Germany.

On December 1, 1934, an assassin shot and killed Politburo member Sergei Kirov, by many accounts the second most powerful man in the Soviet Union and a vocal critic of Stalin's rule. Stalin expressed shock and dismay over the incident and demanded an immediate investigation. Within a hundred hours, nearly one hundred people had been accused and summarily executed for the crime.[56]

Though there has been no conclusive evidence, the Reichstag fire and the Kirov assassination were probably sanctioned by Hitler and Stalin, respectively. More important, each event marked the beginning of absolute rule for each dictator.

Three weeks after the Reichstag incident, SS leader Heinrich Himmler declared the opening of Dachau, the first Nazi concentration camp. The following months witnessed the first application of anti-Jewish laws, disbanding of trade unions, dissolving of all opposition parties, and the creation of a special court with exclusive jurisdiction over cases of treason. Hours after Kirov's assassination, Soviet law forbade appeals to sentences of death and unleashed wave after wave of mass arrests, most of which incarcerated people with no prior record and revealed no evidence of criminal activity. Within years, the number of political prisoners reached six figures in Germany and seven figures in the Soviet Union.[57]

The invasion of Poland in 1939 began on the pretext of a staged incident.
German soldiers dressed up as Polish border guards and faked an attack on
a German radio outpost. Hitler presented the event as fact and launched
his blitzkrieg the following day.

7. BOTH OWNED FEW PERSONAL POSSESSIONS

Insatiable in their lust for authority and conquest, both men expressed profound disinterest in material wealth. Stalin once said to his wife, "I never loved money, because I usually never had any." Hitler told confidant Albert Speer, "I would find a simple little house in Berlin quite sufficient. I have enough power and prestige; I don't need such luxury to sustain me."[58]

Though adamant about living simply, both functioned within a bourgeois lifestyle, with servants, drivers, cooks, and numerous residences. Stalin had several dachas (country homes) at his disposal, leftovers from dispossessed elite of the prerevolutionary era. But their private quarters, whatever the location, were humbly furnished, their wardrobes simple, and their diets basic if not rudimentary.

The state, rather than themselves, was to be the recipient and expression of wealth. Both men supported and at times directed the confiscation of art works and antiquities, but neither kept a single piece for himself. Instead they pilfered in order to amplify the holdings of national museums and galleries. Grander still were their plans to reconstruct major cities. Hitler envisioned a national stadium at Nuremberg holding four hundred thousand spectators, a national assembly hall with a central dome towering nine hundred feet in the air (nearly twice the height of the Washington Monument), and a Berlin headquarters with six million square feet of floor space. Stalin flaunted even greater aspirations, including a Palace of Soviets in Moscow designed to be the largest building on earth. Not unlike their ideologies, almost none of Stalin's or Hitler grandiose architectural visions were completed, interrupted by the outbreak of mutual hostility.[59]

Upon his death, Stalin's personal effects consisted of little more than some uniforms, a few pairs of boots, and a well-worn sheepskin peasant coat. So, too, Hitler passed with a dearth of property to his name, among them a flag and some trinkets acquired during a recent birthday party.

8. NEITHER HAD EXPERIENCE IN MILITARY LEADERSHIP

Franklin D. Roosevelt was Woodrow Wilson's assistant secretary of the navy. From 1922 dictator Benito Mussolini served as his own navy, army, and air force minister. CHIANG KAI-SHEK studied military tactics in Japan and Russia and was commander in chief of Nationalist China since 1925. Longtime soldier Winston Churchill served as an officer, minister of munitions, secretary of war, and first lord of the admiralty before becoming prime minister. Military academy graduate Tojo Hideki worked as chief of military police, chief of staff, and minister of war. Of all the major leaders in the Second World War, only two possessed essentially no background in military authority.

Despite four long years of meritorious service in the FIRST WORLD WAR, Hitler never rose beyond the rank of corporal. Stalin served in the Red Army during the RUSSIAN CIVIL WAR, but only as a political adjutant.

At the end of the war, Hitler declared the German people unworthy of his military genius; Stalin bestowed upon himself the rank of Generalissimo, the medal "Order of Victory," and the title "Hero of the Soviet Union."[60]

9. BOTH AVOIDED THE FRONT FOR THE ENTIRE WAR

When German guns came within twenty miles of Moscow in December 1941, Stalin refused to leave the Kremlin, yet he also never visited any of his troops in the field. War or no war, seclusion was in keeping with his abstracted style of leadership. After taking power in 1928, he rarely ventured out in public, offered a decreasing number of party speeches, and avoided appearing in villages and factories altogether.

Only once, in 1943, did Stalin risk an excursion toward the

fighting, an event he painted in the most gallant terms to Roosevelt and Churchill. His line commanders viewed the occasion differently. Gen. Nikolai Voronov recalled being summoned, driven mile after mile into secluded backwoods to a cottage nowhere near the front, in which a waiting Stalin requested a synopsis of how the war was progressing. "He could see nothing from there," noted Voronov. "It was a strange unnecessary trip."[61]

So, too, Hitler became increasingly detached. Biographer Ian Kershaw notes how the Führer conducted nine public speeches in 1940, two in 1943, and none in 1944. Ebbing tides in North Africa and the Soviet Union convinced Hitler to avoid the German public almost completely. He instead shuttled between his cloistered Eagle's Nest mountain retreat at Berchtesgaden and his dreary concrete Wolf's Lair headquarters in East Prussia. When field commanders spoke of exhausted supplies and faltering troops, Hitler dismissed their reports as defeatist, often adding, "Believe me, things appear clearer when examined at longer range."

A secretary of Hitler's lamented, "We are permanently cut off from the world wherever we are…It's always the same limited group of people, always the same routine inside the fence." By autumn 1944 the Führer had been absent for so long that many of his countrymen began to believe their leader was either seriously ill or dead.[62]

In addition to military arenas, Stalin and Hitler avoided nearly everything else to do with the war. Neither ever visited a field hospital, bombed neighborhood, or concentration camp.

When traveling by train during the war, both Stalin and Hitler insisted that curtains remained drawn so they would not have to see the damage rendered on the surrounding countryside.

---

10. BOTH HAVE BEEN DEPICTED AS THE ANTICHRIST

Christian fears of the "Final Enemy" were propagated with the coming of the Second World War. Signs appeared profuse—a false deliverer, throngs of devout followers espousing a new order, eruption of war between many nations, and genocide.

To many then and now, the apparent embodiment of evil was Adolf Hitler, who spoke of a millennium (the thousand-year Reich), a divine mission (eradication of Jewish Bolshevism), and providential destiny (the rise of the German people). Others found greater evidence of a world dictator in Stalin, who fashioned a rule of idolatry (cult of Stalin), a new church eradicating all others (Marxism), and a promise of paradise (communism).[63]

Without question, both regimes were proficient at killing. Hitler's armies traversed three continents; shot, burned, starved, hanged, and bombed millions; and swept entire towns from the face of the earth. Nazi concentration camps devoured millions more.[64]

Stalin's numbers were even worse. His forced collectivization of Russian farms in the early 1930s starved as many as ten million. His Great Terror of 1936–39 purged nine of eleven of his own cabinet members, more than sixty thousand military officers, and untold millions of ordinary citizens. Between 1941 and 1945, Stalin's Red Army killed more soldiers and civilians than any other military force in the war. Estimates of those killed directly or indirectly during Stalin's entire reign approach sixty million.[65]

The term antichrist *has been applied to many historical figures, including Nero, Martin Luther, Gustavus Adolphus II, Napoleon, Benito Mussolini, Mikhail Gorbachev, Henry Kissinger, Ronald Reagan, Saddam Hussein, and a multitude of popes.*

MILITARY LIFE

LARGEST ARMED FORCES

Never before had so many served in uniform. In 1934, fewer than ten million persons worldwide were in the military. In 1944, the total neared one hundred million. Larger still was the amount of yen, pounds, rubles, marks, crowns, and francs spent to make it all happen. By 1945, several belligerents were allocating 60 percent of their national budgets on the war. In 2005 dollars, the conflict's overall price tag was in the low trillions.

Most citizens in the services were not volunteers. Many never envisioned themselves ever being in the military. Not until the late 1930s, when an ARMS RACE accelerated rapidly, did conscription become endemic. Whatever the commitment level, troops universally expressed a desire to get the fighting over with as soon as possible.

Enlisted soldiers ranged in age from ten to sixty, officers from eighteen to eighty-eight. In a war of unbridled nationalism, most armed forces were not homogenous. Sixteen percent of Lithuania was not Lithuanian. A quarter of Romania and nearly a third of Poland were of varying backgrounds. The largest ethnic group in the United States was (and still is) German.[1]

From this mix of the global family came the biggest assortment and assembly of combatants in history. Listed below, in order of total number of persons mobilized, are the largest national forces in the war.[2]

1. SOVIET UNION (21,000,000)

ENTERED WAR: 1939

PEAK STRENGTH: 13,200,000

The largest country on the planet, the Soviet Union also had the largest armed forces ever assembled under one flag. By 1945, there were as many veterans in the Soviet Union as there were people in Mexico. More Soviet women served in the Red Army than Frenchmen served under Charles de Gaulle.

Often referred to as "the Russians," the Soviets were a multiethnic assembly. In 1940, only half were Great Russians. The rest were Ukrainians, Byelorussians, Lithuanians, Poles, Georgians, Jews, Armenians, plus a hundred other ethnicities. Out of a total population of 190 million, 11 percent served in the military. Of these, the vast majority were in the massive Red Army. Fifteen of sixteen Soviets in uniform were ground troops.

Victory came at an exorbitant price for the Soviets, yet they were fortunate to avoid a two-front war with Japan.

At the start of the war, the Soviet armed forces had an extremely poor reputation internationally. Perceived as undisciplined, unwieldy, and unmotivated, the Red Army confirmed this image with a disastrous performance against greatly outnumbered Finns in the WINTER WAR of 1939–40. Yet as following events would prove, the Soviets may have been poorly trained and at times ineptly led, but they tended to fight tenaciously when placed on the defensive.

Of the roughly twenty-one million Soviet troops that were mobilized, half became casualties.

---

2. GERMANY (17,900,000)

ENTERED WAR: 1939
PEAK STRENGTH: 9,500,000

Restricted by the VERSAILLES TREATY to one hundred thousand ground troops and no navy or air force, Germany began all-out remilitarization in the mid-1930s. By 1939, it had the second-largest army and best air force worldwide. The Kriegsmarine, though far behind, had an adequate submarine arm and was hoping to eventually add aircraft carriers to its fleet.

Nearly a fourth of the population served in the war, the highest percentage of any country. For every German in the Waffen SS, there were two in the navy, four in the Luftwaffe, and twenty in the army. The majority of troops served on the eastern front. Infantry, artillery, and tank crews were five times more likely to be deployed to the East than anywhere else.

Neither the German public nor its armed forces were eager to wage war, especially since the previous contest had rather unfavorable results. But victory in Poland after a mere three weeks brought a great sense of relief if not patriotism. Seven months later, offensives into Western Europe seemed to go even better, capturing six countries in six weeks. Quick Balkan victories the following year only solidified a sense of greatness. Many assumed that the invasion of the Soviet Union would also end quickly and favorably.

Though the reputation of the German soldier remained high

throughout the war, success of the German armed forces began to wither after the massive assault of BARBAROSSA. Numerically, the German army would not peak until late 1944, but their performance had reached a high point in 1941.

Germany had some of the best ground troops in the war but could not replace the numbers they lost.

The Waffen SS was supposed to be Nazi Germany's elite guard of pure Aryans. By 1945, more than half the Waffen SS were not German. One-third were Romanian. The rest were Croatian, Dutch, Hungarian, Italian, and Ukrainian, plus a few Muslims.

---

3. UNITED STATES (16,354,000)

   ENTERED WAR: 1941
   PEAK STRENGTH: 12,000,000

In 1936, Americans spent 1 percent of the national budget on defense and ranked about seventeenth in the world in military power. Less than a decade later they had the second-largest army on earth, by far the largest navy, and the largest air force. The marines by themselves nearly equaled the entire armed forces of Australia.

For every twenty Americans in uniform, ten were in the army, five served in the army air force, four were sailors (of which two served on land), and one was a marine. Overall, Americans were the best paid and best fed service personnel in the world.

Of sixteen million in uniform, only five million served overseas, illustrating how the United States was empowered by logistics and supply.

Each American soldier in the field was supported by four tons of equipment. In comparison, material support for each Japanese soldier averaged out to a few pounds. Distance also mandated a high proportion of U.S. troops committed to supply. The United States stood three thousand to seven thousand miles away from most battle zones.[3]

Reflective of their mountainous support network, only one in three U.S. servicemen served overseas.

Of Americans enlisted in the war, less than half possessed a high school degree.

4. CHINA (14,000,000)

ENTERED WAR: 1937
PEAK STRENGTH: 5,700,000

Although China was the most populous nation on earth with nearly five hundred million inhabitants, it had the smallest percentage of combatants among the major powers. Less than 4 percent of all Chinese served in an army during the war. Never a single "armed forces," China's defense was more of a patchwork of regional militia, CHIANG KAI-SHEK holding the largest collection. His Nationalist forces initially held most of the country, but by 1938, Chiang and company were desperately holding on to the rural center around the city of Chungking (Chonqing).

In northeast China, the Communists were generally effective in winning over the population and debilitating the Japanese. As the empire concentrated troops in cities and along rail lines, the Communists operated around the pockets in between, blending into the local population and employing guerrilla tactics along vulnerable points. Only once did the Communists mount a large, organized offensive, the so-called Hundred Regiments Campaign in 1940. Killing more than twenty thousand Japanese, it also convinced Chiang that his rivals were becoming too powerful. From that point onward, the war was not China versus Japan but the Nationalists versus the Communists versus Japan.[4]

Poorly armed and generally poorly led, the Chinese fought and died in large numbers.

Due to a lack of communication equipment, Chinese officers often had to be at the head of their columns in combat. As a result, the officer class died at a rate five times faster than the enlisted.

5. JAPAN (9,100,000)

ENTERED WAR: 1937
PEAK STRENGTH: 7,500,000

Though it often appeared as if the Japanese navy was the largest branch of the imperial armed forces, the army outnumbered its naval counterpart, on average, three to one. The heaviest commitment had always been China, where Japanese manpower ranged from 800,000 to 1,500,000. The Allies rationalized backing the inept CHIANG KAI-SHEK on the belief that his Nationalists were "tying down" the bulk of the Imperial Army.

It was the army that achieved most of Japan's great successes, conquering Hong Kong, Burma, the Dutch East Indies, SINGAPORE, Malaya (Malaysia), and the Philippines. Of course, these would have been difficult if not impossible without the temporary dominance of the Imperial Navy.

Japanese armadas had a temporary advantage over their opponents. Although the Imperial Navy was the third largest in the world in 1941, it could concentrate its forces, whereas Britain and the United States had to disperse their warships across the globe. This competitive edge allowed Japan to score a string of phenomenal victories in late 1941 and early 1942, highlighted by the attacks on PEARL HARBOR and the sinking of Britain's treasured battleship HMS *Prince of Wales* off of Singapore, both achieved days within each other. Yet success was fleeting, so to speak.

The Imperial Navy had the two largest battleships ever made, the Yamato *and* Musashi. *Each was nearly as long as three football fields and had 30 percent more displacement than the largest U.S. battleships ever built.*

---

6. ITALY (9,000,000)

ENTERED WAR: 1940
PEAK STRENGTH: 3,100,000

Although huge in number, the Italian armed forces were poorly outfitted and unmotivated. Far from cowardly in combat, the Italians were simply not prepared for the job. Tanks were of archaic design with flimsy armor and limited firepower. Artillery was at a tenth of the volume of World War I and outdated. The navy had no radar, no sonar, and no aircraft. The air force, what little there was, consisted of a fair number of biplanes.

Essentially, the military was a metaphor of the country—fragile and fragmented. Mussolini came to power by way of the militia, a.k.a. "the black shirts," not by the support of the military. In twenty years,

Fascist Party influence never took root among the armed forces. In fact, Italian soldiers and sailors were bound by oath to the king, not to Mussolini.

Facing defeat after defeat, the armed forces suffered long after the fall of il Duce. In 1943, the Wehrmacht invaded the country from the north, capturing and disarming more than three hundred thousand Italian soldiers, sending most of them to Germany as slave labor.[5]

One of Italy's defeats actually created an Axis victory. In November 1940, the RAF launched a surprise torpedo attack on Italy's naval base in Taranto, sinking three battleships. Impressed by the results, the Japanese naval high command reasoned the same could be done against a fleet at Pearl Harbor.

---

7. GREAT BRITAIN (5,896,000)

ENTERED WAR: 1939
PEAK STRENGTH: 4,683,000

The British Isles were predominantly a sea power at the outbreak of hostilities, with a navy ranked second in the world, but its navy was the smallest of the three military branches. From an overall population of 47 million, nearly 4 million served in the army, 1.2 million were in the RAF, and 900,000 were in the Royal Navy.

Arguably, Britain's army bore the brunt of the war. In 1939 it numbered 400,000, smaller than the army of Belgium. Climbing to 1.6 million by 1940, Britain's ground forces still went on to amass an extremely poor record, although not for lack of trying. Driven from France and Norway in 1940, then Greece and Crete in 1941, the British nearly imploded when they lost SINGAPORE in early 1942. A following string of losses in Burma and North Africa did not help matters.

With the British armed forces stretched too thin across the empire, lacking reliable tanks and antitank guns, not until SECOND EL ALAMEIN did the royal luck turn for the better, mostly because of vastly superior numbers in vehicles and men. Combined operations with the United States from 1943 onward led to better fortunes in Sicily, Italy, and France.

Like the Soviet Union, Great Britain drafted women into service. By the end of the war, 10 percent of the British armed forces was female.

---

8. FRANCE (3,500,000)

ENTERED WAR: 1939

PEAK STRENGTH: 2,680,000

France was a paradox. At its strongest, it lost. At its weakest, it prospered. In 1940, at its apex in men and equipment, with the fourth largest army and navy in the world, France suffered its worst defeat in the war, beaten in six short weeks on its home turf. Nearly half of France's armed forces went through the war in captivity. The Third Reich captured 1.5 million Frenchmen and French colonials. Those who did not die or escape remained POWs or were slave laborers in Germany for the duration.

At the end of the war, ranking eleventh globally in military strength, playing a tertiary role in the liberation of its own country, France possessed zones of occupation in Germany and Austria.[6]

A substantial cause of both scenarios was France's global positioning. It started the war with three armies—one guarding France proper, one covering North Africa, and one guarding colonies elsewhere—a system heavily dependent on the work and sacrifices of colonial subjects.

In 1940, the setup compromised France's military might on the Continent. In the interim, it was France's savior. The Free French movement started its comeback when French Equatorial Africa decided to back Charles de Gaulle over Vichy France. Other colonies began to switch over, and the momentum changed for good with the Allied invasion of French Morocco and Algeria. By 1945, thanks to shrewd bargaining, the French were again a global power, albeit a military prune.

In 1940, the French army was ten times larger than the British army. In 1945, the British Army was ten times larger than the French.

---

9. INDIA (2,581,800)

ENTERED WAR: 1939

PEAK STRENGTH: 2,200,000

When Britain declared war on Germany, the British viceroy for the colony of India stepped in and proclaimed India at war as well. This did not go over well with the three hundred million Indians who were not consulted. British demands for obedience in the hour of imperial need led to a general breakdown of order. Most of India's prominent civil leaders were arrested, including pacifist Mohandas Gandhi.

When the war started poorly for Britain, London officials moved to secure greater cooperation from the subcontinent, eventually promising to grant India its independence once victory against the Axis had been achieved.

This promise of autonomy spawned an explosion. The Indian armed forces grew from 160,000 in 1939 to more than two million by 1944. All of them were volunteers. Predominantly led by white officers, the poorly equipped but highly motivated army sent divisions to Europe, North Africa, East Africa, the Middle East, and Southeast Asia. Most were stationed as home guard, protecting the geographically vital subcontinent from invasion and providing air bases for Allied air transport to China over "the Hump" of the Himalayas. India's crowning achievement occurred in 1944 and 1945 when it successfully fended off a Japanese invasion from Burma and then secured the country for the Allies. Of the "British" forces in Burma, seven out of ten were Indian.[7]

*One of the problems with organizing the Indian armed forces was com-
munication. At the time of the war, India (which included Pakistan and
Bangladesh) was home to more than eight hundred languages and dialects.*

10. POLAND (2,400,000)

ENTERED WAR: 1939
PEAK STRENGTH: 1,200,000

As with France, Poland had one of the largest armies on earth when
Germany invaded. Unlike France, Poland had no colonies to fall back
on and no victory parades waiting in its future. Yet many Poles went
on to achieve great successes in support of the Allied effort.

Of more than one million troops routed in the blitzkrieg of 1939,
some ninety thousand managed to escape by way of Slovakia and
Romania. Many trained in France and were part of the ill-fated defeat
in 1940, while portions of the small navy, including two submarines,
were able to make it to Britain and assist in convoys and coastal defense. The first bright moment came in the BATTLE OF BRITAIN, in
which the courage and marksmanship of Polish pilots accounted for
one out of every eight German planes brought down.

While an untold number of regular army personnel formed the
core of the resistance movement in and around Warsaw, exiled Poles
served in North Africa, the eastern front, and Western Europe. Part of
the NORMANDY invasion and the less successful OPERATION MARKET-
GARDEN, Poles had their finest hour in Italy, capturing the abbey
heights in the fight for CASSINO, losing thousands of men in the process, but succeeding where three other assaults by other nationalities
had failed.

*While stationed in Palestine, several thousand Polish soldiers of Jewish
descent deserted their units to live in the area. One of them became a
rather proficient militant activist by the name of Menachem Begin.*

WEAPONS

In terms of weapons, the war appeared both astounding and ridiculous. Combatants moved by jet and mule, battled from hundreds of feet beneath the waves to thirty thousand feet above the ground, and killed with atomic radiation and sharpened sticks. The volume of ordnance was, in a word, unreal. For each citizen of the Axis, the United States had three artillery shells. There were enough bullets made worldwide to shoot every living person on the planet forty times.[8]

One consistency: it was a war in motion. Where its predecessor involved armies trying not to budge, the Second World War involved forces trying to move the fastest. The primary cause of this revolutionary change in the nature of warfare was the perfection of the internal combustion engine. When asked his opinion on the most effective weapons of the war, Gen. DWIGHT EISENHOWER cited the Jeep, the C-47 transport aircraft, the bazooka, and the atomic bomb. Fittingly, two of his responses were motorized, and the bomb required a four-engine plane for delivery.[9]

Excluding rockets (see FIRSTS), below is a roster of the prominent weapon types listed by amount procured. Note that the majority were essentially delivery systems exhibiting the changing nature of war, in which mobility equaled power.

1. MINES (600 MILLION)

With speed a decisive factor in fighting, mines were a cheap and easy way to slow down opponents. Categorized as naval, antitank, and antipersonnel, mines appeared in all theaters, destroying bodies and equipment alike.

Most complex and explosive were naval mines, numbering five hundred thousand total. Detonation occurred by contact, magnetic impulse, or sound waves. Planted by ships, submarines, and aircraft, mines were only practical in high-traffic shallow waters such as harbors and bays. To combat them, minesweepers cut cables, noise-making devices burst acoustic mines, and electric currents counterattacked magnetic detonators. Although these mines accounted for a tiny fraction of all ship losses, they were the most effective way to close ports and sea lanes for days at a time.

Land mines were most prominent in the Soviet Union and North Africa, where large areas were void of natural defenses. Some were rudimentary booby traps of grenades or other small explosives. In many instances, artillery shells were simply buried with nose fuses flush to the surface. Mass production allowed for standardized versions to be made in phenomenal quantities. The Soviets claimed to have planted more than two hundred million in their soil. The king of Egypt complained that the Allies left some forty million devices in his country. His estimates were probably not far off. The United States procured more than twenty-four million land mines during the war.[10]

Demolition engineers were usually charged with removal, in many cases while under hostile fire. Detectors were not available until 1942. Most were unreliable because many explosives' casings were made of wood and plastic. The alternatives were to set mines off with airbursts, with tanks fitted with flailing chains, or more often than not, by getting down on hands and knees and prodding the soil with an angled knife or wire.

In Eastern Europe and North Africa, unexploded land mines from World War II were still killing scores of people and animals annually into the 1980s.

---

2. SMALL ARMS (300 MILLION)

World War II marked a fundamental change in the arming of combat infantry. In the nineteenth century the ideal was to have an entire regiment fitted with one type of musket or rifle. By 1940 units worked best when they had a variety of tools. It was not uncommon for a regiment to have twenty or more kinds of weapons, allowing soldiers to fight effectively in different environments and situations.

Bullets could not drop into trenches or lob over walls, but grenades could. Respected were the German "potato mashers" and American "pineapples," but the petrol-filled bottles of "Molotov cocktails" often proved just as effective. In various forms the United States made more than eighty-seven million grenades.

The arrival of tanks required something beefier than a handgun. Most effective were grenade launchers, bazookas, and their German cousins, the Panzerfaust and Panzerschrek. Such devices could save a squad from annihilation, but there were drawbacks. Firing usually gave away a soldier's position, so the first shot had to count.[11]

From left to right, U.S. Marines utilize a Thompson submachine gun, a .30 caliber machine gun, and an M-1 carbine during a standoff at Cape Gloucester in the Solomons.

Submachine guns were popular among airborne and special ops groups. Light and inexpensive, they laid down a menacing rate of fire but also ate ammunition quickly. More effective, though bulkier, were machine guns. The British Bren and U.S. Browning (or BAR) were valuable in offensive and defensive actions. Among the most revered and dependable were German MG-42s. One soldier described its use against a Red Army charge: "swinging backwards and forwards along the brown-coated files, smashing the cohesion of the attack...

[T]he killing was prodigious." Indeed, machine-gun fire of all forms accounted for 10 percent of all combat deaths.[12]

Pistols were largely useless. Adored by souvenir hunters, the German Luger would be hard pressed to stop a charging badger.

The anchor of the infantry was still the rifle, and for nearly every army, it was an archaic bolt-action, single-shot weapon of pre-1914 design. The exception was the semiautomatic U.S. M-1 Garand, the most effective rifle of the war. More than four million were made. Reliable, accurate, just shy of ten pounds, it shot an eight-round magazine using a gas-powered piston. If soldiers had a common complaint, it was the M-1's voice. With a full clip, the rifle spoke with an authoritative and intense "kow kow." But on its final shot, it uttered a distinctive "clank" as it coughed out its empty clip. The sound told the owner to reload, but it also told the enemy that the rifleman was temporarily defenseless.[13]

A deadly small-arms innovation was the German SG-44, a fully automatic rifle. Issued too late to change the course of the war, it was the forefather of the Russian AK-47, the most heavily produced gun of all time.

---

3. ARTILLERY (2 MILLION)

The Russians had a saying: "The artillery is for killing, the infantry for dying." At SECOND EL ALAMEIN, a British tank brigade lost seventy of its ninety-four tanks to field guns. At KURSK, the biggest tank battle in history, there were a total of seven thousand tanks and thirty thousand artillery pieces. British medics calculated that 70 percent of all deaths and injuries in NORMANDY came from mortars. Approximately half of all battle wounds came not from bombs or tanks but from artillery.[14]

Including massive coastal guns, rail guns, antitank guns, mortars, howitzers, assault guns, and recoilless cannon, artillery was the most adaptable and damaging weaponry in World War II. Most numerous and effective were the portable field pieces.

The Soviets depended heavily on their long-barreled 76mm guns. Americans and British produced dual-purpose artillery, capable of lobbing shells like a howitzer and launching straight shots like a cannon.

The most famous, or infamous, gun of the war was the German 88mm Flieger Abwehr Kanone (flak). Introduced in 1934 as an anti-aircraft gun, the 88 was clearly ineffective in its intended role, requiring thousands of rounds just to score a single hit. But in the SPANISH CIVIL WAR, crews aimed the barrel at ground targets and discovered it was a viciously effective tank killer. Intended to hurl projectiles twenty thousand feet into the sky, its muzzle velocity was two times faster than many ground guns, allowing its sixteen-pound shell to crack pillboxes, tanks, bunkers, and vehicles with ease. One trooper calculated that an 88 shell flew three hundred yards ahead of its sound, producing an eerie effect of a cataclysmic explosion followed by the scream of the approaching shell. A wary British soldier said of the 88, "That's the deadliest bastard that's come out of this war so far."[15]

Of the war's artillery, American field gun versions may have rated highest in versatility. Most models could fire more than a dozen different kinds of shells, including armor-piercing, smoke, incendiary, and poison-gas.

---

4. FIGHTER-BOMBERS (450,000)

Single-engine combat aircraft served as metaphors for the war as a whole. Initially, the Axis aircraft were more agile and powerful, but Allied planes caught and passed their adversaries with greater numbers and technology.

Among the hundreds of aircraft makes and versions were several standouts, including the dominant Messerschmitt 109, the most produced German aircraft and chariot of the most prolific aces of the entire war. Not until the British put a Merlin engine in the American

P-51 Mustang were Me-109s summarily tamed. The Mustang was nearly a hundred mph faster and had a range five times that of the German fighter. Mustangs also enabled Allied bomber command to bomb Germany almost at will, having the unmatched ability to escort bomber formations all the way from England to Czechoslovakia and back, whereas the Messerschmitt could barely make a round trip from NORMANDY to London.[16]

In the Pacific, the Mitsubishi Zero, with its featherweight body and ample wings, could outsprint and outturn all of its early adversaries, especially at low altitude. But when a downed Zero was discovered intact in the Aleutians and brought to the United States for study, its innovations helped create the F6F Hellcat. Ultimately faster and more resilient than the Zero, the Hellcat accounted for more air-to-air kills in the Pacific than all other U.S. aircraft combined, although it served for only the last two years of the war.[17]

Altogether, fighters may have been the most adaptable weapons, performing as interceptors, dive bombers, rocket launchers, torpedo launchers, escorts, tank busters, sub hunters, radar and reconnaissance platforms, artillery spotters, and kamikazes. Yet all the adaptability in the world would not help the Axis, who lacked the pilots and planes to stay even with the Allies. For every fighter the Axis produced, the Allies manufactured five.

The top 108 fighter aces in World War II were all German or Austrian.

---

5. TANKS (300,000)

Except in areas of dense jungle, land combat revolved around tanks. By 1940 every country knew the importance of the relatively new weapon. The question was how to use it. Conventional thinking viewed tanks as infantry support to be deployed piecemeal among slow-moving foot soldiers. German blitzkrieg tactics dismantled this logic by massing armored vehicles together and smashing through lines.

Tanks were generally classified as light, medium, and heavy. Light tanks were little more than armored cars, useful for reconnaissance or against poorly armored foes. Most Japanese and Italian tanks were of the light variety, the latter frequently called "self-propelled coffins." Heavies were meant to be indestructible land cruisers, but most were too heavy and came too late to change the war's outcome, the exception being the Russian KV-1. The Third Reich's much celebrated King Tiger was a beast. More than thirty feet long and twelve feet wide, it had frontal armor nearly one foot thick. Unfortunately for the Germans, it drank two gallons a mile and sank in soft ground.[18]

U.S. infantry huddles close to an M-4 Sherman medium tank during the September 1944 advance into Belgium.

The most effective tanks were the mediums, such as the M-4 Sherman. The Sherman's strength came from reliability and huge numbers. Eleven different companies produced more than forty thousand of them. Drawbacks included thin armor and precarious ammunition storage. A German observed that a Sherman would "burn like twenty haystacks."[19]

Workhorses of the German stable were the Panzer III and IV, which functioned exceptionally well until they encountered the Soviet T-34. With sloping armor, wide treads, and high-torque diesel engines, T-34s could punch holes in the panzers from almost a mile away. Most of all, more than sixty-four thousand were made, more than all German tanks combined. Of its shortcomings, it had no radio, which forced commanders to use flags or hand signals or play "follow the leader."

More than anything else, superior numbers ensured Allied dominance. From 1939 to 1944, for every tank the Axis built, the Allies made eight.[20]

Sometimes it took very little to knock out a tank. When a panzer division on the eastern front came under attack, more than two-thirds of the vehicles would not start. Later inspection revealed that throngs of mice had gotten into the engine compartments, probably for warmth, and chewed through the electrical wires.

---

6. MEDIUM AND HEAVY BOMBERS (170,000)

Most bombers throughout the war had one or two engines, with the medium twin-engines being the mainstay of most air forces. Only the United States and Great Britain produced operational four-engine aircraft in quantity.

Japan had three medium bombers as its workhorses, all manufactured by Mitsubishi. Germany's twin-engine Heinkel 111 was as good on paper as the U.S. B-17. Italy's Fiat BR20M could fly nearly as far and as fast as the B-25 Mitchell. Although the Axis suffered from want of payload on their missions, failure came down to lack of protection. The Axis simply did not have the fighter escort capability of the Allies and suffered accordingly. As an example, the B-17G bristled with thirteen machine guns (hence the name "Flying Fortress"), but it still underwent terrible losses when traveling beyond fighter protection.

There were alternatives. Britain's twin-engine De Havilland "Mosquito," of which more than seven thousand were made, consisted of a wood frame and no defensive weapons, yet it had one of the lowest fatality rates of the RAF. Flying at around four hundred mph, Mosquitoes simply outran the competition. The famed B-29 Superfortress, a technological marvel of pressurized cabins and a range of four thousand miles, flew too high for interceptors or antiaircraft fire to reach.

On reputation, the B-17 and B-29 get accolades, but the B-24 Liberator was the most utilized and produced bomber of the war. Ugly as sin, with a fat fuselage, pug nose, and a tail fin that looked like earmuffs on a harmonica, the B-24 worked in all theaters and carried a greater load and flew farther than the B-17. It was also vastly more adaptable than the B-29. More than eighteen thousand were made, outnumbering B-17s and B-29s put together.[21]

Ugly but effective, more B-24 Liberators were manufactured than any other warplane in U.S. military history.

During the war, the versatile B-24 saw service with the U.S. Army Air Force, Navy, and Marines, plus the air forces of Australia, Brazil, Canada, Nationalist China, France, Great Britain, India, liberated Italy, New Zealand, Portugal, South Africa, the Soviet Union, and Turkey.

7. SUBMARINES (2,100)

At the start of the war, no fewer than ten navies possessed submarines. In fact, the largest underwater fleets belonged to the Soviet Union, Italy, and France.

Types were of the extreme. Smallest were "midgets," with crews of one to five. Both the attack on PEARL HARBOR and the D-day landings began with midget-sub reconnaissance. Largest was the I-400 class developed by Japan. Longer than a football field, the I-400s were intended to attack the United States and the Panama Canal but never became fully operational. The prize for endurance went to Germany's Type IXD Ucruiser, capable of sailing around the world, whereas Japan's manned suicide torpedo was designed for much shorter trips. For maximum flexibility, several countries had models that carried floatplanes or collapsible aircraft.

Crews commonly engaged in nonconfrontational pursuits. The low-profile vehicles were ideal for guerrilla and secret operations support, smuggling agents and ammunition as well as money and medicine. Subs also performed a large number of rescue operations. In September 1944, the USS *Narwahl* made an impressive haul by evacuating eighty-two Allied POWs from the Philippine island of Mindanao.[22]

Attack sub USS *Wahoo* claimed twenty kills in the Pacific before she and her entire crew were lost off the coast of Japan in October 1943.

The most common task was hunting merchant ships. The Royal Navy eventually ruled the Mediterranean, choking off supplies to the Afrika Korps. A few hundred German U-boats, operating from the Arctic to the Caribbean, sank nearly two thousand Allied transports. After replacing defective torpedoes in 1943 (initial models swam too deep), one hundred U.S. submarines accounted for more than half of all Japanese ships sunk in the Pacific, including four thousand merchant vessels. In contrast, the Japanese mainly used their small fleet to hunt enemy warships, with costly results. On average, for every enemy vessel sunk, Japan lost one submarine.[23]

The work was perilous. One in four Allied and three of four Axis submariners did not survive.

In September 1944 a TBM Avenger was shot down off the coast of Okinawa. The submarine USS Finback *sailed to the site and managed to save the sole survivor of the three-man crew, U.S. Navy pilot Lt. George Herbert Walker Bush.*

8. DESTROYERS AND CRUISERS (1,700)

A basic measurement of a warship was its main guns. Destroyers had gun barrels of three to six inches in diameter, cruisers five to eight, battleships fourteen to eighteen. During the war, only seven navies possessed battleships, whereas eighteen owned destroyers and cruisers.

Destroyers proved to be the most adaptable of naval vessels. Used mainly to escort merchant and warship convoys, destroyers were simultaneously torpedo boats, sub hunters, rescue ships, scouts, and antiaircraft screens. They also functioned as minesweepers, coastal patrol boats, radar platforms, and support batteries for amphibious landings. The Japanese, with the third-largest contingent of destroyers, used them aggressively in surface battles and paid dearly. The Imperial Navy lost more than three hundred during the war, more than all other Japanese warship losses put together. Britain owned the second-largest fleet, using the vessels predominantly in escort duties and losing almost half as many as the Japanese, mostly to U-boats. The U.S. Navy had the largest collection of destroyers, losing eighty-two, but dominating both the Atlantic and Pacific with superior numbers and radar-sonar capability.[24]

Cruisers were designed to be self-sufficient, long-distance combat ships and convoy raiders, ranging in size from very large destroyers with crews of six hundred to virtual battleships with twelve hundred officers and men. As with destroyers, the United States had the largest fleet, and the Japanese suffered the highest losses. Serving in all naval theaters, cruisers figured predominantly in the Pacific, where they proved faster than battleships and more powerful than destroyers.[25]

The Japanese destroyer *Amagiri* became infamous after ramming and sinking a PT boat skippered by future U.S. president John F. Kennedy.

Days after safely delivering components of the Hiroshima bomb to Tinian Island, the cruiser USS Indianapolis *was sunk by a Japanese sub. Out of 1,196 men on board, 900 were alive when the ship went under. Four days later 317 were rescued. The rest died of exposure, wounds, and shark attacks.*

9. AIRCRAFT CARRIERS (180)

Only Great Britain, Japan, and the United States deployed operational carriers, ranging from "escort carriers" holding a few dozen planes to "light carriers" with thirty to forty aircraft to "fleet carriers" with sixty to ninety fighters, dive bombers, and torpedo planes.

Most were escorts tasked with shepherding convoys to safety. The United States and Britain made many (110) and Japan few (5). The Japanese Empire consequently lost nearly all its merchant shipping in a few short years.

Of the light and fleet carriers, numbers were initially small. In 1940 there were nineteen large carriers in existence. By the end of 1942 thirteen of them were at the bottom of the ocean. Britain and Japan replaced their losses slowly, launching a few flattops each year, while the industrial behemoth United States almost made it look easy, commissioning fifteen new ships in 1943 alone.[26]

The hull sizes of most flattops were equivalent to a cruiser. In fact, many carriers were converted from old or half-built cruisers, including

the Coral Sea casualty *Lexington*, PEARL HARBOR and Midway veteran
Akagi, and all nine ships of the Independence class.[27]

For the Royal Navy, objectives included patrolling the home islands, supporting convoys in the North Atlantic and Indian Oceans,
and flushing the Italians from the Mediterranean. The U.S. and
Japanese large carriers were essentially committed to attacking each
other, either ship-to-ship or ship-to-shore. The battle of MIDWAY
helped tip the scales in favor of the Americans, with the battles around
LEYTE GULF dooming the Imperial Navy for good.

During the war, the U.S. Navy
built nearly three times as many
fleet carriers as did the Empire
of Japan.

The carrier USS Franklin *was a tough nut to crack. In October 1944,
over a period of two weeks in the Philippines, she was hit by a kamikaze,
a bomb, and another kamikaze. Sent to the United States for repairs,
she returned to the Pacific in time for the Okinawa campaign only to be
hit by two more bombs and set on fire. But the carrier never sank.*

10. BATTLESHIPS (50)

Bismarck, Arizona, Prince of Wales, Yamato—it is sad yet symbolic that
the most famous battleships were all sunk. For centuries, battlewagons
were the prestige and soul of the major navies, and there was no reason
to believe otherwise when the Second World War began.

At the height of their influence, the *Arizonas* of the world were
appropriately called "capital ships," top of the line. Brandishing the

largest guns and heaviest armor of anything afloat, they were born to fight other ships for control of the seas, thus their deaths were often interpreted as a serious if not mortal blow to a nation's naval strength.

By the time the conflict officially ended—ironically on the deck of a battleship—it was patently obvious that the grand vessels no longer ruled the waves. In a way, the aforementioned battleships demonstrated the paradigm shift. All four were sunk in part or completely by aircraft.

Just weeks before December 7, 1941, a U.S. Navy publication boasted that America had never lost a battleship to air attack.

Given few opportunities to sink enemy ships, crews adapted to new assignments, primarily battering land targets and protecting air-craft carriers. Direct attacks on other fleets were rare. During the war, U.S. battleships exchanged salvos with enemy vessels in only three en-gagements: Casablanca, GUADALCANAL, and LEYTE GULF. One of several naval actions at Leyte Gulf involved the battle of Surigao Straight, in which Japanese and American armadas traded fire in the early morning hours of October 25, 1944. The fight ended when the imperial battle-ship *Yamashiro* sank from torpedo hits. The USS *Mississippi* trained its big guns on the dying vessel and fired its first and only volley of the affair. It was the last time in history a battleship ever fired on another. Confirming the end of an epoch, the shots missed.[28]

The four largest American battleships ever made—the Iowa, Missouri, New Jersey, *and* Wisconsin—*never took part in a surface engagement during the entire war.*

ITEMS IN A SOLDIER'S DIET

The foundation of morale, food was also the primary determinant of how far troops could march, how fast they could act, how quickly they could recover, and how well they could maintain discipline. The U.S. Quartermaster Corps categorized rations as "Class I," ahead of fuel, clothing, ammunition, and everything else. In 1940 dollars LEND-LEASE sent $5 billion in aircraft and $5.1 billion in food.[29]

Rations were also a direct reflection of a country's ability to wage war. If a link in the food chain broke—such as loss of farmland, surrender of rail lines, or failure of organization—it meant that military and civilian populations did not eat. With their shipping lanes cut, Japanese soldiers stationed on GUADALCANAL began to call it "Starvation Island." Conversely, Allied advances on Germany from both the east and west stalled in late 1944 because they outran their supply lines. German soldiers lost ground in the east about the same time their rations began to perceptibly decrease.

On average, Chinese and Japanese troops were among the poorest fed, and Americans were by far the best supplied. Yet persons aboard ships always had to carefully ration goods, and field units at any moment could find themselves vainly searching for mobile kitchens. Many veterans recalled days when there was nothing to eat, leaving every moment occupied with thoughts of food.

Listed below are the fodders of fighting men, particularly concerning ground troops. Items are ranked by the quantity generally consumed.

I. WATER

A Japanese military training manual stated it bluntly: "When the water is gone it is the end of everything." A soldier could (and many did) survive days without food, but as the booklet added, "Water is your savior."[30]

Men stationed in North Africa or the South Pacific were extremely susceptible to abrupt dehydration, resulting in cramps, headaches, fatigue, sometimes delirium, and sunstroke. In jungle operations, the Japanese calculated that a man required nearly two gallons per day (and a horse could need up to fifteen gallons).

In most regions, water was available. But the problem was fresh water. Oceangoing vessels were in transit for weeks at a time, requiring sailors and passengers to persist on two glasses a day. Snowbound troops at least had a ready supply, provided a fire could be made. In warmer weather, sources near campsites usually contained high concentrations of bacteria, made worse by bathing and the lavatory habits of animals as well as men. Water in combat areas was generally unusable due to spilled fuel and rotting corpses.

A Chinese laborer uses a light bulb as a drinking glass.

Purification came through filtering and boiling. There was also the use of creosote pills or chloride of lime, which permeated every drop with an acrid taste. To make chemically treated sources palatable, Europeans often carried "fizz tablets" (vitamin-enriched bicarbonate flavor capsules). Americans received lemon-flavored powders in their rations, which the men universally hated, until they tried it with hard alcohol.[31]

Only a few wells existed on the volcanic ash island of Iwo Jima. All stank of sulfur, yet the Japanese depended on them for survival. Some of the last Imperial assaults made in the battle were failed attempts to retake two wells lost early to U.S. Marines.

2. BREAD AND RICE

G.I. Joe had white. Ivan and Jerry ate rye. Tommy had his royal wheat. More than half the Japanese diet was based on rice. As the eternal staple, grain fueled the armies of the world, and most countries aimed to provide two pounds of grain per soldier per day.[32]

Installations and cities usually provided numerous bakeries, but frontline activities normally required mobile kitchens. In Europe, Americans adopted the British field kitchen. If the weather was cooperative and supplies adequate, a single German field bakery with a few dough mixers and ovens could produce enough to feed ten thousand men a day.[33]

When fresh loaves were unavailable, the aptly named hardtack became a necessity. Weighing a few ounces each, biscuits, crackers, and blocks appeared in C- and K-rations, tins, plastic, paper, or crates. Usually old and stale, they hurt the jaw and clogged the stomach. Spreads were minimal. Americans sometimes received margarine, which tended to be more like a petroleum by-product. Europeans had jams and marmalades when they were lucky, animal lard (a.k.a. drippings) otherwise, but they frequently had nothing except the dry, coarse brick itself.

By 1944, U.S. forces stationed in the European theater consumed eight hundred thousand pounds of bread every day.

3. SOUP AND STEW

As roasting or grilling took too long to feed thousands at a time, mobile kitchens were designed primarily for boiling. There were porridges of oats, barley, or corn. Russians ate "Kascha" mush and pickled beat borscht. When preserved or frozen beef could be found, the English had Irish stew. The Japanese drank something that loosely translated as "weed soup." Nearly every army fried broth cubes as a substitute when meat or vegetables went missing in action.[34]

Hot meals in wintertime were key to maintaining troop morale.

The universal stereotype of the surly, cold, and indifferent army cook is based largely in fact. The first to hear the soldiers' complaints and the last to control the supply chain, cooks and mess sergeants were often driven to exhaustion while feeding the conveyer belt of impatient mouths. Either making too little or too much food, most started work well before sunup and finished long after sundown. Some combat soldiers thought highly of their commissary chefs, especially the ones who would brave enemy fire to feed the men. Overall, the hardest-worked and least-liked men in the unit were saddled with as much responsibility as officers, but with none of the perks.

During winter on the eastern front, soldiers on both sides recalled seeing bowls of boiling soup freeze solid within two minutes.

4. CANNED MEAT

Watertight, dividable, and easily shipped and stored, canned meats were a modern convenience for commissary officers. Distributed when operations were in motion, the tins had a varied reputation among the grunts. Unlike square ration packages with dried food, cans were awkward and heavy to carry. If served hot, the contents were tolerable. Taken cold, all had the taste and texture of chunky sludge.

Until 1945 C-ration meals (twelve-ounce cans) embodied monotony. There were meat and beans, meat and veggie hash, or meat stew. Germans muscled down their "iron ration" of hardtack and canned pork. Troops of all nationalities disliked corned beef or "bully beef." The runny brown botch of gravy and gristle earned the nicknames "dog food" and "kennel rations."

So overrun with Spam during their stay in England, U.S. servicemen referred to the country as Spamland. But many Yanks tolerated the meatlike loaf in lieu of canned British alternatives such as bacon and liver, fish and egg, or meat and kidney pudding.[35]

Canned fish was prominent in non-American diets. Commonwealth troops had salmon, mackerel, herring, and sardines. The Japanese consumed large amounts of tinned sea eel. Pushing into the Third Reich, hungry American soldiers captured a cache of German canned fish that was oddly gray and flavorless.[36]

Sometimes the troops had no idea what they were consuming. Rain-soaked, sunbaked, and oft-handled cans frequently lost their labeling. Others had ambiguous markings like MV for "meat and vegetables." Unfortunately, opening the containers did not always solve the mystery.

Afrika Korps troops ate cans of meat stamped "AM." German troops claimed it meant "Alter Mann" for "old man." Italian infantry surmised the initials stood for "Asino Morte" for "dead monkey."

5. VEGETABLES

Soldiers received fewer fresh vegetables than they did in peacetime. Soybeans and bean paste were staples for many Japanese Imperial soldiers, eaten less often but providing far more nutrition than rice. Short on meat, Soviets and Eastern Europeans lived on beets, turnips, cucumbers, and cabbage. While Americans consumed large quantities of corn, Germans were less inclined, as they traditionally viewed maize as pig food.[37]

The exception was potatoes, sweet and white in the East, every other variety in the West. For most armies, spud consumption outweighed all other veggie intake combined. In search of a little variety, some stationary units were able to grow their own crops. Allies camped in Britain sowed thousands of acres of peas, carrots, and onions.[38]

The Japanese government encouraged its armies to be "self-sufficient" in their respective theaters, buying or taking what they needed from surrounding areas. The order was easy to follow on the Asian mainland, as Imperial troops held the most productive regions. Life on the Pacific islands was a different matter. The Japanese planted crops just to survive, but volcanic soils and rocky terrains made for poor yields. Shortages and malnutrition plagued garrisons consistently in these areas.[39]

Airmen everywhere learned quickly to avoid most vegetables as well as any food that caused gas. Not a serious problem back at the base, intestinal gas expanded at altitude in nonpressurized aircraft, causing great pain and occasionally serious internal damage.

6. TEA AND COFFEE

A national right among Commonwealth soldiers, Russians, and the Japanese, tea was also the most favored weapon against unsavory water. It came in nags, bulk, cakes, and slabs. The British developed palm-sized "tea tablets" called Service Blend Compressed, which usually sported a bit of a rotted scent and savor. Russians and Chinese usually received miniscule amounts in loose, coarse form. Many Commonwealth charges had the pleasure of getting sugar and dried milk with their ration, but fresh milk was a rarity throughout the war. Sweetened condensed milk was as good as gold, particularly in the China-Burma-India theater.

No nationality downed coffee like the Americans, who continually requisitioned their quartermasters for more. Airmen and sailors had a greater take, while ground troops on the move had to settle for condensed coffee in the C- and K-rations. When torn up and burned, the wax and paper boxes of K-rations usually gave off enough heat to warm a cup or two of joe.

For fresh-ground java, fuel supplies had to be taken into consideration. Mobile coffee production usually required coal-powered roasters and gas- or diesel-driven grinders.

7. FRESH MEAT

When it was on the menu, things were either going very well or very poorly. American troops on the island fortress of Britain sometimes enjoyed a slice of beef and tried to develop a taste for mutton. Most airmen regularly received hot meals with servings of fowl or red meat. This luxury was partly due to the relative permanence and security of air bases and partly because of their line of work, which required good food and plentiful rest to operate their extremely complicated and expensive machinery. Line troops also had the occasional pleasure of dining on something that wasn't canned, pickled, smoked, salted, frozen, or puréed, usually because of a respite in the fighting and open supply lines.

Then there were times when necessity was the mother of ingestion. Poisonous snakes were standard fare to a few jungle-bound troops. Japanese enlisted were instructed to eat the snake liver raw for its nutrients. On several fronts, rats and dogs made their way to the dinner table. When in hurried attack or retreat, cooking was not always an option. Several American units in the BATTLE OF THE BULGE recalled catching farm chickens and eating them freshly plucked. One lieutenant lost in Burma recalled surviving a month solely on bamboo, parsley, and lizards. Lt. Gen. Jonathan Wainwright, in command of the courageous defense of the Bataan Peninsula in the spring of 1942, ordered his starving men to slaughter indigenous water buffalo, later their own horses, and finally their army mules. Horses, being a major form of transportation on the eastern front, also became a frequent part of diets.[40]

In his failed invasion of India, Japan's Gen. Mutaguchi Renya figured he could feed his troops by bringing along goats, cattle, and water buffalo. After most of his "rolling stock" died or disappeared along the treacherous march, his men were reduced to eating grass and monkeys.

---

8. SWEETS

Issued for their high-caloric content and mild stimulant qualities, sugar-laden foods appeared frequently in the hands of Westerners. Conversely, loss of sugar beet and sugar cane crops greatly reduced confectionary opportunities in the East.

Chocolate candies and drinks, chewing gum, and sugar cubes were most common in the European theater. Germans enjoyed brief periods of plentiful chocolate, until they ventured farther east and the confection disappeared from view. A standard in the American kit was the D-ration, a single bitter candy bar also known as the Logan Bar. Appropriately, American soldiers each carried a D-ration on D-day. To be eaten when nothing else was available, the carbo-loaded snack usually consisted of oatmeal, cocoa, sugar, and dried milk. Chalky and concentrated, it was hard to chew and even tougher to pass.[41]

Nothing brought out fresh food like the liberation of small villages and towns.

Dairy-based treats did not fare well in the tropics. Instead, fruit bars, cereal bars, and hard candy were standards among the Allies. Australian rations contained appropriately named "musk lozenges," odiferous little bonbons with a sweet, syrupy taste. Initially most candies were generic in label and flavor, but by 1943 the Allies were seeing and eating a greater number of major brands. By the end of the war, the Japanese rarely ate processed sugar. More than any other commodity, sugar vanished from Japanese warehouses and homes. From PEARL HARBOR to the fall of Okinawa, imports fell 80 percent and production essentially stopped.[42]

By 1944, Lend-Lease was feeding the Soviet war machine large quantities of K-rations filled with brand-name candy, providing many Communists with their first and last taste of Hershey, Pennsylvania.

---

9. ALCOHOL

Just a decade out of Prohibition, U.S. conscripts were surprised by the amount and variety of spirited beverages overseas. They tried to develop a taste for hearty Irish and English stouts, preferring the ales, and choked on whiskeys when they could get some. American naval personnel, forbidden from having drink on board, were comparatively grateful for whatever was available on land.

The march through Northern Europe provided Americans with a veritable tour of spirits. Accepted from grateful locals, "found" in cellars, or slammed in off-duty escapades, G.I.'s had cider in NORMANDY, champagne in Champagne, beer in Holland, and schnapps in Germany.[43]

For the most part, the soldiers were not after the taste. Alcohol quenched a fierce thirst, especially in areas where clean water could not be found. More often, Americans were drinking for the same reasons as their brothers in arms. Ever since the Great War, the British knew the benefit of a rum ration in times of combat. The French and Italians, accustomed to wine since childhood, switched to harder drinks when called for. A German soldier marching through Belgium in 1940 admitted, "Only through alcohol, nicotine, and that never-ending, ear-deafening raging and roaring of the guns are you still able to remain upright."[44]

Two U.S. sergeants display their affection for beer.

In lieu of physical escape, combatants often turned to drink in search of calm, or courage, or to momentarily feel nothing. Drunkenness skyrocketed among Soviet soldiers before they headed into combat. Consumption on the frozen steppes sometimes reached a quart of vodka a day. German troops disillusioned by the war referred to alcohol as Wutmilch, meaning the "milk of fury." Wounded and dying Japanese on SAIPAN slammed lethal levels of sake then hobbled away in the largest banzai attack of the war. One soldier said of drink, "It is the easiest way to make heroes."[45]

When they could not find alcohol, the troops tried to make it, or at least something with a similar effect. Members of a U.S. infantry unit in Germany attempted to get a buzz by mixing grapefruit juice with antifreeze. Soviet soldiers in Stalingrad filtered antifreeze through gas mask filaments then drank it straight. Many went blind.

10. FRUIT

A lack of refrigerated ships, boxcars, and trucks made fresh fruit impractical for field operations. Most of the time, supplies had to be requisitioned, bought, or taken from nearby growers. Marchers ate melons in Sicily, apples in Germany, grapes in France, and dates in Greece, but little of it seemed to fill stomachs. Soldiers and sailors in the tropics gathered pineapples and coconuts for the half-pint of juice inside.[46]

For the leaner months, there were small amounts of preserved fruit. Russians ate dried apricots and raspberries. The Japanese had salted plums. The British supplemented with canned fruit puddings or fruit salads. Americans hesitantly consumed a fair amount of prunes, also known as "Army strawberries."[47]

Though servicemen could live without the bland flavors of dried and salted fruits, they could not live well without the vitamins therein. Absences of B and C were of high concern to medical personnel. Recent inventions of vitamin pills were of marginal help to the worst cases of deficiency, which tended to fall easy prey to the diseases of dysentery and scurvy.[48]

Men stationed in the lush tropics were warned not to forage too readily from the trees. Berries and fruits that were especially colorful, sweet, decorative, low to the ground, or bright tended to be extremely poisonous.

CAUSES OF MILITARY DEATHS

In a war for national defense, soldiers died far away from their country: Poles over Britain, Japanese in Alaska, Brazilians in Italy, Australians in North Africa. Germans died in thirty countries other than the Fatherland.

For the families left behind, the news came belatedly, if at all. U.S. armed forces were among the most efficient in reporting losses, alerting spouses and next of kin within two to four weeks of the event.

Dictatorships in general denied military losses while inflating damages done upon the enemy. In the first six months of their invasion of the Soviet Union, some 750,000 soldiers of the Third Reich were killed. Berlin reported losses of 30,000, whereas Moscow claimed to have wiped out an equally fictitious 4 million.[49]

Accurate totals will be forever unknown, due primarily to incomplete or destroyed records, multiple causes of death, and the inability of governments (particularly the Soviet Union and Nationalist China) to effectively tabulate catastrophic numbers. Ranked here by descending counts are the ten most prevalent causes of military fatalities during the war. Estimates are conservative. The total exceeds the approximately twenty-five million military fatalities due to overlapping causes.

I. KILLED IN ACTION (11 MILLION)

By definition KIA meant any fatality that occurred in a combat zone where death came before the body reached an aid station or hospital. For the United States, the Second World War became the second-bloodiest conflict in its history. Yet with 294,597 battle deaths (about 0.2 percent of the population), Americans fared comparatively well. Perhaps a million Japanese died in combat. Two million Germans were killed in action. For every twenty Germans who fell, seventeen did so at the hands of the Soviet army and air force. In achieving this deadly distinction, the Soviets suffered the worst combat losses of any country. Official estimates calculate 5,187,000 dying in hostile action or on the way to aid stations.[50]

Numerically the army was the branch hardest hit, accounting for roughly eight of every ten servicemen killed in action. Infantry lost the bulk of these. Constituting just 14 percent of the U.S. armed forces, foot soldiers sustained 70 percent of the casualties, a statistic commensurate with other nationalities. The chief cause was artillery, followed by machine-gun fire, rifle fire, mines, bombs, and grenades.[51]

Next highest fatality totals came from the navies, where drowning and fire were principle killers. Work on the high seas had an all-or-none quality. The 1941 sinking of the *Bismarck* left 110 alive out of 2,300, while the HMS *Hood* took a hard salvo from the German battleship and disappeared in seconds, taking all but three of its 1,421 men.

Submarines were proportionally the deadliest service. U.S. submarine losses were 22 percent, Italy 33 percent, Japan more than 50 percent, and Germany more than 70 percent. Deaths came mostly through asphyxiation or implosion. All that was needed was a small fissure of the inner chambers, a failure of pumps, or the breaking of battery acid cells to smother an entire crew.

Scenes like this one on the beach at Tarawa were not unique during six years of fighting.

In the air services, combat was exceptionally lethal. On average, chances of surviving a tour of duty were around 60 percent for fighter pilots (and much lower for Japanese flyers). Air crews in medium bombers had approximately a fifty-fifty chance of seeing the end of the war. Heavy bombers, with little opportunity for evasive action in tight formations, had a survival rate of less than 30 percent.[52]

The worst fatality rate in any battle may go to the Japanese at Iwo Jima. Of 23,000 soldiers and sailors guarding the island in February 1945, not more than 250 survived the fight.

2. UNKNOWN—MISSING IN ACTION (7 MILLION)

With battles transpiring over greater areas and using more destructive weapons than ever before, bodies vanished with alarming frequency.

Water devoured countless casualties. Tides pulled the dead and wounded from amphibious landings into the deep. Plane crews and parachutists sank without a trace in bogs, lakes, and seas. An untold number of Luftwaffe and RAF pilots found their final resting place in the English Channel. Then there were the thousands of lost ships. Half of all USSR navy casualties were categorized as "failed to return from mission." Land was no better. Plane crashes, collapsing buildings, fires, explosions, and rolling tank treads buried or obliterated the living.[53]

Nearly 80,000 Americans were eventually designated as MIA, officially declared as dead a year after their disappearance. German records listed more than 1.3 million missing, most of whom were probably Soviet prisoners, with only 11,000 declared dead in the war. In keeping with Stalin's policy, 4.5 million Soviets were ranked as simply missing when assuredly the majority were prisoners.[54]

As there were names without bodies, there were also bodies without names. Essentially every unknown soldier was a member of the missing found without tags, documentation, or enough of their person left to make a positive identification.

One MIA turned up in 1974 quite alive. Lt. Onoda Hiroo of the Imperial Japanese Army remained armed and hidden on Lubang Island in the Philippines until persuaded to give himself up.

---

3. PRISON (6 MILLION)

The 1929 GENEVA CONVENTION standardized the treatment of prisoners, but the experiences of World War II POWs were anything but consistent. Detained all over the world, captives lived and died in extremes of heat and cold. Some ate well while others starved. Some were held in isolation while others were packed tight in compounds and ship hulls. A few were released in days; many never were.

Death came in a myriad of ways. Survival depended mainly on the ideological and racial policies of the host. Upon entering a German camp, a British detainee had about a 95 percent chance of living, whereas a Russian's prospects were a grim 35 percent. In Japanese captivity, one out of four British died while perhaps nine out of ten Chinese perished. On the sixty-five-mile Bataan Death March of April 1942, Japanese soldiers murdered an average of ten Americans every mile and ten Filipinos every two hundred yards.[55]

Overall, nationalities developed an unspoken practice of mutual response. Few Japanese ever surrendered, preferring to die rather than face the "shame" of capitulation. Allied soldiers, spurred by frequent incidents of Imperial brutality against captives, were only too ready to kill rather than capture Japanese. Germans and Americans exchanged atrocities in the 1944 campaign across France; these usually involved twenty to forty slaughtered prisoners. In the Nazi-Soviet dance of death, the Red Army captured more than three million Germans. About half died. Germans captured nearly six million of the Red Army. More than half of them perished.[56]

Almost universally, belligerents refused prisoner exchanges for fear of replenishing their enemy. Only ten transfers occurred in the European theater between 1942 and 1944, mostly involving at-risk medical cases, totaling twenty thousand Axis for twelve thousand

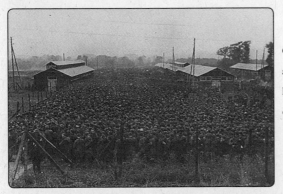

Overcrowding was the least of a prisoner's worries, as disease, hunger, and guards could kill on a daily basis.

Allies. The Soviet Union was extremely reluctant to repatriate captives. Moscow kept many German soldiers until 1957. Of nearly six hundred thousand Japanese taken prisoner by the Soviets in the final weeks of the war, half were still unaccounted for in 1970.[57]

In September 1941, Russians were dying in several Nazi prison camps at the pace of 1 percent every twenty-four hours, a rate three times worse than the American Civil War POW camp of Andersonville.

---

4. DIED OF WOUNDS (4 MILLION)

"Died of wounds" is defined as sustaining mortal injuries in a combat zone and later dying in a medical facility.

Few events misshape the human form with as much grotesque variation as battle, and devices brought to the Second World War seemed exceptionally adept. Yet in many cases, subjects continued to live for many hours, days, sometimes weeks after undergoing mortal deformation. A German soldier on the eastern front recalled walking among Russian prisoners, "many of whom had been badly burned by flame throwers.... Their faces had no longer any recognizable human features but were simply swollen lumps of meat. Another had his jaw shot away."[58]

Survival depended heavily on how one was wounded. Damages to the head and neck were the most lethal. A distant second was trauma to the chest, followed by the abdomen, and lastly extremities. Access to treatment was vital. Wounded commandos and airborne troops, who frequently operated behind enemy lines, survived less often than artillerymen in the rear echelons.

The deciding factor appeared to be to which country an individual belonged. In every company the U.S. had three medics; the Japanese had one. British nationals enforced hygiene with iron discipline in nearly every theater, whereas Russians rarely had the supplies to address the issue. Canadian and U.S. medical teams were among the best equipped with the latest innovations; the Germans had not yet perfected the manufacture of dried plasma or penicillin.[59]

As the war progressed, deaths among the wounded increased for the Axis and decreased among the Allies, primarily because the latter controlled more and more of the sea, land, and air routes along which patients, pharmaceuticals, and food traveled.[60]

Yet on average, medical advances were saving the wounded three times more often than in the previous century. Consequently, a greater percentage of men were able to go right back into the fold. The Red Army calculated it had more than twenty-seven thousand soldiers who were wounded on seven or more separate occasions and returned to duty. The Third Reich actually had a military decoration for soldiers wounded ten or more times.[61]

Surviving wounds for any soldier depended heavily on how quickly he could be evacuated.

Nearly all armed forces gave ribbons or medals to soldiers wounded in combat. The U.S. Purple Heart originated during the American Revolution, where it was initially given as a recognition of valor.

5. DISEASE (1.5 MILLION)

Many soldiers never saw combat, but all were vulnerable to illness. High stress, tight quarters, diet fluctuations, and reduced sleep all contributed to high disease rates. For every U.S. soldier overseas, his chances of getting wounded were 7 percent, injured 11 percent, and sick 70 percent.[62]

Primary causes were contaminated food and water, which invited the perennial guests of wartime: dysentery, diarrhea, cholera, and typhoid. Gnawing lice injected their hosts with typhus, a chief killer everywhere. Pneumonia claimed untold numbers, brought on by damp living conditions and exhaustion.

Swarming in the Mediterranean and tropical regions were mosquitoes, which the Japanese called "the Great Enemy." Various breeds injected several forms of malaria, including cerebral malaria, which produced brain-baking fevers of 110°F. Entire regiments were left prostrate with symptoms similar to severe food poisoning.

In the petri dish of Southeast Asia were skin diseases, including deadly jungle rot. Entering through any break of the skin, an intense bacterium gradually ate away at the flesh, producing golf ball–sized holes in the body. Unless treated with antibiotics, amputation, or aggressive scraping, death was probable.[63]

Along with the above killers, soldiers also succumbed in large numbers to diphtheria, beriberi, tetanus, meningitis, influenza, tuberculosis, and scarlet fever. The Japanese idiom made a strong case when it contended, "To fall in a hail of bullets is to meet a hero's death, but there is no glory in dying of disease."[64]

Survival depended on rest, nutrition, and the correct medication, luxuries commonly available to American and British soldiers but less so among Germans and Russians. Hardest hit were Chinese, Japanese, and colonial troops, who suffered terribly from inadequate supply systems, lack of reinforcements, and poor medical support. In cases of malaria, Japanese soldiers died ten times more often than Americans.

Testament to the variety and severity of illnesses in Southeast Asia during the war, among the diseases reported in the region were leprosy and the bubonic plague.

---

6. ACCIDENT (1.4 MILLION)

From the minute they put on a uniform, officers and enlisted were in danger. Combat training produced a high rate of injuries and sometimes death, especially when live ammunition was used during instructional exercises. Weapons testing was often as perilous as frontline duty. Logistical support was particularly dangerous, as it involved heavy equipment transporting huge amounts of fuel and ammunition over distances of thousands of miles.[65] In July 1944, while U.S. sailors were loading tons of ammunition into ships docked near San Francisco, an explosion detonated the entire cargo and instantly killed more than three hundred men.

Sailing in rough waters was extremely hazardous, more so when ice and wind were involved, taking an untold number of men overboard. U.S. Adm. John W. Wilcox was one of the highest-ranking Americans killed in the war when he was swept from his ship and into the Atlantic in March 1942.[66]

In air operations, collisions, human error, and mechanical or electrical failure tended to have extreme consequences. The Finnish air force lost over half its planes in operations other than combat. The Luftwaffe estimated to have lost 70,000 airmen killed in action and a quarter-million dead in accident-related events. In all, 35,946 American aviators died in accidents, or 43 percent of all accidental deaths of U.S. armed forces. Losses were so high in routine stateside flights that Florida crews coined the phrase, "One a day in Tampa Bay."[67]

Though technically killed in action, victims of friendly fire numbered in the hundreds of thousands. Working in tandem with infantry movements, artillery and bombing runs sometimes fell short, with disastrous effects. Allied soldiers advancing on Caen in NORMANDY were torn apart by Allied bombs intended for the German-held city. To keep warm on the eastern front, Germans wore toasty felt hats captured from the Russians and were summarily mistaken for the enemy and fired upon. Poor communication and low visibility made any fire fight a chance for unintentional fratricide.

Aerial accidents and malfunctions cost the lives of Heisman Trophy winner Nile Kinnick, John F. Kennedy's brother Joseph, and more than a dozen American generals.

7. EXPOSURE (1 MILLION)

During the war, military operations occurred in a range of nearly two hundred degrees. In the "sun's anvil" of North Africa, heat indexes in unventilated tanks broiled to 140°F and higher. The merciless winters of northern Russia brought long periods of −40° and colder.

Ironically, soldiers dying from heat or cold experienced similar ends. First came a brief period of intense pain, which gave way to a numbing state of shock and mental delirium. The victim them slipped into a coma, commonly a point of no return. One by one, organs shut down, ending with heart failure. Of the extremes, cold claimed more lives. Ground troops in Europe experienced frostbite as far south as the mountains near Naples. Sailors swept into the North Atlantic froze long before they drowned. Wounded soldiers on both sides of the eastern front were often evacuated via unheated trucks and railcars. Many casualties arrived at their destinations frozen solid.

Though death by exposure occurred year-round, desert storms and winter blizzards often brought spikes in the toll. Troops caught away from shelter had slim chances of survival. Footpaths and roads disappeared under drifts; trenches filled in an instant. Landmarks, rare in barren areas, became invisible. Soldiers struggling to find shelter sometimes made the fatal mistake of stepping a few feet in the wrong direction, headed off into nothingness, and died slowly from dehydration or frost.[68]

Captured Germans suffer through a blast of Russian winter winds. Hunger and illness increased a soldier's chances of dying from the elements.

Allied bombing raids from North Africa to the Balkans were particularly difficult on the body. Crew members often suited up in 100°F heat, only to fly into the mountainous region at twenty thousand feet, where the air temperature fell to −50°F.

8. STARVATION (800,000)

Although many units underwent periods of shortage, some were emaciated too often and too intensely to ward off fatalities from starvation. In some instances, soldiers witnessed friends turn into something like pack animals, killing civilians, enemies, and each other for pieces of bread.[69]

As always, exact numbers of dead are unknown. Situations decrepit enough to cause famine were normally not conducive to record keeping. Also, acute hunger made victims extremely susceptible to fatal diseases.

Prison camps were the site of most military deaths by starvation, particularly between Berlin and Moscow. Also dangerous was any besieged area. German corpses at STALINGRAD showed clear signs of famine—distended abdomens, gaunt faces, complete absence of subcutaneous fat—but doctors were forbidden to report starvation as a cause of death. The fight for GUADALCANAL, into which Japan fed thirty thousand troops piecemeal, became a supply nightmare. Unable to hold on to ports, pushed to the least accessible corners of the mountainous areas, already undersupplied by Tokyo, the garrisons lost more men from hunger than from American bullets. One Imperial officer wrote in his diary: "Rice. I really want rice…Even when mortars are falling like a squall or the land is reshaped by bombs I don't worry. But I can't stand looking at my men become pale and thin." In several areas and in several instances, soldiers resorted to suicide or cannibalism rather than face hunger any longer.[70]

One German soldier recalled seeing a group of wounded Soviet prisoners on the eastern front. All were begging for food, including several who were wounded in the abdomen, with strands of intestine hanging out.

---

9. EXECUTION (700,000)

In April 1943 the German army came upon forty-four hundred corpses hastily buried in the Polish forest of Katyn. All were Polish officers, and all had been shot in the back of the head. The bodies represented just a portion of opposing officers and men eliminated by the NKVD, the Soviet Secret Police.[71]

Three members of Maj. Gen. Jimmy Doolittle's 1942 bombing raid on Japan were executed, as were untold thousand of captives of the Japanese Empire before and after. Some Japanese camps assigned prisoners to guard duty; if anyone escaped, the guards were executed.[72]

Hitler's infamous commissar order in 1941 condemned political officers in the Red Army to immediate death. Estimates of implementation reach six hundred thousand. His 1944 Bullet Decree stipulated the killing of any recaptured prisoners, excluding Americans and British, which resulted in far fewer deaths.[73]

If armies weren't doing it to each other, they were doing it to their own. Britain executed forty men for various crimes but banned the death penalty for desertion. The United States shot or hanged 146 of its own, mostly for murder and rape. Only one American soldier was killed for deserting. Some 15,000 German soldiers were executed, most for desertion or insubordination. For added effect, the condemned were often left hanging on posts or in trees with placards reading "I am a traitor" pinned to the corpse. The total of Soviet executions is unknown but likely numbered in the tens of thousands.[74]

Soviet records occasionally grouped "accidents" and "sentenced to be shot" in the same category.

---

10. SUICIDE (300,000)

Triggers were innumerable. Drunkenness, severe wounds, "Dear John" letters, hunger, and sleep deprivation were common reasons for men to take their own lives. Thousands of Germans killed themselves during the winter months of the Soviet campaign, incapable of tolerating the horrific cold and creeping frostbite.

A German general ends his life in Leipzig. The damaged canvas of Hitler nearby may have been positioned by the photographer for effect.

Post-traumatic stress disorder was a likely cause in many cases. Rates of self-destruction were comparatively low for armed forces that recognized and treated the malady, namely the United States, Australia, and Britain. Suicide rates were higher among countries that denied the existence of battle fatigue or refused treatment, namely the Third Reich and the Soviet Union.[75]

Suicides were most common in situations involving resistance to capture. In this end the Japanese were proficient. Banzai charges and kamikaze missions notwithstanding (which probably cost 150,000 and 5,000 Japanese lives, respectively), suicides occurred at all military levels in the face of impending defeat. By many accounts, higher ranks preferred death by ritual stabbing or ordered their own beheading. Japanese enlisted frequently opted for explosives, namely grenades held against the stomach.[76]

Annual suicide rates among most civilian populations actually declined during the war, in some countries by as much as half.

MOST SIGNIFICANT BATTLES: EUROPE AND NORTH AFRICA

Importance is in the eye of the beholder. In the early 1980s, a television documentary about the eastern front aired internationally. The program was titled "The Great Patriotic War" for Russian viewers, "The Unforgettable War" for West Germans, and "The Unknown War" for U.S. audiences.[77]

When thinking of World War II, Americans generally focus on England and NORMANDY, placing all other areas a distant second. The tendency is understandable. Of the five million American troops sent overseas, most served in Britain and France. The United States was simply closer to the Old World than to the East, geographically, politically, and historically. The dominant language in the United States was and remains English.

Of course, Western Europe was only a part of the picture. A state of war existed in North Africa for nearly a decade. Most of the fighting and dying happened east of Berlin. Compared to the duration of combat in France, Americans fought twice as long in Italy and four times as long in the skies over Germany.

As reflected by the following list, the war was truly global. Below are the ten most significant military engagements in Europe and North Africa, listed in chronological order and selected for their respective military and political consequences for the entire hemisphere.

1. POLAND (SEPTEMBER 1–OCTOBER 6, 1939)

France and Britain did not declare war when Germany annexed Austria in 1938 or marched into Prague in 1939, but they drew the line when Hitler made threatening demands for Polish territory. It hardly mattered.

Fixated on demonstrating his military might, Hitler intended to take Poland by force. With all risk of Russian intervention eliminated by the unsavory NAZI-SOVIET PACT signed a week earlier, the German Wehrmacht slipped its hand around Poland, with the navy in the Baltic to the north, two armies to the northwest, three to the southwest, and one to the south in Slovakia. In the morning darkness of September 1, the hand closed.

Committed to holding the highly populated west, the Polish military lost unity within hours. Luftwaffe dive bombers severed lines of communication, and tank brigades split armies into isolated pockets. Defending tenaciously, the Poles managed only one successful assault, when two German divisions attempted to cut off the retreat of an entire Polish army. Any chance of survival disappeared when the Soviets attacked from the east on September 17. Fighting officially ended on October 5.

Partitioned for the fourth time in two centuries, Poland suffered nearly 100,000 military and civilian casualties, a fraction of the 5.5 million it would eventually lose in the war. British and French promises of military intervention never materialized. The Polish government escaped and found exile in London, only to be compromised years later during Allied conferences. Citizens who survived went on to endure a lifetime of occupation, five years under the Nazis, and more than forty under the Soviets.

Blitzkrieg was only the beginning of a six-year war in Poland.

The Poles may have surrendered in five weeks, but they put up a harrowing fight. Germany lost more dead conquering Poland than the United States would later lose taking Iwo Jima.

2. FRANCE (MAY 10–JUNE 22, 1940)

Of the six countries Hitler rapidly invaded and conquered in the spring of 1940, five were targeted for their geographic location. Hitler had to invade the Nordic countries of Denmark and Norway, he reasoned, to protect Germany's northern border and access the Atlantic. Luxembourg, Belgium, and Holland were simply in the way of his only true adversary in the West.

As Hitler contended in *Mein Kampf,* "France is and will remain the implacable enemy of Germany." Noting France's stubborn survival during the First World War, imposing reparations, and occupying the Rhineland against international will: "What France has always desired, and will continue to desire, is to prevent Germany from becoming a homogenous Power."[78]

More accurately, France simply did not want Germany to invade again, having involuntarily hosted the Huns in 1870 and 1914. Many credited this fearful and defensive posture as one of the main reasons the country fell so quickly in 1940.

Militarily, France was the zenith of Hitler's success. Never before and never again would Nazi Germany conquer a country of comparable wealth and military size. The improbable and rapid victory also gave Germany submarine pens along the Atlantic, large amounts of cash indemnities, coal and bauxite deposits, and a base for future aircraft and missile operations against Great Britain.

Hitler celebrated the fall of France with a well-documented tour of Paris.

To further humiliate the defeated French, Hitler stipulated that the surrender proceedings take place in a historic railway coach in Compiègne, the same railcar in which Germany signed the armistice of surrender to end the First World War.

3. THE BATTLE OF BRITAIN (JULY 10–SEPTEMBER 17, 1940)

When Hitler's "Nordic cousins" rejected his appeal for a peace agreement after the fall of France, he intended to teach them a lesson: "Since England, despite its hopeless military position, still shows no signs of willingness to come to terms, I have decided to prepare a landing operation against England and if necessary to carry it out."[79]

Invasion first required control of the air. The Luftwaffe promised to deliver, calculating it would take a mere four days to obliterate the RAF's fighter command.[80]

The ensuing battle uncovered several German oversights. Their twin-engine bombers—Heinkel 111s and Junkers 88s—were slow and easy targets with modest payloads. The Stuka JU-87 dive bomber, though menacing with its whaling siren, had the speed of a crop duster. The Messerschmitt 109 was an excellent fighter, but its fuel capacity barely got it to London and back. Yet the weakest aspect of the Luftwaffe was strategy. Bombing ports and ships, followed by airstrips and finally cities, the German air force never eliminated the British radar sites.

Outnumbered four to one, British fighters were able to survive by pinpointing their efforts with an early warning system. In just over two months, the RAF lost 1,100 aircraft to the Germans' 1,800. Thanks to rescue operations on their home turf, though, the British only lost 550 pilots compared to 2,500 German crewmen. On September 17, 1940, Hitler postponed the invasion of Britain indefinitely, choosing instead to punish Britain by way of "the Blitz"—nightly air raids that would last until May 1941 and kill more than 40,000.

The Battle of Britain was numerically an intermediate affair. Both sides replaced their material and crew losses quickly. Britain's resolve fueled a great deal of national pride and a considerable amount of American admiration. Ironically, Germany may have also benefited. Hitler lacked the landing vessels and warships to mount an amphibious assault in force. Any Nazi flotilla likely would have succumbed to an immensely superior British navy.[81]

St. Paul's Cathedral provides a background for a December 1940 bombing of London.

The Battle of Britain was an international fight. RAF pilots in-cluded volunteers from Australia, Belgium, Canada, Czechoslovakia, France, Ireland, Jamaica, New Zealand, Palestine, Poland, Rhodesia (Zimbabwe), South Africa, and the United States.

4. BARBAROSSA (JUNE 22, 1941)

The largest invasion of all time, ten times larger than D-day, the Third Reich offensive into the Soviet Union instantly and completely altered the course of the war. It revealed the absolute limits of blitzkrieg, opened the bloodiest theater of the war, and broke the Nazi-Soviet alliance.

The attack began at 3:00 a.m. June 22, 1941. The front stretched from the Baltic to the Black Sea, a span of more than a thousand miles. Amassed were more than a million horses and vehicles. Three-fourths of the German armed forces—plus divisions from Finland, Hungary, and Romania—totaled nearly four million men. In a letter to his con-fidante Benito Mussolini, Hitler called the order to launch Operation Barbarossa the hardest decision of his life: "We have no chance of eliminating America. But it does lie in our power to exclude Russia."[82]

Hitler was optimistic. Thinking he could "crush Soviet Russia in a quick campaign," he believed a short, massive assault would break the Bolshevik experiment, "and the whole rotten structure will come crashing down." Such was his confidence that winter gear was not procured for the operation.[83]

The plan, such as it was, entailed three great army groups: one to push northeast to capture Leningrad, one to head straight for Moscow, and one to progress southeast to the oil fields of the Caucasus.

At first, the blitzkrieg seemed to be working its deadly will. In six months the Soviets suffered more than 2.7 million casualties and 3.3 million captured, tolls never seen before in history. But the Soviets were able and willing to tolerate such bloodshed—and induce a fair number of deaths in return—while denying Hitler all of his objectives.[84]

The eastern front became a meat grinder for the German army from which there was no break during four years of fighting.

What was supposed to be a six-week operation for the Third Reich turned into nearly two hundred weeks of overextended, unfocused slaughter. Of all the war's military and civilian dead, most were destined to perish between Berlin and Moscow.

Hitler could have picked a better operation code name. Barbarossa was a twelfth-century crusader who died on his way to the Holy Land. While attempting to ford a river on horseback, he fell off midstream and drowned. Barbarossa might have survived had he not been weighted down with armor.

---

5. STALINGRAD (AUGUST 23, 1942–FEBRUARY 2, 1943)

Though enduring delays and setbacks, Germany was still on the advance a year into the Soviet invasion. Nowhere had the Third Reich suffered a true reversal. Yet on the approach to the oil-rich Caucasus, Hitler decided to take Stalingrad. It would be his undoing.

On a map the idea seemed reasonable. A heavily industrialized metropolis, Stalingrad guarded a key north–south rail line and a deep westerly bend to the Volga River, both of which fed Baku's oil to the Soviet Union. The city also loomed over any advance into southeast Russia. For Hitler, the chance to shame the city's namesake was an added incentive. In August 1942 a third of a million Axis troops charged through the Ukraine to smash the city against the Volga. Joseph Stalin ordered his town to be held at all costs. Hell was about to open a branch office.

Germans made quick progress to the outskirts, but the head of their formations dissolved when entering Stalingrad's narrow streets. Progress was suddenly measured not in miles but in blocks. To add force to the blow, Hitler pushed in more troops, dangerously overcommitting himself.

Both sides poured in reserves, but the Soviets had the advantage of much shorter supply lines. Three months into the battle, just as the brutal Russian winter set in, the Soviets smashed through the Axis flanks and encircled the overcommitted troops. Outside the hardening cordon, German tank commander ERICH VON MANSTEIN led an attack to break through and rescue the Sixth Army, but Hitler forbade the Sixth from attempting a breakout to meet the panzers.

German forces laid siege to Stalingrad in the late summer of 1942 but fell victim to the brutal winter that shortly followed.

As the noose tightened, fighting within the city became nothing short of animalistic. Squads of men hunted each other, block by block, room to room, preferring to kill silently with knives and spades but resorting more often to submachine guns and grenades. Flamethrowers were particularly effective in the sewers. Snipers ruled open ground. Tanks hid among the rubble and scythed away at moving targets. Artillery set fire to everything, and the city was wrapped in a perpetual shroud of smoke, noise, and stench. During the battle, ruptured oil tanks bled into the Volga, and at times the river itself was on fire. Luftwaffe transport planes were shot out of the sky—rations stopped coming in, and the German wounded could not get out. In due course, the rat population exploded and grew fat on corpses.[85]

Two months later, with no hope of escape or resupply, a fraction of the original German force surrendered. The rest were dead, wounded, or missing. It was the first major defeat of the Third Reich on land anywhere. Germany lost a fourth of its manpower on the eastern front as well as any reasonable chance to take Leningrad, Moscow, or the oil fields Hitler's war machine so desperately needed. From Stalingrad onward, Hitler's mental and physical health began a precipitous decline, and he was rarely seen in public again.[86]

Germany lost more soldiers in and around Stalingrad than the United States lost in Europe during the entire war.

---

6. SECOND EL ALAMEIN (OCTOBER 23–NOVEMBER 4, 1942)

For the British army the war began with a string of humiliating defeats: France and Norway in 1940, Greece and Crete in 1941, Malay and Singapore in 1942. Aside from liberating Abyssinia, the war had been a bust.

North Africa was no better. IRWIN ROMMEL's Afrika Korps harassed and beat the British Eighth Army out of Libya, then chased it into Egypt. It appeared as if Alexandria would fall, then perhaps Cairo and the Suez Canal. In full retreat, British commander Gen. Claude Auchinleck ordered a halt just west of the shore city of El Alamein, fifty miles from the critical port of Alexandria. It was an ideal move. For Rommel to get beyond this point would require a camel to pass through the eye of a needle, or more correctly, a Desert Fox to squeeze through a bottleneck.

Protected on the north by the Mediterranean and on the south by the impassible chasm of the Qattara Depression, Auchinleck's Australians, New Zealanders, South Africans, and British stood astride a forty-mile pass, the only avenue into Egypt. In July 1942, Rommel tried to push through and failed. In September he tried and failed again. All the while his forces dwindled while his opponent's grew.

Though Claude Auchinleck did most of the preparation work, Bernard Montgomery received most of the credit for the Allied victory at Second El Alamein.

By October, the Eighth Army outnumbered the Germans and Italians more than two to one in men and tanks and owned near complete mastery of the air. After a lengthy wait and extensive planning, the new (and supposedly aggressive) Eighth Army commander Gen. Bernard Montgomery finally decided to start boxing. He jabbed with the left on the south side of the line, forcing the Axis to protect its flank. As soon as the left feint made contact, Montgomery smashed with his right. Initially, the British took heavy losses, but knowing that attrition was a fight Rommel could not win, Monty kept punching.

Down to a few dozen operational tanks, nearly surrounded, running low on everything, Rommel disengaged and began a long trek back across Libya and into Tunisia. Monty cautiously and ineffectually pursued.

Viewed objectively, the battle meant little. Rommel was down to a pittance of resources when the fight commenced. Days after it ended, the Allies had landed in Northwest Africa, dooming the Axis either way. But for the British Empire it was a soul-saving victory, "the greatest in military history." El Alamein also catapulted Montgomery to the top of Allied command, where he would simultaneously help and hinder the war effort with his absolute carefulness and monumental ego.

The United States played a significant role in the British victory at El Alamein. Nearly half of Montgomery's tanks were American-made Grants and Shermans.

7. KURSK (JULY 5–23, 1943)

As the war neared its fourth anniversary, the Third Reich was already dying. North Africa was lost, as was the Atlantic. But an opportunity presented itself on the Russian steppes in the shape of a large bend in the Soviet front lines.

Around the rail junction of Kursk, nearly one hundred miles across, a large horseshoe salient bulged westward into Nazi-held territory; five Soviet armies were at risk. Desperate for a victory, Hitler aimed to slice this salient at its base, attacking from both sides, capturing everyone and everything inside.

For once the Soviet high command anticipated Hitler's moves almost exactly. Inside the salient, citizens and soldiers constructed hundreds of miles of overlapping trenches, dug countless tank traps, and laid four hundred thousand mines. Some areas of the defensive belt were forty miles across. The plan was to lure the Germans into the deadly quagmire, wait for the offensive to wear down, and then crush it with counterattacks.[87]

The nearly three-week-long battle of Kursk included some thirteen thousand armored vehicles and twelve thousand aircraft.

The Germans obliged. North and south of the salient, more than 900,000 Germans launched their pincer move, armed with 2,900 tanks and assault guns, 10,000 artillery pieces, and 2,000 aircraft. On schedule, the offensive broke down, battered by antitank guns, swarmed by infantry, tangled in barbed wire. In turn, the counterattacks came, with Soviet forces totaling twice the number of German soldiers and weapons. But it was no mopping up.

Most of the Germans fought their way out, fiercely inducing 50 percent casualties on the Soviets and higher. For every German killed or wounded, there were more than three Soviet casualties. For each German tank destroyed, the Soviets lost more than five.[88] Altogether, Kursk involved approximately three million combatants with more than four hundred thousand casualties, making it one of the largest and bloodiest battles ever. The Germans viewed the battle as a minor setback, especially compared with the simultaneous invasion of Sicily. The Soviets considered Kursk to be an absolute triumph, the first authoritative combat victory over the Third Reich.

Time would validate the Soviet position. Kursk was the last great German offensive on the eastern front. The Soviets soon replaced their losses; the Germans could not. Most important, Kursk signaled the beginning of a general Nazi retreat that would last twenty months and not stop until the fall of BERLIN.[89]

Involving more than seven thousand tanks, Kursk remains the largest tank battle in history.

---

8. NORMANDY (JUNE 6, 1944)

For two years Churchill argued against a cross-channel attack. Better to go into North Africa, he argued, to gain valuable combat experience and to spread the Germans thin. North Africa turned into Sicily, then Italy, and nearly Greece, Yugoslavia, and northern Norway. Fearing a slaughter reminiscent of the First World War, the prime minister wanted the Allies to go anywhere but France. On June 6, 1944, his fears dissipated.

There were several mistakes. Roughly 90 percent of the U.S. airborne troops failed to hit their drop zones, with some "sticks" (plane or gilder loads) drifting more than twenty miles off course. Most of the amphibious tanks either sank or were blasted off the beaches. Landing craft off Omaha Beach initially unloaded troops more than a quarter mile from shore.

But predictions of 70 percent casualties proved wildly inflated. Overall, the rate was closer to 15 percent, mostly because Operation Overlord was unquestionably the best-planned military operation of the entire war. Secrecy had more than one million men in complete isolation for weeks. Deception plans had Hitler believing, even weeks after the initial landings, that Calais was the true invasion point. Ten sea lanes had been swept of mines. Artificial harbors called "Mulberries" were brought in. Bomb runs had destroyed French rail lines as far as three hundred miles inland. The Allies had a fifty-to-one advantage in aircraft. It was the heaviest ship-to-shore bombardment and largest amphibious landing in history.

In ten days more than four hundred thousand men and ninety thousand vehicles came ashore.

The long-awaited invasion of Europe began with the landings at NORMANDY on June 6, 1944.

Unfortunately for the Allies, post-landing planning was not nearly as precise. Secondary objectives were not clearly defined. The countryside was a maze of hedgerows, making offensive coordination nearly impossible. But a solid beachhead had been established in Nazi-occupied territory, and the end of the war in Europe could be measured in months rather than years.

Often seen in the United States as a primarily American operation, the Allied airborne and landing troops on D-day included eighty-three thousand Americans plus eighty-eight thousand British and Canadians.

9. BATTLE OF THE BULGE (DECEMBER 16, 1944–JANUARY 16, 1945)

Though Hitler visualized launching grand counterattacks until the day he died, his last true offensive mimicked his greatest battlefield success. The outcome, however, did not.

Pulling resources from the eastern front, against the advice of his senior staff, Hitler ordered three panzer armies into the Allied lines on Germany's western border. Assembling in only five days, cloaked under cloudy skies and frigid weather, the Fifth, Sixth, and Seventh German Armies rammed directly into the middle of the Allied front, once again using the "impassible" ARDENNES as the entry point.

German forces stalled the Allied offensive with a reprise of the invasion of France in a surprise attack through the Ardennes in December 1944.

By Christmas Eve the German bulge had reached sixty-five miles into the Allied lines. But clearing skies brought five thousand Allied aircraft and a tenacious American counterattack. The ill-prepared Germans lacked the fuel and ammunition for an extended fight and rapidly lost everything they had gained.

On a map, the front line looked almost exactly the same after the battle as before it started. But the fight involved one million men and cost the Allies more than 70,000 casualties. The Germans suffered more than 120,000 dead, wounded, or missing. The Second Ardennes also critically weakened Germany's east and west fronts, expediting the downfall of the Third Reich. Most likely, Hitler's late commitment to the Ardennes campaign allowed for greater Soviet progress into Central Europe than would have otherwise been achieved.

Allegedly, the German commanding officer, Field Marshal Gerd von Rundstedt, had so little faith in the Ardennes offensive, he put his second in command at the head of affairs and spent the first part of the battle reading novels and drinking cognac.

---

10. BERLIN (APRIL 16–MAY 2, 1945)

By mid-January 1945, the Allies in the West had recovered lost ground from the Bulge, and the Soviets to the east had launched their last final offensive in a driving snowstorm outside Warsaw. The vise was beginning to close.

In rapid succession, Warsaw fell, or what was left of it. In a matter of weeks the Soviets reached the Oder River, the old German border, and began to spread north and south to consolidate their gains. Terrorized German citizens fled to Berlin, only to be struck by thousand-bomber raids. February 13 brought the fall of Budapest and the Dresden fire bombings. By the ides of March the Americans and British began crossing the Rhine.

Then on April 16, four days after the death of Franklin D. Roosevelt, the Soviets entered Germany with more than two million soldiers and began to destroy everything. Looting became widespread, as did murder and arson. The Soviets also conducted rampant molestation. It is believed that 80 percent of all females in and around Berlin were brutally and repeatedly violated by Soviet troops.[90]

The savagery continued into the city center. Artillery battered the remnants of the capital as the Red Army entered from the north and south. The Reichstag was their target, not the Chancellery four hundred yards away, under which Hitler committed suicide on April 30.

On May 7 Gen. Alfred Jodl signed an unconditional surrender to the Allies at Eisenhower's headquarters in Reims, France. Angered that the Americans and British should receive capitulation before the Soviets, Stalin demanded an "official" surrender ceremony be held the following day in Berlin.

Yet one of the most significant events in the battle for the German capital occurred nearly a month before its downfall. On April 11, General Eisenhower ordered the western Allies to halt along the Elbe River, just seventy miles from Berlin, and allow the Soviets to enter the city first. Done to prevent possible deaths from friendly fire between the east and west fronts, and to concentrate on taking as much of southern Germany as possible, Eisenhower's decision infuriated the British and a fair number of Americans. The disappointment soon fostered a widely held belief that the U.S. high command "gave up" Berlin to placate Stalin and thereby lost the first pivotal battle in the Cold War.[91]

Before the fall of Berlin, friendly fire had occurred between the Soviets and the Americans. On March 18, near the German capital, U.S. fighter pilots engaged eight "Focke-Wulf 190s." The single-engine fighters were in fact Soviet air force aircraft, six of which were lost, resulting in two deaths.

MOST SIGNIFICANT BATTLES: ASIA AND THE PACIFIC

There is a tendency in the United States to reduce the Pacific and Asian theaters to Honolulu and Hiroshima and to concentrate instead on the war in France and Germany. But a eurocentric view greatly skews the big picture.

In spite of a "Germany First" strategy, the United States had already engaged in a score of naval engagements, conducted its first offensive, bombed Tokyo, and suffered ten thousand dead in the Pacific before ever launching its first land assault on Nazi-held territory (which in fact was into French Morocco and Algeria). For the rest of the world, the war in Asia and the Pacific involved twice the number of people, was almost three years longer in duration, and covered four times more of the surface of the planet than did the conflict in Europe and North Africa.

The region's battles included the bloodiest in U.S. Navy history, the bloodiest in U.S. Marine history, the longest retreat in British military history, plus numerous incidents of Japanese forces experiencing casualties of 100 percent.

Within these milestones were many thousands of clashes, most lasting a few hours and others enveloping several months. Listed in chronological order are the ten most significant military clashes among them in terms of strategic, economic, and political consequences in the region.

1. SHANGHAI (AUGUST 13–NOVEMBER 9, 1937)

To the surprise of his country and the Japanese military, Nationalist leader CHIANG KAI-SHEK did not offer concessions to Japan after the CHINA INCIDENT along the Marco Polo Bridge. Normally he would back down after such military "disturbances" with Japan's Manchurian Kwantung Army.

Instead, Chiang sent troops into the multinational city of Shanghai. The move was in clear violation of an agreement (one of many with Japan) to keep the area demilitarized. The unarmed city soon became host to 400,000 Nationalist Chinese and 200,000 Japanese troops, slamming away at each other with artillery, bombs, and small-arms' fire. Unburied bodies filled the streets. Blocks burned to the ground. Fighting lasted for nearly three months.

A child wails amid the debris after the Japanese bombed Shanghai.

When the Japanese threatened to cut off his line of retreat, Chiang directed his men to remain in the city, dooming his best and most loyal troops. Only at the last moment did he order a withdrawal, which quickly turned into a terrorized rout westward to Nanking.

The Japanese lost some 70,000 men. Chiang lost at least 180,000. The number of civilians killed or maimed has never been accurately calculated. Chiang's wish for international intervention went unfulfilled, and the war in Asia had officially begun.

At the start of the battle for Shanghai, the Nationalist Chinese air force tried to bomb Japanese ships moored in the city along the Yangtze River. The bombs overshot the targets and struck a busy shopping district, killing 728 civilians.[92]

2. PEARL HARBOR, OAHU (DECEMBER 7, 1941)

Strategically, Oahu loomed on the Japanese navy's left flank. Imperial warships could not hope to move south against resource-rich countries until the military threat to the east was neutralized. From this logic, Japan's naval high command began to view a preemptive strike against the American fleet at PEARL HARBOR as its best chance for success everywhere else.

Planned nearly a year ahead of time and set in motion while diplomatic exchanges continued between the two countries, the Japanese attack on U.S. naval and air installations in Hawaii went better than even the most optimistic had hoped. Shielded by a series of storms on its approach, a flotilla of eighty-eight warships sailed undetected on a five-thousand-mile voyage, launched some 350 planes, and retrieved all but 29 aircraft. In return, the attack crippled nearly every U.S. battleship in the Pacific, sank or damaged a number of other ships, and destroyed or damaged nearly three-quarters of all military aircraft on the island of Oahu. For the U.S. Navy, the first day of the war was the worst, with more than 2,100 dead.

The explosion of the forward magazines of the destroyer *Shaw* produced this dramatic image of the attack on Pearl Harbor.

For all their successes, the Japanese achieved only marginal gains. Their main targets—three U.S. aircraft carriers—were not at PEARL HARBOR. Of the seven battleships sunk or damaged, all but three were restored to full service. For the most part, docks, hangars, technicians, and engineers survived the raid, making for impressive repair times. Precious OIL TANKS were untouched. Above all, a previously isolation-ist American public abruptly became unified and belligerent, inspired all the more by a Japanese declaration of war that was delivered after the PEARL HARBOR attack commenced.[93]

So moved by the stunning success at Pearl Harbor, Japan honored the anniversary of the attack every month for the rest of the war.

---

3. FALL OF SINGAPORE (FEBRUARY 15, 1942)

Winston Churchill called it the "worst disaster and largest capitula-tion of British history." As far as disasters go, Britannia had suffered its share—the Norman Invasion, the Black Plague, and the battle of the Somme come to mind. But the PM was correct in the latter point. The eighty thousand Australian, Indian, Malay, and British troops cap-tured at Singapore constituted the largest surrender in Royal military history.[94]

At the tip of the Malayan peninsula, the 240-square-mile island was the British Empire's linchpin in South Asia. The citadel stood south-east of India, southwest of Hong Kong, and northwest of Australia. Assuming the naval base would be susceptible to attack from the sea, the British constructed massive defenses and batteries along the south-ern coast. The dense Malay jungle to the north was believed to be impenetrable.

An hour before the attack on PEARL HARBOR, Japan invaded "impenetrable" Malay. Battle-hardened from years of fighting in China, the Imperial Twenty-Fifth Army scored repeated routs over Commonwealth infantry, eventually forcing British commander Lt. Gen. Arthur Percival to call a retreat onto Singapore.

Though outnumbering the Japanese more than two to one, Percival did not have tanks or air support. His demoralized troops retreated far-ther and farther into the island, as did hundreds of thousands of refugees.

Despite Churchill's order to "fight to the end," the defenders exhausted their supplies of food and water; yet unbeknownst to Percival, so had the Japanese. Unable to withstand a siege, Percival capitulated.

In Britain news of the surrender plunged the nation into mourning and unleashed a storm of conspiracy theories. A myth erupted that the massive coastal guns could not turn inland (they could, but their shells were only effective for piercing ship hulls). People blamed Parliament for not funding better defenses, though the government had spent many millions already. Percival was portrayed as a hero, a patsy, and an incompetent. In contrast, Japan exploded with pride. The once-mighty British Empire had been humiliated. More so than PEARL HARBOR, Singapore appeared to assure ultimate victory. One newspaper headline declared: "General Situation of Pacific War Decided."[95]

Strategically, the island proved to be marginal, as it was simply bypassed in the long, gradual Allied counterthrust a year later. But psychologically it was the high tide of the war for Japan and by many accounts the beginning of the end of British imperial power in South Asia.[96]

Lt. Gen. Arthur Percival lived through more than three years of imprisonment and was present at the formal Japanese surrender at Tokyo Bay. Many of his fellow captives did not survive. As many as one hundred thousand refugees caught in Singapore eventually died in Japanese captivity.

---

4. MIDWAY (JUNE 3–6, 1942)

In the spring of 1942, while debating whether to invade Australia or push for India, Japan's army and navy staff officers received a rude visit from sixteen B-25 Mitchell bombers, compliments of Col. James Doolittle and the USS *Hornet*, coming in from the central Pacific.

Bomb damage was not extensive (fifty fatalities, one hundred homes destroyed), but the attack spawned a near-unanimous decision to seize the atoll of Midway, draw U.S. carriers to the island, and destroy the Americans in a battle for the heart of the Pacific Ocean.

While sending a diversionary fleet to bite the long Aleutian tail of Alaska, Adm. Yamamoto Isoroku ordered four separate strike forces toward Midway. Thanks to INTELLIGENCE intercepts, Adm. CHESTER NIMITZ was aware of Yamamoto's intentions and moved to stop him, albeit with a smaller force including the carriers *Hornet*, *Enterprise*, and the miraculously repaired *Yorktown*, which had nearly capsized at the battle of CORAL SEA. At first, everything went Yamamoto's way.

Jimmy Doolittle's raid on Japan provoked the battle of Midway.

U.S. planes based on Midway (a miscellany of army, navy, and marine aircraft) flew to intercept the Japanese strike force. More than half the dive bombers and torpedo planes were shot down without scoring a single hit. Fifteen B-17s, soaring at twenty thousand feet, bombed the approaching flotilla but missed every ship. Meanwhile, Japanese aircraft strafed and bombed Midway's defenses and airstrips at will, then returned to their flattops to load up for the killer blow.

Not until Nimitz's carriers launched nearly everything they had, 151 aircraft in all, did the tide of battle turn. First to threaten the Japanese carriers were fifteen Douglas Devastator torpedo planes; slow and bulky, skimming the surface, ready to unload, when all fifteen were annihilated by ZEROS and antiaircraft fire. But their low-level flying pulled down Yamamoto's fighter screen to sea level, allowing a handful of dive bombers to drop bomb after bomb on the Japanese decks. Within minutes, three Imperial carriers, carpeted with rearmed and refueled aircraft, burst into flames and foundered. The remaining Japanese carrier was mortally bombed soon after, at the price of the *Yorktown*, her belly cut open by two aircraft-launched torpedoes.

It was the first clear victory for the United States in the war. Along with losing four carriers, Japan also lost hundreds of irreplaceable pilots and never went on the offensive in the central Pacific again.

> *To cover up the tremendous defeat at Midway, Prime Minister Tojo Hideki hid the truth about the lost carriers from his emperor and the public, simply declaring the battle a great victory. Parades were held in Tokyo to celebrate.*

5. GUADALCANAL (AUGUST 7, 1942–FEBRUARY 9, 1943)

As if slowly pushing a knife into an artery, Japanese forces advanced steadily along the Solomons, a chain of islands that cut across the sea lane between Australia and North America. On the easterly island of Guadalcanal, a few thousand Japanese engineers began building an airstrip, which they believed would make the knife's edge razor-sharp.

In reality, Guadalcanal was not capable of being a major airbase. Though nearly a hundred miles long and thirty miles wide, it was a mountainous, jungle-carpeted, malarial, scorpion-infested steam bath without enough flat land to build a decent graveyard. Still, the local headhunters called it home.[97]

Adding to the misery of Guadalcanal, maps of the British-owned island were inaccurate, making navigation of jungle areas a waking nightmare.

Almost as an afterthought, some ten thousand U.S. personnel were sent to take over the airstrip. The invasion force initially met little opposition. Unwilling to hand over Japan's southernmost possession, Adm. Yamamoto approved a naval counterattack, which abruptly sank four Allied cruisers in the area. The island quickly became a point of escalation.[98]

What began as two thousand Japanese on the island became nine thousand, then twenty thousand. Major naval engagements boiled in the surrounding waters, one of which lasted a mere thirty minutes but cost the Americans six warships. Air battles flared almost daily. Not until the United States amassed fifty thousand troops on the island did fortunes move to its side.

What was supposed to last a few days dragged on for six months. There were seven major naval fights, sinking more than forty major ships (most of them American). Hundreds of planes were lost. More than seven thousand U.S. sailors, marines, and soldiers perished along with thirty thousand Japanese. Guadalcanal was the first major offensive conducted by the United States in the war, and its conclusion signaled the turn of the Solomon knife westward.[99]

Four soldiers won the Medal of Honor on the beaches of Normandy.
Nine marines won the Medal of Honor in the jungles of Guadalcanal.

---

6. ICHI-GO (APRIL 17–DECEMBER 11, 1944)

Tokyo's intentions were ambitious, to say the least. Fifteen to thirty divisions would leave from strongpoints in east central China, head directly south for 1,000 miles, capture and destroy Chinese and American air bases along the way, and link up with Japanese forces in Indochina. The goal was to form a supply line stretching from Manchuria to Singapore. Fittingly, the name given to this bold project was Ichi-Go, "Operation One."

The tactic was brute force—air support, artillery, and light tanks, backed by 140,000 ground troops and 70,000 horses on a front 150 miles wide. At first the offensive made considerable progress. Nationalist and regional Chinese armies often outnumbered the Japanese four to one. Yet poorly supplied and completely outgunned, the Chinese suffered casualties of twenty-to-one in several engagements. At one point, Japan pulled all available reserves from Manchuria and the mainland, creating a massive army of 360,000, its largest mobile force of the war.[100]

A Chinese Nationalist protects American P-40s still sporting the shark's teeth of the Flying Tigers. Ichi-Go's main objectives included the destruction of these air bases in southeast China.

Though a few Chinese regional armies fought with spectacular bravery, the Chinese Nationalist Army did not. Chiang's troops simply melted away in the face of battle. Regional commanders begged the generalissimo and his Allied chief of staff, U.S. Gen. Joseph Stilwell, for weapons, supplies, and food. Both men repeatedly denied the requests; Chiang feared arming a potential rival, and Stilwell believed the Chinese were being driven back by cowardice. Ultimately, Washington lost all discernible confidence in Chiang.[101]

In the end the Japanese did achieve most of their objectives, linking with garrisons in Indochina on December 11, 1944, but a withered supply line halted any further progress, and U.S. victories in the Pacific made most of the gains irrelevant. Tokyo had spent itself in Asia, and Chiang's Nationalists were routed, but another group benefited greatly from Ichi-Go. By watching the two main rivals fight to the death, Mao Zedong's Communists suddenly became major contenders in the fight for China.

Per usual, the Chinese did not have the weapons to stage effective resistance during Ichi-Go. One regiment fought using two rather vintage artillery pieces. The guns previously belonged to the French army and had been used in the First World War.

---

7. SAIPAN (JUNE 15–JULY 9, 1944)

Saipan was the home base of the Imperial Central Pacific Fleet and the headquarters of Vice Adm. Nagumo Chuichi, the man who directed the air assault on PEARL HARBOR. The island was also within heavy bomber range of Japan. In the summer of 1944 the United States was determined to take the island, and the Japanese were just as determined to hold it.

The attackers had advantages. Japanese air cover was almost nonexistent. U.S. submarines were sinking transport after transport of soldiers and supplies heading for the area. American marines and soldiers outnumbered the defenders almost three to one. The Japanese also had to protect more than thirty thousand civilians on the island. But Saipan—fourteen miles long and five miles wide—was littered with swamps, ravines, high peaks, and thickets of jungle, interspersed with caves ideal for defensive positions. Guarding their few beaches were reefs of jagged coral.

Though landing more than twenty thousand troops on the first day, the Americans were under almost constant fire. Units got lost. Fragile battle lines broke, reformed, and broke again. Torrid accusations of incompetence flew back and forth between marine and army commanders. As the battle entered its third week (it was supposed to last only three days), the Japanese launched the largest banzai charge of the war. More than three thousand men, some only armed with grenades, nearly liquidated two American battalions.

Trapped on the island, Nagumo committed suicide, as did several thousand of his men. Of the Japanese civilians, some twenty-two thousand jumped or were forced off the seaside cliffs on the west and north sides of the island. Others killed themselves with grenades or simply walked into the sea to drown. U.S. patrol boats struggled to move through the floating corpses.[102]

In the battle of Saipan, U.S. Marines suffered four thousand casualties in the first two days of fighting.

Back in Japan, the defeat meant the end of Prime Minister Tojo Hideki, who resigned along with his entire cabinet, as did the minister of the navy and the chief of navy general staff. In light of the impending attacks from B-29 bombers, Emperor Hirohito inquired if there was a way to quickly and favorably terminate the war.

Nearby Tinian and Guam islands were taken soon after Saipan fell. The three islands served as a hub for B-29 operations, and Tinian was the take-off point for both the Enola Gay and Bock's Car on their atomic missions.

8. LEYTE GULF, THE PHILIPPINES (OCTOBER 23–26, 1944)

The largest naval engagement of the war began over a fight for land. In October 1944 Gen. Douglas MacArthur fulfilled his promise to return to the Philippines, invading the island of Leyte with 175,000 men under the protection of two U.S. fleets. In response, Adm. TOYODA

SOEMU sent nearly every surface vessel left in the Imperial Navy, more than seventy warships, to crush MacArthur and the U.S. Sixth Army on the Leyte beachhead.

Though complicated, Toyoda's plan almost worked, primarily because Allied INTELLIGENCE had not deciphered the code variation used to coordinate the attack. Using a diversionary force of four carriers, the Japanese lured the U.S. Third Fleet, assigned to protect the landings, northward and hundreds of miles away from Leyte. While the Third Fleet feasted on this sacrificial lamb, the bulk of the Imperial forces descended upon MacArthur and the remaining Seventh Fleet, curling around the island from the north and south.

The southern claw of the Japanese attack broke under the weight of a daring defense. The Seventh Fleet first stunned the attack with waves of PT boats, then stopped it cold with destroyers, and finally crushed it altogether using cruisers and battleships. The northern strike force sailed within range of the landing beaches, then withdrew under the false impression that both U.S. fleets were still in the area.

The landings at Leyte fulfilled Douglas MacArthur's promise to the Philippine people. His "I have returned" address remains one of the most revered speeches in Filipino history.

Leyte Gulf was the implied end of Japanese rule on the expansive Philippines and the irrefutable end of the Japanese navy. It was also the last engagement between battleships ever and, in fact, the largest naval battle in world history. Oddly, it was also the first truly coordinated operation between the two senior officers in the Pacific, Gen. Douglas MacArthur and Adm. CHESTER NIMITZ.

In the battle of Leyte Gulf, the escort carrier USS St. Lô *went down after being hit by a Japanese plane, making it the first of eighty-three Allied ships in the war to be sunk by kamikazes.*

9. IWO JIMA (FEBRUARY 19–MARCH 26, 1945)

Called "Sulphur Island," Iwo Jima was a pear-shaped volcanic creation five miles across and a vital airbase to the Japanese. With rancid water, putrid air, radiating heat, and minimal vegetation, it was a miserable assignment for its defenders and a deathtrap for anyone wishing to invade it.

But by the fall of 1944 the U.S. Joint Chiefs of Staff determined the island to be of absolute importance. Fuel and reliability problems were downing B-29s faster than the Japanese. The only viable landing site on the thousand-mile bombing run from the Marianas to Tokyo was Iwo Jima. Japan's "unsinkable aircraft carrier" had to be taken.

As the Fourth and Fifth U.S. Marine divisions quickly learned, as would the reserves to follow in their wake, days of naval shelling and months of bombing raids had done nothing to push the Japanese from hives of subterranean fortifications and caves. The Americans landed against minimal opposition, gaining several hundred yards and amassing thousands of men on the beachhead. Then the island defenders opened up with mortars, antitank guns, and machine guns. There was no cover; it was nearly impossible to dig foxholes in the soft volcanic ash. Assault vehicles became trapped in the formless soil.

Joe Rosenthal captured an immortal moment in this photo atop Mount Suribachi on day five of the battle, yet Iwo Jima would not be secured until day thirty-six.

By nightfall six hundred marines were dead, but the island had been cut in two. The following day, the Fifth Marines pushed south up Mount Suribachi, and the Fourth Marines fanned north to secure the airfields. Three days later, five marines and a navy medic planted a large American flag atop Suribachi, and photographer Joe Rosenthal captured the most famous image in American military history. In a grand sweep north, the Third Marine Division joined in the fray. Still, a month of brutal fighting lay ahead. Even as B-29s began making emergency landings after long bombing missions against Japan, ground troops were still mopping up heavy pockets of resistance. Not until the end of March was the island finally declared secured.

In killing nearly the entire Japanese force of 23,000, almost 7,000 Americans died. Yet by the end of the war, more than 2,200 B-29s made emergency landings on Iwo Jima, sparing 24,000 U.S. crewmen's lives.[103]

In all, twenty-seven U.S. servicemen won the Medal of Honor on Iwo Jima, twelve of them posthumously, a total more than any other battle in the Second World War.

---

10. OKINAWA (APRIL 1–JULY 2, 1945)

It was the last stop on the island-hopping campaign. Shaped like a serpent heading southwest, sixty-mile-long Okinawa held nearly eighty thousand Imperial soldiers, most of them positioned on high ridges across the serpent's neck. On April 1, 1945, a half-million U.S. servicemen, plus an attack fleet from the British Royal Navy, essentially surrounded the reptile and thrust one hundred thousand men into its right side.[104]

Landings and advances north progressed well for the Americans. Troops reached the snake's tail in two weeks. But the push south quickly turned bloody. Bombings and barrages failed to dislodge the Japanese from caves along the high ground. Mortars and artillery leveled the Americans from afar; grenades and machine guns slaughtered at close quarters. The long delays caused Allied naval support to remain in position, drawing hundreds of successive kamikaze attacks. On land the Japanese held out until an ill-advised banzai charge separated their lines, signaling the beginning of gradual disintegration. The following six weeks witnessed savage fighting in the skull of the snake—storms of artillery fire, roving packs of flamethrowers, and suicides. Discipline evaporated among the surviving Japanese, who began to turn on each other and against civilians. By late June most of the original garrison was dead.[105]

The battle of Okinawa killed or wounded 10,000 U.S. Navy personnel, mostly through kamikaze attacks. American marines and soldiers suffered 40,000 killed and wounded. All told, nine out of ten Japanese troops died. As many as 20,000 pro-Japanese native militia and 60,000 civilians perished.

The empire had lost the last remnants of its navy and most of its remaining aircraft, but that hardly insinuated an easy Allied victory in the impending invasion of Japan. Of the losses in the fight for Okinawa, 90 percent occurred on land.[106]

Along with the U.S. and Japanese banners, a Confederate flag flew over Okinawa. A U.S. marine lofted the Stars and Bars atop Shuri Castle after the stronghold fell to the Americans. Some claim the flag was in honor of the commanding officer, Gen. Simon B. Buckner Jr., whose father was a general in the Confederate army.

HOME FRONT

HARDSHIPS

As a basic measure of noncombatant involvement in a conflict, some comparative history may be useful. In the American Civil War no more than 7 percent of the fatalities were civilian. By the First World War, the rate had climbed to 20 percent. In the Second World War, nearly 60 percent of the dead were not in the military. The phrase "fighting for our lives" had taken on a literal meaning.

Conservative estimates place civilian war deaths at more than thirty million. Of these, the Soviet Union lost at least twelve million. Many historians refuse to guess on China, where the toll was somewhere between two million and fifteen million (probably closer to the latter). Poland suffered the highest percentage, losing 15 percent of its population—nearly six million people. On average, Yugoslavia lost more civilians every two weeks than Britain lost every year.

As expected, war brought far more hardships to the home front than just loss of life. People lost limbs and eyes, their homes, sometimes their countries. Ever present among physical traumas were mental demons of anxiety, fatalism, and fear. Yet people lived on, many through astounding displays of composure and diligence. Survivors from Buchenwald to Nanking recounted how, even in the most desperate times, a pervasive fight for normalcy endured.

Listed below, and placed in no particular order, are some of the more ruthless trials set upon the home front, many of which lasted well beyond the dates of any military cease-fire.

1. HUNGER

It was as if the four horsemen of the apocalypse had come, and famine was leading the way. First to go was prime farmland. While the Soviet Union transported many of its factories east, past the barrier of the Urals, its agricultural base naturally remained rooted where it stood, in the west and southwest. When Germany overran these areas in 1941, the Soviets lost more than one-third of their grain and grazing lands, more than half their potato acreage, and nearly the entire sugar beet region. So, too, China lost its two most cultivated regions to Japanese invasion by 1938.[1]

As with most famines, the greatest harm came not from lack of food but from lack of transportation. Never in the world's history had population centers been so large and so dependent on food shipments to sustain them.

The war sank ships, destroyed roads, killed draft animals, and commandeered trucks that transported food. For countries such as Greece, which imported a half-billion tons of grain annually, the effects were devastating. In the winter of 1941–42, Athens alone lost three hundred residents a day to starvation. Leningraders were dying at a rate of four thousand a day, with survivors reduced to killing and eating pets. In 1943 a famine in China's Honan province sparked a civilian uprising against the Nationalist Army. By 1944 famines erupted in Holland and east India, the latter killing an estimated 1.5 million. Nearly 2 million people in Indochina succumbed to hunger the following year.

Incidents of cannibalism occurred in more than one country. Women everywhere turned to prostitution to feed their families.[2]

While fighting had ceased in most countries by the end of 1945, hunger had not. Russia and China were producing half the grain of prewar years. Germany experienced its worst food shortages in 1946 and 1947. Rationing continued in many countries through 1950.[3]

A mother masks her anguish, while her children are less guarded. As many as a fifth of all civilian casualties were less than ten years old.

In 1944, Japan's petroleum-starved war industry took what precious food was left and literally fed it to their machines. Factory owners confiscated and processed countless tons of soybeans and coconuts for machine oil and used distilled potatoes and rice to make alcohol for engines.

2. GROUND COMBAT

"Battlefield" had become a misnomer by the 1940s. The primary targets of conquest were not the opposing armies but the factories, ports, rail lines, ships, and towns that supplied them. If residents of such areas were unable or unwilling to leave their homes, unspeakable horrors awaited. For many the sight of bombers was not nearly as damning as approaching enemy tanks and infantry.

In addition to the shelling and shooting, there were the added chances of arson, looting, murder, and molestation. The desecration of women occurred with chilling regularity, especially in ethnically charged battles. Nations such as Burma, the Low Countries, France,

Manchuria, the Philippines, Poland, Romania, and the Ukraine had the added curse of being fought over several times.

On local levels, men and machines razed villages, towns, and cities across Africa, Europe, Asia, and the Pacific. By 1944 eight out of ten buildings in Warsaw were leveled or unusable. Yugoslavia, exposed to both international and civil war, possessed a stretch of road more than one hundred miles long where not a roadside building remained standing. By 1945, the city of Manila was barely recognizable. After the war the Soviet Union designated Kiev, Leningrad, Minsk, Stalingrad, and others as "Hero Cities," essentially for undergoing 40 percent or higher casualties. Bonn became the West German capital by default because it was one of the few major German cities with more than 40 percent of its buildings intact.

In April 1945, Kronach, Germany, begins to experience the same kind of devastation that plagued hundreds of thousands of other villages across the globe.

Upon visiting the capital of conquered Germany, Gen. Dwight Eisenhower muttered, "It is quite likely, in my opinion, that there will never be any attempt to rebuild Berlin."

3. IMPRISONMENT

Franklin Roosevelt's Executive Order 9066 forced 110,000 Japanese Americans into relocation camps, though most of Hawaii's 30,000 Japanese residents were not interned. The idea of interning

German-born residents was briefly entertained, until it was calculated there were 600,000 of them.[4]

The thought of handling such numbers did not detract two governments across the Atlantic. The Third Reich detained as few as 25,000 people at the start of the war but abruptly expanded its network of camps to hold several million at once. The Soviet Union, with a long tradition of incarcerating large numbers, also increased its rate of abductions once war began with Germany. Both states singled out ethnic groups. Doomed in the Third Reich were Gypsies, Russians, and Jewish and Catholic Poles. For the USSR the deported included Poles, Germans, Bulgarians, Chechens, Estonians, Greeks, Kurds, Latvians, Lithuanians, Tartars, and more. Rail was the transport of choice for both regimes, inexpensively carting thousands after thousands in suffocating, lice-ridden cattle cars, permitting only a fraction of the survivors to reach their assigned destinations, mostly labor installations.[5]

Political prisoners were a different issue. Accused of anything from collaboration to stealing potatoes, "enemies of the state" as a whole were subject to interrogation. Methods of extraction varied with the arresting parties, but the German Gestapo depended heavily on torture and threats. Soviet interrogators steered toward depriving their subjects of food and sleep.

All told, the number incarcerated by the Soviet Union and Nazi Germany may have exceeded thirty million, with as many as twenty million prisoners not surviving.[6]

Of Poland's 5.5 million war dead, most died in German and Soviet camps.

4. AERIAL BOMBING

In his 1921 treatise *Command of the Air*, Italian Giulio Douhet predicted bombers alone would decide the outcome of future wars. By 1939 his theory had many believers, including HERMANN GÖRING and British air chief Marshal Arthur "Bomber" Harris. Prevalent was the conviction that precise strikes could knock out munitions factories, rail hubs, and key administration buildings, consequently shutting off life support for a mechanized army. As it turned out, bombing was hardly an exact science. A 1941 report in Britain revealed that, on average, fewer than a third of Allied bombs were landing within five miles of their desired targets. Given a factory or railhead as an objective, crews would have to drop around five thousand bombs to destroy it.[7]

Mortified by this revelation, British planners decided to use the same method the Germans employed in the BATTLE OF BRITAIN: to carpet bomb in hopes of breaking the morale of the populace and perhaps hitting a few key targets as well. The United States practiced a similar method of "area bombing" upon Japan.

Postwar studies indicated that this method also failed. Most communities hit by bombing runs became more unified, not less. But destruction came nonetheless. Though Paris and Rome were generally spared, Belgrade, Berlin, Chungking, Manila, Vienna, and many others were not. Bombed cities and towns numbered in the thousands, homes destroyed in the millions.

Most of the civilian deaths in Germany and nearly all in Japan died from bombs, or more correctly, from fires created by bombs. The highest rate of damage occurred in the last two years. France lost sixty thousand citizens in raids for the NORMANDY campaign. Incendiary bombing killed more than forty thousand in Hamburg and seventy thousand in Dresden.

More than half of Japan's bombing deaths occurred in cities other than Hiroshima and Nagasaki.[8]

The most destructive form of civilian bombing involved incendiary devices, which torched high-density housing at thousands of degrees.

To maintain pressure on the government of Japan to capitulate, the United States resumed conventional bombing of the country the day after Nagasaki.

5. REFUGEE LIFE

Some 300,000 Germans were killed by their own government; another half-million died from bombing, but more than two million died while they were refugees.[9]

Officially termed in the West as "displaced persons" or DPs, war refugees flooded roads and overwhelmed towns to such a degree than many military planners began to view them as weapons. Both the threat and the deliverance of violence sent families far from home, mostly with no more than the possessions they could carry. Flight was hardest on the very young and the old, many of whom could not withstand the rigors of constant exposure to the elements and greatly reduced food and rest.

Some three million residents in southern England left their homes in 1939 and 1940. Bombing raids in 1945 left twenty million Japanese without homes. An estimated seventeen million Germans were expelled from Eastern Europe after V–E day.

Refugees were anguished coming and going. Flooding cities and towns with their numbers, they were rarely greeted with open arms, especially in communities already suffering privation. Many who

With some traversing hundreds of miles, the vast majority of refugees traveled mostly or entirely on foot.

returned to their homes recalled being treated as de facto deserters by their neighbors who had stayed and braved the storm.[10]

Arguably none suffered more from the trials of exodus than the Chinese. Shackled by the corrupt Nationalist government and pocked with warlord strongholds, the country proved to be the least able of the belligerent nations to handle its refugee crisis. Estimates of displaced Chinese ranged from twenty million to sixty million people, with an unknown number dying from marches far in excess of a thousand miles.

The total number of civilians temporarily or permanently driven from their homes during the war nearly equaled the entire U.S. population at the time.

6. FORCED LABOR

Either in their own country or elsewhere, at least fifteen million civilians (in addition to several million POWs) were reduced to involuntary labor during the war. Perpetrators in the main were the Soviet Union, Nazi Germany, and Japan.

Much of Soviet industry had been taken piece by piece to the safety of central Russia. Although factories were rebuilt, supporting infrastructure was not. Food, water, and shelter were at deprivation

levels in many areas. Laborers simply ate and lived in rustic munitions factories. Workdays were extended to fourteen hours and beyond, workweeks varied between six and seven days, and absence was
deemed equivalent to desertion. If collective farms did not produce
the state-mandated quota (set at arbitrary levels), laborers were subject
to imprisonment. Soviet citizens were sometimes paid with nothing
more than vouchers for state-issued clothing. Civilians taken from
conquered territories such as Poland and the Baltic states were given
next to nothing while suffering in Ural iron mines, arctic ports, and
on Siberian roadways.[11]

In the Third Reich, involuntary labor was the foundation of better living standards because the hardest labor was reserved for non-
Germans. Coerced into low-wage servitude or taken by force, foreign
labor was at three million in May 1941, four million a year later, and
six million the next. In some factories, eight out of ten workers were
essentially slaves. Reaching 20 percent of the Reich's work force,
these "drafted" Belgians, French, Italians, Poles, Russians, and others
were treated much like machine parts, driven until they broke, then
discarded and replaced. Heinrich Himmler summarized the state's position by saying, "Whether nations live in prosperity or starve to death
interests me insofar as we need them as slaves for our culture."[12]

In the Empire of Japan servitude fell hardest on the people of
Korea. By 1945 there were three hundred thousand Japanese troops
on the peninsula, four times the force stationed on OKINAWA, imposing order on a country from which Tokyo had already taken considerable amounts of grain, livestock, and precious metals. Nearly three
million inhabitants were subjected to forced labor. Many more were
deported. By the end of the war, Koreans constituted a quarter of
the workers in Japan. At least twenty thousand Korean women underwent years of devastating violation as "comfort women" for the
Imperial forces.

One aim of German concentration camps was to provide slave laborers. These men were photographed at Buchenwald near Jena.

Of the dead at Hiroshima, approximately one-fifth were Korean laborers.

7. HAVING FAMILY MEMBERS IN THE SERVICE

Of the major belligerents, all but the United States and China placed a majority of their male citizens aged eighteen to thirty-five into the military. The vast majority of soldiers and sailors throughout the world were draftees, taken from homes and communities to work and perhaps die elsewhere. In democratic countries, conscription was relatively civil and orderly. Nationalist China employed decidedly more aggressive methods. An American witness equated the process to widespread kidnapping, a kind of inverted epidemic that struck down the strongest young men and shuttled them into poorly equipped, barely fed, ineptly trained divisions. In the last six months of the war, Hitler's last-ditch Volkssturm ("Storm of the People") sent young boys and old men against Allied tanks and guns.[13]

Along with the emotional price, departure of a male, and sometimes the only male in the family, was a considerable financial loss. In 2005 dollars, the United States paid its enlisted about $1,000 a month. Other nations paid their enlisted half as much or less. For the women left behind, their earning potential, not to mention professional and political leverage, was extremely limited (women in France, Hungary, Italy, Japan, and Yugoslavia did not yet have the right to vote). Government subsidies for dependents were meager or nonexistent. The exception was Germany, which paid wives a pension equal to a full-time clerical position.[14]

War also broke communication lines between servicemen and their loved ones. Aside from photographs, couples often went years without seeing each other, let alone hearing from one another. Mail was heavily censored, easily lost, and a very low priority for military transport. Letters traveled least when they were needed most, during battles, sieges, and capture. If an American serviceman was wounded in action, he was allowed to receive one message of cheer from a single emergency contact of five words or less.

Lt. Gen. John Wainwright, commanding officer among the captives of Bataan, spent nearly three years in a POW camp. His wife wrote him three hundred times. He received six of the letters.

---

8. INFLATION

Over the span of the war, inflation in Germany reached 700 percent. In Italy it climbed 1,000 percent. In China it hit 11,000 percent.[15]

Currency is fundamentally a reflection of confidence. Governments that collapsed were often preceded by an implosion of their reserve notes. States under German occupation had the added burden of having to reimburse the Third Reich for the financial costs of their occupation. This "security fee," saddled upon the peoples of the Low Countries, France, Greece, Norway, and Yugoslavia, was invariably many times the actual expense of harboring troops. Requiring the handing over of nearly all their revenues, several of the states simply printed more money to cover the margin, which sent the face value of notes in a tailspin.

Pushing prices even higher was the natural phenomenon of supply shortages in wartime. Due to the Japanese invasion and CHIANG KAI-SHEK's confiscation of crops, the cost of rice in China was fourteen times higher in 1941 than in 1939. In 1940 a few pounds of cheese cost about sixty Greek drachmas, but by 1944 the price had jumped to over a billion. Allied officers often forbade their men from buying or taking local food and livestock to prevent a worsening of shortages. The urge was often too much for many soldiers, who discovered their rations of American cigarettes had become the currency of choice in civilian barter and black markets.[16]

Ruthless speculators on the Russian black market made fortunes trading food for people's rubles, jewelry, and government bonds. To keep Moscow from shutting down their operations, these profiteers made small "contributions" to the national defense fund and were consequently hailed as heroes by the state.

---

9. ENEMY OCCUPATION

Invaders generally knew it was in their best interest to stabilize a nation once its armed forces had been defeated. The question was how to achieve stability. In China, the Empire of Japan tried to subdue the population by using terror (Nanking and Shanghai: 1937), puppet governments (east coast: 1937–45), saturation bombing (Chungking: 1939–40), search and destroy (Communist-held northern China: 1939–40), control of infrastructure (eastern provinces: 1940–42), and overwhelming force (everywhere: 1940–44).

Parisians were shocked when German soldiers marched into the city in 1940. Faced with a foreign military presence, many had to decide between capitulation, collaboration, and annihilation.

More than thirty countries experienced partial or complete occupation, undergoing various forms and durations of suppression such as those listed above. To say the least, experiences were mixed, but the general theme was utter disruption. Legally, whatever citizens had in the way of civil liberties were quickly removed, especially concerning speech, press, and assembly. Economically, conditions on the personal scale varied from controlled markets (with ration books and government assistance) to complete chaos. National economics generally devolved into a type of feudalism, in which occupying forces enforced quotas and restricted essentially all physical and professional mobility. Socially, communities and families were torn apart, as some chose the servitude of collaboration while others invited the dangers of resistance.

Regardless of how well people governed themselves, they were still largely at the mercy of their overseers. Even the most settled environments could erupt into bloodshed. Nazi atrocities in Western Europe provided some of the smaller but better documented examples. In 1942 the Gestapo descended upon occupied Televåg, Norway, accused the townspeople of harboring secret agents, and summarily executed eighteen men and carted the rest of the village off to concentration camps. In 1944, days after the Allied landings in NORMANDY, German soldiers entered Oradour-Sur-Glane, France, forced the men into five barns, all the women and children into the town church, and set all six buildings on fire.[17]

Nazi occupation of Paris = 3 years, 67 days. Japanese occupation of Nanking = 7 years, 255 days.

---

10. DEATH OF A FAMILY MEMBER

For those who lost relatives in the armed forces, many found consolation if victory was achieved. Even in victory, an absence of closure haunted many who never knew exactly what happened to their loved ones. The number of American deceased whose remains were returned to the states (by request of the families) roughly equaled the number listed as missing in action or presumed dead. Germans officially listed as missing outnumbered all American fatalities put together. Russians listed as missing outnumbered all Americans who served in Europe.[18]

Yet a person was more likely to lose a family member who was not in the armed forces. Such was the case for the Belgians, losing three civilians for every serviceman. In Poland the ratio was nine for every one. In Holland it was eighteen noncombatant deaths for each soldier killed. Civilian deaths were also likely to be witnessed by a family member, especially in refugee migrations, bombing raids, and concentration camps.

To combat a sinking national morale from the mounting losses in China and the Pacific, the government of Japan implemented a "National Smile Week" in March 1943.

TOP TEN

FORMS OF RESISTANCE

Romanticized and glorified, resistance was a far more fragmented, varied, and rare animal than initially portrayed. Multitudes claimed to have actively fought their oppressors, yet few actually did.

As for the great silent majority, most preferred to rationalize their plight rather than rebel against it. Lacking the organization and firepower of professional armies, civilians expected minimal gain and maximum cost for fighting back. If caught, imprisonment was the least of their worries. Nazis frequently advertised the price of rebellion by publicly hanging captives. Soviets traditionally shot dissenters in the back of the head. Frustrated by heavy resistance in northern China, the Japanese army diligently applied a succinct mantra in 1941 and 1942: "Take all, burn all, kill all."[19]

A small percentage accepted the risks and in many cases achieved measurable success. By biting the hand that terrified them, Greeks and Yugoslavs tied down more than fifteen Axis divisions in the Balkans. Filipinos and Indonesians prevented Japan from securing total occupation. Several resistance leaders eventually became heads of state, such as Hoxha in Albania, TITO in Yugoslavia, de Gaulle in France, and Mao in China.

Ranked here, by level of violence, are the ten most prominent forms of civilian dissent in the war against military repression. Some were more effective than others, but all provided hope against the specter of degrading servitude.

I. COMBAT

By 1943, the Polish Home Army had at least 40,000 members, partisans in the Soviet Union numbered 200,000, and Communist soldiers and militia in China totaled 300,000. There was the Home Front of Norway, the Czech Central Leadership of Home Resistance, Indochina's Viet Minh, and hundreds of other groups. Yet in any given occupied country the number of armed insurgents was less than 1 percent of the population. Exceptions were Albania, Greece, and Yugoslavia, all of which had more than 10 percent (and all three were undergoing civil war).[20]

Paramilitary activity was at first uncommon and minuscule. As the war progressed, persons under occupation began to gather around remnants of army units, political parties, and religious groups. Some outfits were ad hoc gangs of the brutish and vengeful; others became highly structured networks with their own paymasters and medical personnel. Assisting these groups were state agencies, such as the U.S. Office of Strategic Services and Britain's Secret Intelligence Service.

Among the most organized were the Communists, especially in France and China, with well-defined memberships and long traditions of opposition.

Two of the better-documented episodes of guerrilla combat were the Warsaw uprisings. By 1943 a quarter-million Warsaw Jews had died through starvation, execution, or deportation. In April, to honor Hitler's impending birthday, the SS moved in to eradicate the last 60,000. Several hundred Jews, armed with incendiaries, pistols, and a single machine gun, held off the onslaught for nearly three weeks. Fewer than one hundred insurgents escaped alive. In August 1944, 40,000 Poles, most of them in the Home Army, resisted a German advance into the capital. After two months of vicious urban fighting, 250,000 inhabitants were dead, and the Home Army essentially ceased to exist.

In most pitched battles the goal was to stave off defeat rather than achieve outright victory. Yugoslavia was, for all intents and purposes, the only country self-liberated. Even in France, synonymous with "the resistance," freedom came only after the Allied invasion. Reportedly Charles de Gaulle confessed to an associate after the war, "Between you and me, Resistance was a bluff that came off."[21]

Jean Moulin created the Conseil National de la Résistance, a unification of eight major resistance groups and the eventual foundation of Charles de Gaulle's political support. In 1943, Moulin was betrayed, imprisoned, and tortured to death at the hands of Klaus Barbie, the "Butcher of Lyon."

---

2. ASSASSINATION

Along with the sniper shot, assassinations were carried out by ambush, grenade, firing squad, knifing, and demolition. A German commissioner died in his sleep—immediately after the bomb under his bed went off.[22]

German officials and officers were targets. In an effort to curb the attacks, Nazi officials published the consequences for such attacks.

Belgians were told they would lose five countrymen, the French heard fifty, Poles were told one hundred, and Czechs were given no limit. In this the Third Reich was good to its word. The slaying of an officer in France brought a fine of several million francs and the immediate execution of fifty townspeople. The death of a Gestapo agent in Poland resulted in one hundred locals being rounded up and shot. When Czechs assassinated Reinhard Heydrich, architect of the Holocaust, the SS leveled the nearby towns of Lidice and Lezaky and killed at least two thousand inhabitants.[23]

Underground assassins most often aimed for known collaborators. Whereas killing a soldier brought dire consequences, killing a stooge taught locals to stay with the resistance or stay out of the way. The practice was most prevalent in the eastern front and in China, especially against anyone caught figuratively or literally sleeping with the enemy.

Undoubtedly the most famous partisan assassination occurred near Lake Como, Italy, on April 28, 1945. After surviving two previous attempts on his life, Benito Mussolini was captured, taken to the countryside, and shot nine times with a submachine gun.

Then there were the ones who got away. During the war, unsuccessful attempts were made on the lives of Nikita Khrushchev, Maurice Chevalier, Wilhelm Keitel, Rudolfo Graziani, Victor Emmanuel III, Tojo Hideki (twice), and Adolf Hitler (at least three times).

---

3. SABOTAGE

The threat of sabotage was often more menacing than the actual event. This forced militaries to dedicate far more resources to the protection of railways, bridges, and roads than normal. It also led many officials to credit any accident or bottleneck to the work of saboteurs. Stalin and Hitler blamed any breakdown on the work of saboteurs, and the FBI insisted there were more than three thousand acts of sabotage in the United States during the war.[24]

Not to say the paranoia was unfounded. Partisan armies, lone dare-devils, and hard-line terrorists destroyed factories, government buildings, phone lines, airplanes, pipelines, and tanks. A favorite target was rail lines. Rail lines being long and vulnerable, removal of a piece of track or a few spikes could derail a train in seconds and block a route for days. On average, a forced derailment occurred somewhere in Poland every forty hours. But railroad damage was often a double-edged sword. If enemy troops and shells couldn't be shipped, neither could food and coal for everyone else.[25]

Actions didn't have to be explosive to be efficacious. Due to the constant shortage of rubber, slashing truck tires did amazing damage to army logistics. Removal of a firing pin rendered any gun impotent. Mislabeling a shipment manifesto could send vital supplies far astray. The British claimed to have developed an abrasive grease that would rapidly wear out engine parts and factory machinery.[26]

A few saboteurs were fortunate enough to work with cyclotrimethylene-trinitramine, Composition C—a wartime British invention better known as plastic explosives.

---

4. PUBLIC PROTESTS

Vocal and open demonstration was a dangerous undertaking in areas under totalitarian control. In 1942, when told their nation was going to be annexed into the Reich, citizens of the tiny duchy of Luxembourg protested en masse. The Nazis crushed the revolt through widespread executions and deportations.

Two avenues of marginal effect but frequent use were pulpits and schools. In a rare case of civil victory against Nazi atrocities, Bishop of Münster Clemens August Count von Galen succeeded in halting Hitler's euthanasia program on the physically and mentally handicapped, but not until one hundred thousand had perished.[27]

In Norway almost every clergy member of the state Lutheran

Church resigned in protest of the fascist puppet government. From the pulpit, Cardinal van Roey of Belgium beckoned his parishioners to fight "the enemy" and all their collaborators. More than a thousand rebellious French priests were arrested and extradited by the Third Reich.

Among schools and universities, students and faculty rejected closures and censorship. Nearly all teachers in Norway refused the creation of Hitler Youth programs in their schools. Thirteen hundred were summarily arrested. In France and Belgium, students protested the dismissal of Jewish students and professors. Whereas many churches continued to resist, especially at the parish level, academic institutions declined in influence due to forced closures and conscription.[28]

The "White Rose" operated out of Munich University for four years, quietly disseminating reports on Nazi atrocities. In 1943, they "went public," handing out leaflets and protesting in the open. Their leaders were immediately arrested, tried, and executed.

---

5. LABOR STRIKES

In a world where unarmed attacks against totalitarian regimes were tantamount to suicide, labor strikes provided a clever substitute. Strikers masked their assaults by making nonthreatening demands, such as asking for more bomb shelters, shorter workweeks, and safer working conditions. In gathering together, demonstrations also projected a moral unity. Of a more concrete impact, work stoppages curbed production of war materials. Yet several marches turned bloody. In Oslo, Norway, during September 1941, workers demonstrated against milk rationing. The SS addressed the issue by rounding up hundreds of laborers, torturing many, and selecting a few for execution.[29]

Labor uprisings became more aggressive in the last years of the war. In the spring of 1943 Italy's industrialized north erupted in widespread protest. Wracked by inflation, corruption, and a string of military defeats abroad, laborers at the Turin Fiat factory initiated a walkout that grew to hundreds of thousands. The fascist government reluctantly arrested a few hundred and sent a token amount of demonstrators to the front in Sicily. In 1944 French factory walkouts exploded after D-day, Hungarian workers openly demonstrated against the pro-Nazi government, and the Dutch launched a rail strike in concert with OPERATION MARKET-GARDEN.

The United States was not without labor strikes, experiencing nearly fifteen thousand of them during the war. A massive 1944 railway stoppage threatened the war effort enough to make George C. Marshall call it the "damnedest crime ever committed against America."

---

6. ESPIONAGE

More so than government operatives, civilians were the eyes of the war. Rail clerks read train schedules. Dockworkers knew what was being loaded onto ships. Shopkeepers spotted shoulder patches on visiting troops and thus knew which divisions were in the area. Farmers reported on local weather and road conditions—essential information for military ground operations. Residents along sea lanes had clear views of ship convoys and support squadrons.

Some of the best collectors and transporters of information were young women. Unlike healthy young men of military age, teenage girls were rarely suspected of being partisans or spies. Some of the best spy networks consisted predominantly of ordinary citizens, such as France's "Noah's Ark," led by MARIE-MADELEINE FOURCADE.[30]

Occupying powers never fully stopped the flow of information. When Nazis demanded the confiscation of all bicycles in Holland, the Dutch scrounged up and sent in every old rusty bike they could find and simply hid their good ones. The Third Reich also tried, with little success, to eradicate all known homing pigeons.[31]

Though not always heeded by the military hierarchy, citizens offered their scouting services. The Belgian underground supplied most of what the Allies knew about German radar tactics and development. Civilians informed Allied bomber command that Germany's ball-bearing plants were almost exclusively in Schweinfurt. When a V-2 rocket crashed far off course, Poles removed the engine and sent it off to London.[32]

"Rote Kapelle" (Red Orchestra) was a prolific Communist spy ring operating against the Third Reich. In 1942, the Gestapo arrested forty-six of its members, tortured them, then guillotined the women and hanged the men. One Leopold Trepper escaped and made his way to Moscow. Stalin accused him of being a Nazi spy and threw him into prison.

---

7. PROTECTION OF JEWS

Swedish envoy Raoul Wallenberg granted "protective passports" to tens of thousands. Practically the whole villages of Chambon-Sur-Lignon, France, and Nieuwlande, Holland, helped those in need. Diplomat Sugihara Sempo lost his job in the Japanese consulate in Lithuania for granting exit visas to fleeing Jews.

In spite of the obvious danger in doing so, many citizens of Western Europe defied the principle objective of Himmler's SS from 1942 to 1945. In Warsaw the underground had literal meaning; neighbors broke through cellar walls to create a vast grid of subterranean passageways, connecting with sewers and water mains, creating paths to freedom. France had scores of escape routes out of the country. Danes successfully ferried away 95 percent of their Jewish population to neutral Sweden. Even fascist Italy was wholly uncooperative with the Nazis in regard to handing over Jewish citizens.[33]

Through their own volition and the work of others, some 280,000 European Jews left the Continent, while more than 3 million stayed behind and survived the Holocaust.[34]

The State of Israel officially recognizes more than fourteen thousand Gentiles as "Righteous Among Nations" for having risked their lives to save Jews.

8. UNDERGROUND PRESSES

To people under occupation, underground papers were gold in black and white. From scraps of parchment slipped into mail slots to multipage dailies plastered on walls, the written word became the most consistent, visible, and communal expression of the resistance.

Some journals actually prospered. France's *Combat* grew from 40,000 copies per issue in 1943 to 300,000 by 1944. *Défense de la France* went from a circulation of 5,000 in 1941 to almost a half-million by the time of liberation. Ukrainians printed and read an estimated 400 million copies of leaflets and newspapers during the war.[35]

For reasons of safety, most covert prints were small and temporary affairs. Norway had some three hundred different journals, but the majority soon disappeared by force or flight. Shortages of ink and paper, loss of printing machines, plus arrests and executions quieted many more. Yet everywhere the presses continued. Soviets behind the lines read *Death to Our Enemies*. Italians took courage from *Unita*, Belorussians learned of guerrilla triumphs in *Partizanskoye Slovo*. News mattered less than the papers themselves, acting as tangible proof that the resistance was alive and working.[36]

One country where underground presses did not flourish was China. The country's literacy rate of 20 percent may have been a contributing factor.

9. PASSIVE RESISTANCE

After the war, when citizens claimed to be part of the resistance, they most often recalled engaging in labor "slowdowns," a kind of patriotic slacking. Machinists "misplaced" tools, teamsters drove at a leisurely rate, station agents took their time loading trains. Work absenteeism often reached 30 percent in parts of occupied Europe and China. It all had some tangible effect. From prewar levels, Belgian coal mining dropped more than 60 percent; steel and iron production in Luxembourg fell 70 percent.[37]

Barely perceptible but greatly reassuring were symbolic gestures. Devoted Scandinavians refused to talk to suspected collaborators, what became known as the "Ice Front." Dissidents marked sidewalks and walls with patriotic graffiti—"H7" for Norway's King Håkon VII, the Cross of Lorraine in France, and V for victory across Europe. Everywhere, flowers and wreaths, especially those in the hue of national colors, appeared in buttonholes and on monuments.[38]

Citizens often used levity to lighten the weight of oppression. As with speech, press, and assembly, the freedom of humor was also heavily curtailed under totalitarian regimes. Cracks against Hitler and Stalin often brought imprisonment, but the custom endured nonetheless, with its profound ability to both hide and express anguish.

Humor became a tool of survival in many concentration camps. Jewish psychiatrist and author Viktor Frankl kept himself sane in Auschwitz by trying to invent a joke each day.

---

10. DRAFT EVASION

Faced with conscription into factories and the armed forces, literally millions simply refused to go. Nazi Germany demanded seventy thousand young Norwegian men for labor service in the Third Reich; they collected only three hundred. A further eighty thousand went into hiding rather than submit. Before and during the war, countless ethnic Germans and Austrians living in East Europe fled westward to avoid impressments into the Red Army. The largest number escaping mandated service were the Chinese, millions of whom refused to work for either the Japanese or the warlord CHIANG KAI-SHEK.[39]

Governments designated the adamantly uncooperative in several ways. The Third Reich used the term "work-shy elements." Stalin preferred the classification "traitors." The usual reprimand for those so designated was harsh imprisonment. Though no state tolerated "draft dodging," a few countries officially recognized conscientious objection, namely Australia, Holland, the Scandinavian nations, Great Britain, and the United States.[40]

Of these, Britain may have been the most tolerant. Only about 1 percent of those drafted declared objection on moral or political grounds. Some were given jail time and some were excused from obligation, but most "conchies" were assigned to public service. Less than 0.1 percent of American draftees declared C.O. status. The U.S. government granted no dismissals. Options were jail, public service, medical experimentation (such as subjection to typhus, hepatitis, sleep deprivation), and military support.[41]

Both Britain and the United States had C.O.'s take part in combat. A third of Britain's airborne ambulance corps on D-day were conscientious objectors. In a definitive expression of counterviolence, several hundred C.O.'s volunteered for bomb disposal.[42]

In the Second World War, three American conscientious objectors won the Medal of Honor, two of them posthumously.

ALTERNATE NAMES FOR THE WAR

In the early years of the war, when its scope was not yet perceptible, American president Franklin Roosevelt openly asked advisers and colleagues what he should publicly call the conflict. No one offered a satisfactory answer.[43]

Four years later, a month after the war had ended, Roosevelt's replacement asked the same question. With further deliberation, Secretary of War Henry Stimson recommended a term that had appeared often in radio broadcasts, newspapers, and several articles of legislation. The president agreed, and on September 11, 1945, Harry Truman accepted "World War II" as the official U.S. designation.[44]

The term was primarily of German construct, employed by Nazi spokesmen who wished to convey a sense of worldliness to their endeavor. Cultures adopted the title gradually, if at all ("Second World War" was not part of British vernacular until the late 1940s). Around the world, people mainly called it la guerre, voina, senso, der Krieg, the war. Following are the next most common references among hundreds used in print and in public during and immediately after the conflict.[45]

1. HITLER'S WAR

Historically, wars often had surnames attached to them. For example, the Napoleonic Wars, King George's War, Lincoln's War, etc. So, too, with the Second World War, whether in praise or condemnation, people spoke of Roosevelt's War, or Churchill's, or Stalin's, or Hirohito's. In the Western Hemisphere, however, one name dominated the rest.

Historians will perpetually debate the actual extent of Adolf Hitler's role in creating international conflict in 1939 (see CAUSES). Whether people considered him a blathering figurehead or an unequaled mastermind, Hitler certainly declared himself the latter. In private conversations, public speeches, written statements, and military dispatches, he repeatedly emphasized a national destiny for greatness and his crucial role in making it a reality. "Essentially all depends on me, on my existence," he informed his military commanders in 1939.[46]

Socially, politically, militarily, his imprint was everywhere, thanks mostly to the German Ministry of Information and Propaganda. City centers throughout Germany and Nazi-occupied Europe were given a "Hitler Square." Boulevards and buildings were christened in his honor. The prestigious SS First Panzer Division, the National Socialist youth organization, and even public greetings bore his name.

Rather than dismiss his role in the course of world events, his enemies tended to emphasize it. Branding Hitler as an "evil genius," "madman," and "sole cause of the war" not only simplified the escalation of international hostility but also removed all other governments from any shared responsibility for the collapse of peace.[47]

A wartime Czech joke stated: "In India, a person starves because of all the people. In Europe, all the people starve because of one person."

---

2. THE PHONY WAR

In early September 1939, in response to the Nazi invasion of Poland, both France and Britain declared war on Germany, called up reservists, and mobilized their armed forces.

In major cities, women and children piled into railcars and buses carrying food, clothes, and gas masks, evacuating en masse to private homes, farms, schools, and hotels. Across Western Europe, as many as two million children were abruptly relocated. Many Frenchmen assumed they would be attacked by both the Germans and Soviets, just as Poland had been. Britain's Parliament legislated a flood of emergency acts, including forced blackouts, rationing, and the closing of dance halls and movie theaters for fear of bomber strikes. Hospitals turned away heart patients to free up beds for anticipated battle casualties.[48]

Then nothing of substance happened. Aside from France's advance into German territory near Saarbrücken and sporadic German bombings of English and French positions, all sides avoided provocation. Only on the high seas was there much action, mostly via U-boats. Days turned into weeks, then months. A partially relieved, partially annoyed British public cried "Phony War." Clever journalists labeled the apparently baseless scare Sitzkrieg. Cynical Parisians called the whole situation Drôle de guerre.

In Britain, by late spring of 1940, 40 percent of all children and 90 percent of mothers and babies had returned to their original residence. Similar percentages returned in France and the Low Countries. Americans as well suspected the worst was likely over. A promising Harvard student named John Fitzgerald Kennedy, son of the American ambassador to Great Britain, adroitly observed, "Everyone is getting much more confident about our staying out of the war, but that of course is probably because there is such a lull over there."[49]

British soldiers killed in the first three months of World War I: 50,000.
British soldiers killed in the first three months of World War II: 1.

3. THE PEOPLE'S WAR

In an attempt to unite their disparate populations, leaders frequently presented their national struggle as a "people's war." Rich and poor, left and right, young and old were brought together with an "us against them" approach. The title was almost automatic in Communist-held northwest China and the Soviet Union. Though used occasionally elsewhere, it took root deeply in an unlikely place.

When war erupted in 1939, the British were in no way enthusiastic about marching back into the breach, especially with recollections of Flanders fields. Many asked, "Why die for Danzig?" while twenty-two out of Europe's twenty-seven countries remained neutral.

Yet the traditionally class-divided British began to find unity in hardship. Large-scale urban evacuations, worker shortages, and homeland defense operations created an intermixing of previously separate castes. Laborers of all levels of skill and education worked together in munitions plants. Citizens from every station joined in the original melting pot—the armed forces. Bombs were not selective about which class they fell on. With misery came interaction and interdependence, the likes of which peacetime did not provide.[50]

The nation truly found its war footing with the abrupt and

China lost more than five citizens for every soldier killed, whereas the United States lost hundreds of soldiers for every civilian who died.

astonishing fall of France in 1940 and its climactic "Miracle of Dunkirk." Over the course of ten days, a flotilla of ships and boats—French, Belgian, Dutch, and Commonwealth British—came together to rescue more than one hundred thousand French and two hundred thousand British troops from almost certain Nazi capture. Thereafter, "People's War" was in common use. Though far less harmonic or selfless than was commonly portrayed, the war was quite possibly "their finest hour," when the crowd rather than the Crown became the substance of the kingdom.[51]

Three out of four rescue ships at Dunkirk were civilian, many of them simple fishing boats.

4. THE WAR OF RESISTANCE

Unlike Australia, Britain, Japan, and the United States, most of the war's combatants experienced periods of either partial or total foreign military occupation. Many used "War of Resistance" to describe their struggle.

The Kremlin heartily promoted "Resistance to Fascist Oppression." After the fall of Paris in June 1940, Charles de Gaulle appointed himself the leader of the Free French and declared, "The flame of French resistance should not be extinguished." Among other subversive groups in occupied Holland was the Raad van Verzet, or Resistance

Council. Both Mao Zedong's Communists and CHIANG KAI-SHEK's Nationalists called their fight Kanri zhanzheng (the War of Resistance).

As with the last case, foreign invasion often provided a common enemy, bringing bitter rivals together. In France, Communists and nationalists joined in combating the Germans. Josip Broz, better known as TITO, brought together Serbs, Croats, and Muslims in his resistance movement. Communists, nationalists, and royalists in Greece joined the resistance against fascist Italy and Nazi Germany. Unfortunately, this sense of unity often disintegrated once the invaders departed.

Few cities or villages in northern France don't have a plaza or street named "Le Résistance."

5. THE HOLY WAR

Religion, history's baptismal font of conflict, was not a major cause of World War II. Participants nonetheless sought the heavens for divine inspiration and claimed their own mission as the most righteous. Americans sang "Onward Christian Soldiers" almost as often as they crooned "Praise the Lord and Pass the Ammunition." The British Royal Navy ordered all ships of cruiser size and above to install chapels. In their fight against "godless Bolsheviks," the German Wehrmacht wore belt buckles stamped Gott Mit Uns ("God is with us").

Secular and clerical circles presented the war as a showdown between good and evil. Nearly every national leader used the pious term "holy war" several times in public, along with other dutiful tags such as "sacred cause" and "crusade." Officially agnostic *Pravda* printed V. I. Lebedev's poem "Holy War" just two days after the German invasion, and its stanzas were set to music soon after. Stalin, a former seminary student, christened the "Sacred War" with sermons on "Holy Russia."[52]

More than any other nation, Japan defined the global conflict as a divine test of souls. "Holy War" remained central in word and deed,

Through religion, civilians sought salvation while governments sought justification.

anchored by a faith in an emperor seen as the embodiment of providence upon earth. In a far less reverent medium, Japanese cartoons often illustrated the "Holy War" concept. Whereas American and British propaganda often drew the Japanese as toothy, bespectacled simians, Japanese illustrators advertised their enemy as purely satanic. Caricatures of Roosevelt, Churchill, Uncle Sam, and John Bull invariably featured horns, tails, clawed forelegs, and hoofed hindquarters. Allied soldiers and sailors were also drawn in devilish guise, presented as poised and ready to instill wicked wrath upon sacred Asia and the whole world.[53]

During the Second World War, 8,896 chaplains served in the U.S. Army.

---

6. THE GREAT PATRIOTIC WAR

Czarist Russians referred to Napoleon Bonaparte's 1812 march on Moscow as "the Patriotic War." When Adolf Hitler repeated the march in 1941, Soviet leaders declared the new struggle Velikaia otechestvennia voina ("the Great Patriotic War").[54]

Suddenly, warm nostalgia replaced cold ideology. Rather than comrades fighting for communism, "brothers and sisters" were fighting for "Mother Russia." Instead of Lenin and Marx, movies glamorized Russian heroes like Alexander Nevsky and Ivan the Terrible.

Speeches and songs recalled triumphs over foreign hordes, particularly German ones.[55]

Most Russians expressed their patriotism in words as well as deeds during the war. Soldiers marched into battle without weapons. Civilians transported factories brick by brick to the security of the Urals. In foundries and on farms, people labored fifteen hours a day and more, subsisting on near-starvation diets. Many willingly suffered "for country and home." Of course, along with this jingoist fervor, Russians also had two additional motivations: fear of Hitler and fear of Stalin. To this day, "the Great Patriotic War" remains the official Russian title of the conflict.[56]

> *All in all, Hitler fared better against the Russians than Napoleon. Der Führer lost approximately 60 percent of his forces in three years, whereas the Little Emperor lost 90 percent of his Grande Armée in six months.*

7. ANOTHER THIRTY YEARS' WAR

Connecting 1914 with 1944, Europeans labeled the period "another Thirty Years' War." Public usage of the term emanated from Winston Churchill, Charles de Gaulle, and exiled Czechoslovak president Edvard Benes. To them and others who personally experienced two massive wars in one lifetime, World Wars I and II were essentially the first and second acts to a tragedy in which Germany was the continual antagonist. The only difference seemed to be the cast of characters.[57]

There were definitely similarities between the seventeenth-century war and its twentieth-century counterparts. The 1618–48 version also featured Germany, cost millions of lives, occurred in phases, and introduced new and unwelcome methods of warfare, including mobile artillery and rapid-firing infantry.

To some observers, history verified Germans as inherently militaristic. Scholars hypothesized of a German Sonderweg or "peculiar path," whereby the Fatherland failed to follow the "natural progression" of modern nation-states, somehow remaining fundamentally barbaric. In turn, German nationalists countered the Sonderweg theory by reminding Britain and France of their own particularly bloody histories wrought with ruthless revolutions, civil wars, ventures of conquest, and centuries of less-than-benevolent-treatment of colonial subjects.[58]

In the First and Second World Wars put together, approximately 14 percent of the German population died. In the Thirty Years' War of 1618–48, at least 25 percent of the German population was killed.

---

8. THE GREATER EAST ASIAN WAR

Beginning with the RUSSO-JAPANESE WAR, Japan rationalized its territorial expansion as the natural progression of an industrialized country, much in the same vein as "manifest destiny," "Lebensraum," or "Rule Britannia." These paths went from parallel to confrontational in 1941, when Tokyo's designs targeted European and American holdings in Asia and the Pacific.

Any chance to share the spoils ended on December 7, when Imperial air and naval forces launched simultaneous attacks on British Hong Kong, the American Philippines, Honolulu, and elsewhere. From then on, the empire officially called the conflict Dai Toa senso ("the Greater East Asian War") and presented the conflict as a grand "counteroffensive of the Oriental races against Occidental aggression."[59]

Initially, some sincerely believed the Japanese were acting as liberators. Several thousand Burmese, Malayans, Filipinos, Okinawans, and others assisted or fought in concert with Imperial forces. Others collaborated in hopes of removing the Western presence from their midst. But over time the Japanese demonstrated an equal or greater talent for repression. Consequently, most Asians turned against their Japanese "saviors," aiding the downfall of an empire that at its peak stretched from the Indian Ocean to the Aleutians.[60]

In December 1945, Gen. Douglas MacArthur's occupation

headquarters forbade the use of "Greater East Asian War" in Japanese public discourse because its meaning was viewed as inherently nationalistic. Henceforth, the only acceptable term was to be Taiheiyo senso ("The Pacific War").[61]

Today, an ongoing feud continues within Japan's school system on what to call the Second World War. Educators who wish to emphasize national pride call it "the Greater East Asian War," whereas others who wish to present Japan as a member of the international community teach it as "the Pacific War."

9. THE FIFTEEN YEARS' WAR

Time may heal all wounds, but it also functions as a naming convention for historical events. Such was the case in the 1940s when people grieved over "the interminable war" and later applied more precise measures to its elements. Leningraders suffered through "the Nine Hundred Days" when German forces surrounded and nearly leveled the Baltic city. Allied bombers flew more than three thousand sorties in "Big Week," in actuality a six-day hammering of German aircraft factories in February 1944. Westerners still refer to the Allied invasion of NORMANDY as "the Longest Day."

After 1945 Asians spoke of "the Fifteen Years' War," especially those who wished to enunciate the duration of Japanese military aggression. Measuring from the 1931 MANCHURIAN INCIDENT, the term encompassed the plethora of subsequent "incidents" between Chinese and Japanese troops in the 1930s, the full-fledged invasion of China in 1937, pitched battles with the Soviet Union along the border of Outer Mongolia in 1939, and the spread of war into the Pacific in December 1941. A few former members of the Japanese military also used the title, in part because it implied that Japan lasted twice as long as its Axis partners.[62]

Though most Americans considered PEARL HARBOR the beginning of war in the Pacific Rim, official Allied policy coincided with the

fifteen-year view. In trying Japanese for war crimes, the International
Military Tribunal for the Far East allowed evidence dating back to 1931.[63]

---

*In the San Francisco Peace Treaty of 1951, Japan had to concede not
only everything it had acquired since 1931, but also all the areas it had
gained since 1895. This included Manchuria, Formosa (Taiwan), Korea,
and the Marshall, Mariana, Palau, and Caroline islands. The lost land
was equivalent in area to California, Arizona, New Mexico, Utah, and
Colorado put together.*

---

10. THE GOOD WAR

It is said there is no such thing as a good war or a bad peace. To many
Americans, the Second World War stood as a plausible exception. For
starters, the United States could boast the moral high ground, having
been attacked without a declaration of war. Further, both sides committed atrocities, but Japan's rejection of the GENEVA CONVENTION and
Germany's pursuit of genocide were bona fide crimes against humanity.

Utilized occasionally during the conflict, "the Good War" term
became a more prevalent moniker afterward, stemming largely from
the harvest of favorable results. Americans and their allies conquered
tyrannical regimes in Berlin, Rome, Tokyo, and Vienna. In their stead,
peaceful, democratic republics took root. To accomplish this, the
United States suffered no invasion, nearly doubled its gross domestic
product in five years, and became an undeniable global superpower.

"The Good War" may have reached its apex in the 1960s and
1970s, as the situation in Vietnam left many Americans nostalgic for
the comparatively clear objectives and unified effort brought to bear in
the early 1940s.

---

*In a 2003 Gallup Poll survey, 90 percent of Americans considered
World War II a "good war." The same survey revealed only 50 percent
knew that the D-day invasions took place in Normandy.*

SONGS

Cultural historians and music scholars note the absence of a defining anthem to the Second World War. Missing was an "Over There," a "Battle Hymn of the Republic," or a "La Marseillaise." Not to say that countries didn't try to find one. In 1942, the *Chicago Daily Times* held a "War Song for America" contest. Out of eight thousand entries, the best was a forgettable trench tune entitled "Mud in His Ears." The Soviet Union in 1943 sought a new national anthem. Of more than two hundred entries from composers and poets, nobody won.[64]

At best, music and the war had an uneasy relationship. The Japanese government forbade the playing of Western songs and promoted native patriotic ballads such as "Wife on the Home Front" and "Rise, Imperial Army." Germany's Reich Chamber of Culture vilified jazz tunes as the "impudent swamp flowers of Negroid pandemonium." Nazis also brutally repressed the German "Swing Youth" movement, burning songbooks, confiscating albums, and jailing dancers.[65]

Governments also capped production of record albums to save war-vital wax and shellac and restricted the sales of consumer electronics, including radios and phonographs. What laws failed to destroy, combat often finished off. Bombs and shells crushed dance clubs, concert halls, instrument factories, and music companies. German soldiers entered the historic home of Peter Ilyich Tchaikovsky in November 1941, and to keep warm, they threw piles of rare original sheet music into a burning stove.[66]

Yet music prospered nonetheless. In the dead of Russian winters, musicians played in unheated venues, bedecked in overcoats and fingerless gloves. British and American communities resurrected the dance marathons of the Great Depression. In private, Japanese citizens played forbidden ballads about love and sadness. Among the litany were numerous standouts, some of which remained popular to the present. Listed below are the most common songs of the era, based on amount of orchestral and vocal group performances, radio and jukebox play, sheet music and record sales, and longevity through the war.[67]

1. "WHITE CHRISTMAS" (1942)

At the apex of his long and prolific career, songsmith Irving Berlin crafted flag-waving tunes for the war effort. Yet his most popular hit possessed neither patriotic intent nor lofty aspirations. Written almost as an afterthought for the movie *Holiday Inn*, "White Christmas" found life in the smooth baritone of Bing Crosby and a huge audience in the South Pacific.[68]

U.S. soldiers, stuck in fierce fighting and stifling jungles, immediately took to the song's imagery of home, winter solitude, and peace. It was also an instant classic back in the states, winning the 1942 Academy Award for best song and selling millions of copies in sheet music and recordings. Crosby's rendition alone sold nearly twenty million albums. It became the longest-running song in the history of the American radio program Your Hit Parade, the number-one-selling song in the United States for decades, and rivaled the eighteenth-century German creation of "Silent Night" as the most endeared Yuletide composition ever made.[69]

To date, "White Christmas" has sold nearly two hundred million copies worldwide, in more than thirty languages.

---

2. "LILI MARLEEN" (1938)

A sonnet written in 1915 by a German soldier before he set off for the Russian front, its simple stanzas described an all-too-brief love affair of a soldier and his "Lili Marleen." In 1938, Hans Leip's words were set to a soft and heartfelt melody, and Swedish singer Lale Anderson introduced it to a marginally interested German population. In 1941 the sweet romantic ballad became a surprise favorite of Wehrmacht soldiers stuck in North Africa. Nearby British and Australian troops of the Eighth Army became fond of it as well, often singing it in its native tongue.[70]

Uncomfortable with the thought of their troops harmonizing in German, the British government asked famous lyricist Tommy Connor to fashion the tune into English. Eventually almost every language in Europe had its own version, with the French rendition becoming particularly popular. Many Americans got their first taste in the aptly titled 1944 movie *Lili Marlene*, starring German-born bombshell and ardent American patriot Marlene Dietrich. Hardly offended at the world adopting at least a piece of their culture, Germans played the song on national radio almost every night for three years.[71]

The music of "Lili Marlene" would return to the silver screen in 1961 as a paradoxical score piece in the film Judgment at Nuremberg.

---

3. SHOSTAKOVICH'S SEVENTH "LENINGRAD" SYMPHONY (1941)

Most symphonic composers continued to produce in spite of the war, although their new works were often about past epochs of violence: Jericho, the French Revolution, and the American Civil War. Some chose to write music about the current crisis. Grief-stricken by the Nazi reprisals at Lidice, Czech composers crafted no fewer than a dozen symphonies dedicated to the slaughtered city. A few harkened toward tomorrow, quite literally in the case of Dutch-born Gunnar Johansen, who claimed to have finished his PEARL HARBOR Sonata just hours before the fateful attack.[72]

One shy benevolent man, Dmitri Shostakovich, produced a synthesis of past memory, present misery, and future hope and inspired half the world with his music's inherent force. His Seventh Symphony, depicting the Nazi invasion of the Soviet Union, won him instant international fame and music immortality.

Just thirty-four years old in 1941, Shostakovich and his family were trapped with three million others in Leningrad, bombed, shelled, and surrounded by the German army. As food and any reasonable hope of survival began to run out, the composer began to write a symphony. Three movements were completed in a matter of weeks. After he was flown out of the besieged city by order of the Soviet government, Shostakovich completed the fourth and final movement in an abandoned schoolroom in Moscow.[73]

First performed in the Russian capital, the Leningrad Symphony began with a long sullen march, followed by a drone of heavy instruments, with piccolos and flutes whispering in fragile defiance. The piece concluded with all sections charging forth with a host of major chords, pronouncing a lasting triumph of light over darkness. The seventy-minute opus soon played to packed audiences in Britain, Hungary, Poland, France, and the United States.

Shostakovich's likeness graced the cover of *Time*. He became an honorary member of the American Academy of Arts and Sciences, an object of adoration to the Russian people, and a hero to the antifascist movement.[74]

The Soviet air force smuggled sheet music for Shostakovich's Seventh back into besieged Leningrad. An orchestra was assembled, including musicians hastily pulled from the front, and on August 9, 1942, the symphony played to a live audience, including the German army who heard via loudspeakers blasting from inside the city.

4. "CH'I LAI" (1933)

Because of the Japanese invasion, China's ballads of protest and patriotism were one and the same. Several folk songs were somehow adept at celebrating the simple life while promoting harsh reprisals against foreign attackers. The popular "Farmer's Song" insisted, "Our ancient nation must arise and rid the fields of the weeds." In "Husband Goes to War," a female voice assured, "If, alas, you meet your death, your hero soul will cry us on."

Most common were marching songs, many of which were rather direct in their message, such as "Wrath of the Warrior" and "Song of the Guerrillas." By far the most popular was "Ch'I Lai" ("March of the Volunteers"). Written as the theme song to the film *Children of the Dark Clouds,* the lyrics proclaimed: "China's masses have met the day of danger...Brave the enemy's gunfire. March on! March on!"[75]

A young man from southwest China named Nieh Erh wrote the melody for "Ch'I Lai." In 1934, he went to Japan to study music and write more patriotic songs. The following year, just before he planned to leave, the twenty-four-year-old was found dead in a body of water.

5. "CHATTANOOGA CHOO CHOO" (1941)

In a patriotic push to manufacture jingles as fast as weapons, tune-smiths often faltered in quality. Tin Pan Alley's products were less than riveting. For example, a post-PEARL HARBOR pep tune proclaimed, "You're a sap, Mr. Jap, to make a Yanky cranky. Uncle Sam...is gonna spanky."[76]

Most nationalistic songs, cheesy or not, had the unromantic rhythm of a military march. More attractive to the general populace were the swing and sway of the big bands, inviting patrons to dance to songs of enchantment. No band was internationally bigger than the Glenn Miller Orchestra, and its biggest hit was a stylish, churning boogie called "Chattanooga Choo Choo."

Premiered in the movie *Sun Valley Serenade,* the tune dominated jukebox sales, a "nickel nabber" extraordinaire that became the highest grossing RCA Victor seller of all time and the first gold record ever, selling more than a million copies by 1942.[77]

Miller went on to serve in the U.S. Army Air Force, achieving the rank of captain in the official capacity of band leader. He and his uniformed orchestra toured the United States and overseas, doing more than eight hundred live and radio shows, playing hits such as "Chattanooga Choo Choo," "In the Mood," "That Old Black Magic," and "Pennsylvania 6-5000." But Miller did not finish his tour of duty. On December 15, 1944, he boarded a plane for a flight from England bound for Paris to make arrangements for an upcoming performance. Taking off in foggy weather, the aircraft disappeared somewhere over the English Channel and was never seen again.

> In selecting his U.S. Army Air Force orchestra, Miller rejected a nineteen-year-old pianist named Henry Mancini, future composer of the "Pink Panther Theme," "Moon River," and the score to the film The Glenn Miller Story.

6. "GOD BLESS AMERICA" (1918)

If the United States were to choose a commanding officer of morale for the war, Russian-born Irving Berlin (whose real name was Israel Balin) would have made the short list. Among his repertoire of hits were "Arms for the Love of America," "Any Bonds Today?" and "Song of Freedom," from which he contributed all royalties to charity. He created, wrote, produced, and starred in a musical revue called This Is the Army, featuring a cast of hundreds of enlisted personnel. The show toured the United States and overseas, raised millions of dollars for the Army Relief Fund and British War Charities, and became a movie. His songs and shows earned him the U.S. Medal of Merit and a Medal of Honor.[78]

But the one patriotic tune for which he was best known was the ballad "God Bless America," written long before the Second World War and debuted on Armistice Day in 1938. Simple, brief, with a grandiose crescendo, its lyrics paid homage to an idyllic and expansive countryside. After 1941, it played consistently before or after radio programs, public functions, and sporting events. The tune became a virtual second national anthem. One young listener recalled, "We listened to the radio and heard Kate Smith sing 'God Bless America' more times than we recited the Lord's Prayer or Pledge of Allegiance in school each morning." In keeping with his practice of donating royalties of patriotic tunes, Berlin gave every penny he earned on the song to the Boy Scouts and Girl Scouts of America.[79]

Berlin composed and played purely by ear. In all his 101 years of life, he never learned to read or write music.

---

7. "THERE'LL ALWAYS BE AN ENGLAND" (1939)

After learning of the astounding success of "God Bless America," a London publicist asked a pair of songwriters, Hughie Charles and Ross Parker, to compose a British equivalent. Borrowing heavily from Irving Berlin's references to placid fields and wholesome folk, the two managed to pump out "There'll Always Be an England" in about three hours, but the song failed to take off.[80]

Months later, while Hitler invaded Poland, Britain braced for attack. A buzz developed around an obscure nationalistic ballad about country lanes and fields of grain, and the song became a full-fledged hit when King Charles VI mentioned it in a somber radio message to his subjects. Sheet music flew off the shelves. BBC airwaves rang with its cheery chords. The title appeared on bumper stickers in Canada, and Londoners sang it in bomb shelters: "There'll always be an England, and England shall be free, if England means as much to you, as England means to me."[81]

The drag of the ensuing PHONY WAR period diminished its luster, but the syrupy refrain made a comeback with the BATTLE OF BRITAIN in 1940. By 1942, it played less often than romantic songs like "The White Cliffs of Dover" and Hughie Charles and Ross Parker's own "We'll Meet Again," but "England" matured throughout the war to be an old standard of the Commonwealth.[82]

> *In tribute to the occasion, British schoolchildren once again bellowed the lyrics of "There'll Always Be an England" at the coronation of Queen Elizabeth II in 1953.*

8. "THE HORST WESSEL SONG" (1930)

Like their opponents, Germans preferred sentimental classics, jazz, and pop tunes to brash, banging martial compositions. Amid personal dreams and the daily grind, "Awake, German Fatherland" and "Tomorrow We March" simply lacked the appeal of a good dance number or love song, such as "Do You Remember the Beautiful May Days?" Even in the darkest hours, citizens of the Reich cared for "No More Beautiful Death in the World" before "Deutschland Über Alles."[83]

But in the Third Reich, orchestral works by the German masters (Hitler preferred Wagner) and military ensembles were the order of the day. Dominant among the latter was "The Horst Wessel Song."

Wessel was a twenty-three-year-old member of the Nazi Sturmabteilung, the SA, a.k.a. "Brownshirts." In his spare time he wrote marching tunes and attended rallies. He also bullied Communists, until one came to his apartment and shot him (his compatriots maintained he was struck down in a street brawl). When Wessel subsequently died weeks later, Nazi propaganda director Joseph Goebbels hailed him as an angelic martyr and adopted one of the deceased's poems, originally titled "Raise the Flag on High," as the official anthem of the Nazi Party.[84]

The drum-tinged vocal-dominated tribute to belligerence received numbingly repetitive play on state radio and in official assemblies. The music may have been lifted from an old Salvation Army tune, but the imposed words were far from charitable: "SA men march with bold, determined tread, Comrades felled by Reds and Ultras in fight, March at our side, in spirit never dead."

By 1942, many Germans were clearly unenthused with such nationalist themes and the constant reminders of war. Fearing he was going to lose his audience completely, Goebbels mandated a return to light music, which soon took up 70 percent of programming. From then on, Horst's march played infrequently, but extreme departures like jazz remained verboten (forbidden).[85]

Because of its connection with the Nazi Party, it is currently illegal to sing or play the "Horst Wessel Song" in the Federal Republic of Germany.

---

9. "DON'T SIT UNDER THE APPLE TREE" (1939)

East and West, some of the most popular songs centered around three themes: love, loneliness, and a plea for abstinence. The Chinese sang "Wait for Me," French voices echoed "Wait for Me, My Love," and English singers assured "I'll Be Seeing You" and "I'll Walk Alone." A favorite German hit was "Come Back to Me," while Russians asked "Are You Waiting?" Topping them all in circulation was the peppy American ditty "Don't Sit Under the Apple Tree (with Anyone Else but Me)."[86]

Written in 1939, the earnest tune became the rage when the Andrews Sisters sang it in the 1942 movie *Private Buckaroo*. Number one on Your Hit Parade from October 1942 to January 1943, no other war-related tune in the United States spent as much time at the top as the one that asked a sweetheart to wait "until I come marching home."[87]

Unfortunately for Americans and everyone else, many lovers did not wait. Years of separation, uncertainty, and a sense of fatalism placed exceptional stresses on relationships. By necessity, military training for most armed forces included lectures and films on sexual hygiene. Socially transmitted diseases were major contributors to unit casualties, and many women left behind also pursued physical companionship.

Americans received "Dear John" or "Dear Jane" letters confessing infidelity. Germans wrote of "suitcases" (secret lovers). In countries where divorce was permitted, separations doubled over the course of the war. In Britain, illegitimate births more than doubled, and separations filed because of alleged adultery quadrupled. But songs of faithfulness remained popular for the duration.[88]

The International Red Cross in Geneva had a department to handle divorces for prisoners of war.

---

10. "AH! LA PETIT VIN BLANC" (1943)

Call it pragmatism, call it denial, but most citizens in occupied France tried to make the best of a bad situation, to create a sense of security in a very insecure time. Vichy culture embodied this pursuit by glorifying traditional male-female roles, villages, rural life, folk art, and music.

Sounding this retreat into the past was the most popular melody of the occupation era, "Ah, La Petit Vin Blanc," sung by the general of joie de vivre, Maurice Chevalier. Paying grand homage to a little bottle of white wine, a romantic getaway in the countryside, and bright carefree optimism, the leisurely waltz was just one of many French songs with a blatantly escapist theme.

Countering was an artistic resistance of sorts. Citizens were attentive to double entendres within lyrics, poems, or plays, searching works for anti-German messages. In reality, most works did not have such hidden meanings. Artists such as Spanish exile Pablo Picasso and playwright Jean-Paul Sartre continued to produce works high in emotional content but evasive in political meaning. Music was generally submissive as well. Frenchmen may have sung the resistance march "Le Chant des Partisans" in public after liberation, but before that time, "La Petit Vin Blanc" had already sold 1.5 million copies of sheet music.[89]

For playing to German audiences, Maurice Chevalier was later accused of being a collaborator, an affront he shared with thousands of other conspicuously cooperative French citizens, including the mistress of a German officer, Coco Chanel.

5

IN RETROSPECT

FIRSTS

The Greek philosopher Heraclitus proclaimed, "War is the father of all things." Compelling as his words may be, reality speaks otherwise. Historically, wars tend to constrict if not consume incubators of innovation, such as laboratories, libraries, universities, and human beings. Over the course of major conflicts, everything from architecture to literature stagnates as resources are diverted to issues of more immediate security.

Exceptions come from the science of survival, exemplified by inventions made between 1937 and 1945. Allied airmen witnessed the first pressurized cabins, autopilot systems, and rubber-coated "self-sealing" gas tanks that could take a bullet and not explode. Nutritionists synthesized vitamins and high-calorie meals. Although blood types were known since the beginning of the century, blood banks were used for the first time, as were nonperishable plasmas.[1]

For every novelty made to preserve a body, there seemed a dozen invented to tear it apart. During the war, a team of Harvard researchers

concocted a gummy liquid called Napalm. U.S. weapons designers fashioned handheld rocket launchers nicknamed "bazookas." Nazis created
nerve gas. Several countries introduced a host of new bombs, bullets,
fuses, land mines, shells, and torpedoes. For better or worse, the conflict
deserved Winston Churchill's classification as "the wizard war."[2]

Following in chronological order are the first of their kind in world
or American history. Some are events; others are objects of warfare.
Most played significant roles in the course of the war. All exercised
equal or greater effect on history after 1945.

1. FIRST FULLY MOTORIZED ARMY (SEPTEMBER 1939)

World War II often conjures images of German armor and American
industry. But the first entirely mechanized armed forces belonged to
Great Britain. All other combatants utilized beasts of burden, many of
them extensively.

Infantry officers of numerous countries rode on horseback during
the war's early years. Almost every army possessed horse cavalry, such
as the U.S. Second Cavalry Division deployed to Morocco in 1943.
Draft horses hauled supply wagons, ammunition, and the wounded.
Most of Italian and German artillery was horse-drawn. Because of the
rugged terrain in Sicily, the U.S. Army routinely employed pack
mules. Red Army draft animals numbered in the millions.[3]

The fully mechanized British
war machine motors across
Libya while the vast majority
of German and Italian infantry
travels on foot.

In contrast, the British army traveled by fuel oil rather than fodder, thus becoming the first modern army. Regardless of its reputation for conservatism, rigid class structure, and resistance to change, Britain's military was often a vanguard of innovation. Colonial troops used machine guns in the Zulu Wars (1871, 1879). The Royal Navy was among the first to switch from coal to oil engines (1913). The RAF was the first independent air force ever created (1918). Much of these adoptions came from a long-standing realization that Britain attained and maintained its vast empire by virtue of superior technology.[4]

Horses used in the successful British invasion of Germany: 0.
Horses used in the failed German invasion of the Soviet Union: 625,000.

---

2. FIRST USE OF RADAR IN WARTIME (SEPTEMBER 1939)

Owing to the static nature of trench warfare, finding an enemy during World War I was hardly a challenge. Tracking one's opponent during World War II, however, was like trying to find a fast, mobile, deadly needle in a haystack.

Enter radar, or "Radio Detection and Ranging." Years before the outbreak of hostilities, private and governmental agencies in Britain, Germany, Italy, Japan, and the United States experimented with radio signals and echoes, mostly for tracking airplanes. Results were limited. Once the war started, radar technology progressed rapidly, especially in the United Kingdom and Nazi Germany. The British perfected a network of coastal stations that helped direct the RAF's meager fighter reserve with maximum effect in the BATTLE OF BRITAIN. Germany answered with a guidance system for bombers, using intersecting radar beams to indicate bomb targets. The British quickly learned how to jam these signals, which the Germans then overcame by using variable frequencies.[5]

Britain then introduced an improvement the Axis never matched. In 1940, two scientists from Birmingham University successfully tested the cavity magnetron, a transmitter that reduced radio waves from several feet to a few inches, increasing radar accuracy tenfold.

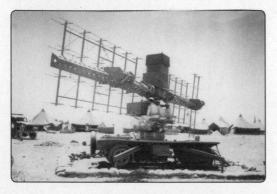

At the dawn of the information age, superior radar technology enabled the Allies to gain an unassailable edge over the Axis.

Of all the sought-after "superweapons," the cavity magnetron–equipped radar deserved the title. By 1943 the microwave system found its way onto Commonwealth and U.S. bombers, fighters, antiaircraft batteries, ships, and early warning stations. Impressively sensitive (it could detect a submarine periscope) and difficult to detect or jam, the new device enabled the Allies to "see" faster, farther, and more precisely than their opponents ever could. Virtual command of the sea and sky followed. In January 1944 Hitler cursed this leap in radar technology as the worst blow to his plans for victory.[6]

After receiving cavity magnetron radars in 1943, Allied destroyers and planes sank three times more U-boats than in the previous year.

3. FIRST PEACETIME DRAFT IN U.S. HISTORY (SEPTEMBER 1940)

It took the Civil War to instigate military conscription in the United States and World War I to temporarily resurrect it. Yet Americans universally disdained the draft. Even after Japan invaded China and

Germany swept through Poland, national opposition to conscription remained steadfast.

In March 1940, more than 96 percent of Americans opposed the idea of declaring war against the Axis. Yet when Hitler conquered Denmark in a single April day and proceeded to take Norway, France, Belgium, Holland, and Luxembourg in a matter weeks, attitudes began to shift. By June 65 percent of the American population believed that if Britain fell, the United States would be next. A sense of urgency erupted, since the United States possessed only the eighteenth-largest army in the world.[7]

Initial calls for a draft did not come from the White House or the military but from congressmen and grass-roots organizations. Even isolationists such as aviator Charles Lindbergh demanded a heightened state of readiness. Senator Ted Bilbo of Mississippi summed up their convictions bluntly: "We are not going to send our boys to Europe to fight another European war, but we are going to get ready for the 'Big Boy' Hitler and 'Spaghetti Mussolini' if they undertake to invade our shores."[8]

In June 1940, two days before France fell, a bill was proposed in Congress that all male citizens between the ages of twenty-one and thirty-six should register for possible conscription. Draftees, chosen by lottery, would train in the military for one year and remain on active reserve for a decade. On September 16, 1940, after months of bitter public debate and national introspection, the measure became law.

While Japan carved into China, Italy invaded Egypt, and the Luftwaffe bombed London, millions of American men registered under the Selective Service Act. Just six weeks later the War Department started drawing numbers. Eventually ten million draftees served in uniform, and despite promises to the contrary from senators, congressmen, and the president, half were sent overseas.[9]

World War II restarted the draft. Another war helped stop it. Following the unpopular and ultimately unsuccessful police action in Vietnam, President Richard M. Nixon ceased national conscription in 1973.

4. FIRST U.S. PRESIDENT ELECTED TO MORE THAN TWO TERMS (1932, 1936, 1940, 1944)

Months before the 1940 presidential contest, Franklin Roosevelt assumed he would follow George Washington's example and resign after two terms. Unfortunately for his Democratic Party, there appeared to be no viable replacement, and Roosevelt reluctantly chose to break precedent and run again.

To oppose him, the Republicans owned even fewer prospects. They eventually placed their hopes on a political rookie, Indiana businessman Wendell Willkie. The Grand Old Party's nominee had much in common with the president, as he too was well educated, tall, handsome, and exceedingly charismatic. Although he was selected by the GOP, Willkie was a lifelong Democrat.

In spite of growing international unrest, domestic issues dominated the campaign. Willkie agreed with most of FDR's foreign policy, condemning totalitarianism and pledging to keep America out of war. Willkie instead attacked the bureaucratic beast of the New Deal, labeling such big-government programs as inefficient and ineffective against a stagnant economy. Republicans also condemned Roosevelt's pursuit of a third term, calling it an act of hubris, if not dictatorship. Roosevelt triumphed nonetheless, bolstered by huge victory margins from key voting blocks, namely farmers, organized labor, and women. He also won a majority of votes from African Americans, who had traditionally sided with Republicans since the days of Lincoln.[10]

In 1944, Roosevelt's health began to fail, yet he rallied enough to convince the public that his sixty-two-year-old body could withstand another election, especially against the Republican's nominee, brilliant but smug forty-two-year-old Thomas Dewey of New York. Two key factors aided Roosevelt. He dumped his liberal and pro-Soviet vice president, Henry Wallace, for moderate, unknown Harry Truman, and he could point to the recent invasion of NORMANDY as proof that the long and horrid war was finally nearing an end. Roosevelt won again, though in his four elections, the fourth was his narrowest margin of victory.[11]

Wary of another era of one-man domination, in 1951, Congress passed the Twenty-Second Amendment, setting a two-term limit on the presidency. Years later, ardent supporters of fortieth president Ronald Reagan unsuccessfully lobbied for its repeal.

5. FIRST CARRIER BATTLE (MAY 1942)

In the spring of 1942 a Japanese fleet of three carriers and a complement of supporting cruisers, destroyers, and transports headed southeast around New Guinea and into the Coral Sea. Their mission was to capture key ports and installations in the area, setting the groundwork for an intended attack on Australia.

After intercepting transmissions of the Japanese plan, U.S. naval forces closed in, strengthened by the carriers *Lexington* and *Yorktown*. On May 7, aircraft from the U.S. carriers struck and sank *Shoho*, the smallest of the three Japanese flattops. The following morning and almost simultaneously, a swarm of planes from both fleets found their targets. Bombs and torpedoes fell in scores. Japan's carrier *Zuikaku* escaped unscathed, protected by the veil of a storm. The *Shokaku* and *Yorktown* each took several bombs but remained afloat. The *Lexington* did not survive, gutted by torpedoes on its port side and set ablaze by three direct bomb strikes. By early afternoon, the contest ceased by

The flight deck of the carrier *Lexington* is strewn with debris from an attack. Too damaged after the battle, *Lexington* was scuttled—the first U.S. carrier to be lost in the war.

mutual withdrawal. Both sides claimed victory, although Japan failed to gain the ports it sought, and the great Imperial assault on Australia never came to pass.[12]

The battle of the Coral Sea provided a host of maiden events: the first encounter of Japanese and U.S. naval airmen, the first sinking of Japanese and U.S. carriers, and the first time in the war Japan's navy failed to achieve an objective. But this brief clash in an otherwise placid corner of the globe was nothing short of a revelation, a harbinger of things to come.[13]

For the first time in three thousand years of naval warfare, a sea battle transpired completely by air. Not once did enemy ships come within sight of each other. No deck guns ever hit their opposition. From that point onward, ruling the waves required control of the skies.[14]

Flying back from a mission on the night of May 7, a Japanese pilot from the Zuikaku *spotted a flattop and attempted to land, only to be shot out of the sky. Having lost his way in the darkness, he had accidentally tried to set down on the deck of the* Yorktown.

---

6. FIRST OPERATIONAL JET AIRCRAFT (JULY 1942)

In the fight for air supremacy, speed was critical. Designers tinkered with engine types, fuel mixtures, wing shapes, prop design, and weight reduction to squeeze more velocity from their aircraft. But physics limited propeller planes to just over 400 mph. After British aeronautical genius Frank Whittle produced the first jet engine in 1937, engineers hypothesized this new propulsion system could reach 500 mph and more. The main problem involved getting a jet engine and an airframe to work in concert.

In this pursuit, German engineers caught and passed the British, developing a working prototype in August 1939: the Heinkel 178. Yet neither the He-178 nor British prototypes could surpass the speed and performance of existing prop-engine fighters. Then, after three years of development, the sleek twin-engine Messerschmitt 262 flew on July 18, 1942, nearing 100 mph faster than anything aloft.[15]

Despite its initial success, the Me-262 would not see combat for another two years. The German jet suffered from the same problems afflicting American, British, and Japanese programs: poor engine reliability, shortage of engineers, and lack of precious metals.

Ingenious but unreliable, Me-262s revolutionized aeronautics but had negligible effect on the war.

Overall, four types of jet planes flew in combat, three German and one British. The RAF's twin-engine Gloster Meteor was used primarily to shoot down V-1 buzz bombs. In seven months, sixteen operational Meteors scored just thirteen V-1 kills.[16]

7. FIRST FLYING BOMB
(JUNE 1944)

Predecessor to the cruise missile, the V-1 represented the most effective of Germany's secret weapons. It also exemplified the crippling lack of coordination within the Third Reich.

Resentful of the funds and attention granted to the army's rocket program, air force marshal HERMANN GÖRING pushed development of a pilotless flying bomb. Rather than share technicians and facilities, the Luftwaffe openly competed with the army, slowing down production on both projects and further damaging a military wrought with petty quarrels and overlapping responsibilities.[17]

Less expensive and simpler than the army's rocket, the Luftwaffe's experiment reached completion first. Looking like a bird of prey with wings outstretched, it flew by the power of a pulse-jet engine (ironically a French innovation), which produced a spine-rattling metallic flutter, earning it the nickname "buzz bomb" or "doodlebug." The German Ministry of Propaganda dubbed it "die Vergeltungswaffe" or "Vengeance weapon," V-1 for short.[18]

A V-1 buzz bomb, its pulse jet shutting off, slowly turns over as it descends into a London neighborhood.

Vengeance first materialized on June 13, 1944, just days after the Allied invasion of NORMANDY. Four bombs fell on London. Two days later, two hundred came, then thousands in the following weeks. One landed directly on a chapel during services, killing 121 churchgoers almost instantly. Winston Churchill confessed the V-1 brought "a burden per-haps even heavier than the air-raids of 1940 and 1941. Suspense and strain were more prolonged. Dawn brought no relief, and cloud no comfort."[19]

Overall, Germany launched more than twenty-two thousand V-1s, with nearly seven thousand reaching their targets in Britain, Belgium, France, and Holland, killing an average of two people per bomb.[20]

On June 17, 1944, one buzz bomb strayed far off course and hit a German bunker in eastern France. Though shaken, the shelter's oc-cupants escaped uninjured, including one Adolf Hitler.

---

8. FIRST LIQUID-FUELED BALLISTIC MISSILE (SEPTEMBER 1944)

In late August 1944 the Allies liberated Paris, but the euphoria was short-lived. On September 6 an altogether new weapon terrorized the city, falling from the sky faster than sound. Two days later the same deadly device hit London. Suddenly no point in Allied Europe ap-peared safe.

After nearly a decade of development, German engineers success-fully transformed Robert Goddard's 1926 invention for interstellar exploration into the first operational liquid-fueled ballistic missile, called the A-4, renamed "Vengeance Weapon 2." Nearly four stories tall, capable of traveling two hundred miles in five minutes, and armed with a one-ton warhead, the rocket was unsurpassed in its ability to induce fear. One young boy in London recalled, "Of all the Nazi's weapons, we were most afraid of the V-2 because there was no way to stop it."

Though the V-2 ultimately played a secondary role in the war, the weapon signaled the beginning of an entirely new type of warfare and inspired the U.S. and Soviet governments to capture—and then employ—as many of its creators as possible.[21]

Wernher Von Braun worked as the chief guidance system engineer for the V-2. He later became deputy associate administrator of NASA.

9. FIRST ATOMIC BOMB (JULY 1945)

Six weeks after the Nazi invasion of Poland, Roosevelt received a letter from Albert Einstein. The renowned physicist suggested the possibility of constructing a bomb using fissionable material, namely uranium: "A single bomb of this type, carried by boat and exploded in a port, might very well destroy the whole port together with some of the surrounding territory. However, such bombs might very well prove to be too heavy for transportation by air."[22]

A series of recent findings influenced Einstein's prediction. The neutron was discovered in 1932, as was Uranium-235 in 1935. In early 1939 French and American scientists theorized that a chain reaction of U-235 neutrons was possible and would release "vast amounts of power."[23]

A radioactive plume ascends from devastated Hiroshima, the second-ever atomic detonation.

German, Japanese, Soviet, British, and American governments all sponsored investigations into the feasibility of atomic weapons. By 1943 Germany and Japan opted out due to critical setbacks in research and resources. Soviet progress lagged from two years of land war with Germany. Only British-American cooperation found success, fostered by secure U.S. manufacturing sites and massive funding.[24]

A budget of two billion dollars, a work force of forty thousand people, and nearly four years of continuous work resulted in the construction of three devices. The first, armed with plutonium (U-238 with an additional neutron), tested successfully on July 16, 1945, outside Alamogordo, New Mexico. Three weeks later came the first atomic weapon used in wartime. Contrary to Einstein's assumption of its required size, the entire apparatus could be carried by a four-engine aircraft, but his estimation of its force was on target. The U-235 bomb, nicknamed "Little Boy," detonated above the port city of HIROSHIMA, Japan, decimating four square miles and killing at least one hundred thousand people. Three days later a plutonium bomb, called "Fat Man," exploded above Nagasaki, killing at least seventy thousand. Enough plutonium was available for a fourth bomb, but it remained unused when the Japanese Empire surrendered on August 14, 1945.[25]

Just before the blast at Alamogordo, some of the participating scientists feared the chain reaction would persist uncontrollably, destroying all of New Mexico if not the entire global atmosphere.

---

10. FIRST WAR IN WHICH MORE AMERICAN SOLDIERS DIED FROM COMBAT THAN FROM SICKNESS (DECEMBER 1941–AUGUST 1945)

In the First World War, two doughboys succumbed to ailments for every one killed in action. In the American Civil War, the ratio was closer to four to one. In the American Revolution, nine out of ten military deaths occurred away from the battlefield. And so it went for most soldiers in nearly every conflict in history.

Over the course of the Second World War, a number of momentous innovations changed this pattern, the greatest of which was penicillin. Discovered in 1929, its benefits were not fully evident until 1939, when a team of Oxford biologists noted its peculiar ability to destroy internal bacteria yet not harm human tissue. After the British perfected a stable and concentrated strain, they arranged for American companies to mass-produce it, and the age of antibiotics was born. Used sparingly in the North African theater in 1943, penicillin became widely available to Allied soldiers (mostly American and British) in 1944. The Axis never created an equivalent, save for a much weaker medicine called Prontosil made by the German consortium I. G. Farben.[26]

Also late in the war, the Allies achieved major victories against disease-carrying insects. To stave off malaria, troops stationed in the mosquito-infested South Pacific consumed newly synthesized quinine (a bitter yellow powder called Atabrine), while their Japanese counterparts often went without such preventive medicines. Consequently, malaria alone reduced many Imperial fighting units by a third or more.

Ground troops everywhere were subject to typhus, compliments of gnawing little fleas, lice, mites, and ticks. Allied soldiers fought these biting bugs with liberal applications of DDT, an insecticide called "the atomic bomb of the insect world" before it was discovered to be nearly as caustic against animals.[27]

Armed with better hygienic training, better food, cleaner water, and more extensive medical care than their opponents, American servicemen finally stood a fighting chance against life-threatening illness.[28]

In the American Civil War, Union infantry had one medic per five hundred men. In World War II, U.S. infantry had one medic per forty men.

TOP TEN

BEST MILITARY COMMANDERS

Nazi Germany had seventeen field marshals, thirty-six full generals, and three thousand additional generals and admirals. More than twenty-four hundred star-shouldered officers served in the U.S. armed forces. By the end of the war, the Soviet Union had enough dead generals to fill a battalion and enough live ones to fill a brigade.

Ranking these commanders depends on criteria. For level of commitment, few can match U.S. Army air chief Henry "Hap" Arnold, who suffered three heart attacks during the war yet refused to retire. On field tactics, there was the flashy IRWIN ROMMEL. U.S. Adm. Raymond Spruance had a freakish gift of knowing when to attack and when to hold back. Despite a selfish, divisive ego, Douglas MacArthur boosted morale on the home front like no other.

The wisest among them all realized that no man was an island, that success depended on a multitude of people, from politicians and spies to mechanics and merchant marines. Following are the best commanders based on their respective achievements in directing support through logistics, morale, communications, and overall strategy. Most of all, they are measured by the magnitude of their contribution to the success of their side.

1. GEORGI ZHUKOV (USSR, 1896–1974)

He was considered by some to be cruel, egocentric, and brutal. Others suggested he was lucky, that his victories came from timely winter storms and enemy hesitation. Still others believed him to be unmatched in his will to win. All charges were true.

Georgi Zhukov was in his midforties when war erupted. Profane and blunt, he often took full credit for ideas not totally his own, demoted officers with impunity, and threatened dissenters with firing squads. Yet he told people how to fight, inspired them to use every weapon, resource, and moment at their disposal, and allowed subor-

dinates latitude in carrying out orders. He was one of the few generals who could stand up to Stalin, and he slowly convinced the dictator to let the generals run the front. Last but not least, no commander from any country ever approached Zhukov's phenomenal record in the war.

In 1939 he led the Red Army against the Japanese in the battle of Kalkhin Gol on the border of Outer Mongolia. Using superior force through armor, his battalions inflicted more than 70 percent casualties, including eighteen thousand dead. Imperial Japan never ventured against Soviet Russia again. Promoted to the general staff, he warned of an impending German invasion and called up seven hundred thousand reservists months before his prediction came true. Assigned to save surrounded Leningrad, Zhukov redoubled defenses and pulled guns off of Baltic warships and used them as artillery. He also pushed soldiers into relentless counterattacks. Aided by Hitler's last-minute decision to lay siege rather than enter the city, Zhukov became Leningrad's savior.[29]

Shuttled to Moscow while German panzers were within sight of the city, Zhukov re-formed flagging lines in the suburbs, drafted women and children to dig rifle pits and build roadblocks, and lofted balloons to snare low-flying planes. Several times Stalin expressed doubt that Moscow would hold; Zhukov assured him it would. Throwing reserves against the German center, Zhukov sacrificed thousands but spared millions in the process.[30]

Though not the sole architect of the plans, he helped design the counterattacks that saved STALINGRAD and KURSK. When the Red Army marched on BERLIN, Zhukov directed the middle of a three-pronged offensive, took the city, and accepted the formal surrender.[31]

Vaunted as "St. George," Moscow's patron saint, the marshal fell fast at war's end. Burning with covetous suspicion over Zhukov's international fame, Stalin demoted him to a backwater command and swept his name from official histories. But Zhukov's success would not be forgotten. Though callous and vainglorious, he was at the head of affairs for every major Soviet victory. GEN. DWIGHT EISENHOWER befriended the man and said of him: "In Europe the war has been won and to no man do the United Nations owe a greater debt than to Marshal Zhukov."[32]

Like Hitler and Stalin, Georgi Zhukov was the son of a cobbler.

---

2. GEORGE C. MARSHALL (U.S., 1880–1959)

His was the literal translation of a soldier's code of conduct. Humorless, cold, and formal, Marshall believed wholeheartedly in self-discipline

and the pursuit of perfection. His commander in chief called him "George" once and never made the mistake again. He left no memoirs, feeling that any self-promotion was unbecoming an officer.

A graduate of the Virginia Military Institute, George C. Marshall performed logistical miracles in the First World War and later served as Gen. John Pershing's top aide. Though he longed for a field command, Marshall excelled at staff work and was named U.S. Army chief of staff the day war started in Poland. Roosevelt selected him over thirty-four senior candidates.

Widely respected and utterly credible, he personally convinced an isolationist Congress to pass the first PEACETIME DRAFT in U.S. history. Before PEARL HARBOR, he helped transform a paltry army of two hundred thousand into a modern force of nearly two million. From the outset, he endorsed a cross-channel attack as the surest way to defeat Germany. He considered assaults on North Africa a waste of time and resources, if not a British ploy to maintain imperial control. But he accepted consensus and executed his orders to the utmost, regardless of whether he agreed with the directives or not.

When the time came to invade France (the strategy and tactics of which Marshall helped formulate), the general was the obvious choice to command. But Roosevelt decided against it, unwilling to part with his chief military adviser for any length of time.

Throughout the war, Marshall exacted from others what he demanded from himself: commitment, action, and accountability. Under his direction, the U.S. armed forces went from the eighteenth most powerful in the world to the first and achieved victory in large part because of his ability to direct, delegate, and inspire. Secretary of War Henry L. Stimson once said to the general, "I have seen a great many soldiers in my lifetime, and you, sir, are the finest soldier I have ever known."[33]

As Truman's postwar secretary of state, Marshall helped rescue Europe once again, coordinating the economic aid program that became known as "the Marshall Plan." For this, he was awarded the 1953 Nobel Peace Prize.

---

3. HEINZ GUDERIAN (GERMANY, 1888–1954)

"When his eyes flash," a fellow officer said of Heinz Guderian, "Wotan seems to hurl lightning."[34] Inventive, unassuming, and good to his men, Guderian was also intense and driven to the point that he became known as "Hurrying Heinz."[35]

A middle-ranking officer during the reformation of the German army, Guderian pioneered the blitzkrieg concept.  He envisioned the use of tank brigades as spearheads, backed by mobilized infantry and field guns, with dive bombers acting as a form of artillery. He believed the orchestra could stay in unison, as well as be flexible to new movements, by using something he had been studying since the First World War: radio communication.[36]

Promoted up the command chain for his initiative as well as innovations, Guderian led a panzer corps in the scything of Poland in 1939 and was one of the most successful commanders in the 1940 invasion of France, where his tactics became de facto Wehrmacht policy. He repeated his performances in leading the 1941 advance on Moscow until Hitler intervened and redirected Guderian's divisions southward toward Kiev. Guderian's armor helped capture six hundred thousand Soviets, but the commander was incensed at the lost opportunity to take Moscow by storm, and he let his Führer know it. Guderian was relieved of duty soon after for withdrawing troops from an exposed position without Hitler's approval.[37]

For more than a year, the alchemist of blitzkrieg sat on the sidelines, until a desperate Hitler made him inspector general of armored troops. What Guderian saw repulsed him.

In the factories, tank production had slowed to a crawl, each overcomplicated design worsening with endless modifications. In the field, Hitler schemed to renew the failed Russian offensive near KURSK, with neither the armor nor the right plan to accomplish the task. The general demanded an end to such wasteful practices. He streamlined tank production, endorsed gradual withdrawal from the East, and insisted on stronger defenses in the West, the front on which an Allied attack was sure to come. Yet every idea the general put forth his war-lord either rejected or altered beyond recognition. The relationship ended in March 1945 when Hitler dismissed Guderian for good, just weeks before the fall of BERLIN.[38]

A prisoner of the Allies until 1948, Guderian spent the next two years writing his memoirs. Titled Panzer Leader *for English audiences, the book became a worldwide bestseller and was translated into ten languages.*

---

4. DWIGHT D. EISENHOWER (U.S., 1890–1969)

A no-name lieutenant colonel when war began in Europe, Dwight Eisenhower was nonetheless the owner of a pristine reputation among

elite figures. Creator of the U.S. Army's first-ever tank units during World War I, he went on to serve under Gen. John Pershing after the war and then graduated first in his class at the U.S. Army Staff College. He served in the Philippines, where he earned hard-fought admiration from his command-ing officer and polar opposite, Douglas MacArthur. GEORGE C. MARSHALL only met him twice and was so impressed by his humble yet responsible demeanor that the chief of staff assigned the Kansan to the War Plans Division immediately after December 7, 1941.[39]

By June 1942, Eisenhower was in London as the commanding gen-eral of the European theater of operations. British officers noted that the American had never heard a shot fired in anger, a fact that vexed Eisenhower to no end. But he proved to be a quick study. When his North Africa and Sicily campaigns faltered from low morale and disunity, Ike reacted straightaway. He fired poor generals, promoted the best ones, took greater control of strategic planning, and, above all else, he forced cooperation.

Ike hit his stride with the NORMANDY invasion, to which he committed months of planning. From stubbornly independent branches of air, army, and navy, he forged a force involving more than 4,000 ships, 10,000 aircraft, and a landing force of 150,000 international troops. Despite imperfections, the invasion was an unqualified success. However, Eisenhower's true greatness showed in the months that followed, when limited resources and a tenacious enemy nearly brought the campaign to a standstill.

His infectious smile and pleasant demeanor disappeared when he encountered infighting or defeatism. When British Gen. Bernard Montgomery pushed him one too many times, Ike scolded back, "Good will and mutual confidence are, of course, mandatory." His frequently criticized broad-front strategy kept fragile alliances together and likely minimized casualties. Only once did he permit a diversion from his grand strategy, OPERATION MARKET-GARDEN, and it broke down with disastrous results.[40]

His levelheaded, meticulous nature helped prevent a similar breakdown during the BATTLE OF THE BULGE, where he turned a problem into a victory. His methodical push into Germany, also frequently criticized as too hesitant, may have prevented an armed confrontation with the Soviets, whose leader viewed the American and British presence as a threat as much as a blessing.

Overall, those who liked flash and bravado tended to dislike Eisenhower's steady and diplomatic methods. But Eisenhower knew better than anyone else that cavalier charges did not win battles.[41]

Dwight Eisenhower, the supreme commander of the largest American assault force ever assembled, was raised by parents who were pacifists.

5. KONSTANTIN ROKOSSOVSKY (USSR, 1896–1968)

Konstantin Rokossovsky was brilliant and humble, clever and level-headed. In 1937 he was a Red Army corps commander when he was

arrested during Stalin's military purges. Enduring torture and imprisonment, he avoided probable execution by deftly dismantling evidence brought against him. Released after nearly three years, he returned to his command.[42]

During the initial phases of the 1941 German invasion, Rokossovsky led fierce but futile opposition against the southern wing of the attack. Redeployed to the center in front of Moscow, Rokossovsky's mechanized infantry corps again threw themselves against the Germans and greatly blunted the momentum of the assault. His troops also took part in the counteroffensive that failed to destroy the German advance but succeeded in driving it away from Moscow.

In the battle for STALINGRAD, Rokossovsky's men led a wide northern sweep that encircled and eventually crushed the German Sixth Army. At KURSK, he commanded the successful defense of the critical salient's northern side. In the final advance on Berlin, the general led the push through Poland and secured the right wing of the Soviet assault, eventually meeting up with U.S. troops two hundred miles northeast of the German capital.

On the whole, Rokossovsky preferred maneuver to Zhukov's brutish pounding and counterattack to frontal assault. Considerate of the needs of his men and generally humane to captives, Rokossovsky demanded a greater level of professionalism than most commanders. Officers and enlisted respected him equally, as well as a good number of his opponents, many of whom considered him the finest general in the Red Army.[43]

Konstantin Rokossovsky became momentarily famous in the United States on August 23, 1943. He was on the cover of Time *magazine.*

6. JOSIP BROZ TITO (YUGOSLAVIA, 1892–1981)

In 1939, Josip Broz Tito became general secretary of the Communist Party of Yugoslavia, yet the title was almost meaningless. At the time the

Communists were a small, illegal outfit in the constitutional monarchy. No one—including Tito (an alias he took as his permanent name in 1934)—believed he would soon be the most powerful man in the country.

Though energetic and charismatic, Tito had only four years of primary education, was born a Catholic Croat in an Orthodox Serb–dominated state, possessed only a few weapons at the start of the war, and had at most five thousand loyal party members. He would fight not one but several enemies: the Germans who invaded in 1941 and the Bulgarians, Hungarians, and Italians who helped occupy the country. Internally, he faced a pro-Nazi puppet state in Croatia, guerrillas loyal to the Serb crown, and ethnic and religious separatists. Yet it was this fractured, chaotic environment that allowed his courage and leadership to shine.

Personally heading guerrilla sabotage operations with a few thousand supporters, Tito learned quickly to replace Communist rhetoric with a more patriotic message. As the region disintegrated into bloody civil war, Tito preached unity against the Axis and its collaborators, inviting people of all religions and ethnicities to join his "People's Liberation Movement." By 1943 he counted twenty thousand under his command. Recognizing his rising status as the one potential leader in Yugoslavia, both the Soviet Union and the Western Allies began lending political and material support. Tito soon had enough armor and artillery to equip several divisions.

With the help of the Red Army, Tito's partisans liberated most of Yugoslavia by the end of 1944. He was also the head of a provisional government and commanded more than one hundred thousand troops. Yet Marshal Tito saved his strongest move for last.

Citing Red Army atrocities against his people (many Soviet soldiers were fond of murder and pillaging), Tito began to break with Moscow. Rejecting London's support of the old royalist government, he held elections in which nearly every name on the ballot was Communist. He became prime minister, defense minister, and supreme commander of the army and began to ruthlessly hunt down potential adversaries. Years later he would declare himself "president for life," a position he held until almost his ninetieth birthday.[44]

In 1944, several British special operations commandos parachuted into Yugoslavia to assist Tito's headquarter operations. One of the officers was Randolph Churchill, son of the British prime minister.

---

7. CHESTER W. NIMITZ (U.S., 1885–1966)

Above Chester Nimitz was the hard-drinking, womanizing (although brilliant) Adm. Ernest King. Beneath him was a tough school

of seadogs, including brash Adm. William "Bull" Halsey, the tantrum-prone Adm. Richmond Turner, and the aptly nicknamed marine, Holland "Howlin' Mad" Smith. Before him was a smoldering Oahu, a victorious Japanese navy, and millions of square miles of Pacific Ocean. Somehow the affable and soft-spoken Nimitz took it all in stride.

Immediately named Adm. Husband Kimmel's replacement at PEARL HARBOR, Nimitz first set about rebuilding morale and assessing damage. He kept Kimmel's able staff and noted that much of the naval base was either intact or salvageable, including the submarine base he helped create in the 1920s. The installation recovered quickly under his direction.[45]

A submariner from his early days, Nimitz instructed his modest undersea force to target merchant shipping, which nearly eliminated Japan's surface lifelines by 1945. He understood the primacy of carriers in modern war, and many of his victories came by way of flattops. Nimitz also paid close attention to INTELLIGENCE, unlike some commanders (such as MacArthur), which enabled him to plan the attack on GUADALCANAL, stage the pivotal victory at MIDWAY against superior forces, and shoot down his adversary, Yamamoto Isoroku, the following year.

Like JOHN C. MARSHALL, he refused to write memoirs or sing his own praises. Like DWIGHT D. EISENHOWER, he pressed for calm assessment and steadfast unanimity, a necessity when many of his operations (such as OKINAWA) involved army, navy, and marine personnel. Unlike many commanders, Nimitz was able to win nearly every engagement he entered.[46]

Studious and disciplined, Chester Nimitz was accepted into the U.S. Naval Academy at the age of fifteen.

---

8. FREDERICH ERICH VON MANSTEIN (GERMANY, 1887–1973)

A general's general, Erich Manstein was a slim, astute, dignified Prussian with a military pedigree and a talent for modern tactics. Born the tenth child of an officer, Erich was adopted by his uncle, also an officer, and entered military school in his teens. He would grow to be one of the most respected commanders in the German army.

His sharp mind was the root of his visible confidence. But he also had a vicious emotional side, which he tried to control his whole life. His orders were clear and calculated. He believed in staying adaptable in a fire fight, which endeared him to his officers. He also hated frontal assaults and refused to be trapped or overcommitted, which won the trust of his men.[47]

Manstein is best known for an alteration. Hitler's initial plan for invading France involved going through Belgium and then southwest to Paris, retracing Germany's path in the First World War. A staff officer at the time, Manstein suggested going through the heavily forested ARDENNES, catching the French by surprise, and heading northwest to cut their defenses in half. The idea appealed to Hitler, and the attack transpired nearly as Manstein suggested.[48]

Obviously a gifted strategist, Manstein achieved most of his victories as a tank commander on the eastern front. Assigned to take the Crimean Peninsula in the Black Sea, he succeeded, thus becoming the only German general to achieve a major objective against the Soviet Union. He also scored one of the last German victories anywhere by retaking the rail hub of Kharkov in March 1943, stemming a gradual collapse of the southern front.

By 1944 Manstein staged a series of steady withdrawals, which cost the attacking Soviets heavily and saved his own ranks from annihilation. But increasing disagreement with Hitler over battle plans eventually cost him his job, and he was permanently relieved of command in March 1944.

The Western view of Manstein is highly polished. His true image is less than gentlemanly. He heartily endorsed the Anschluss (annexation) of Austria, used Russian POWs to clear land mines, and sent thousands of prisoners to Germany as slave labor. Concerning the popular litmus test applied to all German generals, Manstein was indeed critical of Hitler, but his most adamant opposition came after 1945. During the war he was one of the most able and effective commanders at Hitler's disposal.[49]

In 1949, a British tribunal sentenced Erich von Manstein to eighteen years' imprisonment for war crimes, of which he served four. In 1956, the West German government hired him as a military adviser.

---

9. GEORGE S. PATTON JR. (U.S., 1885–1945)

Most of the flamboyance was for show—the ivory-handled revolvers, the vulgarity, the self-promotion. As a rule, George S. Patton ran an

orderly and efficient headquarters, encouraged input from his subordinates, and planned his operations studiously. A firm believer in destiny, he shared many traits with Confederate Gen. Thomas J. "Stonewall" Jackson in that he was extremely pious and eccentric, a devout believer in discipline, unloved but respected by his men, and the most successful field commander of his country.[50]

Assigned to lead the U.S. assault on Casablanca in the 1942 Allied invasion of North Africa, Patton secured the area in less than a week. He took over the U.S. Second Corps after its demoralizing defeat in Tunisia, quickly establishing discipline and morale. Leading the U.S. Seventh Army in the invasion of Sicily, Patton and his troops traveled twice as far and twice as fast as the British, securing most of the island in less than a month.

Two separate incidents in Sicily, one of which was heavily publicized, nearly wrecked Patton's career. He verbally and physically assaulted two soldiers suffering from combat fatigue, and the public backlash greatly embarrassed the U.S. high command. Biographers commonly refer to Patton's outbursts as temporary "meltdowns" on the general's part. Viewed on the whole, his outbursts epitomized his character. Willful and belligerent, Patton neither understood nor tolerated hesitation in combat. His aggressiveness (which Gen. DWIGHT EISENHOWER worked diligently to harness) was a constant mental state, one that handicapped him on a personal level but empowered him in command.[51]

Patton redeemed himself at the head of the U.S. Third Army in France. Activated seven weeks after D-day, his men swept west and secured most of the Brittany Peninsula, then raced east on an abrupt charge to the German border. The surprise German offensive in the BATTLE OF THE BULGE failed in large part because Patton cut it off at its base. In the advance into the Third Reich, Patton's was the most successful army in grabbing territory, plowing through southern Germany and seizing parts of Austria and Czechoslovakia before being ordered to halt. In less than a year his men advanced more than one thousand miles across enemy-held territory, moving farther and faster than any other unit in the operation.

Patton survived the war but was mortally injured in a car accident in Germany months after the peace.

Having served his country in Mexico, World War I, and World War II, George S. Patton Jr. also donned a U.S. uniform in the 1912 Summer Olympics in Stockholm, where he finished fifth in the modern pentathlon.

---

10. BERTRAM RAMSAY (UK, 1883–1945)

Ramsay was humble and diligent among his peers yet venomous against incompetents. A naval veteran of the First World War, Bertram Ramsay came out of retirement to serve as the ranking flag officer at Dover. It was from this channel city, from tunnels beneath Dover Castle, that Ramsay and his staff directed the emergency evacuation of British, French, and other troops from embattled Dunkirk. Prime

Minister Winston Churchill, himself a former lord of the admiralty, estimated 45,000 troops could be saved. Sailors, the RAF, civilians, and Ramsay rescued more than 330,000.[52]

Duly knighted for his actions, Ramsay was later the deputy naval commander of the invasion of North Africa. The task was at best daunting, requiring the transfer of U.S. soldiers from New York directly to Casablanca and the passing of more than 300 British ships through the Straits of Gibraltar. Out of all the vessels, the Allies lost only one transport and landed more than 65,000 troops. Ramsay also served as deputy commander in the amphibious invasion of Sicily in 1943, involving nearly 2,600 ships tasked with escorting soldiers ashore.

In 1944, Ramsay was in charge of Operation Neptune, the naval portion of the NORMANDY invasion. Pulling together battleships, cruisers, destroyers, submarines, tugs, hospital ships, minesweepers, landing craft, and other vessels (totaling four thousand ships, mostly British), loading divisions from across the English southern coast, rendezvousing the armada in the Channel, and directing it across hostile waters, Ramsay and his subordinates delivered five divisions to the northwest shores of occupied France.

Under Ramsay's guidance, the Allies hauled and assembled two artificial ports, laid an underwater oil pipeline, and shuttled more than seven hundred thousand men plus vehicles and supplies in a matter of weeks. Longtime friend of Winston Churchill, object of esteem among servicemen of all ranks, the steadfast Ramsay helped orchestrate the largest amphibious invasion of all time.[53]

Adm. Sir Bertram Ramsay did not get to see the fruition of his great efforts. The day after New Year's 1945, en route to a meeting with Field Marshal Montgomery, Ramsay died when his plane went down over France.

WORST MILITARY COMMANDERS

The fortunes of war can tarnish the finest brass, just as misfortunes, extenuating circumstances, and politics can negate diligent and able service. RAF air chief Marshal Hugh Dowding saved Fighter Command, and possibly England, by using his pilots sparingly in the BATTLE OF BRITAIN, but his shrewd methods won few fans, and he was removed from his post. Lt. Gen. Walter Short and Adm. Husband Kimmel, both competent and professional soldiers assigned to command in Hawaii, were made to take the blame for the damage leveled on PEARL HARBOR.

But there were chieftains who had no excuse, who repeatedly wasted, endangered, and failed their countrymen despite being given liberal amounts of public support, military hardware, skilled subordinates, ample INTELLIGENCE, time, and virtual autonomy of command. Following are ten prime examples of habitual underachievers among the high-ranking, selected for the degree to which they squandered chances, created problems, and generally contributed to their nation's demise.

1. ADOLF HITLER (GERMANY, 1889–1945)

In a decade he took a minuscule army in a bankrupt country and developed it into the strongest and most feared military power in the world. Had he only stopped after the defeat of France, he might have been heralded as the brightest military mind of the twentieth century. But the halcyon days after the armistice of Compiègne soon faded into darkness as Hitler began to exercise an unnatural degree of control over a system fraught with limitations, and few components of Hitler's war machine were more limited than himself.

Though a gifted orator, Hitler was a phenomenally poor communicator. He preferred to lecture rather than listen. He gave vague orders, refused to delegate tasks, and invalidated opinions divergent of his own.

On military concerns, he was almost completely ignorant of air and naval operations. Logistics confused him. He assumed any shortage of

fuel or ammunition was a matter of supply rather than transportation. Strategically he had a strange habit of halting offensives just before they reached their objectives, demonstrated outside of Dunkirk in 1940 and within miles of Leningrad in 1941.

If Hitler did not know when to move forward, he also refused the option of pulling back. He first issued a "no retreat" order in November 1941 to tank commanders in the Caucasus. He would repeat the directive for the rest of the war, dismissing or executing any general who moved anywhere but forward.[54]

When men failed him, Hitler placed an increasing faith in machines. By 1943 he assumed the next V-weapon or supertank was all that was required to reverse his losses. As with logistics and people, he did not understand the limitations of technology. He once demanded the construction of a missile with a ten-ton warhead. A rocket engine capable of such thrust would not exist for another twenty years.[55]

Examples abound of his miscalculations, baseless reprisals, and ever-widening separation from reality. Arguably his weakest characteristic as a military commander was his vacillation, notably pertaining to war aims, indicating that this leader of the "master race" had no master plan.[56]

For his tombstone, Hitler stated he wanted the epitaph: "He was a victim of his generals."

---

2. HERMANN GÖRING (GERMANY, 1893–1946)

On top of his corpulent ego, his unceasing repression of political opponents and Jews, and his art pilfering, narcotics bingeing, palace  squatting, jewelry hoarding, and other related acts of Nero-esque debauchery, Hermann Göring was also a bungling air force officer.

A World War I flying ace and last commander of the Richthofen Squadron, the starved-for-action Göring joined the fledgling Nazi Party in 1922 and quickly climbed its ranks. In 1935 Hitler named him Luftwaffe commander in chief. Heading the most technical branch of the German armed forces, Göring had little understanding of engineering and production. He once said half-jokingly that he did not know how to operate his radio.[57]

Göring summarily appointed yes-men and incompetents, failed to develop an operational long-range bomber, and led his Führer and country to believe the Luftwaffe could achieve anything. Initially it could. The Luftwaffe was exceptionally effective in bombing the undefended city of Warsaw in 1939. After the action, Göring received the fabricated übertitle of Reichsmarshal.[58]

The high-flying dirigible garnished his Polish success with baseless proclamations—his Luftwaffe could crush the evacuation of Dunkirk, destroy Britain's air defenses, supply besieged Stalingrad completely by air, etc. In only one prediction was he technically correct. Before the war he proclaimed, "The Ruhr will not be subjected to a single bomb." The Allies eventually dropped far more than a single bomb on the industrial mecca.[59]

As if the air force wasn't enough, Göring also meddled in army affairs. By 1941 his Luftwaffe ran half of Germany's antiaircraft batteries, competing with army batteries for ammunition, guns, and spare parts. After 1942 the largest and best-equipped tank unit belonged to the Reichsmarshal, the "Panzerdivision Hermann Göring." All of Germany's eight paratroop divisions were under the jurisdiction of the Luftwaffe. Of Germany's 150 infantry divisions on the eastern front, twenty-two of them wore Luftwaffe uniforms.[60]

By 1943, Göring's bloated sun had finally set, his Luftwaffe all but shot out of the sky or beaten into the ground. As Allied bombers flew deeper and deeper into German territory, he accused his fighter pilots of cowardice, a strange recrimination. The top U.S. fighter scored forty kills in the war, while fourteen German pilots notched more than two hundred confirmed kills each.[61]

Göring lived to be indicted in the Nuremberg trials, a slimmed-down, detoxed rebirth of his young pre-Nazi self. Defiant and bombastic throughout the proceedings, he was convicted on all counts. He swallowed poison just hours before he was to be hanged.

Only three Germans ever received the Grand Cross, the eighth and highest grade of the Iron Cross: Gebhard von Blücher for routing Napoleon at Waterloo, Paul von Hindenburg for defeating Russia in the First World War, and Hermann Göring.

---

3. KLIMENT VOROSHILOV (USSR, 1881–1969)

A Bolshevik long before the 1917 revolution, Kliment Voroshilov was a Red Army commander in the RUSSIAN CIVIL WAR when he met and befriended Stalin. Though lacking in intellect and military aptitude, Voroshilov impressed the Georgian with his dogmatic zeal. As years progressed, he displayed an ever-growing loyalty to Stalin, for which he eventually had a military academy, a tank (the heavy KV-1), and a city named after him (Voroshilovgrad, currently Lugansk). He also served as defense commissar from 1934 to 1940, during which the vapid sycophant developed a gift for inflicting terrible damage.

Through Stalin's bloody purges, Voroshilov assisted in liquidating 80 percent of the Soviet Union's senior officers, later bragging, "During

the course of the cleansing of the Red Army in 1937–1938, we purged more than 40,000 men." He further destroyed military readiness by improperly supplying and training Russia's western armies. Few war games transpired while he was in office. Deployment plans were almost never issued. Many divisional headquarters lacked basic maps. Between extolling the leverage of heroism and dismissing the importance of tanks, he predicted that the next war would only take place in enemy territory and any battles therein would be brief and relatively bloodless.[62]

When war broke out, Voroshilov "coordinated" the invasion of largely defeated Poland in 1939 and an attack against Finland in the "WINTER WAR" of 1939–40, netting marginal victories and horrendous losses. During the latter affair the Soviets had six times as many soldiers as the Finns. But poorly motivated and without winter clothing, the Red Army suffered eight times the casualties. Nikita Khrushchev, then a political commissar, dubbed Voroshilov, "the biggest bag of [expletive] in the army."[63]

In 1941, Stalin incredibly placed Voroshilov in charge of defending besieged Leningrad. Though the inhabitants courageously held out month after month, Voroshilov became convinced that defeat was near, so he wandered up to the front in the hopes of getting killed. He failed in that venture as well, and Gen. GEORGI ZHUKOV arrived the following day to secure the city's defenses. Voroshilov was summarily removed and promoted to the Soviet Defense Committee.[64]

The inept Kliment Voroshilov was to have one more distinguished post before retirement. From 1953 to 1960, he was president of the Soviet Union.

4. CHIANG KAI-SHEK (CHINA, 1887–1975)

It says something about a man if Germans, the Soviet Union, the United States, Britain, and Mao Zedong fight on his side and he still can't win.

By 1936, a narcissistic, petty, oppressive but charismatic Generalissimo Chiang Kai-Shek had established a military academy with the help of German advisers. He also purchased German weapons and began to modernize a massive army of at least two million. At the same time, the Chinese Communists negotiated a "united front" with Chiang to oppose the looming power of Japan. When the Japanese invaded China proper in 1937, first to assist were the Soviets, who provided weapons, ammunition, even pilots and fighters. By 1942 the Allies designated Chiang supreme commander of the China theater and sent billions of dollars in LEND-LEASE.

With all this, Chiang was able to amass an army of three million and more, but he failed to score a single major victory in eight years. Only twice did Chiang direct serious opposition, both times in 1937. In July he initiated a fight over SHANGHAI, primarily to gain international attention by placing the multinational port—and China's richest city—in harm's way. The event sparked a three-month battle, during which his forces were eventually routed. He immediately followed the devastating loss by jamming two hundred thousand troops in his indefensible capital of Nanking to the west. Both the cream of his army and his capital were demolished in weeks.[65]

For the rest of the war, he regressed into China's primitive back-country, establishing a new capital in Chungking (Chongqing), six hundred miles from the Pacific coast. He forced millions of peasants into an undisciplined rabble of an army and presided over a ring of corrupt officials and regional warlords while hoarding money, weapons, and ammunition for an anti–Communist campaign he was aching to resume.

The popular stance in the pro-Chiang camp is that he traded space for time, letting Japan overextend itself into China and subsequently wither on the vine. Such a view overlooks a few basics. The space Chiang surrendered contained 80 percent of his industrial base, including nearly every major city and port in the country. The time he gained he did not use, even when his enemy was locked in a Pacific struggle against the United States.

As for the Communists, their armies never numbered more than a tenth of his force. However, they maintained a much greater level of discipline, conducted far more guerrilla operations, and were more willing to implement tax, rent, and land reforms than the rigid and remorseless Chiang. When two able and progressive Nationalist generals, Pai Chunghsi and Li Tsung-jen, begged the generalissimo to adopt similar methods, Chiang rejected them outright.

In the end, Chiang sacrificed more than a million Chinese soldiers and well over ten million Chinese civilians in his bid to stay in power. In 1949, the West was somehow surprised when the warlord also lost China as well.

Repulsed by Chiang's limited intellect, his Allied chief of staff, Gen. Joseph Stilwell, referred to the generalissimo as "Peanut."

---

5. RODOLFO GRAZIANI (ITALY, 1882–1955)

He was the youngest Italian colonel in the First World War and showed great promise, but Rodolfo Graziani's long tenure in Mussolini's fascist regime provided little beyond pointless cruelty and military failure. A general by the early 1930s, stationed in the Italian colony of Libya, he attempted to crush an independence movement by closing religious shrines, executing thousands, destroying villages, and throwing almost the entire population of east Libya into concentration camps. In the 1935–36 war with ABYSSINIA, he granted military contracts to personal friends, endorsed ruthless behavior among his troops, and used poison gas on essentially defenseless Ethiopians.[66]

Graziani's Second World War career varied little from his preceding record. Just as Germany was about to secure an armistice with defeated France, Mussolini wanted to rush into the Alps and claim up to a quarter of France for himself. Several advisers rejected the scheme. Army chief of staff Graziani cheered the idea and assured Mussolini his troops were ready. They were not. Invading the mountains without adequate ammunition, air support, or winter clothing, the Italians managed to advance just a few miles. They soon lost more men to frostbite than to bullets.[67]

Graziani's crowning achievement transpired in autumn 1941. At the head of Mussolini's forces in Libya, he reluctantly led 150,000 soldiers into Egypt against 30,000 British subjects, mostly Indians. Gains were modest until the Commonwealth counterattacked, which sent the Italians reeling. Heading the retreat was Graziani himself, at times more than 300 miles behind the front lines. He lost all but 20,000 of his troops. Upon hearing the news, British foreign secretary Anthony Eden said, "Never had so much been surrendered by so many to so few."[68]

Yet Graziani's pitiful career was not yet complete. When Nazi Germany rescued the deposed Mussolini in 1943, il Duce set up the Italian Social Republic in the northern half of the country and selected the ever-loyal Graziani as chief of staff and minister of defense.

> *In 1940, Graziani "earned" the position of overall commander in North Africa when his predecessor, Air Marshal Italo Balbo, was accidentally shot out of the sky and killed by Italian antiaircraft guns.*

6. TOYODA SOEMU (JAPAN, 1885–1957)

In the Samurai code of bushido, a warrior must be willing to sacrifice his life if needed. When Toyoda Soemu inherited the Imperial

Combined Fleet in May 1944, he believed the time had come to demand such a sacrifice. In the year that followed he pressed the Japanese navy into a number of poorly planned engagements in search of a "final and decisive battle." None of the battles were final or decisive, but all reduced a once-daunting force into a ghost of its former self.

A desk officer until appointed naval headmaster, the intelligent but insular Toyoda directed the Imperial Fleet into an all-or-nothing interception of the American attack on SAIPAN. Before his pilots left their carriers, he radioed: "The rise and fall of Imperial Japan depends on this one battle. Every man shall do his utmost." Outgunned, undertrained, and outnumbered two to one, his air arm flew into what Americans later called "the Great Marianas Turkey Shoot." Eighty percent of Toyoda's planes were shot down, more than three hundred aircraft. The U.S. lost fewer than thirty planes. The admiral also lost seventeen of twenty-five submarines and three of nine carriers.[69]

In October 1944, he pushed again for a "final battle" at LEYTE GULF in the Philippines. Plucked of his planes and submarines, Toyoda soon forfeited the bulk of his surface ships. His strike forces totaled an astounding six carriers, nine battleships, twenty cruisers, and thirty-five destroyers. A few days later only six battleships and a handful of cruisers remained above water. Afterward Toyoda fully endorsed the use of kamikaze in a desperate attempt to hold on to the Philippines. To ensure the best results, he ordered the use of Japan's best pilots.[70]

And still there was one more try in him. To the battle of OKINAWA Toyoda sent the *Yamato*, the largest battleship ever constructed. Legend states that the warship and its small complement of support vessels were given enough fuel for a one-way trip. Regardless, they had no air cover. Dismembered by direct hits from twenty torpedoes and bombs, the *Yamato* sank to the bottom of the ocean.[71]

Removed from his post, Toyoda was promoted to navy chief of staff. Serving in Tokyo up to the end, he passionately argued for a continuation of the war, even after the second atom bomb fell on Nagasaki.[72]

Brought to trial for war crimes, Toyoda Soemu was one of the few senior officers of the Japanese Empire to be acquitted on all counts.

---

7. IRWIN ROMMEL (GERMANY, 1891–1944)

Yes, *the* Irwin Rommel. Chivalrous, charming, aggressive, and perceptive, Rommel was a phenomenon in the First World War. A mere low-grade officer, he personally led raids in France, Romania, and Italy, capturing thousands with a fraction of the troops. As a high-ranking leader in the Second World War, his maverick, reckless exploits were lethally out of place. He routinely disobeyed orders, displayed a contempt if not ignorance of logistics, and all but refused to cooperate with fellow officers.

Assigned to Libya in February 1941 to head the newly formed Afrika Korps, Rommel was ordered to stay on the defensive. Instead he launched an attack on the British protectorate of Egypt. Though he won ground and frightened the Commonwealth, he captured no major ports or key cities. He managed, however, to waste fuel and equipment earmarked for the impending invasion of Russia. Upon hearing of Rommel's escapade, chief of staff Franz Halder fumed that Rommel had gone "stark mad."[73]

Eventually beaten back to Libya, Rommel at least captured its vital port of Tobruk (after four bloody attempts), which strengthened his supply line from Italy and Germany. Instructed to remain there, he headed eastward again. In the summer and fall of 1942, he lost three successive battles, including SECOND EL ALAMEIN, which began while he was on sick leave. His withdrawal of one thousand miles west to Tunisia, though often described as "brilliant," saved only a fraction of his command. It was also the longest continuous retreat in German military history up to that time.

Later scoring a modest victory against inexperienced U.S. and French troops at Kasserine Pass along the Algeria–Tunisia border, he failed to coordinate with fellow commander Gen. Hans Jürgen von Arnim and lost the initiative. He returned to Germany, but his troops could not follow. Rommel's desert adventures compromised Axis strength in the Mediterranean, leaving no viable route for evacuation. The Axis subsequently surrendered more men in Tunisia (two hundred thousand) than at STALINGRAD (ninety-one thousand).[74]

Later in 1943, while his cohorts fought for their lives on the eastern front, Rommel transferred to quiet northern France, where he wasted time and resources on the tactically futile ATLANTIC WALL. In 1944, when INTELLIGENCE and climactic conditions indicated a May–June window for an Allied invasion, he left for Germany to visit his wife on her birthday—June 6, 1944.

Overall, German historians think little of Rommel. His reputation stands high in the West partially because he was stationed in the West. Except for a brief staff job in the invasion of Poland, he served in France and Africa, where he initially faced green troops and commanders who vaunted his "brilliance" rather than admit to their own shortcomings. Rommel vaingloriously augmented his inflated status by courting journalists and photographers throughout his tenure.[75]

Time and again Rommel's reputation remained intact because, in truly critical moments, he was usually absent. He also took leave of another important event. Conspirators asked him many times to support the July 1944 bomb plot against Hitler. But contrary to legend, Rommel strongly opposed murdering his Führer.[76]

Constantly paired with U.S. Gen. George S. Patton Jr., the two never met in battle. Rommel left Tunisia, Italy, and France before his armies engaged Patton's.

---

8. JEAN FRANCOIS DARLAN (FRANCE, 1881–1942)

An American officer described J. Francois Darlan as "a short, bald-headed, pink-faced, needle-nosed, sharp-chinned little weasel." Still,

the French admiral could be reduced to a single word: indecisive.[77]

Chief of the navy at the time of France's surrender, Darlan initially hinted that he would enjoin his fleet, the fourth largest in the world, to the Allies. He instead sent his European-based vessels to French colonial North Africa. Britain retaliated by bombarding the warships on the Algerian coast, sinking the battleship *Dunkerque* and killing more than a thousand sailors.

Infuriated, Darlan forged closer French relations with the Third Reich. For a time he favored German victory, which he believed would enable France to control the oceans and overtake the British Empire. For his work, Darlan was promoted to commander in chief of Vichy's armed forces.

Darlan was in Algiers in November 1942 when the Allies invaded, and he ordered French troops to fight back. When American envoys arrested him two days later, Darlan denied having any military authority. After further negotiations, he relented and ordered his men to cease fire. But when he heard that the Vichy government was angered by his capitulation, Darlan announced a resumption of the fighting. Twenty-four hours later, when Germany invaded southern France, Darlan hinted he would help the Allies.[78]

Weathering these bizarre U-turns from his headquarters in Gibraltar, the normally patient DWIGHT D. EISENHOWER finally cracked. "What I need around here," seethed Ike, "is a damned good assassin." Eisenhower's offhanded wish came true. For unknown reasons, an obscure young Frenchman visited Darlan at his palatial Algiers office on Christmas Eve, 1942, and shot him dead.[79]

Darlan's family had a legacy of contesting Britain. His great-grandfather was killed by the British in the battle of Trafalgar.

---

9. WILHELM KEITEL (GERMANY, 1882–1946)

A competent staff officer with no particularly outstanding qualities or achievements, Wilhelm Keitel was as surprised as anyone when he was

promoted in 1938 to chief of staff of the high command of Germany's armed forces, in charge of all military strategy. In an instant, he had become the second-highest-ranking member of the German general staff, right below der Führer.

Whatever latent talents Keitel possessed remained in hibernation, as he quickly became Hitler's most blindly loyal servant. So repugnant were his kowtowing antics, other officers began to call him "Laikeitel"—a German play on the word "lackey."

But this lackey simultaneously protected Hitler from voices of dissension and crushed morale and communication among Germany's high command. Between stroking his leader's confidence, he occasionally informed Hitler of "defeatist" voices among general officers.

On one instance he demurred. When Hitler expressed a desire to invade the Soviet Union in 1940, the normally spineless Keitel criticized the idea. Troops were too entrenched in France. Necessary tanks, planes, and winter gear were not available. The attack would have to happen early in the spring to avoid the Russian winter. Yet when the same conditions applied the following summer, Keitel succumbed to Hitler's bidding and enthusiastically supported the invasion.[80]

Though the field marshal often neglected to stand up for his military, he found time to initiate atrocities in the name of his boss. He endorsed the shooting of captured Soviet political commissars, authorized SS extermination programs, and ordered civilians to murder downed Allied airmen. "Any act of mercy," he insisted, "is a crime against the German people."[81]

Found guilty in Nuremberg of crimes against peace, war crimes, crimes of international conspiracy, and crimes against humanity, Keitel was executed in 1946.

At Nuremberg, Wilhelm Keitel requested to be shot, as it was the proper method of execution for officers. They hanged him.

---

10. MUTAGUCHI RENYA (JAPAN, 1888–1966)

"I started off the Marco Polo Incident, which broadened out into the China Incident, and then expanded until it turned into the Great East Asian War." Humility was not a strongpoint of Japan's Lt. Gen. Mutaguchi Renya. Neither were patience, foresight, troops, morale, matters of supply, etc. And it is entirely possible his regiment did initiate the CHINA INCIDENT in 1937. Mutaguchi was one of the more rabid officers of Japan's rogue Kwantung Army in Manchuria.[82]

Later, at the head of a division, he performed admirably in the

February 1942 conquest of SINGAPORE. But at the time he was under the guidance of the cunning and reliable general Yamashita Tomoyuki.

When he was later promoted to lead the Fifteenth Army in Burma, Mutaguchi did not fare so well. Tokyo directed him to hold the country, the only viable land avenue between India and China as well as a producer of rice and petroleum. At first he complied, but then he began to harbor dreams of great conquest. Eying India, he believed a thrust into the subcontinent would inspire a domestic uprising against British rule. If India fell, perhaps Britain itself would be shaken to its core and sue for peace.

Given approval to mount a modest advance across the border, Mutaguchi aimed for the British base at Imphal, a heavily defended city reachable only through fast rivers, dense jungle, and rugged mountains. With 155,000 troops and 20,000 draft animals, he headed west with a minimal amount of food, medicine, and ammunition. The whole operation, thought Mutaguchi, would take about two weeks.[83]

Four months later, his troops wandered back, defeated by privation and dissension as much as by the Indians and British. All of the pack animals were lost or eaten, and a third of his force was dead. Then the monsoons came. Beaten men, too exhausted to march on, fell in the mud and drowned. Maggots swarmed in the wounds of the living and the dead. Some men ate grass to stay alive; others begged for grenades to end their torment. In all, 65,000 died.

In losing his troops in India, the routed Mutaguchi also lost his ability to hold onto Burma, which in turn lost his empire's hold on southern Asia. For the ignominious failure, the general placed all the blame on his subordinates.[84]

His India adventure was arguably the worst defeat in the history of the Japanese army. Yet instead of being tried or demoted for his actions, Mutaguchi Renya was transferred to Tokyo and promoted to the army general staff.

MILITARY BLUNDERS

Yesterday's battle is tomorrow's board game. Too often the present views the past with an air of condescension. This is especially true concerning the treatment of command decisions in the Second World War.

Of course, later observers see the war from a comfortable vantage point, armed with benefits their objects of study did not enjoy: plentiful information, ample time to contemplate options, freedom from danger, and foreknowledge of results. Judging a decision is easier than making one, especially when armies and countries are at risk.

Still, leaders and commanders made a number of bumbling mistakes during the war, decisions from which their enemies benefited greatly. These blunders usually emanated from one of four factors: ego, shortsightedness, wishful thinking, or panic. These are human traits to be sure, but they often resulted in needless loss of life and destruction. Listed here are the worst strategic and tactical failures conducted between 1937 and 1945, ranked by time, resources, morale, and lives wasted. Probably none of them changed the war's final outcome, but all significantly altered its course and duration.

1. THE ATLANTIC WALL
(GERMANY'S COASTAL DEFENSES, 1942–44)

From Denmark to Spain, pressed tight against the meandering Atlantic coastline, stood the wall to Hitler's Fortress Europe: bunkers, trenches, pillboxes, siege guns, machine-gun nests, barbed wire, thousands of antitank and antiship obstacles, and five million mines. The defensive perimeter ran more than seventeen hundred miles, equivalent to the distance from Boston to Denver. It required three years and half a million workers to erect, and it was the largest construction project ever attempted since the Great Wall of China. It was also almost completely useless.[85]

Poland attempted to defend its entire thousand-mile western border in 1939, only to have Germany abruptly puncture the line in a matter of hours. History repeated itself eight months later when Germany made a mockery of French border fortifications, easily going around or over supposedly impregnable defenses of the Maginot Line. Strange that the chief advocate of the Atlantic Wall, IRWIN ROMMEL, had personally taken part in these two invasions and never made the connection.

Placed in charge of the Atlantic Wall in late 1943, Rommel accelerated construction and demanded more infantry, artillery, and nearly every available tank in the western theater. His commanding officer, Field Marshal Gerd von Rundstedt, advocated keeping forces farther back, waiting for a landing point to become known, and then smashing the invasion with a concentrated counterattack. Precedent favored von Rundstedt. When defenders employed focused counterattacks, invasions were almost always contained, as demonstrated by the Greeks against the Italians in 1940 and the Germans against the Allies at Anzio in 1943. Hitler ordered a blending of Rommel's and Rundstedt's strategies, allowing Rommel's expansion plan to continue. The bastions rapidly grew, as did their insatiable appetite for resources the Third Reich could not spare.[86]

Judgment day came with the invasion of NORMANDY. The Allies

broke through the wall at its strongest point in less than ten hours, turning the entire immobile, expensive wall into one giant relic.[87]

Huge coastal guns along the Atlantic Wall—expensive, inadequate, and immobile.

From 1942 to 1944, Nazi engineers used twice as much concrete to fortify the Atlantic Wall as they used to build factories, air bases, submarine pens, and oil-storage facilities combined.

2. STALIN'S STUNNED SILENCE (OPERATION BARBAROSSA, JUNE 1941)

A furious Gen. Ivan Boldin screamed into the telephone, "Cities are burning and people are dying!" The deputy commander of the Western Military District begged Moscow for orders in the first horrific hours of the German invasion. More than three million German soldiers, plus another million from supporting nationalities, were rolling eastward, demolishing airfields, towns, and divisions at will. Stationed far from the chaos, the voice on the other line responded to Boldin with cold detachment: "I am informing you…comrade Stalin has not authorized artillery fire against the Germans."[88]

At the time, Stalin refused to authorize much of anything. After a few days in Moscow, hearing report after disastrous report from the front, he retired to one of his country villas outside the capital. Those close to him suspected he had suffered a nervous breakdown, as he somehow believed the largest invasion in world history was just a ruse, concocted by a rogue Nazi general—or more likely, Winston Churchill—to trick the Soviets into attacking Germany.[89]

A week passed before Stalin returned full-time to the Kremlin, and nearly another week went by before he addressed his people by radio, commanding them to stand firm. In those two weeks, his air force lost half its planes, most while on the ground, and his army lost nearly a million men (killed, wounded, or captured) of its five million total. The invasion had sliced deep into Stalin's domain, two hundred miles in places, and showed no signs of slowing.

Certainly the Soviet armed forces in 1941 were not well trained or equipped. The Red Army as a whole lacked cohesion and morale and had undergone a devastating purge that killed or jailed nearly every senior officer during the later 1930s. But whatever potential the Soviet defenses had in June 1941 was severely and almost fatally compromised because of one man's terrible and terrified hesitation. The lost territory would be won back, but not until three years had passed.

While Stalin brooded over conspiracy theories, his Red Army stood virtually helpless against the largest invasion in history.

Germany attacked the Soviet Union with 170 divisions. Soviet postwar history books later inflated this to 208 divisions.

3. CHIANG DROWNS HIS OWN PEOPLE (YELLOW RIVER, CHINA, JUNE 1938)

The three-thousand-mile-long Hwang Ho, or Yellow River, was also known as "China's Sorrow." Over the centuries, the mainland artery had burst time and time again, flooding the vast east central plains, killing thousands and occasionally millions of people. In an ongoing effort to cure the problem, the Chinese constructed stalwart dikes hundreds of miles long to nurse the staggering, murky Yellow River eastward into its namesake sea.[90]

In 1938, China was undergoing an altogether new sorrow. Driving south from Manchuria, armed with tanks, bombers, and artillery, Japanese Imperial forces appeared as if they could drive through to Indochina and cut China in half. To stop them, Generalissimo CHIANG KAI-SHEK ordered the severing of the Yellow River dikes. None of the residents in the doomed flood plains were warned ahead of time.[91]

Witnesses described a storm of mud and water heading south and east. Crops, buildings, homes, roads, and wells were soon buried under a great swath of liquid earth. An estimated six million became homeless. The number of drowning victims was never determined.[92]

Flooding did slow the Japanese, but only temporarily. Far greater was the lasting damage rendered upon the Chinese. Along with eleven major cities and four thousand villages, precious farmland was destroyed and remained unusable for years. Widespread famine ensued, killing exponentially more than the actual flooding and earning Chiang millions of lifelong enemies.[93]

As a result of the flood, the Yellow River changed its course by 250 miles, the equivalent of having the Mississippi River sweep over to the Alabama-Georgia border and out through the panhandle of Florida.

4. HITLER'S SIXTH ARMY SACRIFICE
(BATTLE OF STALINGRAD, NOVEMBER 1942–FEBRUARY 1943)

Soon after hearing of Rommel's crippling defeat at SECOND EL ALAMEIN, Hitler received intelligence of an even greater crisis. Soviet forces, during a frigid and whirling blizzard in late November 1942, launched major counterattacks north and south of STALINGRAD, threatening to encircle Gen. Friedrich von Paulus and 250,000 soldiers of the Sixth Army.

Sentenced to die at Stalingrad, the German Sixth Army paid the ultimate price for its leader's hubris.

Fixated on holding the city, Hitler adamantly refused withdrawal. Three days later the two claws of the Red Army closed forty miles west of Paulus and began to curl inward. As Soviet artillery rained down on the German, Romanian, Italian, and Hungarian troops, pockets of Russians still within the city chewed away at Hitler's men like a cancer. Adding to the misery, temperatures fell below freezing. Immediately Paulus started to run low on ammunition, medical supplies, and food. HERMANN GÖRING assured Hitler his Luftwaffe could supply Paulus from the air. Instead, a lack of planes and landing sites, the relentless weather, and Göring's ineptitude assured failure. The army did not receive a tenth of the supplies it needed.

Twice the Soviets offered surrender terms. Twice Hitler ordered Paulus to refuse, demanding he fight to the last man for "the salvation of the Western world." Hitler even promoted Paulus to field marshal, knowing that never in history had a German of that rank ever been taken alive. Nonetheless, after months of cruel fighting, Paulus capitulated, and Hitler lost all of an army that could have been saved.[94]

The German Sixth Army started the Soviet campaign with 285,000 men. After Stalingrad, it numbered 91,000. After years of imprisonment, only 5,000 members survived to return to Germany.

---

5. THE UNTOUCHED OIL TANKS (PEARL HARBOR, DECEMBER 7, 1941)

In the attack on PEARL HARBOR, the Japanese lost just twenty-nine planes and five midget submarines. They destroyed seven battleships, three cruisers, three destroyers, and more than three hundred aircraft. But they missed one huge, vital target.

Opposite Battleship Row, adjacent to the submarine pens and main naval station, sat two sprawling fields of oil tanks, the sole cache of lifeblood for every Corsair and carrier in the U.S. Pacific Fleet. Every drop had to be transported from California, more than two thousand miles away. And every three-story storage tank was vulnerable to .50-caliber bullets.

Big, full, and overlooked oil tanks skirt the water's edge at Pearl Harbor.

Technically, the oversight was not the fault of the Japanese dive bombers and fighters. Responsibility rested with the usually meticulous

Adm. Yamamoto Isoroku, architect of the assault. He had simply failed to include the hillside of oil tanks in his list of primary targets.[95]

To what precise extent the damaged reservoirs and lost fuel might have hindered the U.S. war effort cannot be determined, but an authority on naval operations suggested the effect would have been considerable. By his estimation, Adm. CHESTER NIMITZ calculated that the loss of the PEARL HARBOR oil field "would have prolonged the war another two years."[96]

Japan attacked Pearl Harbor in retaliation for something that happened on August 1, 1941. To curb Imperial aggression, President Franklin Roosevelt imposed a total oil embargo on the empire.

---

6. OPERATION MARKET-GARDEN (HOLLAND, SEPTEMBER 17–25, 1944)

The Allies had stalled along Germany's western border, but Field Marshal Bernard Montgomery convinced Gen. DWIGHT EISENHOWER to try a radical solution: push north into occupied Holland, then east into the industrial heart of Germany, then on to Berlin. The plan would secure the Belgian port of Antwerp and shorten Allied supply lines by hundreds of miles, avoid Nazi fortifications in the Siegfried Line (a.k.a. the West Wall), and, if all fared well, end the war by Christmas.[97]

Though the premise was tempting, the specifics left much to be desired. Crossing Holland meant traversing a myriad of canals, streams, and rivers, the last being the deep and expansive Rhine. No fewer than nine bridges had to be secured behind enemy lines. To do this, Monty proposed airdropping the U.S. 101st and 82nd, the Polish 1st, and the British 1st Airborne Divisions to secure the bridges while the British Armored Thirty Corps attacked northward and covered seventy miles to link them all up.

Adding to the challenge, the Allies did not have enough planes to carry all the paratroopers at once, radio equipment was inadequate and faulty, and Thirty Corps had but one narrow road that could handle the weight of its twenty thousand vehicles. In addition, intelligence reports gave conclusive evidence of German heavy armor units deployed where the Allied attack was most vulnerable—along the Rhine.[98]

Soon after it started, the operation unraveled. Thirty Corps planned to make thirty-six miles on the first day. Caught in a series of firefights, it advanced only six. Radios failed. Fog rolled in and delayed supporting airdrops for days, leaving paratroopers without supplies and reinforcements. German resistance was tougher than expected around every bridgehead, especially at ARNHEM, where the 1st Polish and 1st British Airborne were nearly wiped out in less than a week. The Allies had achieved little more than moving sideways along the border of the Reich at a cost of more than ten thousand casualties. Stopped cold in Holland, the Allies would not cross the Rhine until March of the following year.[99]

Bird's-eye view of Arnhem bridge. Reconnaissance photos and reports also showed the presence of German armor, but Allied planners went ahead with the attack.

The Allies lost more soldiers in Operation Market-Garden than they lost in the first week of the Normandy invasion.

7. BLITZKRIEG STRIKES TWICE
(BATTLE OF THE BULGE, DECEMBER 16, 1944)

During April 1940, from Switzerland to the North Sea, French and Belgian defenses deployed to withstand a German offensive. Fortresses, batteries, men, and armor were at the ready—everywhere except directly in the middle, west of the ARDENNES. Topographically, the minimalist treatment seemed logical. Densely forested, the ARDENNES was also the only area in all the Low Countries dominated by steep hills and deep basins through which only a few narrow roads passed. To practically every observer, it seemed to be a natural barrier.[100]

A GI guards German prisoners near Bastogne. He was a lucky survivor in a battle that cost sixty thousand American casualties.

Adjacent to this region, France placed nine divisions, or about a tenth of its army. Through this area, in May 1940, Germany thrust forty-five divisions, taking France and much of the Western world by surprise.

By November 1944, the Allies had returned to the German border with three massive army groups. But in the middle, in the "impassible" ARDENNES, the United States had just six divisions. On December 16, 1944, twenty-five German divisions came barreling through.

The Allies responded rather brilliantly once the attack began. Eisenhower treated the battle as an opportunity, and Patton rapidly counterattacked from the south. The tenacious fight offered by frontline and reserve troops all prevented a grave mistake from turning into disaster. The price for initial indiscretion was, however, exceedingly high, especially for the Americans. Hitler's 1944 Ardennes offensive killed more U.S. soldiers than any other battle in the war.[101]

The U.S. lost more men in the Battle of the Bulge than at Pearl Harbor, Midway, D-day, and Iwo Jima combined.

---

8. THE INVASION TEST
(DIEPPE, FRANCE, AUGUST 19, 1942)

Barely hanging on against the bulk of the German army, Soviet leaders became incensed by London's vacillation on opening a second front in Europe. American military and public opinion also clamored for action. To satisfy their allies, Churchill and company presented an offering. In the summer of 1942, ten thousand troops would land in northern France and establish a beachhead for future operations. This was later scaled down to six thousand troops to perform a brief "reconnaissance in force" at the port city of Dieppe.

In the planning phase, information on enemy strength was sketchy. Adequate landing vehicles were not available. Sheer cliffs one hundred feet high dominated the landing zones. The area would not be bombed beforehand. Dismayed, Gen. Bernard Montgomery recommended canceling the operation indefinitely. But a youthful, glory-hunting vice admiral, Louis Mountbatten, personally adopted the project. Impressing Churchill with his vigor, Mountbatten was allowed to proceed with the raid.[102]

Approaching the French coastline at 3:00 a.m. on August 19, 1942, the armada of eight destroyers and scores of landing vessels, shepherded by hundreds of fighter planes, lost the vital element of surprise when a German patrol convoy spotted their advance. Rushing to hit the shoreline, landing craft arrived in the wrong places at the wrong times. Previously undetected German batteries slaughtered advancing columns while Luftwaffe and infantry poured into the area. It took only six hours for the British operation to fail completely.

From an invasion force of 6,000, the losses were 3,369 killed, wounded, or captured, most of them Canadian. The Royal Navy lost an additional 550 men plus one destroyer and more than thirty smaller ships. More than one hundred RAF fighters fell from the sky. The defenders lost less than half their planes and a sixth of their men and began to redouble their defenses for the larger invasion to come.[103]

If anything, the tragedy of Dieppe provided an opportunity for heroics. Chaplain Maj. John Foote carried thirty wounded men to rescue ships, then swam back to be with his regiment as it entered captivity.

---

9. GERMANY'S GIANTS (NAZI LARGE WEAPONS PROGRAM, 1937–44)

Along with some of the most effective designs in trucks and artillery, Hitler's arsenal also included a cast of the big and bizarre, none of which worked well, unless their purpose was to devour materials, money, and manpower.

From his experience in World War I, Hitler respected the destructive effect of artillery. Figuring bigger was better, he endorsed production of a colossal rail howitzer christened the "Gustav Gun," or as its crews dubbed it, "Big Dora." Weighing nearly fifteen hundred tons and measuring fifty yards in length, it could only be moved in pieces and on two parallel railroad tracks. Assembly required two more adjacent tracks for cranes. Big Dora took five hundred men to load and fire, plus nearly a division to maintain. The entire contraption, used sparingly in the capture of Sevastopol and against Warsaw, was comically inaccurate and profoundly ineffective.[104]

Another überhowitzer was the V–3, a cannon 170 yards long, designed to shell London from Continental Europe. Hitler ordered fifty, each to be buried within the French coastal limestone, their exposed muzzles aiming directly at the British capital. Testing was a failure. Shells fell short, the goliath barrels cracked and exploded during firing, and the complex subterranean bunkers were never fully completed. But twenty-five thousand shells were made, and thousands of technicians and artillerists worked on the project for a year before Allied bombers and demolition experts entombed the guns and bunkers under a blanket of rubble.[105]

Good props for shooting photos but not for much else, the Third Reich's mammoth railroad guns never justified their consumption of resources.

Not to be outdone, the Luftwaffe failed to develop an adequate four-engine bomber program but did create a six-engine lumbering behemoth made to span the Atlantic and bomb New York, which it never did. German engineers also produced a tank that weighed 180 tons (the workhorse Sherman tank weighed a fifth as much). Slow and costly, with a fickle transmission and engines to match, the tank was too wide and heavy for nearly every road in Europe, and it served as solid proof that the leaders of the thousand-year Reich were not adept at thinking ahead.[106]

Among the designers working on Germany's supertanks was a Mercedes engineer who also helped develop the Volkswagen: Ferdinand Porsche.

10. MUSSOLINI'S BALKAN EXCURSION (ITALY INVADES GREECE, OCTOBER 28, 1940)

Benito Mussolini became envious of (and definitely overshadowed by) Hitler's lightning successes in Poland, Scandinavia, Belgium, Holland, Luxembourg, France, and Romania. In comparison, il Duce's

Continental empire began and ended with Albania. Aspiring to greater conquests, he targeted Greece, a politically fragmented country, albeit a good source of olive oil and only one-fifth the size of Italy.

Expecting an easy victory, he ordered a demobilization of nearly half his army just two weeks before the invasion. Claiming to have planned out every detail, he had obviously missed a few. Most of the troops assembled for the invasion were barely trained and very inexperienced. His estimate of Greek army strength was low—by a factor of ten. Greece's mountainous terrain apparently was not taken into account, nor was its impending winter weather. Yet there was little opposition to the plan, mostly because Mussolini neglected to inform Hitler, his own air force, and his own navy of the operation until a few days before it was set to begin.[107]

Not only did the attack fail, but the Greek army also pursued Mussolini's paltry force of seventy thousand back into Albania. Mussolini later added four hundred thousand troops to the effort with no positive effect. In the face of such blatant ineptitude, an Italian public began to turn against the dictator. The following year, an angered but sympathetic Hitler invaded Greece for Mussolini and, in doing so, may have fatally delayed the invasion of the Soviet Union.

Hours before he killed himself, Hitler reflected on the great catastrophes that plagued his reign. Among the failures he listed was Mussolini's "useless campaign against Greece."[108]

HEROINES

It is said that wars are man-made. Whether warfare is a natural pursuit of either gender is debatable, but women were involved in every arena of World War II.

Most nations discouraged women from joining the service until the totality of war dictated otherwise. Eventually one out of fifty Americans in uniform was female. In Poland the ratio was one in twelve, and in Britain one in ten. Unlike their male counterparts, most women served in noncombat roles, a point emphasized by recruiting slogans. American naval auxiliary posters read, "Enlist in the Waves, Release a Man to Fight at Sea." In nearly every culture, the order was, "Be the woman behind the man behind the gun." Even in the Soviet Union, where by necessity nearly a half-million women served in combat, the initial battle cry was "men to the front, women to the home front."[109]

Guerrilla warfare offered greater opportunity for frontline work. Conservatively, 10 percent of underground combat units in France, Italy, and Yugoslavia were women. Fifteen percent in Russia and Poland were female. Directly involved in the fighting, their losses mounted accordingly. While the U.S. Army lost sixteen female nurses killed in action, Yugoslavia lost nearly ten thousand woman partisans, approximately one out of every four who served.[110]

Behind the lines, women were the backbone of aid societies, such as the International Red Cross, Women's Volunteer Service of Britain, and the Greater Japan Women's Association. Most prevalent was the female presence in the work force. "Rosie the Riveter" symbolized a doubling of American women in factories. By 1945 36 percent of the American labor pool was female, 37 percent in Britain, and 50 percent in Germany and the Soviet Union.[111]

Regardless of the degree of service, official recognition was not forthcoming. In 1944, France awarded the Compagnon de la Libération medal to 1,057 individuals, only 6 of whom were female. Germany granted tens of thousands of Iron Crosses throughout the war, with a paltry 29 going to women. America's 100,000 WAVES (Women Accepted for Volunteer Emergency Service) would not receive veterans benefits until 1977.[112]

Many risked their lives, but few achieved widespread influence and adoration in the service of their country. Listed here are ten exceptions. They are just ten out of some half-billion women who persevered through the largest and bloodiest of wars yet "made by man."

1. ELEANOR ROOSEVELT (U.S., 1884–1962)

The "First Lady of the World," Eleanor Roosevelt utilized her unique station, sharp intellect, unbendable will, and the modern media to be-

come the most visible woman on the globe and arguably the most influential female in the Western Hemisphere since Catherine the Great.

Venomous to the corrupted, altruistic to the downtrodden, intense, vocal, and uncompromising, Eleanor Roosevelt was an idealist driven to action. She was the first wife of a president to hold press conferences, write syndicated columns, and speak regularly on radio, "fighting for democracy at home" when the pressures of war threatened to reverse social gains. She unsuccessfully protested the internment of Japanese Americans and lobbied for granting visas to European Jews. In the name of equality and the war effort, she successfully lobbied for increases in the number of women in the workplace and African Americans in the military.[113]

Though she intensely hated to travel, Roosevelt flew to Britain and the South Pacific during the war, often in rickety bombers, to speak with dignitaries, address civilians, and visit the sick and wounded in uniform. In one month she managed to traverse twenty-five thousand miles.

Her brash and relentless character offended many, including white conservative southerners, anti–New Deal Republicans, and a fair number of women. But others grew to revere her, particularly minorities, British civilians, and American servicemen. Accompanying her on a hospital tour in Guadalcanal, the stoic Adm. William "Bull" Halsey marveled at her determination and tenderness and greatly respected the way "she went into every ward, stopped at every bed, and spoke to every patient." Winston Churchill said she had "a spirit of steel and a heart of gold." Joseph Goebbels, angered by her popularity and influence, forbade German papers to write about her.[114]

Immediately after the war, at the insistence of President Truman, Eleanor Roosevelt became a U.S. delegate to the United Nations.

While visiting wounded soldiers at Walter Reed Hospital, Eleanor Roosevelt came upon a young man severely burned while fighting in North Africa. He mentioned he played the piano. To encourage him, Mrs. Roosevelt said he could practice on the Steinway in the White House, which he did for a year, and he recovered.

---

2. MARINA RASKOVA (USSR, 1912–43)

Soviet Aviation Group 122 consisted of standard-issue bombers, fighters, uniforms, and equipment. Formed in late 1941, there was little to distinguish the group from any other air-combat unit in the war, except that nearly all of its pilots, mechanics, navigators, and support personnel were women, assembled under the leadership of Marina Raskova.[115]

The first professional female navigator in the Soviet Union, Raskova was a famous endurance pilot before the war and became an air force officer. The young and cheerful Raskova also knew Stalin, which enabled her, in the face of much social and professional opposition, to demand and lead the formation of a female air-combat unit.[116]

Diligent, inspiring, and practically inexhaustible, for nearly a year she trained what would become three air regiments within the group: the 586th Fighter, 125th Dive Bomber, and 46th Night Bomber. Altogether, the thirty-year-old managed hundreds of officers and enlisted, but she never lived to see combat.

In late 1942 Moscow assigned Raskova's 125th Dive Bomber Regiment to STALINGRAD at the height of the winter battle. Piloting one of the regiment's twin-engine Pe-2s, Raskova and three crew members flew to the front when a sudden blizzard engulfed them. Facing thrashing winds and falling darkness, she attempted to land in an open field and crashed, killing everyone on board.[117]

Testament to her leverage and inspiration, her body was interned in Red Square. Streets, schools, village centers, and newborns were named after her. Not surprisingly, Raskova's group went on to fight with distinction. From 1942 to the war's termination, the group logged thirty thousand sorties, two of her fighter pilots attained the status of ace, and her night-bomber regiment fought in the battle of BERLIN.[118]

During the war, thirty-three women flyers received the highest decoration, "Hero of the Soviet Union." All but three of them were in Raskova's Aviation Group 122.

---

3. YVONNE NÈVEJEAN (BELGIUM, 1900–1987)

Famed Moravian Oskar Schindler rescued more than twelve hundred Jews from the Holocaust. Lesser-known Belgian Yvonne Nèvejean spared more than four thousand, mostly children.

She was head of the Oeuvre Nationale de l'Enfance (National Agency for Children) and directed the state-sponsored children's homes

 throughout her country. As the SS began to round up and export Belgium's sixty-five thousand Jews in 1942, the nation's underground Jewish Defense Committee turned to Nèvejean for assistance. When asked to help children who had become orphaned or separated from their parents, Nèvejean vowed to save any child and immediately employed her agency to that end.

As the JDC found children for rescue, Nèvejean dispatched social workers and nurses to pick them up. Housing her charges in state facilities, she worked tirelessly to find permanent homes for all, either with foster families or Christian organizations. To pay for the operation, she collected funds from the JDC, banks, private donors, and the exiled Belgian government in London. She and her assistants also gathered food, medicine, clothes, ration books, and forged documents.[119]

On one occasion, the Gestapo raided a children's home in Wezembeek, seized a number of Jewish children and adults, and transported them to Mechelen camp, a train embarkation point for AUSCHWITZ. Nèvejean hurriedly contacted Belgium's Queen Mother Elisabeth and, with the help of the national department of justice, negotiated the release of all the detainees.[120]

Over the course of two years, Nèvejean and her associates saved approximately a quarter of Belgium's Jewish population below the age of ten, known thereafter as "Yvonne's Children."

Yvonne Nèvejean's rescue of the children from Mechelen was a miraculous achievement. Of the 26,500 Jews deported from the camp, only some 500 are known to have lived.

4. LUDMILA PAVLICHENKO (USSR, 1916–74)

Tiny, bitter, and blunt, Sgt. Mila Pavlichenko was one of the most prolific sharpshooters in the Red Army and a legend on the eastern

front. Her fellow Soviets called her the "Death Sniper." To the Germans she was the "Bolshevik Valkyrie," killing with impunity in her native Ukraine and Crimea. During the 1941 siege of Odessa alone, she allegedly tallied more than 180 kills.

Wounded four times and losing her husband in combat, she desired to kill as many Germans as possible. But as news of her exploits reached Moscow, Soviet officials decided to use her in a different capacity. They promoted her to lieutenant, made her the subject of a documentary, and in 1942 sent her on a speaking tour. In Canada, England, Wales, and the United States, she regaled audiences with stories of her assassinations and lectured them on the need for a second front in Europe. She met with students, factory workers, Ukrainian-American groups, and was one of the first Soviets ever to be invited to the White House, a personal guest of ELEANOR ROOSEVELT.[121]

When telling audiences of her daring occupation, she recalled one incident most often. Near the city of Sevastopol, she became locked in a duel against an opposing sniper that lasted nearly two days. After finally getting in the last and fatal shot, she investigated her prey and found a booklet containing a tally of more than four hundred kills. One version of the story contends the ledger read "Dunkirk." Whether this was added to stir the emotions of British audiences is unknown.

What could be confirmed was her own incredible total. In her brief but prolific career, Pavlichenko was credited with 309 enemy fatalities.[122]

According to Soviet records, female snipers of the Red Army scored more than eleven thousand kills during the Second World War.

5. GISI FLEISCHMANN (SLOVAKIA, 1897–1944)

A diehard Zionist working for the Jewish Center of Slovakia before the war, Gisi Fleischmann was in charge of arranging emigrations to

Palestine. As Hitler's power grew, she knew enough to send her two children to the British mandate, but she repeatedly refused to go herself. Instead she spent the rest of her short life saving others.

In the spring of 1942, as the SS began wholesale roundups, extraditions, and executions of the Continent's Jews, Fleischmann and others formed a clandestine rescue operation code-named "Working Group." Members of the underground society decided to bribe regional Gestapo chief Dieter Wisliceny to stop the deportations. Fleischmann raised the ransom money through Jewish foundations in Geneva and New York and led the negotiations with Wisliceny. The attempt succeeded. From the fall of 1942 to the fall of 1944 extraditions effectively ceased in Slovakia.

Encouraged by their success, Working Group outlined a "Europa Plan," whereby the Third Reich would spare all Jews in exchange for money and goods shipped in from outside the Continent. While presenting the arrangement to Nazi authorities, Fleischmann was arrested and jailed for four months. After her release, she again refused to leave the country. In October 1944 the SS swept up nearly every member of the outfit, including Fleischmann. Taken on one of the last trains to reach AUSCHWITZ, she was pulled from the boxcars, sent directly to the chambers, and gassed.[123]

When she was deported to Auschwitz, Gisi Fleischmann was designated "R.U." for Rückkehr unerwünscht, meaning "Return undesirable."

---

6. YELENA FEDOROVNA KOLESOVA (USSR, 1917–42)

A Moscow grade school teacher, tall, athletic, Yelena Kolesova volunteered for military service immediately after the German invasion. Hastily trained in demolitions, Kolesova led a small group of female fighters behind enemy lines in November 1941. Over the course of nineteen days they set fire to buildings, conducted reconnaissance, and killed several German soldiers. For her initiative and courage, she received the Order of the Red Banner, the third-highest decoration available to Soviet citizens.[124]

In May 1942, she survived a behind-the-lines airdrop that killed three of her female compatriots. Undeterred, Kolesova proceeded with her diminished group. With the help of local civilians, she derailed trains, abducted enemy soldiers, and destroyed bridges. Germany offered thirty thousand Reichmarks (about seven thousand dollars in 1942) for her capture and estimated her unit to be six hundred strong, where in fact it only numbered a half dozen. She went on to receive the Order of Lenin, the highest decoration in the Soviet Union.[125]

On September 11, 1942, while leading an attack on a heavily defended German outpost in the town of Vydritsa, Kolesova charged a machine-gun nest and was torn apart by return fire.

Along with several schools and museums, avenues in four Russian cities bear the name Yelena Kolesova.

---

7. MARGARET BOURKE-WHITE (U.S., 1904–71)

She was the first woman editor of *Fortune* magazine, one of the first photographers from the West allowed into the Soviet Union, a founding member of *Life* magazine, and the only U.S. photographer in Moscow at the start of the German invasion. Not only did she break new ground and champion higher standards in a male-dominated industry, but she also risked her life to show the war to the United States.

After her return from the eastern front in 1942, she published a book titled *Shooting the Russian War* and sought assignment in the European theater. The first woman correspondent officially accredited  by the U.S. armed forces, she was also the first to accompany a B-17 crew on a bombing run. Bourke-White narrowly escaped death when a torpedo sank her ship off the coast of North Africa, only to follow U.S. troops through the mountains astride Naples and CASSINO. She then went with GEORGE S. PATTON's Third Army on its march through northern France.

Arguably her most revolutionary contribution to photojournalism occurred in the last days of the war, when she took part in the liberation of Buchenwald, a forced-labor camp in central Germany. Going against governmental censorship and an unwritten agreement among media members to suppress disturbing images, Bourke-White and *Life* magazine printed her photos of Buchenwald's emaciated and dying inmates. The images were the first graphic confirmation of Nazi concentration camps ever published for the American public.

Though a woman of many firsts, Margaret Bourke-White took the last known photograph of Mohandas Gandhi, just hours before he was assassinated in 1948.

---

8. MARIE-MADELEINE FOURCADE (FRANCE, 1909–89)

She was the only woman to head a major network of the French underground, a spy ring the Gestapo called "Noah's Ark" for the animal code names given to its operatives. Secretary to the Ark's founder, Marie Madeleine Fourcade (a.k.a. Hedgehog) took over when her boss was arrested in 1941. Under her direction, the network became the largest and most prolific civilian espionage system in Western Europe.

Positioned across France, at one time numbering more than three thousand operatives, her beasts of burden collected details on troop movements, bunker locations, unit strengths, and supply routes.

Information was then fed through a score of radio transmitters to the British Secret Intelligence Service. When maps, images, and volumes of material were collected, Fourcade arranged to have the RAF fly them out.[126]

Moles infiltrated the Ark on several occasions. Fourcade herself was arrested twice and escaped both times, once by squeezing through the window bars of a Gestapo holding cell. Every time the network collapsed, she rebuilt it. Though she and her network survived the war, more than five hundred of its operatives died along the way.[127]

In Paris is the Foundation of Memory and Hopes of Resistance at Place Marie-Madeleine Fourcade.

9. ANDRÉE DE JONGH (BELGIUM, 1916–2007)

Twenty-four-year-old Andrée De Jongh became furious when her country capitulated after only eighteen days of fighting. She vowed to

work for victory and set upon the idea to rescue Allied soldiers and airmen caught behind the lines. Creating a chain of safe houses in Belgium with her father, she laid the foundation for a network that would rescue some eight hundred military personnel.

In 1941, she and two accomplices smuggled a British airman out of Belgium. Andrée and her entourage proceeded through France, across the Pyrenees, and into Madrid. Meeting with British officials, she convinced them to support an underground railroad from Brussels to Gibraltar. The system was soon to be known affectionately as the "Comet Line." Fierce and untiring, she was dubbed "La Petit Cyclone" and "the Postman." De Jongh personally delivered 118 pilots, navigators, gunners, and engineers to safety, many of whom returned to the service.

In the course of their work, several conductors on the Comet Line were arrested and executed, including Andrée's father, Frederich. The Gestapo caught up with Andrée in January 1943 and sent her to prison in Paris. They later sent her to Ravensbrück concentration camp. She survived the internment and was liberated by Allied troops in April 1945. After the war, she worked as a nurse in impoverished areas of Africa.[128]

For creating the Comet Line and for her courageous work, Andrée De Jongh received the American Medal of Freedom and the George Cross (Britain's highest civilian decoration) and was made a Belgian countess.

10. HANNA REITSCH (GERMANY, 1912–79)

A natural-born flyer, Hanna Reitsch earned her pilot's license by age twenty. Impressing the public at air shows, she also broke distance and

altitude records. Before the war she had not particularly cared for the Nazi regime, going so far as to publicly criticize its ethnic policies. But the opportunity to fly the latest and fastest machines had her working as a test pilot for the Reich by 1938.

Weathering a number of crashes, she nearly died in a 1942 incident. She suffered a dislocated jaw, cracked vertebrae, and skull fractures but won much sympathy and attention from Hitler. After ten months of recuperation, Reitsch was again in the air, testing the Messerschmitt 163 rocket plane and a prototype of the V-1 buzz bomb.

She became a national icon, gracing the pages of newspapers and magazines. Far from the Nazi ideal of an obedient homemaker, Reitsch nonetheless served as a symbol of German courage and achievement, a status she did not take lightly. When Allied air raids and Soviet offensives began to tear into the German heartland, Reitsch approached Hitler and offered to lead a suicide mission, piloting modified V-1 rockets to key targets. He halfheartedly consented. Though nothing came of the idea, the gesture ensured her place as one of the last and most trusted members of Hitler's entourage. She would be one of the last people to see him alive.

In April 1945, as the Red Army stormed into the center of Berlin, Reitsch and Luftwaffe Gen. Robert Ritter von Greim flew through Soviet gunfire to reach the Chancellery bunker. Upon seeing his cherished pilot, Hitler exclaimed: "Brave woman! So there is still some loyalty and courage left in the world!" Yet the Führer refused her offer to fly him out of Berlin. She and von Greim left the bunker two days before Hitler's suicide.[129]

Arrested and detained after the war, Reitsch returned to condemning the Third Reich. Released after a year's incarceration, she toured the world, met Jawaharlal Nehru and John F. Kennedy, and set more flying records.[130]

Hanna Reitsch is the only woman in German history to receive both a second- and first-class Iron Cross.

TOP TEN

REASONS THE ALLIES WON

The old axiom "God is always on the side with the biggest battalions" has an appealing simplicity to it. But history is full of examples where the largest army did not prevail: the American Revolution, the Chinese Revolution, and the Korean War, to name a few.

Any event contains an interplay of infinite variables, as exemplified by the Second World War. Perhaps the best that can be done, when investigating why one side succeeded and the other failed, is to discern what the major differences were and determine which of those differences played a significant role in the progression of the conflict.

The following are ten key distinctions between the Allies and the Axis. Some were centuries old. Others were recent developments. By themselves, none could have swayed the war to its particular conclusion. In concert, however, these facets greatly affected the chances of the warring parties.

1. OBJECTIVES

Succinctly stated, the Axis had to conquer more than thirty countries while the Allies had to defeat three. Moreover, the Axis did not have a definitive endpoint to its military ambitions, whereas the Allies did.

Japan's "Greater East Asia Co-Prosperity Sphere," a weak attempt to define imperialism as "unity under one monarch," targeted Manchuria and China. But the sphere soon expanded to include Indochina, Burma, the Dutch East Indies, and the Philippines. Early success fostered dreams of incorporating Australia, India, and parts of North and South America. For Italy, il Duce dabbled with imperialism by fits and starts and momentarily believed he could conquer most of southern Europe. Part of Hitler's early success came from convincing his country and most of Europe that his goals were limited. But as demonstrated by invasions of Czechoslovakia, Poland, France, and the Soviet Union, Hitler's aims continually grew.

In contrast, starting in 1943, the Allies adopted the war aim of UNCONDITIONAL SURRENDER, vowing to cease fighting immediately after the governments of Germany, Italy, and Japan capitulated absolutely.

There had been much public criticism (which continues to the present) of the Allies' goal, arguing that unconditional surrender forced the Axis to fight to the death rather than negotiate, thereby elongating and intensifying the war unnecessarily. Though there is no way of knowing what any alternative plan may have produced, the Allies' aim was probably a productive move. First, allowing negotiations would have implied concessions. Negotiating certainly failed in the prewar era. In addition, there was little historical evidence that negotiations necessarily shortened any war or created much postwar stability, the Versailles debacle being only one example.

On the point of forcing the Axis to fight to the finish, both the Japanese and Germans were making public declarations of "annihilating the enemy" well before 1943. Events such as the Rape of Nanking and SS death squads on the eastern front suggested the Axis fought viciously, no matter what position the Allies took.

As for the Allies, unconditional surrender reduced the chance of any one government opting for a separate peace. It also gave soldiers and the home front a clear reason for their sacrifices and granted the Allied war effort a focus other approaches would not.

Franklin Roosevelt summed up the Allied objectives when he announced the capture of Rome: "One down. Two to go."

---

2. INDUSTRIAL CAPACITY

In a heavily mechanized war between industrialized countries, the Axis had the early edge. Against the rising power of Germany and the yet underdeveloped Italy, Great Britain probably could have stayed even in manufacturing. But with the freakish bond between Hitler and Stalin in the NAZI-SOVIET PACT, the British were clearly outmatched. Their detached partner, China, although home to four hundred million people, by 1939 had lost most of its factories and foundries, holding onto less heavy industry than Belgium.

Everything changed in 1941. Germany's assault on the Soviet

Union and Japan's attack on the United States swung the pendulum in favor of the Allies, uniting the globe's top three industrial powers against the Axis. In 1942 Britain produced nearly eight times the number of tanks as the Japanese, and the Soviets made ten thousand more aircraft than Nazi Germany. The United States alone manufactured more war materials than the entire Axis combined. In fact, the United States surpassed the Axis close to the time HERMANN GÖRING claimed Americans "could only produce cars and refrigerators."[131]

The Allies also practiced greater economy of effort compared to the Third Reich. As the Soviets concentrated on producing two basic kinds of tanks of relatively simple design, the Germans experimented with dozens of tank versions, making hundreds of prototypes and tinkering with thousands of modifications for each one. While Americans had the versatile jeep, Germans made one hundred dissimilar models of motorcycles. By the end of the war, Americans could produce fifteen B-17s in fewer man-hours than the Germans took to construct a single Tiger tank.[132]

U.S. production easily outpaced the whole of the Axis, demonstrated here by the efficient assembly line manufacture of B-17 bombers.

Of all the manufactured goods produced in the world in 1945, half were made in the United States.

3. COORDINATION BETWEEN COUNTRIES

Born out of propaganda from both the Allied and Axis camps, the image of a unified German-Italian-Japanese war machine contained marginal basis in fact. Aside from mutual hostility toward international

Communism and the British Empire, the three main Axis states shared little during the course of the war.

In the summer of 1939, while Japan fought the Soviet Union in a series of increasingly bloody battles along the Manchuria-Mongolia border, Hitler's foreign office secured the NAZI-SOVIET PACT. In 1941, weeks before Hitler planned to invade Russia, Japan agreed to a five-year Soviet-Japanese Neutrality Pact. Japan never signed the "Pact of Steel" agreement of mutual assistance penned in May 1939 between Germany and Italy.

It is also fair to say that the Allies had their own divisive issues. There were personality clashes, particularly between British commander Bernard Montgomery and almost everyone else. There were strategy disagreements, such as where and when to invade Western Europe. Yet the Allies generally coordinated their efforts through numerous military and political conferences, plus several major summit meetings including TEHRAN, YALTA, and Potsdam. Churchill himself traveled to four separate continents to confer with other heads of state. In contrast, Germany and Japan never conducted a single high-level exchange during the course of the war.

Indicating how little they communicated with each other on major issues, Imperial Japan viewed Hitler's invasion of the Soviet Union the same way Hitler viewed Japan's attack on Pearl Harbor—with complete and utter surprise.

---

4. ACCESS TO RAW MATERIALS

Within their peacetime borders the Axis possessed limited amounts of the materials needed to wage war. Italy led the world in the supply of mercury, used in detonating explosives. Germany was number one in the production of potash, which made fertilizer. Otherwise, resources were scarce.[133]

Among Axis leaders, this dearth in raw materials compounded a sense of vulnerability and added to the incentive for regional conquest. At the time, Malaya held almost half of the world's rubber supply and a quarter of its tin. Most titanium ore came from India or Norway. China and Burma owned the largest known deposits of tungsten, a vital alloy component of armor. France possessed considerable bauxite for aluminum production.

Most of the earth's coal, copper, lead, nickel, sulfur, and zinc were deep within Allied territories. In one resource the Allies were completely dominant, creating an expression among the Japanese: "A drop of petrol is a drop of blood."[134]

In 1940 the United States accounted for two of every three gallons of gasoline made in the world. Of the Axis, only Romania possessed a large number of wells, and the Germans had no efficient way to transport or process the oil the Romanians produced.[135]

When Japan's oil reserves began to run dry in 1943, the military greatly reduced pilots' training, making them easy targets against well-practiced Americans. By 1944 the Imperial Navy found itself disengaging or avoiding fights altogether for lack of fuel. For the Wehrmacht, worn-down tanks began to drink oil five times faster than before. In February 1945, the Luftwaffe had only enough aviation fuel to keep fighting at full capacity for two more weeks.[136]

By the end of the war, when the United States produced millions of barrels a day, Germany procured only a few thousand a week, most of it "synthetic oil" slowly and expensively extracted from coal. Japan began converting cars, buses, and ambulances to run on charcoal, and its military experimented with a fuel made of alcohol and turpentine.[137]

Petroleum haunted Axis leaders right to the end. The bodies of Mussolini and his mistress were hung upside down at a Milan gas station. Hitler wanted to be cremated after his suicide, but there was not enough fuel available to complete the job.

5. TECHNOLOGY

Initially behind on a number of engineering fronts, the Allies eventually attained superiority in aeronautics, radar, sonar, ballistics, medicine, nutrition, and radio communication. Among their innovations were the proximity fuse, demagnetized ship hulls, synthesized quinine, a predecessor to the computer, and thermonuclear weaponry. The Allies simply had more money, more engineers, and safer work facilities than the Axis.

In contrast, only Germany made significant strides in technology, some of which were revolutionary. Yet advancements were largely negated because the Third Reich failed to emulate the Allies in teaming scientists with soldiers.

Traditionally, the German scientific community depended more on individual genius than teamwork to achieve its breakthroughs. Similarly, the German military tended to be conservative and closely guarded against intrusion. Barriers to cooperation remained through most of the war, resulting in slow response times to serious problems and impressive but impractical innovations.

Examples of this are endless. The Luftwaffe lacked a quality bombsight. Rather than coordinate with engineers to make a better aiming device, the air force demanded stronger wing construction so aircraft could withstand the strain of dive-bombing. Technicians designed the sleek and fast Messerschmitt 262 jet with low-slung engines that sucked up dirt and debris on takeoff. It proved to be a bit of a problem since most combat airfields were unpaved. V-rockets, though impressive to watch, were too inaccurate for any tactical application. In the entire war, there was only one documented case of a direct conference between a German field commander and a team of scientists.[138]

Meanwhile, the Allies perfected "Operational Research," in which engineers studied military equipment in the field to measure performance and seek areas of improvement. Both the British and American leadership had scientific advisers. The Allied apex of achievement was undoubtedly the Manhattan Project, in which tens of thousands of individuals, working in tightly controlled environments at more than a dozen locations, went from abstract subatomic theory to a working device in three years. (Whether that was a good thing is open for debate.)

During the Battle of Britain, RAF Spitfires were able to boost engine performance 25 percent through the use of an American invention: 100-octane gasoline.

---

6. POPULATION

Before the industrial revolution, population equaled power. Afterward, industrialized countries gained a considerable edge in business, diplomacy, and military engagements. Yet in a war of attrition, numbers still counted.

For every person in an Axis uniform, there were nearly three Allies. For every civilian in an Axis state, the Allies had five. The Soviet Union alone had more people than Germany, Italy, and Japan combined.

This supremacy in numbers provided two profound advantages: the Allies could replace military losses faster than the Axis, and the Allies could commit larger numbers to logistics and manufacturing. Wherever there were shortages, the Allies were generally more willing to employ women, such as in heavy industry and agriculture, than were the more gender-traditionalist Axis states.

One statistic in particular illustrated which side was more capable of enduring a battle of attrition. Overall, the Allies lost twice the number of combatants as the Axis and still achieved victory.

"Providence is always on the side of the last reserve." —*Napoleon Bonaparte*

7. INTELLIGENCE

Knowledge is power, and through spy networks, reconnaissance, and resistance movements, the Allies knew more and gave away less than the Axis.

The largest disparity came by way of code. The United States made considerable strides in decoding Japanese diplomatic and naval messages. The British, with considerable help from Polish and French operatives, were able to decipher large portions of German communications, especially those of the Luftwaffe.

Both the Japanese and Germans believed their systems were unbreakable, and considering the complexity of the setups, their assumptions were not unreasonable. Both the main Japanese enciphering machine (based on phone switches) and the German "Enigma" machine (based on electromagnetic rotors) produced nonrepeating letter patterns that had possible combinations numbering in the trillions. Even when letters were correctly deciphered, the words they formed were in code, and their meanings varied between agencies. German enciphering was also based on alterable key systems, which changed monthly, weekly, and sometimes daily.[139]

Yet the Americans were able to fabricate a Japanese enciphering machine without ever having seen one, and the British procured several captured or copied Enigma machines. With the work of military personnel, translators, etymologists, mathematicians, statisticians, chess champions, and others, the Americans and British were able to uncover numerous vital pieces of information. The greatest breakthroughs provided Luftwaffe combat strength in occupied France, the time and place of Japan's attack on MIDWAY, disposition of U-boat wolf-pack patrols in the North Atlantic, and the flight itinerary of Japanese navy commander in chief Adm. Yamamoto Isoroku, whose plane was subsequently ambushed and Yamamoto killed.[140]

For security reasons, the Allied governments waited until the 1970s to reveal that they had broken Axis codes. The news shocked many former Axis cryptologists.

8. GEOGRAPHY

Although their war performances differed greatly, the Soviet Union and China shared a weapon that helped them stave off defeat: land. Attacked from one direction, both states were able to relinquish territory and not be overtaken, both were able to transfer large numbers of people and machinery to hinterlands, and both were subsequently able to endure long strings of losses without being totally overrun. Such luxuries were not available to less sizable countries such as Belgium and Singapore.

Japan and Great Britain possessed the advantage of being sizable island states shielded by wide bands of water and functioning as giant and unsinkable aircraft carriers. As it turned out, neither one would be invaded during the war. But their natural barrier also made both countries dependent on shipping for material survival. In this regard, Britain eventually secured the assistance of the United States, while Japan stood completely isolated from its nearest advocate, separated by oceans and land masses in either direction.

Well-suited for the defensive, Italy had limited offensive potential, with its navy bottled in the Mediterranean by the Suez Canal and Gibraltar and its army simultaneously shielded and dangerously separated by its mountainous terrain. Of all the major powers, Germany was probably the most vulnerable, situated between its declared adversaries. Aside from the Alps to the south, it also possessed almost no natural barriers.

No country benefited more from geography than the United States. Bordered by two vast oceans and resting between two cooperative neighbors, the nation was effectively in its own world. Safe from attack by land or air and far too large to be taken by amphibious assault, the United States may have been at war, but vast distances allowed its factories and government to function in relative peace.

The forty-eight United States were not entirely free from hostile fire. In February 1942, a Japanese submarine shelled an oil refinery near Santa Barbara, California. Late in the war, thousands of Japanese "balloon bombs" floated to North America, with several hundred reaching land and killing a dozen people.

---

9. "THE DECISIVE BATTLE"

Wars are rarely decided by a single event. Most involve extenuated, inglorious bouts of tedium and attrition, punctuated on occasion by sharp spikes of armed engagement. Though World War II followed this pattern to the letter, both Hitler and several members of the Japanese high command developed a counterintuitive faith in a last "decisive battle."

History may have contributed to this reasoning. Later in the war, Hitler habitually brought up how Prussia's Frederick the Great pulled out an unlikely eleventh-hour victory in the Seven Years' War against Austria, France, Russia, and Sweden. In Japan a favorite "lesson" from the past was the pivotal naval battle of Tsushima in the RUSSO-JAPANESE WAR. More recent memories conjured up thoughts of instant glory, namely Hitler's dizzying successes in 1939 and 1940 and Japan's sweep into the Pacific in December 1941.[141]

Nostalgia turned into military strategy late in the war. In 1944, Japan launched extremely large ground offensives in China and India, an air assault off Saipan, and naval offensives in LEYTE GULF. In each case, the commanding officers expressed the desire to win the war in a single blow. Hitler's last great offensive, known as the BATTLE OF THE BULGE to Americans, was a vain attempt to relive his greatest and most decisive victory.[142]

In all cases, though inflicting heavy casualties, the Axis lost a disproportionate number of troops. For Hitler's attack, the losses were nearly two to one. For the Japanese, the deficits averaged out to six to one. The battles were decisive to a certain extent: the massive casualties facilitated defeat, which would have likely come much later had a more defensive posture been taken.

The Japanese Mitsubishi Zero was an excellent fighter plane, but it was purposely built without armor. The rationale was that protecting the pilot made him act less aggressively.

---

10. THE "ARMY-NAVY GAME"

Interservice rivalries are as old as military history. Branches often fight each other as much as the enemy for prestige, assets, and autonomy. While the major Allied powers were able to temper internal discord through leadership and communication, the Axis states were not.

Case in point: aircraft. HERMANN GÖRING and Benito Mussolini believed their air forces should have a monopoly on combat planes, which was a fundamental reason why neither navy developed a working aircraft carrier and why Italian and German armies often lacked timely air cover. In contrast, the U.S. Army, Navy, and Marines each had its own combat aircraft, which could be used as needed in any given situation.

Axis intelligence processing remained strictly segregated among the armed services, creating what can be best described as schizophrenic paranoia. The German army, for example, often spent more time spying on the Luftwaffe than on the Allies.

Undoubtedly, the biggest internal rivalry existed in Japan. One of the major incentives for the Imperial Navy to strike into the Pacific was to stem the growing power of the Japanese army, which siphoned much of the military budget with its expanding war in China. The branches also conducted their own work on INTELLIGENCE, radar development, and jet propulsion yet refused to share their findings with each other. The divisive practice wasted money, resources, and time, all of which the empire could not afford to lose.[143]

One American military rivalry that continued uninterrupted was the annual Army-Navy football game. Navy won in 1942 and 1943; Army triumphed in 1944. The official program for the 1941 game, played nine days before Pearl Harbor, contained a photo of the doomed USS Arizona.

PURSUING THE WAR

GENERAL HISTORIES

There are at least 175,000 books about World War II. Approximately half are in English. On average, a bound volume concerning the conflict is published somewhere in the world every four hours.[1]

In the first postwar decade, publications were principally memoirs, diaries, and battle accounts. Most read askew, penned by individuals validating themselves while belittling their opponents. Authors desiring to create balanced works suffered from want of reliable information. Letters, diaries, dispatches, and statistics were available only in small amounts. Military INTELLIGENCE, especially in the outbreak of the Cold War, was off-limits. Most archives were either destroyed, in disarray, or under lock and key.

Over time, accessibility to information increased, treatment of the subject matured, and several excellent publications emerged. Listed below are just some of the best overviews for general audiences, selected for their accuracy, cited evidence, readability, and most of all, for their capacity to thread complex events into a comprehensive tapestry.

1 . *WORLD WAR II*
JOHN KEEGAN (1989)

Eloquent and effortless, John Keegan's writing is that of a craftsman wholly familiar with his medium. The venerable authority on military history, he expounds upon Machiavellian axioms and modern artillery with equal ease. Keegan's *World War II* outshines the two standard general texts on the subject: Peter Calvocoressi and Guy Wint's encompassing but argumentative *Total War* and Gerhard Weinberg's scholarly but impersonal *A World at Arms*.

Simultaneously expressive and succinct, Keegan's single-volume work vividly demonstrates how war is more than a meeting of brigadiers and battalions. For example, other overviews may mention the Italian campaign involving the U.S. Fifth and British Eighth armies. Keegan reminds readers that those armies consisted of Texans, Londoners, and Canadian volunteers, plus crack units from India and vengeful émigrés from Poland, and that they fought swollen streams, a bitter winter, and jagged mountains, as well as Germany's best reservists. Drawing upon his vast knowledge of the past, Keegan also points out how these men were up against history itself, noting that Italy had only fallen twice to rapid invasions in the last thousand years.

Excluded are endnotes. Keegan offers a small remedy by including a collection of suggested readings. But the absence of supporting materials does not diminish his credibility, as Keegan has a well-earned reputation for factual and impartial work.

Concerning military events, Keegan's coverage is not exhaustive. He highlights only six engagements: the BATTLE OF BRITAIN, the airborne operation of Crete, the naval engagement at MIDWAY, the armored battle around Falaise, urban fighting within BERLIN, and the amphibious attack on OKINAWA. But by using case studies, he defines the Second World War as a whole, not as a ledger of names and dates, but as a leviathan conflict of human beings empowered by science and inseparable from nature.

In 2000, in recognition of his great and many contributions to the field of history, John Keegan was knighted.

2. "THE GOOD WAR": AN ORAL HISTORY OF WORLD WAR TWO
STUDS TERKEL (1984)

Chicagoan Studs Terkel possessed an astounding gift for extracting gems of memory. Though trained in law, Terkel developed a talent for reading people through years of work as a radio actor, disk jockey, and television emcee. *Hard Times*, his 1970 interview anthology of the Great Depression, remains one of the most humanistic reflections on a topic often treated as purely economic. He repeats the accomplishment with greater effect in a compilation of a hundred reminiscences in the Pulitzer Prize–winning *The Good War*.

Contributors cover the spectrum: generals and privates, homemakers and hospital nurses, politicians and shopkeepers, Americans, Germans, Japanese, and Russians. From venerable economist John Kenneth Galbraith's controversial views on aerial bombing to poet Oleg Tsakumov's childhood memories of living through the siege of Leningrad, each monologue is potent in its unpolished candor. Two of the most moving excerpts come from Maxine Andrews of the Andrews Sisters singing trio and army nurse Betty Hutchinson. Both tenderly recount working with soldiers who suffered multiple amputations and extensive facial destruction.

Missing from this great litany is an overall conclusion. After displaying the harrowing stories of others, Terkel (who served in the army air force) downplays his own experiences. Yet in leaving his subjects and audience to their own conclusions, Terkel divulges his subtle genius. He simply listens.

In 1953, Senator Joseph McCarthy and the House Committee on UnAmerican Activities accused Studs Terkel of being a Communist. Terkel refused to name names and was subsequently blacklisted and fired from his job in television.

3. THE OXFORD COMPANION TO WORLD WAR II EDITED BY I. C. B. DEAR AND M. R. D. FOOT (1995)

Containing thousands of subject entries, statistical tables, a chronology of each military theater, and more than 120 detailed maps, *The Oxford Companion* is the outstanding single-volume encyclopedia on the war.

Credibility rests firmly on its faculty of contributors, a who's who of World War II historians, including the above-mentioned Gerhard Weinberg, preeminent Eastern Europe authority Norman Davies, and the ever-popular Stephen Ambrose. More than 130 scholars and military commanders from more than a dozen countries provide succinct information on leaders, battles, weapons, logistics, communications, etc. Cross-references link related topics, and suggestions for further reading direct readers to reputable works.

The Oxford Companion's shortcomings are few. Treatment is not always proportional. For example, a synopsis of Australian involvement receives ten pages of text, whereas the Ukraine gets four. Yet Ukrainians underwent German and Russian invasion and experienced 150 times the casualties as the Aussies. Subject headings are not always self-evident: casualty figures are listed under "demography"; songs can be found under "marching songs."

Organizational nuances aside, the work is exceptionally accurate and inclusive. Strong in the traditional focuses of Germany, Britain, the United States, the Soviet Union, and Japan, it also gives attention to commonly bypassed regions, such as East Africa, the Balkans, Scandinavia, and the open seas. It is aptly titled a companion, as it helps readers navigate through other works that might be heavy in detail but light on definition.

Collectively, the contributors to The Oxford Companion *earned more than three hundred academic degrees and spent more than a thousand years attaining them.*

4. *U.S. ARMY IN WORLD WAR II*
U.S. ARMY CENTER OF MILITARY HISTORY (1946–)

In 1943, for purposes of posterity and analysis, the U.S. Army formed its own historical department. Consisting of professional historians, cartographers, linguists, and support personnel, the unit began to chronicle the operations of the largest and most involved branch of the U.S. armed forces (two out of three Americans in uniform were in the army). At war's end, writing of the official histories began. The end result was the famous "green books."

Every major American university has (or should have) the lion's share of these seventy-eight texts. Most popular are the ten European theater of operations volumes, detailing everything from the NORMANDY invasion in *Cross-Channel Attack* to the conquest of western Germany in *The Last Offensive*. All are thoroughly researched and widely respected. John Eisenhower, son of the supreme commander, depended on nearly the entire theater series for his rendition of the BATTLE OF THE BULGE titled *The Bitter Woods*.

Written of, by, and for the military, some of the works stumble from the sheer weight of military formation details and dry statistics. But each volume is enlightening in its own way. The most candid volumes may be the four on the Medical Department, the most alarming are arguably the three on the Chemical Warfare Service, and the most censored appear to be the three pictorial records gleaned of casualty images.

Also available are the multivolume sets of *The Army Air Forces in World War II* and *The History of U.S. Marine Corps Operations in World War II*. Supremely written is the fifteen-volume *History of U.S. Naval Operations in World War II*, created under the direction of Harvard professor Samuel Eliot Morison.

During the war, the U.S. Army produced seventeen thousand tons of records—equal to the weight of ten brigades of Sherman tanks.

5. RUSSIA AT WAR, 1941–1945
ALEXANDER WERTH (1964)

Churchill described Russia as "a riddle, wrapped in a mystery, inside an enigma." But a working knowledge of the Second World War requires at least a basic understanding of the Soviet Union's role. The Allies landed in NORMANDY with nine divisions; Hitler attacked the Soviet Union with 170 divisions. Of all the war's dead, roughly half were Russian or Ukrainian. Of Germany's four million military fatalities, the Red Army and Air Force could take credit for 80 percent of them.

Since the end of the Cold War, there has been a marked increase in available information on and objective treatment of the "mystery." One of the best examinations of the Red riddle is one of the oldest. *Russia at War* was written by a journalist born in Russia, educated in Britain, and present in the Soviet Union for almost the entire duration of World War II. Alexander Werth witnessed firsthand the privations in Moscow. He also saw starvation in his birthplace of Leningrad (now St. Petersburg), combat on battlefronts, desperate resolve in factories, and liberation of concentration camps. He maintained connections with generals and the Kremlin yet remained grounded among citizens and soldiers. Werth wrote *Russia at War* as both a holistic and personal account of the darkest years in Russian history.

From his observations, the author credits the battle of KURSK rather than STALINGRAD as the turning point against Germany. He considers Stalin deserving of accolades and vilification for the demands he placed upon his people. Most valuable is Werth's presentation of the Russian perspective on invasion and retreat, on home life and battle casualties, and on victory and the atomic bomb, not from the official line of the Communist Party, but from the independent and dynamic viewpoints of everyday people.

In 1944, BBC correspondent Alexander Werth accompanied the Red Army in liberating the Nazi death camp at Maidanek, Poland. His description of the place was so horrific, the BBC dismissed the report as an exaggerated piece of Soviet propaganda.

6. THE RISING SUN: THE DECLINE AND FALL OF THE JAPANESE EMPIRE
JOHN TOLAND (1970)

His 1982 book on PEARL HARBOR conspiracies is unconvincing. His 1976 biography on Hitler reads well but is not at the top of its class. But John Toland's *The Rising Sun* is arguably the most lucid and engaging presentation of the Japanese military perspective yet available in English. The effort rightly landed him a Pulitzer Prize.

To assemble the account, Toland went through the standard sources of transcripts, diaries, and records. He and his Japanese wife also interviewed nearly five hundred veterans, politicians, and civilians, including Harry Truman, members of Japan's royal family, and members of Tojo Hideki's cabinet.

Unveiled through extensive quotes and dialogue is the empire's often lethal infighting—between the royalty and cabinet members, between ultranationalists and cautious conservatives, between the army and navy. Also poignantly illustrated are the flesh-and-blood experiences of individuals: Adm. Yamamoto Isoroku's fatalism after PEARL HARBOR, Lt. Ohno Toshihiko's struggle to stay alive in the caves of IWO JIMA, and Dr. Akizuki Tatsuichiro's attempt to treat the dying of Nagasaki.

Scholastic purists may dismiss Toland's narrative style as "storytelling," but the fact remains he can paint a scene and thereby transport an American reader to the deck of a Japanese flagship or general staff meeting or a Hiroshima hospital. That he builds these moments upon the words of the actual participants only adds to the authenticity.

Of John Toland's interviewees, twenty-one died before The Rising Sun *was published. Among them were Prime Minister Clement Attlee, Fleet Adm. Chester Nimitz, CIA Director Allen Dulles, and Hiroshima mayor Hamai Shinzo.*

7. *THE CHRONOLOGICAL ATLAS OF WORLD WAR TWO*
CHARLES MESSENGER (1989)

Maps in historic atlases are frequently too convoluted or too basic to be functional. *The Chronological Atlas of World War Two*, however, strikes a solid balance. With prudent economy, the atlas manages to incorporate the essentials of an operation without tangling the image in superfluous detail, primarily by matching subject and substance.

Panoramic views concentrate on panoramic conditions, such as areas of occupation, shipping lanes, and aircraft ranges of operation. Where greater detail is required, as in the marine assaults upon IWO JIMA, the cartography zooms in to pinpoint marine formations, their movement (over weeks, days, even hours), and the topography over which they traveled.

Air operations are especially well portrayed, showing not only where fighters and bombers flew, but also what their specific targets were, such as factories, submarine pens, and railroad depots. Also of tremendous benefit are maps addressing the commonly ignored but strategically vital battlegrounds of Austria, Burma, Crete, and Indochina.

To clarify the big picture even further, illustrations are accompanied by a day-by-day account of the war's progression. With ample text, the atlas describes not only the military overview of any given moment, but also the economic and political atmosphere in which it existed.

Arguably the work's weak point is its conclusion, which grossly underestimates the human losses and overall importance of operations in continental Asia, an arena otherwise well covered in the body of the book. Regardless, few works match this one in providing visual navigation through a long, churning tempest.

Charles Messenger wrote the text for The Chronological Atlas. *He had been a cadet at Sandhurst, where he studied under John Keegan.*

8. *THE SECOND WORLD WAR*
WINSTON CHURCHILL (1948–53)

Winston Churchill's six-volume series *The Second World War* cements his reputation as an artisan of English and a celebrator of empire. It also reveals a man wholly convinced of his own greatness.

Volume one, *The Gathering Storm,* discusses the era in which he was largely an outsider heavily critical of military caution against rising Nazism. Following is *Their Finest Hour,* featuring Churchill's ascendancy to prime minister and a passionate recollection of the Battle of Britain. *The Grand Alliance* addresses operations in North Africa and the Middle East as well as PEARL HARBOR. *The Hinge of Fate* focuses on the devastating loss of SINGAPORE. Volume five, *Closing the Ring,* begins with the invasions of GUADALCANAL and proceeds to the eve of D-day.[2]

The final volume rushes through the last year and a half of the conflict, but the title itself, *Triumph and Tragedy,* summarizes Churchill's ultimate view of the British national experience. He presents his beloved kingdom as victorious in war but relegated in peace, a diminished, bankrupt, international also-ran. Evident throughout, he sets this bitter tone in the series introduction, warning the two superpowers that eclipsed his: "Woe betide the leaders now perched on their dizzy pinnacles of triumph if they cast away at the conference table what the soldiers had won on a hundred blood-soaked battlefields."[3]

For those repulsed by his militant verbiage, his blatant Anglocentrism, and his ornate and self-idolizing style, Churchill's *The Second World War* is still worthy of full attention for one supreme reason: it is the only memoir completed by one of the "Big Three." Stalin and Roosevelt left no equivalent written legacy.

Churchill completed his monumental series despite three strokes, one after publication of Their Finest Hour *and two after releasing* Closing the Ring.

9. *INSIDE THE THIRD REICH*
ALBERT SPEER (1970)

Defeat was lethal for the Nazi elite. Suicide eliminated Hitler, Joseph Goebbels, HERMANN GÖRING, Heinrich Himmler, and a host of generals. Hangings for war crimes subtracted ten more. Highest-ranking among survivors was the minister for armaments, Albert Speer, who was sentenced to twenty years' imprisonment.

While incarcerated he began to write, as he said, "to relieve some of the burden that pressed so heavily upon me." Speer was one of the few defendants at Nuremberg who accepted responsibility for his actions, which included procuring and using thousands of slave laborers to manufacture weapons. Strangely, his admission of guilt led some Americans and British to label him "a good Nazi."

Within a decade, Speer completed a rough draft of his manuscript, *Inside the Third Reich.* Technically an autobiography, it is the most intimate account of the Nazi privileged from their early days in Bavarian beer halls to their final pleas in an international tribunal. In between, Speer details his unexpected and sudden rise in the party, the concrete and ethereal aspirations of an inherently inefficient system, and Hitler's eventual loss of control over the war, his country, and his physical and mental health.

Naturally, Speer's view is incomplete. Sheltered from armed service, claiming to be ignorant of death camps, Speer was also absent from the Berlin bunker at the end (the best account of which is Hugh Trevor-Roper's *The Last Days of Hitler*). But his is a compelling elucidation of how a talented, educated person can rationalize, if not eagerly seek, participation in a regime he knew to be immoral and destructive.

At Nuremberg, opinions varied on what Speer's sentence would be. Some American jailers predicted acquittal. His defense lawyer thought he would get four years. Speer assumed he would be condemned to death.

10. *ORDEAL OF TOTAL WAR, 1939–1945* GORDON WRIGHT (1968)

The big picture often reveals more than microscopic scrutiny. Few histories demonstrate this better than Gordon Wright's examination of Europe in *Ordeal of Total War*. Through a mere three hundred pages, Wright manages to cover everything from Polish tank production to French existentialism. Touching many subjects, he employs a central theme: war consists mostly of intangibles.

Wright observes how both sides grossly overestimated the effects of area bombing, whether by planes or rockets, upon civilian morale. Instead of "breaking" the opposition, aerial bombardments often created solidarity among citizens. Case in point: Churchill's popularity was never higher than when London was under the Blitz.[4]

Regarding weapons production, in which the Americans and British prospered and the Germans foundered, Wright credits dialogue more than economics. Allied manufacturers and military men were frequently one and the same, well versed in engineering and willing to exchange ideas. In Germany, scientists and the general staff worked within cliques and were consequently ignorant of each other's basic needs and abilities. In comparison, the Allies eventually perfected torpedoes, landing craft, high-altitude bombers, and an atomic weapon, whereas the Germans could not make a tank that ran well in mud.

The study of armaments can be reassuring in a way. Guns, ships, and planes are solid things. They can be drawn, measured, weighed, and counted. In contrast, elements such as motive, hope, fear, anger, and aspiration are far less containable, but as Wright demonstrates, they have a much greater leverage upon war than any weapon.

In 1944, while working for the U.S. State Department, Gordon Wright led a supply convoy from Lisbon in an attempt to reinforce the American Embassy in Paris. Wright made it, even though fighting was still going on and his superior believed he had no chance of succeeding.

FILMS

Nearly as soon as it erupted, the Second World War appeared on the big screen. Studios released a burst of patriotic pictures, and some managed to make a film a week, motivating and entertaining their respective countrymen. Among hundreds of flag-waving morale boosters were *Victory in the West* (Germany, 1941), *Eagle Squadron* (U.S., 1942), and *We Dive at Dawn* (UK, 1943). Story lines varied, but the overriding theme was predominantly "good versus evil."[5]

After the war, moviemaking struggled. Companies in Asia and Europe suffered from want of equipment and money. Usually the only lighting and backdrops available were daylight and ruined landscapes. Thus productions from 1945 to 1948 were commonly called "Rubble Films." The United States also bade farewell to its golden age of the silver screen. From 1945 onward, ticket sales plummeted, largely due to the advent of television. For people who still went to the movies, their preferences spoke volumes. After years of self-sacrifice, Americans developed a taste for Westerns, with stories of rugged individualism and the great wide open plains.[6]

World War II movies slowly regained popularity in the 1960s, but almost exclusively within victorious countries. Most productions were action flicks, with pyrotechnics and heroics galore, typified by

The Longest Day (U.S./UK, 1962), *The Dirty Dozen* (U.S., 1967), and *Kelly's Heroes* (U.S., 1970).

Adventure turned to anguish during the extenuated struggles of Vietnam, Afghanistan, and the nuclear arms race. Films began to characterize warfare as paradox, a fight between duty and disillusionment, as shown in *Hope and Glory* (UK, 1987), *Prisoners of the Sun* (Australia, 1991), and *The Thin Red Line* (U.S., 1998).

Overall, the fight between the Axis and the Allies has seen literally thousands of renditions, many of which have achieved critical and commercial success. To date, nine films about the war have captured the Oscar for best motion picture. Following are the best of the ages (available to Western audiences), based on quality of writing, directing, acting, cinematography, and historical accuracy.[7]

1. *DAS BOOT* (1981)
BAVARIA ATELIER/RADIANT
PRODUCER: GÜNTHER ROHRBACH
DIRECTOR: WOLFGANG PETERSON
STARRING: JÜRGEN PROCHNOW, HERBERT GRÖNEMEYER, KLAUS WENNEMANN

A war reporter in the Third Reich, Lothar-Günther Buchheim survived numerous U-boat missions. Decades later he eventually brought himself to write a distressing, honest depiction of U-boat service and the German war experience as a whole. Deeply moved by Buchheim's 1973 novel, director Wolfgang Peterson translated the print into pictures. The result was one of the most raw, cognizant, and genuine war films of all time.[8]

The story follows the exploits of U-96, a fictional amalgam subjected to factual miseries, patrolling the hostile waters of the North Atlantic and Mediterranean. In shots of tight and dismal quarters, moldy food, and crowded and unwashed men, one can almost feel

the weight of the sea upon the hull. The sub itself is eerily real, made
for the movie by a German company that actually produced U-boats
during the war.[9]

Scenes of engagement are especially astute: the cold sequence of
a torpedo launch, the echoing groan of a sinking ship, the sight of
drowning survivors. In depicting mortality of German crews, the film
is brutally truthful. Of the thirty-eight thousand officers and men who
served on U-boats during the war, fewer than eight thousand survived.

After the collapse of the Third Reich, German cinema wallowed
for decades in bewilderment. Films either treated the war as some
out-of-body nightmare or avoided the subject altogether. *Das Boot*
reestablished the reality that everyday Germans were active participants, serving, fighting, and suffering horribly with their chosen vessel
of war.[10]

---

*Due to mounting production costs, the project was nearly offered to a
pair of American studios, both of which intended on making* Das Boot
*into an action-adventure picture, starring either Paul Newman or Robert
Redford.*

---

2. *SCHINDLER'S LIST* (1993)

AMBLIN/UNIVERSAL
PRODUCERS: STEVEN SPIELBERG, KATHLEEN KENNEDY, BRANKO
            LUSTIG, GERALD MOLEN, LEW RYWIN
DIRECTOR: STEVEN SPIELBERG
STARRING: LIAM NEESON, BEN KINGSLEY, RALPH FIENNES

Critics often hesitate to administer praise upon a Spielberg film, as the
director has a penchant for tugging heartstrings and granting tidy end-
ings. The conclusion of *Schindler's List* does little to break the filmmak-
er's habit, exhibiting a row of Schindlerjuden honoring the Jerusalem
grave of their paradoxical savior.[11]

Throughout, Spielberg does much to cleanse the factual Oskar

Schindler (played by Liam Neeson), the Catholic businessman who spared more than twelve hundred Jews by employing them in his own factories. Instead of a changed man, the historical Schindler remained adulterous, alcoholic, and opportunistic for the rest of his days, even selling the gold ring he received from grateful survivors. Schindler's departing speech in the film, where he lamented his failure to save more people, is a fabrication.[12]

In spite of presenting a simplified Schindler (dispensed with greater accuracy in Thomas Keneally's historical novel), Spielberg unleashes the finest and most legitimate work of his career. Shot in high-contrast black and white, strengthening shadows while bleeding faces pale, the film does nothing to hide or glamorize issues of violence. Most directors present the Holocaust as an event of untouchable extremes, of automatic behavior from convenient stereotypes. Spielberg humanizes all involved, showing persecutors and the persecuted as equally capable of fear, cowardice, strength, guilt, and gratitude. The result is history made utterly tangible.

The governments of Egypt, Indonesia, Jordan, Lebanon, and Malaysia banned Schindler's List *for its allegedly pro-Jewish stance. Brigham Young University censored the movie for its sexual content.*[13]

3. *THE BEST YEARS OF OUR LIVES* (1946)
RKO
PRODUCER: SAMUEL GOLDWYN
DIRECTOR: WILLIAM WYLER
STARRING: MYRNA LOY, FREDERIC MARCH, HAROLD RUSSELL,
              DANA ANDREWS

Strangers during the war, three discharged veterans meet while returning to their quiet Midwest hometown. As reinstated civilians, they encounter a public largely indifferent to their harrowing service oversees. In turn, the men find solace in each other.

To a postwar European or Asian audience, the scenario would appear ideal, coming home to a family, a home, a city physically untouched by combat. Yet the film must be taken in context. Made less than a year after the fighting ceased, the work addresses issues too unpleasant for popular consumption but all too real for many American veterans: unemployment, alienation, mental trauma, alcoholism, and adultery. Indeed, there were merely a half-dozen American films about veterans before *Best Years* and more than three hundred after.[14]

The outstanding performance belongs to Harold Russell, playing the part of Homer, a sailor who lost his hands in battle. Having no acting experience other than the military training film in which he was discovered, Russell brilliantly underplays the role, revealing the doubt, sadness, and perseverance of a wounded man rummaging through a broken life, debating whether there is anything to salvage. His presence is all the more moving in that Russell was a veteran and a double amputee.

Adding significantly are the female characters. While most World War II films have little or no female presence (save for the obligatory love interest), the wives and daughters in *Best Years* are an exception. On the surface they appear tucked away, brought out for brief moments of reactionary dialogue. Under closer inspection, they are the strongest characters, supporting, challenging, and defining their severely tested relationships, exemplified by Homer's reticent fiancée Wilma (Cathy O'Donnell), who looks upon his handless arms and treats them not as deformations but as proof of fragile beauty and unbreakable courage.

Harold Russell won two Oscars for his performance—one for best supporting actor and an honorary award for inspiring his fellow veterans—yet he never acted in a major motion picture again.

---

4. *PATTON* (1970)

20TH CENTURY FOX
PRODUCER: FRANK MCCARTHY
DIRECTOR: FRANKLIN SCHAFFNER
STARRING: GEORGE C. SCOTT, KARL MALDEN

A screen biography of the controversial and flamboyant American general had been in the works since 1951. Yet producer Frank McCarthy failed to garner support from either the Defense Department or the Patton family, as both groups anticipated a wholly negative treatment of the bellicose commander.[15]

Not until the mid-1960s did McCarthy receive tacit approval, and production was on. Unfortunately, so was the Vietnam conflict and a growing public aversion to all things military.

Armed with a gifted writing team (including Francis Ford Coppola), a healthy budget, and a top-flight cast and crew, plus three thousand extras from the Spanish army equipped with World War II surplus tanks and artillery, McCarthy achieved the near impossible. *Patton* opened in 1970 to rave reviews and mass approval. Hawkish viewers (including President Richard Nixon) praised its depiction of courage and patriotism in trying times. Doves proclaimed the film an excellent portrayal of military hubris.[16]

There are discrepancies and omissions. Spanning Patton's service from North Africa in February 1943 to France in October 1945, the work makes no mention of his blatant anti-Semitic rants, the slapping of a second soldier, or an affair with his niece by marriage. And the British contribution to victory in Africa is nearly ignored. Concerning artistic expression, the real Patton was a much smaller man than Scott, sporting a high-pitched voice that screeched even higher in his many moments of agitation. Far less excusable was the treatment of animals on the set, where several were poisoned or shot for visual effect.[17]

5. *A BRIDGE TOO FAR* (1977)

UNITED ARTISTS
PRODUCERS: JOSEPH AND RICHARD LEVINE
DIRECTOR: RICHARD ATTENBOROUGH
STARRING: JAMES CAAN, MICHAEL CAINE, SEAN CONNERY,
           ELLIOT GOULD, GENE HACKMAN, ANTHONY HOPKINS,
           LAURENCE OLIVIER, RYAN O'NEAL, ROBERT REDFORD

Based on Cornelius Ryan's informative though heavily anecdotal book of the same name, *A Bridge Too Far* portrays OPERATION MARKET-GARDEN, the September 1944 Allied attempt to capture vital bridges deep inside Nazi-occupied Holland.

Much like the failed attack, the film is plagued from the beginning. Martial music, needless subplots, and an excessively famous cast are inappropriate and distracting. Poor continuity and uninspired acting further erode the production.

Nonetheless, *Bridge* is largely accurate and an invaluable lesson in modern warfare, aptly demonstrating the monumental complexity of combat. Hastily assembled, the actual Market-Garden operation lacked adequate INTELLIGENCE, cohesion, and leadership. Inclement weather, obstructed roads, insufficient weaponry, and broken communications added to the debacle, making all the courage in the world count for little. This tragic picture becomes considerably clearer when the film is viewed with a battle map in hand.

Despite the movie's impressive portrayal and blockbuster lineup, *Bridge* fared poorly at the box office. Evidently a detailed account of a military catastrophe held minimal appeal for a post–Vietnam audience.

Actor Dirk Bogarde, who played Lt. Gen. Frederick Browning, knew the story of Market-Garden well. He had participated in the actual battle as a member of British intelligence.

6. *TORA! TORA! TORA!* (1970)
20TH CENTURY FOX
PRODUCER: ELMO WILLIAMS
DIRECTORS: RICHARD FLEISCHER, TOSHIO MASUDA,
          KINJI FUKASAKU
STARRING: E. G. MARSHALL, SOH YAMAMURA, JASON ROBARDS,
          JAMES WHITMORE

Taking objectivity to an extreme, the quasi-documentary of the PEARL HARBOR attack ranks as one of the most balanced and accurate screenplays of the genre. Originally intended to be two films (one American, one Japanese), escalating costs forced a hybrid production, resulting in a rare case of equal time for both sides of the story.[18]

In step-by-step fashion, the mechanics of the raid come into view, with the accompanying U.S. intelligence failures to detect its approach. Shown in great detail is the critical breakdown of communications, where links between governments and their armed forces (and even within each branch of service) played a dominant role in the outcome of events.

Unquestionably, the picture's limited scope has cost and gain. Focusing purely on PEARL HARBOR, there is no reference to simultaneous attacks upon Malaya, the Philippines, Guam, and elsewhere. Nor is there mention of Japan's aging war with China. Yet by concentrating on PEARL HARBOR, the dramatization provides a concise snapshot of a tragic moment in time.

Perhaps of equal value is the film's indication of Japanese-American relations in 1970. The concerted effort required to make the film, and its message of courage under fire, demonstrate how once-mortal enemies can eventually achieve mutual respect.[19]

Commercially successful in Japan, the picture fared poorly in the United States, so 20th Century Fox recouped losses by selling impressively staged attack scenes to other studios. Thus footage of Tora! Tora! Tora! *appears in* Midway *(1976) and* MacArthur *(1977).*

7. *SAVING PRIVATE RYAN* (1998)

DREAMWORKS/PARAMOUNT
PRODUCERS: STEVEN SPIELBERG AND IAN BRYCE
DIRECTOR: STEVEN SPIELBERG
STARRING: TOM HANKS, MATT DAMON

The story: News reaches the U.S. high command that three of four brothers in uniform have perished in quick succession. To rescue the sole-surviving sibling, a squad fresh from the slaughter of D-day enters the French interior. On the way, the team faces its own battles and losses, only to find Pvt. James Ryan (Matt Damon) and a few other soldiers guarding a key river viaduct in enemy territory, setting up a climactic fight against all odds to spare brother and bridge.

The reality: It took weeks rather than hours for casualty manifests to reach headquarters. The June 1944 NORMANDY countryside contained far more hedgerows and hostile Wehrmacht than was depicted. U.S. Army captains tended to be much younger than John Miller (Tom Hanks) and much less willing to tolerate insubordination, engage overwhelming forces, or repetitiously divert from their assignment.[20]

As frail as the story line may be, the manner in which it is presented rivals all other war films ever made. Contrary to the teachings of traditional filmmaking, battles are chaotic, mangling affairs of ultraviolence. Per Spielberg's design, engagements become cauldrons of rolling smoke, stinging shells, and tearing flesh. Cinematographer Janusz Kaminski's use of handheld cameras, close-ups, and fast-action shutter speeds incorporate the viewer into the fold. The twenty-minute rendition of Omaha Beach alone may be the most realistic vision of combat ever re-created.[21]

> Saving Private Ryan *was inspired in part by the story of the Sullivan brothers. Serving in the Pacific theater on the light cruiser USS* Juneau, *all five Iowa brothers perished when enemy torpedoes sank their ship near Guadalcanal on November 13, 1942.*

8. *KANAL* (1956)
JANUS FILMS
PRODUCER: STANISLAW ADLER
DIRECTOR: ANDRZEJ WAJDA
STARRING: TERESA IZEWSKA, TADEUSZ JANCZAR

The second installment of Andrzej Wajda's war trilogy (*A Generation, Ashes and Diamonds*) follows a dwindling platoon of Polish resistance fighters in the final days of the 1944 Warsaw uprising. Surrounded, outgunned, and outmanned, the unit's ragged mix of soldiers and civilians enter the sewers (kanaly) in hopes of escape.

An otherwise moving tale suffers from an awkward musical score, tepid special effects, and poor sound quality. Actors blatantly unfamiliar with their weapons (such as a bazooka crew who stand behind their gun while firing) cause further reduction of authenticity.

Yet the director refuses to let his story falter into cliché. The platoon does not band together in unified triumph (per American war films of the 1940s), nor is there a celebration of heroic sacrifice (per Soviet Bloc war films of the 1950s). Instead, the dark and claustrophobic stench of the sewers unmasks everyone, revealing the heights and depths of human behavior under inhuman conditions and the ruinous fate of a people trapped between two military giants.[22]

Perhaps the strongest scene ever shot in Wajda's long and celebrated career comes in the final moments of *Kanal*, when the bright and beautiful Daisy (Teresa Izewska) and her wounded love, Jasek (Tadeusz Janczar), reach the end of a tunnel. They are inches away from freedom only to find their exit blocked by a metal grate. A master of metaphor, Wajda manages to symbolize war-torn Poland in this single moment, a country barely surviving years of Nazi onslaught only to be caught behind an Iron Curtain.

The director's father, Capt. Jakub Wajda of Poland's Seventy-Second Infantry Regiment, was one of approximately forty-four hundred Polish officers executed by the Soviets in the Katyn Forest massacre of 1940.

---

9. *THE STORY OF G.I. JOE* (1945)
UNITED ARTISTS
PRODUCER: LESTER COWAN
DIRECTOR: WILLIAM WELLMAN
STARRING: BURGESS MEREDITH, ROBERT MITCHUM

Generally, World War II veterans envisioned themselves as neither heroes nor victims. Rather, most reasoned they had a job to do, unpleasant as it was, and addressed their uninvited challenge to the best of their abilities. Few films represent this soldierly self-assessment better than *The Story of G.I. Joe*, released while the war was still in progress.

Tagging along with a fictional outfit marching through Italy is the factual war correspondent Ernie Pyle (played brilliantly by a middle-aged and genial Burgess Meredith). Pyle was one of the few reporters who ventured to the front lines, and his experiences in Africa, Europe, and the Pacific forged a grave respect for the unsung and virtually unknown soldiers of lower rank.

Filmed in black and white, the movie portrays vividly the muddling grayness of infantry service, in which mire, boredom, and exhaustion are constants in life, and death is neither glamorous nor unexpected. Second only to Meredith in this candid picture of subtle acting and bold honesty is Robert Mitchum (as Lieutenant Walker) in his first starring role.

Despite its inglorious tone, the film was well received by war-weary Americans. Commanding general and future president

DWIGHT D. EISENHOWER called *The Story of G.I. Joe* the best war movie he had ever witnessed.[23]

Though Ernie Pyle inspired its creation, the prolific and straightforward journalist never saw the film. In April 1945, while on assignment near Okinawa, he was killed by Japanese gunfire.

---

10. *BLACK RAIN* (1988)

FOX LORBER
PRODUCER: IMAMURA SHOHEI
DIRECTOR: IMAMURA SHOHEI
STARRING: TANAKA YOSHIKO, ISHIDA KEISUKE

For such a pivotal time in Japan's history, there are relatively few indigenous films directly addressing the atomic bombings. In fact, *Black Rain* was the first major Japanese feature on the subject in thirty years. Yet the piece well represents the treatment of the war as a whole within the national cinema.

Laden with imagery and allegory, the tale begins with the unleashing of atomic fire upon HIROSHIMA. Just beyond the doomed city, fallout descends upon the faces of women, including the young, angelic Yasuko (Tanaka Yoshiko). Ever after she is an unwilling witness to the disintegration of her village, her family, and her body.

In this epic story of a half-life, *Black Rain* weaves supreme performances, a haunting score, and transcending symbolism. In 1989, the film rightly won Best Technique at Cannes and Best Picture in Japan. Yet hidden within its frames is a theme often repeated in Japanese war films. Though condemning militarism and warfare, it is void of context, making no mention as to why so much suffering befell a populace. Devastation appears almost as happenstance rather than harvest, as if the fire purged a nation of its recent memory.[24]

Recognizing the power of images, both the Imperial Government of Japan and the American Occupation Forces confiscated every print and negative of the atomic bombings. Decades passed before unedited photos of the aftermath were publicly released in Japan.

POPULAR MYTHS AND MISCONCEPTIONS

Mysteries and conspiracies tend to be more alluring than cold facts and hard truth. Such is the case with the Second World War, a veritable factory of compelling fiction. Rumors had squadrons of Japanese bombers over California, German armies marching through Moscow, and Hitler dying several times before his actual suicide. Often the sources of mythology were government propaganda machines. For years Washington contended that only the *Arizona* had been sunk at PEARL HARBOR while Tokyo proclaimed that virtually the whole U.S. fleet had been destroyed.[25]

Over time, information becomes available, evidence emerges, governments declassify documents, and sometimes accuracy topples illusion. But like slag from a cauldron, falsehoods continue to rise from history and reside within the general psyche as assumed truths. Assembled here in chronological order of their origination are the most enduring myths and misconceptions of the war still widely held in the West.

I. HITLER WAS INTO THE OCCULT

Mysterious, fanatical, and laden with symbolism, the Third Reich appeared to many as an ideological cult led by its author, Adolf Hitler. Yet Hitler was personally indifferent to religion. Although Catholic all his life, he felt annoyed by Germany's attachment to Christianity and its messages of love and forgiveness. He once lamented, "Why did it have to be Christianity with its meekness and flabbiness?" But the occult never interested him.[26]

A few individuals within the Nazi hierarchy attempted to replace Christianity with something more "Germanic." None were more active in this pursuit than SS chief Heinrich Himmler. As leader of Hitler's elite bodyguard, which grew to be a political and military entity unto itself, Himmler tried to plant the seed of a state religion, a mixture of monotheism and paganism. He sponsored archaeological digs, started a porcelain factory that produced pre-Christian idolatry, and formed academic societies to research the roots of Nordic culture. In private ceremonies Himmler tried to introduce Germanic baptisms and marriages, with candles, chalices, and vows loosely based on folk history.[27]

Except for the most indoctrinated of the SS guard, the "Death's Head" extermination units, the experiment found no root or respect. Most Germans, including the majority of the SS, remained with their church. Few were more critical of Himmler's projects than Hitler.

"What nonsense," fumed der Führer. "Here we have at last reached an age that has left all mysticism behind it, and now he [Himmler] wants to start that all over again." On excavations, Hitler added, "Isn't it enough that the Romans were erecting great buildings when our forefathers were still living in mud huts; now Himmler is starting to dig up all these villages of mud huts and enthusing over every potsherd and stone axe he finds."[28]

Of the world's religions, one that Hitler admired but knew very little about was Islam, which he viewed as "faith by the sword."

2. ROOSEVELT KNEW IN ADVANCE ABOUT PEARL HARBOR

The assumption pervades that a pro-war President Franklin D. Roosevelt knew of an impending Japanese attack on the Pacific Fleet in Honolulu and allowed it to happen, thus provoking isolationist America into war. Assuming FDR and others were somehow willing to sacrifice thousands of American lives, the bulk of the navy, and national peace in exchange for a two-front war, the charge of conspiracy falters under its central argument: that the president learned of the imminent raid by way of decoded Japanese messages.

True, the United States had been intercepting Japanese diplomatic and military exchanges since September 1940. But INTELLIGENCE successfully deciphered less than 10 percent of all Imperial code traffic, due primarily to a limited peacetime staff of cryptographers and linguists. Also true, the U.S. Departments of State and War strictly curtailed access to the decoded information. Far from a plot to keep American troops and the public in the dark, the intense secrecy was instead a shrewd and ultimately successful effort to prevent the Japanese from discovering their code had been broken.

Regardless, the Japanese attack fleet had just started using a new code variation called J-25b, which U.S. intelligence had yet to crack. Unable to track specifics, Roosevelt and the War Department sensed enough on November 27 to issue a clear warning to posts in the Pacific theater[29]: "Japanese future action unpredictable but hostile action possible at any moment. If hostilities cannot, repeat cannot, be avoided the United States desires that Japan commit the first overt act. This policy should not, repeat not, be construed as restricting you to a course of action that might jeopardize your defense."[30] U.S. intelligence correctly predicted the attacks on Guam and the Philippines but did not expect simultaneous assaults on PEARL HARBOR, Wake Island, MIDWAY, Hong Kong, Malaya, and the Chinese coast.

From December 1941 to February 1946, the U.S. government and military conducted eight extensive and highly publicized investigations as to why the attacks caused such surprise and devastation. Most in-quiries appeared more interested in leveling blame than improving an obviously deficient INTELLIGENCE process. Contrary to the hopes of anti-Roosevelt Republicans and staunch isolationists, several of whom were on the probe committees, no evidence of a Roosevelt conspiracy ever emerged.

In short, it can be said that the U.S. executive and military were ultimately guilty of the same offense at PEARL HARBOR as Neville Chamberlain was at Munich, Adolf Hitler at STALINGRAD, and Tojo Hideki at MIDWAY—they dangerously underestimated their adver-sary. As one Atlanta columnist curtly observed, "The Japs caught us unprepared because we were unprepared."[31]

In the summer of 1941, Japanese prime minister Prince Konoye offered to meet Roosevelt and discuss ways to ease tensions between the two countries. For a summit location Konoye suggested the Oahu city of Honolulu, home of Pearl Harbor. The meeting never took place.

---

3. FRENCH SOLDIERS READILY SURRENDERED IN 1940

The butt of innumerable jokes in Europe and the United States, the French military fought with much greater ferocity against the Germans in May and June 1940 than was ever recognized. France was not con-quered by cowardice but by convoluted chains of command, outdated military faith in static defenses, a vastly better organized enemy, and an exceedingly defeatist government.

In spite of their detriments, French forces continued to battle the invaders. To the north, the Fourth Armored Division under Col. Charles de Gaulle blunted the spearhead of the German attack, while French and Belgian infantry divisions fought to buy time for a British evacuation in the "Miracle of Dunkirk." To the south, soldiers suc-cessfully repulsed an Italian invasion of the French Alps despite being outgunned and outmanned seven to one. To the east, the much derided Maginot Line never fell. Overall, French opposition to the Germans increased as the invasion progressed, exemplified by valiant though tactically unwise last stands along the Somme and Aisne rivers to the northeast of Paris.[32]

The City of Lights fell nonetheless on June 14, and France officially surrendered on June 22. Comparatively speaking, the "cowardly French" fared better than their neighbors by holding out for forty-two days. Belgium fell in eighteen days, Holland five, and Denmark one.

Of France's 200,000 military deaths in the Second World War, nearly half of them occurred in the six weeks of the German invasion of 1940.

---

4. BLITZKRIEGS SUCCEEDED BECAUSE OF OVERWHELMING NUMBERS

Ironically, it was Germany's lack of numerical superiority that compelled its high command to employ "lightning war" tactics. Any alternative meant a war of attrition, which Hitler and company well knew they had neither the resources nor reserves to endure.

Poland in 1939 had one of the largest armies on the Continent, and for that matter the world, with about 1.3 million effectives. Germany attacked with a similar number. In 1940 France equaled Nazi Germany in troops, tanks, and planes. With the British Expeditionary Force of ten divisions, the French possessed clear majorities in every category except antiaircraft guns.[33]

But by using velocity over volume, German air and ground forces were able to slice through and get behind their opponents, essentially stunning them into submission. Heavy tanks did the cutting, planes and artillery severed lifelines, and light tanks and infantry mopped up.

Hitler believed the system would also succeed against Russia, where once again the balance sheet showed relatively equal sides. The invasion did in fact reap immediate rewards. In three months the Soviet Union lost more than half its armed forces, all but seven hundred of its fifteen thousand tanks, and two thousand of three thousand combat aircraft. So rapid was the German advance, many (including the U.S. and British chiefs of staff and the U.S. secretary of war) believed that the Soviet Union would collapse in a matter of weeks. Of course, the Soviet Union did not fall, primarily because the German blitzkrieg accomplished everything but its most important objective. It never got behind the enemy.

The word blitzkrieg *is probably not of German origin. Some Western journalists claimed to have coined the term, but its exact time and place of invention has never been conclusively determined.*[34]

5. HITLER'S JET FIGHTERS COULD HAVE CONTROLLED THE SKIES

Much has been made of Hitler's "mistake" in changing the FIRST OPERATIONAL JET AIRCRAFT from a fighter into a fighter-bomber, thus negating its superior speed. If allowed to attack a bomber instead of trying to be one, so the logic goes, the abundantly fast Messerschmitt 262 would have always won.

Actually, the first Me-262s were pure fighters, as were most of the fourteen hundred made. But their performance against Allied bombers was not outstanding. In a straight line, the jets were magnificent. Dogfights and bomber interceptions were another matter. Me-262s accelerated slowly, turned poorly, and had difficulty pulling out of dives. The aircraft were also prone to catastrophic failure, especially engine fires. Overall, the German wonder birds had a kill-to-loss ratio of about one to one.[35]

Along with other major roadblocks—Allied bombing of jet factories, scarcity of nickel and chromium for engine construction, lack of qualified technicians—nothing slowed deployment more than the Me-262s themselves. The highly sophisticated planes were difficult to build and maintain. Their touchy handling in flight required the skills of experienced pilots, of which Germany had precious few in the later stages of the war. Their gas–guzzling engines provided brief flying time, fifty minutes at best, barely adequate for search–and–destroy missions. In the end, Germany's fighter jets were more of a marvel than a menace, accounting for less than 5 percent of the Luftwaffe's operational fighter force and less than 1 percent of confirmed kills.[36]

Due to a lack of fuel, pilots, parts, and reliability, only 220 Me-262s (about 17 percent of those manufactured) ever saw action.

---

6. ROCKETS COULD HAVE WON THE WAR FOR GERMANY

At first, Hitler was extremely skeptical of a proposed long-range rocket, but when he saw film footage of V-2 test launches, he became rapturous. "This is the decisive weapon of the war," he told Albert Speer, "and what is more, it can be produced with relatively small resources."[37]

Der Führer was wrong on both counts. A single rocket cost more to produce than fifteen fighter planes. Also, its one-ton warhead was meager. Four rockets equaled the bomb load of one B-17. Of the four thousand V-2s launched against Belgium, England, and France, their combined explosive power was less than a single Allied air raid. In addition, guidance systems and electronics were a consistent problem, sending hundreds of missiles into the sea. Midair explosions were also commonplace. In the end, more slave laborers (at least 10,000) died constructing the V-2 and its facilities than British citizens perished from some one thousand strikes (2,724).[38]

Though just as horrifying as V-2s to intended targets, V-1 buzz bombs were as unreliable. More than a third failed in flight. They were also slow, noisy, and low–flying, consequently making them easy targets for fighters and antiaircraft guns. Some RAF pilots managed to fly next to the flying bombs, tip their wings, and send them back to their place of origin. The V-1 killed nearly three times as many people as the V-2 but still accounted for approximately 0.5 percent of all air-raid fatalities in the war.[39]

Though relatively ineffective, the V-2 served as the principle design for two future rockets: the U.S. Atlas and the Soviet Scud. The latter possessed virtually the same range and payload as the V-2 but was about three times more accurate.

---

7. ONLY JEWS PERISHED IN NAZI CONCENTRATION CAMPS

The Third Reich murdered an estimated eleven million men, women, and children, consisting of at least six million Jews and five million non-Jews. Nazis applied the same methods of extermination to both groups: shootings, torture, privation, medical experimentation, and gassing, much of which occurred in a network of concentration camps.[40]

The first camps opened in 1933 and were primarily for detaining and "reeducating" political and cultural prisoners—Communists, intellectuals, Jehovah's Witnesses, homosexuals, Freemasons. First to die in large numbers, however, were the mentally and physically handicapped in 1939. More than seventy thousand were killed, mostly through carbon-monoxide poisoning. Not until the invasion of the Soviet Union in 1941 did widespread extermination of all targeted groups begin.

Slated for total annihilation were Jews and Gypsies. The former referred to this systematic genocide as Shoah (the Holocaust); the latter called it Porrajmos (the Great Devouring). Killed outright or subjected to slave labor were Slavs (Czechs, Poles, Russians, Ukrainians, etc.). Czechs and Ukrainians were considered potential candidates for hard labor, but the Poles, in the words of SS chief Heinrich Himmler, were to "disappear from the world." In addition, the Nazis intensified persecution of political and social detainees. The Third Reich lasted for twelve years, but most of its Jewish and non-Jewish victims died between 1942 and 1944.[41]

Decades after the war, these murdered millions received little public consideration. Traumatized survivors, silent perpetrators, and incomplete information left much of the concentration camp system sheltered from heavy academic scrutiny. But the early 1970s witnessed a massive upsurge of Holocaust studies, concentrated almost exclusively on the Jewish experience. The ground swell of films, poems, songs, documentaries, and novels led some to call the phenomenon "the Shoah business." While illuminating the loss of six million lives, such works largely overshadowed the fate of millions more who were not Jewish and only recently have received scholastic attention.[42]

The first to die in the gas chambers of Auschwitz were Polish and Russian POWs.

---

8. JAPAN WAS READY TO SURRENDER BEFORE HIROSHIMA

When the "Big Three" gathered in mid-July 1945 in the aristocratic Berlin suburb of Potsdam, Stalin informed Truman and Churchill that Japan had offered, by way of its ambassador in Moscow, to stop the war. But this initiative was far from the UNCONDITIONAL SURRENDER demanded by the Allies.

The cabinet of Prime Minister Suzuki Kantaro agreed to a cease-fire but not capitulation. Japan volunteered disarmament, yet insisted it would disarm itself. There was to be no foreign occupation, and all war criminals would be defined, tried, and prosecuted by the Japanese. In addition, the government would remain in place, as would the existing boundaries of the empire, including Formosa, Korea, and Manchuria, which encompassed three times the land and twice the population of Japan proper.[43]

On both sides, there was little military indication that an end was soon coming. The United States was already shuttling divisions from Europe and North America to the Pacific. In all, two million troops were assigned to take part in the eventual invasion of Japan's main islands, scheduled to begin in November 1945 at the southern island of Kyushu and in early 1946 onto the main island of Honshu. Japan also persisted militarily, retaining large portions of eastern China, sending kamikaze flights from Kyushu into approaching U.S. ships and arming soldiers and civilians alike with anything available for the impeding invasion. The main islands possessed at least two million regular troops.

In addition, fighting intensified the closer the U.S. forces came to Japan. Retaking Manila cost 11,000 American and Japanese dead. IWO JIMA resulted in 25,000 total dead. OKINAWA, the last major island south of Japan, cost at least 112,000 American and Japanese deaths, plus another 80,000 native Okinawans.[44]

With this in mind, Truman decided without much consultation to use atomic devices. He ordered the two available bombs dropped just days apart to give the impression the United States had a cache of such weapons (and believed, as did Gen. GEORGE C. MARSHALL and Henry Stimson, that more than two would be needed to defeat Japan). The tactic worked. Immediately after Hiroshima, Tokyo's high command debated whether the event was indeed atomic. Some argued the United States had only the one bomb. But reports came in of an additional explosion at Nagasaki, and the hawks faltered. Minister of War Anami Korechika, previously committed to a fight to the end, feared the Americans had "one hundred atomic bombs."[45]

In an unprecedented move, Hirohito ordered his subjects to accept immediate surrender. Even this stunning interdiction failed to persuade everyone. Army officers and Imperial guards launched a coup d'état on the night of August 14. Raiding the palace, soldiers attempted to find and destroy a recording of the EMPEROR'S SURRENDER SPEECH, set to be broadcast nationally the following day. Failing in their mission, several of the conspirators committed suicide in the palace.[46]

Some believed War Minister Anami Korechika, the second most power-
ful man in Japan, was behind the coup against the emperor. Anami did
nothing to dispel this theory when, just hours after the coup failed, he
slashed open his stomach and throat and slowly died.

9. USE OF THE ATOMIC BOMB WAS RACIALLY MOTIVATED

Racism was a prevalent reality in midcentury America. With the exception of the merchant marine, the armed forces were segregated.
The U.S. government placed 110,000 Japanese Americans, most of
whom were full and legal U.S. citizens, in internment camps for more
than two years. Truman himself was not averse to using the word *Jap*
in private discourse.

For American servicemen, the war in the Pacific contained definite
racial hatred surpassing anything expressed in Europe. The Rape of
Nanking, the surprise attack on PEARL HARBOR, and the grotesque
abuses of prisoners of war led many U.S. soldiers, sailors, and marines
to view the Japanese as beastlike.

But for all the official and unofficial discriminatory practices in the
United States, the atomic bomb was created and intended for use against
Germany. When it looked as if the Third Reich would collapse before
the devices were ready, Japan became the target by default. Germany
returned to primary status during the 1944 ARDENNES OFFENSIVE, only
to be removed from consideration after the fall of BERLIN.[47]

In the end, Roosevelt's successor decided to use the devices on
Japan, not based on a racial premise, but in the firm belief that atomic
weapons would end the war sooner than any other option available.

In his August 9, 1945, radio announcement of the destruction of
Hiroshima, Truman explained the bomb was a successful "race of dis-
covery against the Germans."[48]

10. TRUMAN "GAVE UP" EASTERN EUROPE

In the West a postwar sentiment quickly emerged: Truman was too soft on Stalin and thereby allowed communist systems to take root in Eastern Europe. In comparison, Churchill recommended that the Allies occupy Prague by force, and GEN. GEORGE S. PATTON stated to U.S. Undersecretary of War Robert Patterson, "If you wanted Moscow, I could give it to you."[49]

Yet nearly a year before Winston Churchill's 1946 "Iron Curtain" speech in Fulton, Missouri, Truman all but threatened Soviet foreign minister Vyacheslav Molotov with retaliation if Poland were not allowed its freedom. At Potsdam, Truman repeatedly argued for guarantees of Polish, Bulgarian, Greek, and Romanian independence, to which Stalin said that any government not fascist was a democracy.[50]

Unfortunately for the American president, the war itself limited his options. For all intents and purposes, Eastern Europe was not Truman's to give. The eventual demarcation between democratic and communist Europe closely resembled the positions of the victorious armies on V-E Day, making the Soviet domination of Eastern Europe a harsh fait accompli.[51]

To be sure, Stalin did break his agreement at YALTA to allow free and unfettered elections in postwar Europe, condemning nearly half the continent to communist dictatorship. In the larger view, Truman fared considerably well, to the point where many in the Soviet Union believed Stalin had failed immensely against the Americans. Conquered by the Red Army, Berlin remained mostly in the hands of the West. The French, playing a marginal role defeating the Third Reich, were allowed to occupy a large portion of western Germany. Soviet-occupied Vienna and east Austria soon fell completely within the Western sphere of influence, as did heavily communist Greece. On the world stage, vehemently anti-communist nations held four of the five Security Council seats in the newborn United Nations, and most significantly, Britain and the United States shared atomic secrets with each other but not with the Soviet Union.

Potsdam was Harry Truman's first and last international conference of his presidential career.

HISTORIC SITES

To crawl inside the cavity of a U-boat and smell the grease and diesel, to peer through the slit of a pillbox and feel its chilling breath, to stare upon the enormity of a military graveyard and read the names aloud. To experience such places is to walk through history.

Unfortunately for the World War II traveler, formidable obstacles await. First is distance. Unlike the relatively compact engagements of previous wars, events in the machine-driven Second World War covered hundreds of square miles, many of them in the ethereal environs of sea and sky. Furthermore, key locations couldn't be farther apart. The war began at a bridge near Peking and at a signal station in Poland and ended in a schoolroom in France and on a battleship off the coast of Japan.

There is also the matter of destruction. Total war, with its relentless force, tended to crush whatever it handled most: flying fortresses, grand battleships, entire cities. That which was not burned or blasted away often succumbed later to drifting sands, blanketing jungles, scrap hounds, thieves, and real estate developers.

Despite the challenges, the physical legacy of the war can still be found. Among the many hundreds of possible destinations, the following drop zones are the most favorable for an effective campaign of exploration for the North American traveler. Rank is based on preservation of natural landscape and man-made structures, overall accessibility (transportation, nearby lodging, guided tours, etc.), plus quantity and quality of supporting museums and monuments.[52]

I. THE BEACHES OF NORMANDY

"D-day" is an operational term for the launch date of any active engagement. But to older generations in North America, Britain, and France, the word *D-day* can only mean June 6, 1944, when nothing was guaranteed but casualties and when perhaps the liberty of the entire free world depended on the outcome of one attack at one place on one day.

Visiting the beaches of NORMANDY is not so much a trip as it is a pilgrimage, and stations of reflections are bountiful. Foremost is Omaha Beach. To understand why this landing sector was the bloodiest of the five, one needs only to walk to the shoreline and turn around. Vertical bluffs to the left and right; a jagged, narrow, steep ascent to the center; concrete gun nests and pillboxes all around. Add mines, barbed wire, smoke, obstacles, and deafening weapons fire, and imagine having to run through a quarter-mile of water and sand to reach it.

Spanning fifty miles of France's north coast, the landing zones code-named Omaha, Utah, Gold, Juno, and Sword provide haunting visuals to what the Americans, British, and Canadians faced. The area contains lasting evidence of this great battle. Situated on a high cliff between Utah and Omaha is the strategic German position of Pointe du Hoc, which still bears the shattered bunkers and overlapping craters from Allied bombing, shelling, and direct assault. Ominous are the concrete-and-metal remains of "Mulberry B," the artificial harbor constructed off Gold Beach after the landings. Every U.S. citizen should see the American Military Cemetery and Memorial overlooking Omaha, with its 9,386 marble grave markers and a wall containing 1,557 names of the missing.

Museums of the invasion are all around, ranging from modest private collections to large, state-run facilities. Chief among them are the Musée des Troupes Aéroportées in Ste.-Mére-Eglise featuring the exploits of the U.S. 82nd and 101st Airborne operations, the Exposition Permanente du Débarquement just off of Gold Beach with heavy military equipment and emphasis on the British landings, and most important, the spectacular Musée pour la Paix (also known simply as "Memorial") in Caen, with its massive collections of hardware and state-of-the-art audiovisual displays.

Small hotels cover the coast, and larger ones of every price range can be found farther inland. Guided tours for groups and individuals are easily arranged through major hotels, museums, and online. June and July are the busiest months, so make reservations far in advance or go in early autumn when crowds are modest and the weather most favorable.

Utah Beach is not where it was supposed to be. The Seventh U.S. Corps wanted to land two miles farther north, but tides and misdirection put them off course. Just as well, since the Germans constructed much stronger defenses at the intended landing zone.

---

2. PEARL HARBOR

For Americans, PEARL HARBOR embodies the beginning and the end. The end appears in the form of the USS *Missouri*. Anchored here since 1998, the largest U.S. battleship ever built hosted the official Japanese surrender on September 2, 1945. The beginning is the harbor itself, main target of the surprise attack that drew the United States fully into the war.

Remnants of the December 7, 1941, air assault traverse Oahu, but the event is encapsulated in the somber, bone-white monument resting near the *Missouri*. Constructed in 1961, the USS *Arizona* Memorial straddles the fated battleship's sub-merged hull; only the iron base of Gun Turret Number 3 rises from the water. Containing the bodies of more than eleven hundred sailors, the *Arizona* entombs half the military dead of Pearl Harbor.

Along with this poignant alpha, Oahu possesses many stories in between. Within the harbor is the USS *Bowfin* Submarine Museum, which pays tribute to the thirty-five hundred U.S. submariners killed in World War II. A tour through the *Bowfin* is highly recommended. Launched a year after the attack, the three-hundred-foot-long submarine scored forty-five kills in nine missions.

Excellent overviews of Hawaii's military history and the Pacific War can been seen at the Fort DeRussy U.S. Army Museum, seven miles east in Honolulu, just behind Waikiki Beach. Also just east of Honolulu is the National Memorial Cemetery of the Pacific, a.k.a. "the Punchbowl." Situated in the mouth of an extinct volcano, the cemetery holds the graves of thirty-three thousand servicemen and the names of eighteen thousand missing from World War II. It is the largest U.S. military resting place outside Arlington National Cemetery.

Transportation, hotels, guides, and group tours are abundant in this tropical paradise. For the more adventurous, a few organizations offer scuba excursions to sunken World War II boats and planes away from the naval base. Excellent in its convenience and accommodations, PEARL HARBOR is supreme in its vivid illustration of the American purpose, victory, and price paid.

Of all the historic sites in the Hawaiian Islands, the most visited is the National Memorial Cemetery at Honolulu.

3. AUSCHWITZ–BIRKENAU

From Yad Vashem in Israel to Washington, D.C., there are twenty and counting major museums and memorial centers to the Holocaust.

Though these facilities can induce chilling reminders with photographs, graphic text accounts, and somber audiovisual displays, they are subdued and tepid in comparison to a walk through a death camp.

Forty miles west of beautiful Krakow, Poland, near the town of Oswiecim, stands the remnants of the largest and deadliest of the six major extermination centers of the Third Reich. Here, through hard labor, starvation, disease, medical experiments, shootings, and gassings, ten thousand Russians and other nationalities, well over one hundred thousand Poles, and at least one million Jews perished between 1942 and 1945. Initially a labor and incarceration facility, Auschwitz eventually grew into a leviathan of forty subcamps designed to kill and cremate. Today the two largest sections, Auschwitz I and Auschwitz II–Birkenau remain relatively intact and are open for public viewing.

Miles of barbed-wire walls, guard towers, and a dead-end rail line greet visitors to this cold, still, colorless landscape. Auschwitz I is the nucleus, holding the commandant's and SS quarters, medical facilities, and prison barracks. Situated two miles to the west is Birkenau, where most exterminations took place. The gas chambers and crematoria lay in ruins, destroyed by SS guards just before Soviet liberation of the camp in January 1945. Still standing are rows upon rows of buildings, mostly barracks, which once housed skeletal inmates stacked like cordwood upon hard, cold shelves.

Guides are available. During the warmer months bus shuttles run hourly between the two former camps. A few moderately sized hotels are available in Oswiecim, but Krakow forty miles to the east has better accommodations. Take a car or bus from Krakow to reach the site. Rail service stops within a mile of the facility; unlike during the Nazi era, trains do not enter the camps.

Auschwitz–Birkenau averages about two thousand visitors per day. At their peak, the four Birkenau gas chambers could "process" six thousand prisoners per day.

---

4. LONDON

Winston Churchill made it a point to call the Allies "the United Nations." Bitter differences over war aims and resources tested this union, but without doubt the city of London served as its capital. The monarchs of Belgium and Denmark, the elected heads of Poland and Czechoslovakia, and a host of other governments in exile came to call London their wartime home. Thousands of Commonwealth soldiers also converged there. In early 1944 more American men bivouacked in and around the English city than resided in Nebraska.

For all that was done in and to the city during the war, very little external evidence remains of a struggle. London's World War II history resides mostly in display cases, museums, and hangars. Fortunately, the city has easy access to a multitude of such sites and is one of the most tourist-friendly regions on the planet.

The mother of military collections is the Imperial War Museum. Focusing primarily on the First and Second World Wars, its highlights include Marshal Montgomery's command tank for the African campaign, remnants of Rudolf Hess's plane, a Spitfire, intact V-1 and V-2 rockets, numerous tanks and artillery pieces, visiting authors and displays, and a section of track from the India-Burma rail line built by Allied POWs.

Anchored in the Thames within the shadow of London Bridge is the HMS *Belfast*. The Royal Navy cruiser ran support missions for arctic convoys and laid down fire support off the NORMANDY beaches on D-day. A self-guided tour reveals almost the entire inner workings of a fighting vessel—its main guns, hospital, mess, communications, and its three-story pipe-labyrinth of a boiler room. Unfortunately, much of the ship is inaccessible for people with physical disabilities.

Among other sites are the National Army Museum and the Cabinet War Rooms. The latter (thirty feet below King Charles Street near Number 10 Downing) was the actual bunker from which Churchill and company directed the country during the war.

Hotels are abundant, as are restaurants, historic and entertainment attractions, and tour packages. If time is available, travel fifty miles north of the city to Duxford Imperial War Museum. It boasts perhaps the finest collection of historical military aircraft in the world and features every major type of fighter, bomber, and cargo plane used in the Second World War.

When traveling through London, the Underground provides quick and easy access to nearly every place of interest. The Tubes are important to see for another reason—the subterranean stations served as bomb shelters during the war.

---

5. CORREGIDOR

On Christmas Eve 1941, Gen. Douglas MacArthur, Philippines president Manuel Quezon, and supporting troops left besieged Manila

and headed for the safety of Corregidor. Three and a half miles long, crowned with artillery, and veined with underground tunnels, the mountainous island fortress and its thousands of soldiers were poised to protect vital Manila Bay and the Bataan Peninsula.

Though no explosive could penetrate the deep man-made caverns, hope was limited. MacArthur and Quezon left for Australia in February 1942. By April, Bataan had fallen, allowing the Japanese to bomb and shell Corregidor almost continuously. In May, the Japanese landed. Short of food, water, and ammunition, Lt. Gen. Jonathan Wainwright and eleven thousand troops and civilians surrendered, facing years in Japanese internment.

Today, the island is dedicated to the preservation of the fortress and to the memory of its defenders. A day tour is available, though the traveler is at the mercy of its tight schedule. A wiser use of time is an overnight trip, with a stay at the island's hotel or resort (both operated by Sun Cruises). Several gun emplacements, memorials, caves, old barracks, monuments, and scenic ocean views are within reach of rigorous walks, jeepney rentals, and open-air bus rides. The island's pièce de résistance is eight-hundred-foot-long Malinta Tunnel, which served as arsenal, head-quarters, and a thousand-bed hospital for the Allies and the Japanese.

A night tour of Malinta Tunnel is amazing but not for the claustrophobic or squeamish. In 1945, Japanese soldiers killed themselves in the tunnel rather than capitulate to the returning Allies.

---

6. THE ARDENNES

Scattered and diminutive monuments, comparatively small museums, and a dearth of road markings make this region a touring challenge, to say the least. But here the landscape becomes the story.

Covering southern Belgium and northern Luxembourg and con-sisting of tightly folded hills, carpets of fir trees, thin and wandering roads, and deep vocal rivers, the Ardennes appear to be impassible for a logging truck, let alone a panzer division. Viewing the area as a natural barrier, the French did not bother to extend the Maginot Line behind it. But through this vast tank trap Hitler launched his two major western offenses in 1940 and 1944. On both occasions he caught his opponents by complete surprise for obvious reasons.

As stated above, museums are few. Principal among them are the small but impressively equipped December 1944 Museum in La  Gleize, Belgium, with a rare Tiger tank parked outside; the Musée D'Histoire 1944–45 in Diekirch, Luxembourg, hosting numerous tanks, artillery pieces, and life-size military dioramas; and the Historical Center in Bastogne, Belgium, with an average collection of weapons and uniforms, a superior film showing footage from the actual BATTLE OF THE BULGE, and the three-story outdoor monument called Mardasson, touching in its sheer gratitude to the American liberation of Belgium.

Less visited and more important are the American, British, German, and Polish cemeteries in the area, and there are several. The Bulge was the bloodiest battle of the war for the United States, with nineteen thousand dead, most of whom are buried near Neuville en-Condroz and Henri Chapelle, Belgium, and just outside of Luxembourg City, Luxembourg.

In recognition of the courageous American defense of Bastogne during the Battle of the Bulge, every major road entrance into the city is "guarded" by a Sherman tank turret.

7. VOLGOGRAD (STALINGRAD)

Mamayev Hill was vital high ground during the battle of STALINGRAD. A perpetual target of artillery, air strikes, tanks, and close-quarter fighting, its soil was often reddened with blood and forever inundated with shrapnel.

Today nearly a square mile of the rise is home to Mamayev Memorial, commemorating the tremendous losses and immeasurable gains of the Soviet victory at STALINGRAD. Opened in 1967, the memorial is an elaborate progression of monuments lining the famous hillside.

Winding upward on granite walks (signifying permanence), through rows of poplar trees (the stalwart defenders), past flower beds and pools of water (eternal life), stand a series of statues and sculptures, each dedicated to a particular facet of the fight. Among other effec-  tively titled places for reflection are the Square of Those Who Fought to the Death, the Square of Heroes, and the Square of Sorrow. Past the last station, a gravesite holding tens of thousands killed in the battle, stands one of the most striking sculptures ever constructed. Towering from the top of Mamayev Hill is Motherland, a saintly female figure brandishing an enormous saber. Colossal, idyllic, and awe-inspiring, it is the most visited memorial in Russia.

Also in Volgograd is Russia's second most complete World War II museum (behind the sprawling Great Patriotic War Museum in Moscow). Refurbished and recommissioned on the fortieth anniversary of V-E Day (simply known as V-Day in Russia) in 1985, the seventy-year-old Volgograd State Panoramic Museum houses four thousand displays set in eight galleries, most of which exclusively feature the battle of STALINGRAD. The museum also has a lifelike panoramic painting two stories tall and the length of a football field entitled the "Defeat of Fascist Armies at Stalingrad."

From the United States, it costs twice as much and takes three times as long to fly to Volgograd as it takes to reach Paris. Getting around the Russian city is not the easiest endeavor for English-only tourists, though a few tours are available. Yet the effort is rewarded in full, if only to see where history profoundly and unquestionably changed course against the "Thousand-Year Reich" of Nazi Germany.

At more than three hundred feet in total height, Volograd's Motherland is the tallest freestanding statue on earth.

8. ARNHEM

In the September 1944 OPERATION MARKET-GARDEN, the British First Airborne plus elements of the First Polish Airborne along with Dutch

Resistance planned to take the town of Arnhem by air drop and then secure its priceless bridge across the Rhine until help arrived. Unfortunately, the plan went "a bridge too far." Today the key stop on this tour is the Airborne Museum, housed in the hotel that served as battle headquarters for the British First Airborne. It boasts an excellent collection of uniforms, relics from the battles, dioramas, video presentations, and a comprehensive 3-D map.

In Arnhem proper, Museum 40–45 depicts the desperate four years of occupied Holland and the fight for the city during Market-Garden. Also significant is the bridge itself. Destroyed after the battle and rebuilt to the same blueprints in 1950, it is now known as the Col. John Frost Bridge, named after the brigade commander who led the doomed attempt to take the span.

The Airborne Museum and other organizations offer walking and coach tours. In September paratroopers reenact an airdrop. To truly appreciate the difficulty facing the British Armored Thirty Corps, it may be enlightening to drive the seventy miles to Arnhem from the Belgian border (Highway N69 to N271) over its single narrow road crossing nine bridges.

In September of each year, the children of Arnhem gather at the Airborne Cemetery just west of town and adorn the British and Polish gravestones with flowers in honor of their sacrifice.

9. CASSINO

One look at Italy begs the question why the Allies considered this the "soft underbelly" of Europe. A spine of mountains down its length, a choice few roadway arteries up its coasts, and a thick skull of frigid Alps, the country was born for defense.

Deep in the shin of the Italian boot, between Naples and the capital, stands Cassino, where the Allied march on Rome came to a bloody halt. To wrest this high ground from the Germans, the Allies launched attack after attack—Americans in January 1944, New Zealanders in February, Indians in March. Finally, Poles and French in May.

The city today should be called New Cassino. The original town rested higher up the hill and was erased during the battle. Crowning the hill is Montecassino, the sixth-century monastery that was controversially and—as it turned out—pointlessly destroyed by Allied bombers in February 1944; rubble from the raids made for better defenses. Fortunately, the sprawling, looming abbey has been nearly restored and can be visited today, provided the tourist arrives properly attired (no shorts or short-sleeved shirts). Some of the original religious trappings survived the battle and are on site.

Surrounding the abbey are grave reminders of the international struggle that took place. Nearby is a Polish cemetery, accessed by stairs, holding more than one thousand troops. Just outside of town is a Commonwealth cemetery with more than four thousand resting places, plus four thousand names of the missing. Farther north is a German cemetery with twenty thousand bodies.

The site is an hour south of Rome. Hotels are plentiful, but the land is rugged and steep. If walking is undesirable, renting a car may be the best option, although Italian motorways are not for the timid.

Ten miles southeast of Cassino is the village of San Pietro Infine. Though tourists visit, it has no inhabitants. All its residents were killed or driven off during a fierce battle there, and the ruins of the town remain as they were in 1943.

10. HIROSHIMA

On any given day, the atmosphere at Hiroshima's Peace Park is strangely relaxed, surrounded as it is by a bustling metropolis of one

million people. Straddling the river Motoyasu, about five hundred yards square, the park is a collection of memorials, a burial mound, temples, and other shrines of solemnity. Most of them impart the "Spirit of Hiroshima," an internal and international appeal for ever-lasting peace. Across the river in the park's northeast corner stands the decaying cadaver of the "The A–Bomb Dome," once known as Hiroshima Prefecture Industrial Promotion Hall, above which occurred the air burst. Just north is the T-shaped Aioi Bridge, used as the aiming point for the Enola Gay.

Central to the complex is the three-story Hiroshima Peace Memorial Museum. Engrossing may be the operative word here. Text is in English and Japanese. There are charred and melted relics of the blast, before and after pictures of human bodies, films of the damage, and video testimonials from survivors. Present is a rare acknowledgment of the Japanese army's 1937 Rape of Nanking. Of the Hiroshima bomb itself, the museum implies that its use was racially motivated. A heavy emphasis is placed on the ensuing nuclear arms race.

Hiroshima is on the largest Japanese island of Honshu. Direct flights to the city are expensive. The better route is by way of bullet train from Tokyo, then by streetcar to the park. Though everything can be covered in a day, the city is home to a bustling nightlife and a major baseball team. Many signs are in English, and hotels are abundant.

In 1946, several prominent Japanese from the Hiroshima area gathered to discuss plans for reconstructing the city. One person suggested preserving the vast wasteland as it was to serve "as a memorial graveyard for the sake of everlasting world peace."[53]

WAYS TO GET INVOLVED

Americans treated the Civil War and World War II almost exactly the same. When the conflicts ended, so ended much of the attention they commanded. Citizens generally bade each calamity a hasty good riddance and moved on. Not until decades had gone by and the war generation began to pass away did the country as a whole turn to see each event for its great magnitude.

For Americans in the early twenty-first century, there are abundant prospects to connect with the Second World War. Established organizations, extensive documentation, and global communications provide far-reaching networks of opportunity. Following are ten among many activities available for newcomers and diehards, students and educators, anyone interested in experiencing history beyond the confines of the bookstore and cable television. Ranking is according to the minimum investment in time and funds required for participation, from least to most.

1. INTERVIEW A VETERAN

Sixteen million men and women served in the U.S. armed forces during World War II. Just over a third were still alive at the start of the twenty-first century. These individuals are dying at a rate of twelve hundred per day. As is too often the case, many depart and take their memories with them, having never recorded their unique and irreplaceable stories for generations present or to come.

Thankfully, in a measure that passed both houses unanimously, the U.S. Congress appropriated the creation of the Veterans History Project. Administered by the Library of Congress American Folklife Center, the program has evolved into the central database for written, audio, and video testimonials of those who witnessed and took part in the largest war of all time.

Along with the veterans themselves, the pillars of this noble endeavor are the people who are willing to take time to conduct interviews and send them in. To date, submissions have topped the fifteen thousand mark, including interviews of Holocaust survivors, civilians involved in the war effort, and veterans from other conflicts. In addition to thousands of enlightening and priceless narratives, participants have sent in copies and originals of wartime photos, maps, drawings, and letters, preserving for the foreseeable future artifacts that would have otherwise been easily lost or forgotten.

To learn more and to download all necessary instructions and forms, visit the Veterans History Project Website (http.loc.gov/folklife/vets), or write: The Veterans History Project, American Folklife Center, Library of Congress, 101 Independence Avenue SE, Washington, D.C. 20540-4615.

One U.S. World War II veteran has died in the time it takes to read this entry.

2. SUPPORT THE JOINT POW/MIA ACCOUNTING COMMAND

The U.S. Government lists eighteen hundred Americans as missing from the Vietnam War. In comparison, seventy-eight thousand Americans are listed as missing from the Second World War. Of these, thirty-five thousand bodies have been determined to be recoverable.

A military unit activated in 2003 helps bring these missing patriots home and helps bring closure to grieving families. It is the Joint POW/MIA Accounting Command (JPAC).

Stationed at Hickham Field in Hawaii, JPAC consists of highly trained military and civilian specialists who spend thousands of hours researching leads and records, negotiating with foreign governments, investigating sites, recovering the fallen, and identifying remains. Their many destinations have included Burma, China, Okinawa, and Germany. In 2004 the outfit conducted several successful operations, including the retrieval of six sets of remains from Caen in NORMANDY, believed to be five Americans and a British serviceman who had been missing since 1942.

The process is considerably expensive. Detection, retrieval, and identification can take two or more years for each case, and funding of this noble work depends heavily on appropriations from Congress.

Help draw greater attention to the program by voicing support. Begin with contacting your representative and senators and urging them to help JPAC in every way possible. Go to the websites of the U.S. House (www.house.gov) and Senate (www.senate.gov). Also write to the president, the Senate Foreign Relations Committee, and the Armed Services Committee, so JPAC can continue its noble work and fulfill its mission.

JPAC's Central Identification Laboratory is the largest forensic anthropology lab on earth.

3. HELP A VETERANS SERVICE ORGANIZATION

Driving a car, sending a check, writing a letter, manning a phone… simple things move mountains. As World War II veterans age, their needs increase accordingly, and so does their appreciation for friendly help.

Orchestrating goodwill into a concerted effort are scores of veterans service organizations who help care for others and society as a whole. Several reputable foundations are specific to the Second World War, including the American Defenders of Bataan and Corregidor, the U.S. Submarine Veterans of World War II, and the Women Air Force Service Pilots of World War II.

Whether through time or money, a person can help someone make a doctor's appointment, stay in contact with old friends, build a monument, or receive the benefits and medals they have earned. For volunteers with talents in health care, there are many great opportunities in the Blinded Veterans Association, Disabled American Veterans, and the Paralyzed Veterans of America, among others.

To see what can be done and what needs to be done, go to the U.S. Department of Veterans Affairs website and review its more than forty partner organizations (www.va.gov).

Although they are passing away rapidly, veterans of the Second World War still outnumber the veterans of the Vietnam War by almost two to one.

4. DONATE TO A MUSEUM

Operational costs continue to climb and plague the caretakers of history. Building and grounds maintenance, artifact tending and restoration, display climate control, and insurance gut the budgets on a daily basis. In addition, many facilities are in desperate need of new or updated security systems, as few places have been spared the work of thieves, and more than one institution has been forced to close after repeated hits.

Even when museums are operating in the black, a little extra capital helps them host new or annual programs, such as veterans' reunions and traveling exhibits.

If a friend or family member was a veteran in the war, look to the places where they served. Some units and bases have their own museums, as do the four branches of the military service. The U.S. Army has a few museums—thirty-four of them. The honoree does not have to be far off. Community historical societies often have collections commemorating the local war effort. In many places modest donations can buy membership into trusts, which often bring free admission, newsletters, plus special programs and tour opportunities to contributors.

For an extensive listing of museums and contact information, see Steve Rajtar and Francis E. Franks, *War Monuments, Museums, and Library Collections of 20th Century Conflicts: A Directory of United States Sites* (2002).

One of the more eclectic museums is in Deming, New Mexico. Along with a touching display commemorating the Bataan Death March, the Luna Mimbres Museum also has a cowboy exhibit, antique cars, and a collection of fine art.

---

5. JOIN OR START A WORLD WAR II ROUND TABLE

World War II round tables are few and far between. Some of the more established groups are in Atlanta, Columbus, Emporia, Minneapolis, and New Orleans. But their numbers are growing.

Round tables are one of the best ways to share experiences and information, to talk of movies, books, and programs, and to hear guest speakers. Many times, people feel too intimidated to join in, believing that a person has to be an expert with encyclopedic knowledge to take part. In reality, the best round tables welcome newcomers and contain all levels of knowledge. The only prerequisite is interest.

If a round table or discussion group is not nearby, consider starting one. Contact local historical societies, collegiate history departments, and veterans organizations to seek out meeting places and potential recruits. All it takes is two or more people, a box of doughnuts, and something to talk about.

Although there were a modest number of World War II round tables sixty years after V-J Day, there were no Civil War round tables seventy years after Appomattox.

---

6. COLLECT ARTIFACTS

On the move, troops tried to carry as little as possible. But when it came time to come home, many of them turned into the biggest pack rats this side of the Smithsonian. What the soldiers, sailors, and marines brought back constitutes a healthy portion of the war artifacts circulating in the United States today.

Objects d'art of war are plentiful and wide-ranging: medals, music, helmets, stamps, newspapers, weaponry, flags, photographs, etc. Where there is curiosity, there is probably a curio to go with it. Ammunition casings are not hard to find, nor should they be. Munitions plants made bullets by the billions. Bulkier items include radios, uniforms, airplane parts, or whole planes. Traditionally, some of the more popular items have been autographs, period posters, and original battle maps.

To get educated on what is available, try auctions (including online sites), swap meets, and antique shows. These venues tend to be expensive for purchasing but are good places to pick up information. To look for hidden treasures, estate sales and tag sales require footwork but sometimes harvest great rewards.

The best defense against mistaking replicas for the real thing or overpaying for authentic pieces is prudence. Work with reputable dealers, research heavily before big ventures, and start with the following: Henry-Paul Enjames, *G.I. Collectors Guide* (2003); Robin

Lumsden, *Detecting the Fakes: A Collectors Guide to Third Reich Militaria* (2000); Patrick Newell, *Military Collectibles* (2000).

Obtaining certain artifacts from Europe might have legal ramifications. Though Internet sales are difficult to regulate, most European states have strict laws against the sale and purchase of Third Reich memorabilia.

---

7. VISIT A HISTORIC SITE OR MUSEUM

A passport is not needed to see the European or Pacific theaters. New Orleans has the National D-day Museum. The National Museum of the Pacific War floats on seven arid acres of Texas Hill Country in Adm. CHESTER NIMITZ's hometown of Fredericksburg.

All fifty states have museums, monuments, and memorials. Many host bona fide locales of World War II history, such as Building D of the SAC Air Force Base south of Omaha, where the famous B-29s Enola Gay and Bock's Car were built. Their infamous cargo was tested near the National Atomic Museum in Albuquerque, New Mexico. Several historic warships returned to the states in one piece, and more than thirty are open to public viewing, including LEYTE GULF veteran USS *Alabama* moored in Mobile, IWO JIMA witness USS *Massachusetts* in Fall River, plus the aircraft carrier and kamikaze-survivor USS *Intrepid* in New York. Among destroyers, cruisers, and landing craft, there are also sixteen submarines, among them U-505 in Chicago, captured from the Third Reich in 1944.

Across the country, hangars and airfields have B-17s, B-24s, and B-29s, Hellcats, Warhawks, and Zeros, plus tanks, half-tracks, and artillery. There is the Women's Army Corps Museum in Anniston, Alabama; the Engineers-Seabees Museum in Port Hueneme, California; and the just plain huge Museum of World War II in Natick, Massachusetts. For World War II buffs, the world is at your doorstep.

For domestic destinations, see Richard E. Osborne, *World War II Sites in the United States: A Tour Guide and Directory* (1996) and Rajtar and Franks, *War Monuments, Museums, and Library Collections of 20th Century Conflicts* (2002).

If the opportunity arises for overseas travel, first read John T. Bookman and Stephen T. Powers, *The March to Victory* (1994) and Chuck Thompson, *The 25 Best World War Two Sites: European Theater* (2004). Also by Chuck Thompson is *The 25 Best World War Two Sites: Pacific Theater* (2002). The British publication *After the Battle* gives in-depth analysis of World War II sites and associated travel opportunities. Its website is www.afterthebattle.com.

The U.S. First Armored Division Museum is excellent, but it is a bit of a commute. The museum, which features dioramas, photos, and a tank park, is in Baumholder, Germany.

---

8. TRACE GENEALOGY

There is still much to learn from those who are gone. Retracing family members and their role in the war can reveal what the event was really like and how we are truly connected to it.

A little work can unearth very deep roots. Hiding in hope chests, photo albums, attics, and journals are links to personal heritage. Archives, veterans organizations, and unit histories also hold considerable information. Most important, there are still a precious few years left to seek out the most valuable resources of all: the deceased's living friends and relatives.

To organize the search, consider purchasing genealogy software. Try the following for guidance: How to Trace Your Family Tree, American Genealogical Research Institute Staff (1998), and the National Archives and Records Administration, Washington, D.C. (www.nara. gov). An excellent source of additional information is a website entitled "Dad's War: Finding and Telling Your Father's World War II Story" (www.members.aol.com/dadswar).

American genealogy suffered a blow on July 12, 1973. At the National Personnel Records Center in St. Louis, a fire broke out and destroyed more than sixteen million official military files. Approximately 80 percent of files on persons discharged from the army between 1912 and 1960 were lost. No index or duplicates were ever made.

9. SPONSOR A PRESERVATION PROJECT

In 2001, Ford Island in PEARL HARBOR made the "11 Most Endangered" list of the National Trust for Historic Preservation. More than six hundred POW camps holding more than 400,000 Axis soldiers once dotted the United States but are now steadily fading into the landscape. Age, neglect, and the elements are devouring historic sites, monuments, and artifacts. Some of the more intricate items, such as aircraft, require expert handling, expensive equipment and materials, rare replacement parts, and a hefty amount of work hours just for maintenance. Harbored ships require routine dry-dock work.

Fortunately, there are friends associations, dedicated museums, and preservation grants to combat loss of the irreplaceable. The Strategic Air Command Museum in Omaha, Nebraska, and the Combat Air Museum in Topeka, Kansas, among many others, continually refurbish World War II aircraft. The San Francisco Maritime National Park dry-docks its Pacific submarine USS *Pampanito* once every six or so years. The Friends of Camp Hearne in Hearne, Texas, are one of a select few groups trying to preserve a World War II–era POW camp.

A person can dedicate a few dollars or a few thousand hours in helping restore and preserve the past. For direction, inspiration, and some fascinating stories, consult the following: the National Trust for Historic Preservation (www.nthp.org); Lou Thole, *Forgotten Fields of America: World War II Bases and Training, Then and Now*, volumes 1 and 2; Kit Bonner and Carlyn Bonner, *Warship Boneyards* (2001); and Nicholas A. Veronico et al., *Military Aircraft Boneyards* (2000).

One World War II site that has endured but was not supposed to was the Pentagon. Hurriedly built in 1942, it was intended as a temporary facility to house the voluminous staff of the War Department. The onset of the Cold War greatly extended its lease on life.

10. REENACT

It's not just for Civil War buffs anymore. Since the 1970s, World War II reenacting has grown from a few enthusiasts into a worldwide assortment of living history groups. Most portray specific combat units, such as the U.S. Second Armored Division (based in California) and A Company, First Battalion, Royal Ulster Rifles (fine blokes mostly from Mississippi and Arkansas). There are Czechs impersonating U.S. Airborne, Belgians acting as Canadian paratroopers, French portraying themselves, and Americans duplicating British infantry. Some groups depict Soviet and German units but strive to be apolitical, focusing instead on the physical, technical, and communal aspects of soldiering.

Participants work to know as much as possible about their historic unit—what the soldiers ate, where they served, how they fought—to better appreciate and understand the military experience of the war. To share what they've learned, many reenacting outfits take part in public demonstrations, parades, restoration projects, and battle reenactments.

Be warned: World War II reenacting takes a great deal of time, study, and fitness. It is also a pricey pursuit. Uniforms, mock weapons, rations, camp gear, and travel can easily cost a few thousand greenbacks. Some units even maintain working historic vehicles.

To learn more, go to the Military History Reenactment website (www.reenactor.net). Also, find a nearby event, speak with the participants, and take note of the rigors involved. It is hard work and hard play, but there is nothing quite like lugging a forty-pound pack, slogging on a long march through a cold rain, wearing wet wool, and downing C-rations to bring a person a little closer to living history.

Several airborne reenactment groups like the 507th Parachute Infantry Regiment out of Detroit are pretty serious. They actually use period equipment and jump out of planes.

EPILOGUE

———•———

The wars within the Second World War died just as they were born—one by one. By mid-1943, organized fighting ceased in North Africa, and U-boats quietly withdrew from the North Atlantic. In late 1944 Greece, Hungary, and Romania succumbed to the Red Army. Through the spring of 1945 Germany underwent a long, slow, bloody implosion, crushed between two grand armies totaling five million troops. The Third Reich would outlive its master by a mere week. By August 1945, the Empire of Japan was no longer an empire—beaten, starved, surrounded, and finally eradiated into capitulation.

In Europe, commonly observed endpoints to the war were May 7, 1945, when Gen. Alfred Jodl surrendered to the Western Allies in Reims, France, and the following day, when Field Marshal WILHELM KEITEL repeated the ceremony with the Soviets in Berlin. In the Pacific the Japanese government unconditionally surrendered on August 14, 1945. Allies recognized the next day as V-J Day, although formal victory came on the deck of the battleship USS *Missouri* on September 2, 1945.

Of more than one hundred nations and colonies involved in World War II, the highest death toll belonged to the Soviet Union. Moscow initially estimated 20 million dead, a number viewed with much skepticism in the West. More recent evidence suggests the assessment was in fact too low; a count of 28 million is more accurate. Unlike most countries, the Soviet Union did not replace its losses quickly. By 1950 the nation still had 12 million fewer citizens than in 1939. China suffered the second highest number of fatalities with perhaps 15 million dead, but its overall population increased by more than 100 million during the course of the war. Germany lost 7 million, with Poland next at 6 million. At least 2.5 million Japanese died. Yugoslavia lost 1.5 million, followed by Czechoslovakia, France, Italy, and Romania each losing approximately 600,000 citizens.

Great Britain, losing 300,000 military personnel and 61,000 civilians, stood fourteenth among the worst subtracted nations. The United States ranked fifteenth globally in total losses with 407,318 military and several hundred civilian fatalities, or about 0.2 percent of its overall population. In all, the Axis lost nearly 13 million people. Allied nations lost approximately 45 million.

Of the war's innumerable legacies, there were a great many positives. The war fostered leaps in medicine, particularly in the fields of antibiotics, synthesized pharmaceuticals, and psychology. Rudimentary data machines became the first step to the creation of computers. Soon after the war, women in France, Italy, Hungary, Japan, and Yugoslavia gained the right to vote. Ultramilitarist regimes in Germany, Italy, and Japan all but disappeared, slowly and steadily replaced by stable representative democracies. In international affairs, previously diehard independent states acknowledged the need for greater cooperation. The United Nations came into formal existence in October 1945, greatly expanding upon the powers and membership of its predecessor. The International Monetary Fund and World Bank, formed in December 1945, were designed to prevent the possibility of another global economic depression. Signaling a return of faith in collective security, twelve countries joined in creating the North Atlantic Treaty Organization (NATO) in 1949, countered by eight nations conglomerating into the Warsaw Pact in 1951. Though many viewed the two alliances as caustic threats to world unity, the institutions proved to be stabilizing forces in a bipolar standoff.

Of course, there were many changes of questionable merit. Before the war there were no such things as nerve gases, proximity fuses, cruise missiles, napalm, intercontinental ballistic missiles, and atomic bombs.

Arguably, no legacy was as obstinate and enduring as the war itself. In many ways the global conflict did not end in 1945. Several Nazi concentration camps remained open under Soviet management. Buchenwald, Sachsenhausen, Ravensbrück, and others in the eastern sector continued operation well into 1950, interning former Nazis and others deemed menacing to international security. Evidence suggests some ten thousand people died in Buchenwald alone.

The refugee crisis worsened after the war. There were seven million Japanese in China, Korea, Malay, and the Pacific, and more than eleven million Germans in Poland, Czechoslovakia, the Ukraine, and elsewhere. Perhaps five million imported slave laborers and camp inmates were still alive in Germany by the time Berlin fell, along with untold numbers of Koreans forcibly detained in Japan and Manchuria. There were displaced persons of all nationalities, soldiers in remote outposts, and POWs, all numbering in the millions. Exact numbers are unattainable, but deaths from postwar migrations likely matched or exceeded the lives consumed by the Holocaust.

A lasting misery was the war's incredible depth of devastation. With the exception of the United States and Canada, national economies took years—in some cases decades—to return to prewar levels. Factories, bridges, dams, canals, roads, boats, and vehicles were destroyed, not to mention millions of draft animals and farms. Major centers of civilization had been reduced to ashes and rubble. Families that had once thought of owning a radio or perhaps an automobile were reduced to searching daily for food, water, and shelter. Unexploded bombs, shells, and mines continued to deform and kill for decades to come.

Although peace came to Germany and Japan, fighting continued well after 1945 in China, Greece, India, Indochina, Indonesia, and Palestine. Inspired by the weakening of empires, colonies throughout Africa and South Asia vied for independence, many of them through armed insurrection. The Red Army remained in Eastern and Central Europe for forty-five years after the fall of the Third Reich. The U.S. armed forces never left Okinawa, Japan, or Germany.

The Allies conducted war-crimes trials regularly into the 1960s. In the West, more than 5,000 Germans were brought to trial, over 800 were sentenced to death, and 486 of these sentences were carried out. Soviet courts tried 87,000 Germans, jailing or executing the majority. Israel, which did not exist at war's end, convicted alleged Nazis into the 1990s. By and large, war criminals on the Allied side were not prosecuted or punished, including many within the Red Army who proved just as capable of unspeakable crimes against humanity as their Axis counterparts.

The most lethal consequence of the war came in the shape of the Cold War. In the 1930s, the United States and Soviet Union were generally isolationist and little more than aloof to each other. By the end of the 1940s the two states had transformed into superpowers, well-armed, mutually hostile, and positioned directly against each other in East Asia and across the heart of Europe. The following decades witnessed an open contest for hegemony, ballooning expenditures on defense programs, and the stockpiling of enough nuclear, biological, and chemical weapons to destroy the world several times over.

Fittingly, the Cold War ended in peace at the same time, and with the same document, that officially ended the Second World War. On September 12, 1990, Britain, France, the Soviet Union, and the United States signed a peace agreement with West and East Germany, the Treaty on the Final Settlement with Respect to Germany. The accord enabled the parties "to overcome the division of the continent" and to effectively bring to an end the costliest and bloodiest conglomeration of wars in human history.

The question arises whether another world war is possible. Unsettling is the fact that no one truly expected World War II to happen. Certainly no one could have predicted the level or lethality of its consequences.

In 1939, Americans hoped to stay out of several small wars, aspiring instead to concentrate on domestic issues. By 1945 the United States was the world's largest arsenal and most advanced fighting machine, with an armed presence in more than half the time zones of the planet, supporting forty countries with weapons and machinery, and sole owner of the most powerful weapon ever devised.

Japan's militarists created a Greater East Asia Co-Prosperity Sphere stretching from the tail of the Aleutians to the edges of Australia. In three years the reckless experiment died by the sword, leaving many of the warmongers dead and previously undefeated Japan under foreign occupation.

Nazi heads professed their rule would endure for a thousand years—it lasted twelve. A demonic former corporal thought he could divide and conquer nations, taking each one after a few weeks of intense military assault. But after six years of war, he had lost everything, including his life. His plans to eradicate Zionism and Bolshevism fell short, to say the least. By the end of 1945, Israel was soon to become a political reality, and communism had spread from one country to ten, including the eastern third of Germany.

Hubris and miscalculation may again permit a collection of wars to merge into a worldwide conflict. As Hitler's confidant Albert Speer noted in 1947, global chaos may be unthinkable, but it is not improbable. While serving a twenty-year sentence for war crimes and crimes against humanity, Speer reflected upon the Second World War and observed: "The build-up of negative impulses, each reinforcing the other, can inexorably shake to pieces the complicated apparatus of the modern world."

TIME LINE

1937

July 7	Japan invades China
August 13–November 9	Battle for Shanghai
December 13–30	Rape of Nanking

1938

March 11	Germany annexes Austria
September 29	Munich Agreement signed

1939

March 15	German army enters Prague, Czechoslovakia
May 22	Italy signs "Pact of Steel" with Germany
September 1	Germany invades Poland
September 3	Australia, Britain, France, and New Zealand declare war on Germany
September 17	Soviet Union invades Poland
September 27	Warsaw, Poland, falls to Germany
October 16	First German bombings of England
November 30	Soviet Union invades Finland

1940

April 8	Germany attacks Denmark and Norway
April 10	Denmark surrenders to Germany
May 10	Germany invades Belgium, France, Holland, Luxembourg
May 10	Winston Churchill replaces Neville Chamberlain as British prime minister
May 14	Holland falls to Germany
May 27–June 4	British forces evacuate France in "Miracle of Dunkirk"
June 9	Norway falls to Germany
June 22	France surrenders to Germany
July 10–October 12	Battle of Britain (Allied victory)
August 25	RAF bombs Berlin
September 16	U.S. Congress passes Selective Service Act
September 22	Japan occupies northern Indochina (Vietnam)
September 27	Axis forms with Germany-Italy-Japan Tripartite Pact
October 7	Germany enters Romania

1941

March 8	U.S. Senate passes Lend–Lease Bill
March 9	Italy attacks Greece
April 6	Germany invades Yugoslavia and Greece
April 13	Soviet Union and Japan sign neutrality pact
April 17	Yugoslavia falls to Germany
April 24	Greece falls to Germany
May 27	*Bismarck* sunk by British Royal Navy
June 22	Germany invades Soviet Union

August 12	Churchill and Roosevelt create Atlantic Charter
September 15	Germans surround Leningrad, nine-hundred day siege begins
October 17	Tojo Hideki succeeds Konoye Fumimaro as prime minister of Japan
October 19	Germans lay siege on Moscow
December 6	Soviet Union launches counterattack on Germans
December 7	Japan attacks Pearl Harbor, Guam, Wake Island, the Philippines, Malaya, and Hong Kong
December 8	United States declares war on Japan
December 9	Nationalist China declares war on Japan and Germany
December 11	Japan invades Burma; Italy and Germany declare war on the United States
December 23	Wake Island falls to Japan
December 25	Hong Kong falls to Japan

1942

January 2	Japan takes Manila
January 11	Japan invades Dutch East Indies
February 15	Singapore falls to Japan
April 9	U.S. and Philippines troops surrender at Bataan; death march begins
April 18	Doolittle leads sixteen B-25s on Japan raid
May 7	U.S. troops surrender at Corregidor
May 7–8	Battle of Coral Sea (Japanese victory)
May 20	Japan conquers Burma
June 4–7	Battle of Midway (U.S. victory)

June 9	Japan conquers Philippines
July 1–27	First Battle of El Alamein, Egypt (British victory)
August 7	U.S. forces land at Guadalcanal
August 9	Mohandas Gandhi begins civil disobedience campaign in India
August 14	Allied invasion at Dieppe, France (German victory)
August 24	Germans enter Stalingrad
August 30–September 2	Battle of Alam Halfa, Egypt (British victory)
October 23–November 4	Second Battle of El Alamein (British victory)
November 8	Allies land in northwest Africa (Operation Torch)

1943

January 14	Allied Casablanca Conference
January 23	Allies capture Tripoli, Libya
February 2	More than ninety thousand Germans surrender at Stalingrad
February 19–23	Axis inflict heavy losses at Kasserine Pass, Tunisia
April 18	Adm. Yamamoto Isoroku (commander in chief of the Imperial Combined Fleet) shot down and killed over Solomon Islands
April 19–May 16	Jewish uprising in Warsaw ghetto
July 5–23	Battle of Kursk (Soviet victory)
July 10	Allies invade Sicily
July 23	Allies capture Palermo, Sicily
July 25	Benito Mussolini falls from power

September 8	Italy surrenders to Allies
October 13	Italy declares war on Germany
November 3	German Field Marshal Irwin Rommel takes command of Atlantic Wall
November 28– December 1	First Allied "Big Three" Conference— Tehran, Persia

1944

January 16	Gen. Dwight Eisenhower becomes supreme allied commander in Europe
January 22	U.S. forces land at Anzio, Italy
January 26	Leningrad freed of German siege
February 15	Allies begin bombing Monte Cassino monastery, Italy
April 3	Soviet forces enter Romania
June 5	Rome falls to Allies
June 6	D-day, NORMANDY
June 13	First V-1 buzz bomb hits Britain
June 15	First B-29 raid on Japan
July 9	U.S. takes island of Saipan
July 18	Tojo resigns as Japan prime minister
July 20	Bomb plot fails to kill Hitler
August 1–October 2	Polish Home Army and militia launch Second Warsaw uprising and are defeated
August 10	U.S. retakes Guam
August 25	Paris liberated
September 4	Antwerp, Belgium, liberated
September 15	U.S. attacks Peleliu
September 17–25	Allied Operation Market-Garden (German victory)

October 13	Allies retake Greece
October 21	Aachen becomes first German city to fall to Allies
October 23–26	Battle of Leyte Gulf (U.S. victory)
December 16–	
January 16	Battle of the Bulge (Allied victory)

1945

January 17	Soviet Union captures Warsaw, Poland
February 4–11	Yalta Conference
February 13	Soviet Union captures Budapest, Hungary
February 19–March 26	Battle of Iwo Jima (U.S. victory)
February 25	U.S. firebombs Tokyo
March 9	U.S. firebombs Tokyo again
April 1–June 22	Battle of Okinawa (U.S. victory)
April 6	Organized use of kamikazes in Okinawa
April 12	U.S. president Franklin D. Roosevelt dies
April 28	Mussolini killed by partisans
April 30	Hitler commits suicide in Berlin
May 2	German forces surrender Italy; Soviet Union captures Berlin
May 7	Germany surrenders to Allies
July 16	First atomic bomb tested at Alamogordo, New Mexico
July 17	Potsdam Conference—outside Berlin, Germany
August 6	Atomic bomb is dropped over Hiroshima
August 8	Soviet Union declares war on Japan, invades Manchuria hours later
August 9	Atomic bomb is dropped over Nagasaki
August 14	Hirohito announces surrender
September 2	Japan formally surrenders

NOTES

CHAPTER 1: "THE GATHERING STORM"

1. Paul Kennedy, *The Rise and Fall of the Great Powers* (New York: Random House, 1987), table 15.

2. J. N. Westwood, *Russia Against Japan, 1904–1905* (New York: State University of New York Press, 1986), 6–7.

3. Mikiso Hane, *Modern Japan: A Historical Survey* (Boulder, CO: Westview Press, 1992), 160.

4. Although the United States made few political or military maneuvers internationally between 1868 and 1898, there was growing commercial activity. Some historians consider this a period of "U.S. economic imperialism." See William A. Williams, ed., *From Colony to Empire* (New York: Wiley, 1972).

5. Norman Davies, *Heart of Europe* (New York: Oxford University Press, 1986), 112–13; Michael Howard, "The Legacy of the First World War," in *Paths to War*, ed. Robert Boyce and Esmonde M. Robertson (London: Macmillan, 1989), 38; Martin Kitchen, *Europe Between the Wars: A Political History* (London: Longman, 1988), 22–24.

6. Evan Mawdsley, *The Russian Civil War* (Boston: Allen and Unwin, 1987), 252.

7. Sheila Fitzpatrick, "The Legacy of the Civil War" in *Party, State, and Society in the Russian Civil War*, eds. Diane P. Koenker, William G. Rosenberg, and Ronald Grigor Suny (Bloomington, IN, Indiana University Press, 1989), 388–91.

8. Davies, *Heart of Europe*, 118; Mawdsley, *The Russian Civil War*, 250–51, 258–60.

9. Mawdsley, *The Russian Civil War*, 253.

10. Yoshihisa Tak Matsusaka, *The Making of Japanese Manchuria, 1904–1932* (Cambridge, MA: Harvard University Press, 2001), 383–87.

11. Ibid., 384.

12. Maurice Baumont, *The Origins of the Second World War* (New Haven, CT: Yale University Press, 1978), 144–46.

13. Ibid., 166.

14. Stephen J. Lee, *European Dictatorships, 1918–1945* (London: Routledge Press, 2000), 3.

15. Chinese estimations place the dead at Nanking at three hundred thousand. Japan officially claimed the death toll to be in the tens of thousands.

16. Republican quote from Clay Blair, *Hitler's U-Boat War: The Hunters, 1939–1942* (New York: Random House, 1996), 25. See also Erik Goldstein and John Maurer, eds., *The Washington Conference, 1921–1922* (Essex, UK: Frank Cass, 1994); Raymond J. Sontag, *A Broken World, 1919–1930* (New York: Harper & Row, 1972), 86–110.

17. Denis Winter, *Death's Men* (Middlesex, UK: Penguin, 1985), 120–22.

18. Leo P. Brophy, Wyndham D. Miles, and Rexmond C. Cochrane, *The Chemical Warfare Service: From Laboratory to Field* (Washington D.C.: U.S. Army Office of the Chief of Military History, 1959).

19. Briand quoted in Hans Mommsen, *The Rise and Fall of the Weimar Republic* (Chapel Hill: University of North Carolina Press, 1996), 206.

20. Marshall Lee and Wolfgang Michalka, *German Foreign Policy, 1917–1933* (New York: St. Martin's Press, 1987), 80–85; Mommsen, *The Rise and Fall of the Weimar Republic*, 199–208.

21. David H. Miller, *The Peace Pact of Paris* (New York: G. P. Putnam's Sons, 1928), 7.

22. Robert H. Ferrell, *Peace in Their Time: The Origins of the Kellogg-Briand Pact* (New Haven, CT: Yale University Press, 1952), 207.

23. Blair, *Hitler's U-Boat War*, 24–26; Christopher Hall, *Britain, America, and Arms Control, 1921–1937* (London: MacMillan, 1987), 101–3.

24. Piers Brendon, *The Dark Valley: A Panorama of the 1930's* (New York: Knopf, 2000), 208–10; Hall, *Britain, America, and Arms Control*, 107–8; Stephen Pelz, *Race to Pearl Harbor: The Failure of the Second London Naval Conference and the Onset of World War II* (Cambridge, MA: Harvard University Press, 1974), 2–3.

25. Richard Lamb, *The Drift to War, 1922–1939* (New York: St. Martin's Press, 1989), 70–71.

26. Anthony P. Adamthwaite, *The Making of the Second World War* (London: Allen and Unwin, 1977), 78.

27. See also Philip Noel-Baker, *The First World Disarmament Conference, 1932–1933* (Oxford, UK: Pergamon, 1979).

28. Rodney J. Morrison, "The London Monetary and Economic Conference of 1933: A Public Goods Analysis," *American Journal of Economics and Sociology* (July 1993): 309–10.

29. R. J. Overy, *The Inter-War Crisis, 1919–1939* (London: Longman, 1994), 50.

30. Morrison, "London Monetary and Economic Conference," 312–15.

31. Richard Collier, *Duce* (New York: Viking Press, 1971), 124.

32. Mussolini quoted in ibid., 125.

33. Ibid., 120–21.

34. Hitler quoted in William L. Shirer, *The Rise and Fall of the Third Reich* (New York: Fawcett Crest, 1988), 496.

35. See also Maya Latynski, ed., *Reappraising the Munich Pact* (Washington D.C.: Woodrow Wilson Center Press, 1992).

36. Roosevelt quoted in Pelz, *Race to Pearl Harbor*, 157.

37. Kitchen, *Europe Between the Wars*, 25.

38. John W. Dower, *War Without Mercy: Race and Power in the Pacific* War (New York: Pantheon Books, 1986), 4–5; Yukiko Koshiro, "Japan's World and World War II," *Diplomatic History* (Summer 2001): 426–28.

39. P. M. H. Bell, "Another Thirty Years War?" in *World War II: Roots and Causes*, ed. Keith Eubank (Lexington, MA: D. C. Heath, 1992), 20; Norman M. Naimark, *Fires of Hatred: Ethnic Cleansing in Twentieth-Century Europe* (Cambridge, MA: Harvard University Press, 2001), 6–7.

40. Andrew J. Crozier, *The Causes of the Second World War* (Oxford, UK: Blackwell, 1997), 179–81.

41. Lamb, *The Drift to War*, 4–6; Gerhard L. Weinberg, *A World at Arms* (New York: Cambridge University Press, 1994), 14–16.

42. Bell, "Another Thirty Years War?", 17. Quote of British MP Eric Geddes in Erik Goldstein, T*he First World War Peace Settlements, 1919–1925* (London: Longman, 2002), 15. Foch quoted in Richard Overy, *The Road to War* (London: Penguin Books, 1999), 122.

43. Goldstein, *First World War Peace Settlements*, 83.

44. Lamb, *The Drift to War*, 6.

45. Lee, *European Dictatorships*, 1–4, 18.

46. Robert Boyce, "World Depression, World War: Some Economic Origins of the Second World War," in *Paths to War*, ed. Robert Boyce and Esmonde M. Robertson (London: MacMillan, 1989), 62.

47. Angus Calder, *The People's War: Britain, 1939–1945* (New York: Pantheon, 1969), 27.

48. Jakob B. Madsen, "Agricultural Crises and the International Transmission of the Great Depression," *Journal of Economic History* (June 2001): 328.

49. Margaret Lamb and Nicolas Tarling, *From Versailles to Pearl Harbor* (New York: Palgrave, 2001), 82–83. See also Dietmar Rothermund, *The Global Impact of the Great Depression, 1929–1939* (London: Routledge, 1996).

50. Jonathan Marshall, *To Have and Have Not: Southeast Asian Raw Materials and the Origins of the Pacific War* (Berkeley and Los Angeles: University of California Press, 1995), x, 2–12.

51. Boyce, "World Depression, World War," 57–59. Denis M. Smith, *Mussolini's Roman Empire* (New York: Viking Press, 1976), 41; Fortune mentioned in Marshall, *To Have and Have Not*, 3. See also William Carr, *Arms, Autarky and Aggression: A Study in German Foreign Policy, 1933–1939* (New York: Norton, 1972).

52. Baumont, *Origins of the Second World War*, 40–41.

53. Ibid., 3.

54. Concerning Hitler's ultimate aims, historians' opinions are widely varied. Maurice Baumont, Norman Rich, Gerhard Weinberg, and others of like mind view Hitler's objectives as fully premeditated and mapped out. See Baumont, *Origins of the Second World War*; Norman Rich, *Hitler's War Aims* (New York: Norton, 1973–74); Gerhard Weinberg, *The Foreign Policy of Hitler's Germany*, vol. 2 (Chicago: University of Chicago Press, 1980).

55. Roosevelt quoted in Robert G. Kaufman, *Arms Control During the Pre-Nuclear Era* (New York: Columbia University Press, 1990), 182.

56. Ibid., 179.

57. Ibid., 207–8; Walter Laqueur, *Stalin: The Glasnost Revelations* (New York: Scribner, 1990), 210.

58. Gordon Wright, *Ordeal of Total War* (New York: Harper & Row, 1968), 11. Admiral Nagano quoted in James W. Morley,

ed., *The Final Confrontation: Japan's Negotiations with the United States, 1941* (New York: Columbia University Press, 1994), 267.

59. John Toland, *The Rising Sun* (New York: Random House, 1970), 75.

60. Stalin quoted in Alexander Werth, *Russia at War, 1941–1945* (New York: Carroll and Graf, 1964), 49.

CHAPTER 2: POLITICS

1. Stalin quoted in David McCullough, *Truman* (New York: Simon & Schuster, 1992), 445.

2. J. Denis Derbyshire and Ian Derbyshire, *Political Systems of the World* (New York: St. Martin's Press, 1996), 590.

3. Ibid.

4. F. L. Carsten, *The Rise of Fascism* (Berkeley and Los Angeles: University of California Press, 1982), 47.

5. Winston Churchill, *Their Finest Hour* (New York: Bantam Books, 1974), 21.

6. Ibid.

7. Philip Goodhart, *Fifty Ships That Saved the World* (Garden City, NY: Doubleday, 1965).

8. Matsuoka quoted in John Toland, *The Rising Sun* (New York: Random House, 1970), 81.

9. James M. Morley, ed., *The Final Confrontation: Japan's Negotiations with the United States, 1941* (New York: Columbia University Press, 1994), 308–9.

10. Joseph P. Lash, *Roosevelt and Churchill, 1939–1941* (New York: Norton, 1976), 264.

11. For more detail on the implementation of Lend-Lease, see Raymond H. Dawson, *The Decision to Aid Russia*, 1941 (Chapel Hill: University of North Carolina Press, 1959); Warren F. Kimball, *The Most Unsordid Act: Lend-Lease, 1939–1941* (Baltimore, MD: Johns Hopkins Press, 1969).

12. Lash, *Roosevelt and Churchill*, 398–99. Churchill quoted in Kimball, *Forged in War*, 137.

13. Roosevelt quoted in Steven Casey, *Cautious Crusade* (New York: Oxford University Press, 2001), 199.

14. William L. Shirer, *The Rise and Fall of the Third Reich* (New York: Fawcett Crest, 1988), 1176.

15. Christian Gerlach, "The Wannsee Conference, the Fate of the German Jews, and Hitler's Decision in Principle to Exterminate All European Jews," *Journal of Modern History* (December 1998): 762.

16. Ibid., 759–812.

17. Roosevelt quoted in Doris Kearns Goodwin, *No Ordinary Time, Franklin and Eleanor Roosevelt: The Home Front on World War II* (New York: Simon & Schuster, 1994), 408.

18. Kimball, *Forged in War*, 188–89.

19. Casey, *Cautious Crusade*, 109–29.

20. Keith Eubank, *Summit at Teheran* (New York: William Morrow, 1985), 253–54, 308–9.

21. Roosevelt quoted in H. McNeill, *America, Britain, and Russia: Their Cooperation and Conflict, 1941–1946* (New York: Johnson, 1970), 373. Churchill quoted in Kimball, *Forged in War*, 244. Anecdote of Stalin's behavior at Churchill's dinner from Eubank, *Summit at Teheran*, 343.

22. Pierre de Senarclens, *From Yalta to the Iron Curtain* (Oxford, UK: Berg, 1995), 12.

23. P. M. H. Bell, *The World Since 1945* (London: Arnold, 2001), 16–22.

24. Hitler quoted in Alan Bullock, *Hitler: A Study in Tyranny* (New York: Harper & Row, 1964), 794.

25. Stalin quoted in Richard Overy, *Russia's War* (New York: Penguin, 1997), 326.

26. Goebbels quoted in David Welch, *The Third Reich: Politics and Propaganda* (London: Routledge: 1993), 30.

27. Shirer, *Rise and Fall*, 1256.

28. Text of Hitler's speech from Bullock, *Hitler*, 503.

29. Weygand quoted in Jack Le Vien and John Lord, *Winston Churchill: The Valiant Years* (London: Bernard Geis, 1962), 48.

30. Martin Gilbert, *Winston S. Churchill: Finest Hour, 1939–1941* (Boston: Houghton Mifflin, 1983), 571.

31. Text of de Gaulle speech from Houston Peterson, ed., *A Treasury of the World's Great Speeches* (New York: Simon & Schuster, 1965), 783–85, and Jean Lacouture, *De Gaulle: the Rebel, 1890–1944* (New York: Norton, 1990), 224–25. Churchill quoted in William Safire, *Lend Me Your Ears* (New York: Norton, 1992), 815.

32. Robert T. Oliver and Eugene E. White, eds., *Selected Speeches from American History* (Boston: Allyn and Bacon, 1966), 250–51.

33. Ibid.

34. Molotov quoted in Dmitri Volkogonov, *Stalin: Triumph and Tragedy* (New York: Grove Weidenfeld, 1988), 407. Text of Stalin's speech in Peterson, *A Treasury of the World's Great Speeches*, 786–89.

35. Roosevelt quoted in James M. Burns, *Roosevelt: The Soldier of Freedom* (New York: Harcourt Brace Jovanovich, 1970), 163.

36. Text of Roosevelt's speech from Erik Bruun and Jay Crosby, *Our Nation's Archive* (New York: Black Dog and Leventhal, 1999), 645–46.

37. Ralf G. Reuth, *Goebbels* (New York: Harcourt Brace, 1993), 313–19.

38. Helmut Heiber, *Goebbels* (New York: Hawthorn Books, 1972), 287.

39. Tojo quoted in Edwin P. Hoyt, *Warlord: Tojo Against the World* (Lanham, MD: Scarborough House, 1993), 201.

40. Hirohito's speech text taken from David Rees, *The Defeat of Japan* (Westport, CT: Praeger, 1997), 182.

41. Courtney Browne, *Tojo: The Last Banzai* (New York: Holt,

Rinehart and Winston, 1967), 204–7; Richard B. Frank, *Downfall: The End of the Imperial Japanese Empire* (New York: Random House, 1999), 320–21.

42. For further comparisons and contrasts of the two leaders, consider Alan Bullock, *Hitler and Stalin* (New York: Knopf, 1992).

43. Edvard Radzinsky, *Stalin* (New York: Doubleday, 1996), 12.

44. Isaac Deutscher contends that Stalin's mother, Ekaterina, had four children. Robert McNeal reports three. Edvard Radzinsky writes Joseph was the "third boy," but his mother "gave birth regularly." See Isaac Deutscher, *Stalin: A Political Biography* (New York: Vintage Books, 1960), 2; Robert H. McNeal, *Stalin: Man and Ruler* (New York: New York University Press, 1988), 3; Radzinsky, *Stalin*, 19–20.

45. Hitler's words from *Mein Kampf* (London: Hurst and Blackett, 1942), 17. Most biographers find six children born to Klara Hitler, whereas Alan Bullock surmises there were five. See Bullock, *Hitler*, 28–29.

46. Hitler, *Mein Kampf*, 79.

47. Ibid., 14–15; Walter Laqueur, *Stalin: The Glasnost Revelations* (New York: Scribner, 1990), 104.

48. Hitler, *Mein Kampf*, 22; Deutscher, *Stalin: A Political Biography*, 24.

49. Barbara Baumann and Birgitta Oberle, *Deutsche Literatur in Epochen* (Munich: Max Hueber Verlag, 1985), 217–20; Mikhail Heller and Aleksander M. Nekrich, *Utopia in Power* (New York: Summit Books, 1986), 272–73.

50. Anton Antonov Orseyenko, *The Time of Stalin* (New York: Harper & Row, 1980), 210; Roman Brackman, *The Secret File of Josef Stalin* (London: Frank Cass, 2001), 311; Radzinsky, *Stalin*, 80, 87.

51. Toland, *Adolf Hitler*, 121.

52. Bullock, *Hitler*, 112–22.

53. Lothar Machtan, *The Hidden Hitler* (New York: Basic Books, 2001), 30–60.

54. Volkogonov, *Stalin*, 10.

55. Bullock, *Hitler*, 394–95.

56. Heller and Nekrich, *Utopia in Power*, 279. See also Robert Conquest, *Stalin and the Kirov Murder* (New York: Oxford University Press, 1989).

57. Ian Kershaw, *Hitler* (London: Longman, 1991), 211–12; Heller and Nekrich, *Utopia in Power*, 279.

58. Stalin quoted in Volkogonov, *Stalin: Triumph and Tragedy*, 102. Hitler quoted in Albert Speer, *Inside the Third Reich* (New York: Bonanza Books, 1982), 157. See also Elizabeth Simpson, ed., *The Spoils of War* (New York: Harry N. Abrams, 1997).

59. Bullock, *Hitler and Stalin*, 385; Volkogonov, *Stalin: Triumph and Tragedy*, 102.

60. Seweryn Bialer, ed., *Stalin and His Generals* (New York: Pegasus, 1969), 563.

61. Deutscher, *Stalin: A Political Biography*, 468–69; Bradley F. Smith, *The War's Long Shadow: The Second World War and Its Aftermath* (New York: Simon & Schuster, 1986), 94. Voronov quoted in Bialer, *Stalin and His Generals*, 243.

62. Ian Kershaw, *Hitler 1936–1945: Nemesis* (New York: Norton, 2000), 500, 565, 614, 741. Hitler quoted in ibid., 454. Secretary Christa Schroeder quoted in ibid., 397.

63. Frederic Baumgartner, *Longing for the End: A History of Millennialism in Western Civilization* (New York: St. Martin's Press, 1999), 201–2, 208–11. See also Bernard McGinn, *Antichrist: Two Thousand Years of the Human Fascination with Evil* (New York: HarperCollins, 1994).

64. On numbers killed by the Nazi government, see Raul Hilberg, *The Destruction of the European Jews* (New York: Holmes & Meier, 1985), and Martin K. Sorge, *The Other Price of Hitler's War: German Military and Civilian Losses Resulting from World War II* (New York: Greenwood Press, 1986).

65. Heller and Nekrich, *Utopia in Power*, 511.

CHAPTER 3: MILITARY LIFE

1. P. M. H. Bell, "Another Thirty Years' War?" in *World War II: Roots and Causes*, ed. Keith Eubank (Lexington, MA: Heath, 1992), 21.

2. Mobilization numbers from John Ellis, *World War II: A Statistical Analysis* (New York: Facts on File, 1993), 227.

3. Gavan Daws, *Prisoners of the Japanese: POW's of World War II in the Pacific* (New York: Morrow, 1994), 275.

4. Arthur Waldron, "China's New Remembering of World War II: The Case of Zhang Zizhong," *Modern Asian Studies* (1996): 971.

5. For Italian POW statistics and forced labor in Germany, see I. C. B. Dear, ed., *The Oxford Companion to World War II* (New York: Oxford University Press, 1995), 384.

6. For an examination of France's struggle with national self-worth, see Eugene Webber, *The Hollow Years: France in the 1930s* (New York: Norton, 1994).

7. See also Pradeep Barua, *Gentlemen of the Raj: The Indian Officer Corps, 1817–1949* (Westport, CT: Praeger, 2003).

8. For U.S. production figures, see Harry C. Thomson and Lida Mayo, *The Ordnance Department: Procurement and Supply* (Washington D.C.: U.S. Army Office of Military History, 1960).

9. Norman Polmar and Thomas B. Allen, *World War II: The Encyclopedia of the War Years, 1941–1945* (New York: Random House, 1996), 164.

10. Karl C. Dod, *The Corps of Engineers: The War Against Japan* (Washington D.C.: U.S. Army Office of Military History, 1966), 352–53; Thomson and Mayo, *The Ordnance Department: Procurement and Supply*, 152.

11. James Lucas, *War on the Eastern Front, 1941–1945* (New York: Bonanza Books, 1982), 158.

12. Ellis, *Statistical Analysis*, 257; Lucas, *War on the Eastern Front*, 24.

13. Ian V. Hogg, *Encyclopedia of Infantry Weapons of World War II* (New York: Thomas Y. Crowell, 1977), 35.

14. John Erickson and David Dilks, eds., *Barbarossa* (Edinburgh: Edinburgh University Press, 1994), 261; Richard Overy, *Russia's War* (New York: Penguin, 1997), 244.

15. Peter McCarthy and Mike Syron, *Panzerkrieg: The Rise and Fall of Hitler's Tank Divisions* (London: Constable, 2002), 61. British soldier quoted in Gerald F. Linderman, *The World Within War: America's Combat Experience in World War II* (New York: Free Press, 1997), 56.

16. Williamson Murray, *Strategy for Defeat: The Luftwaffe, 1933–1945* (Maxwell AFB, AL: Air University Press, 1983), 224. See also Roger A. Freeman, *Mustang at War* (Garden City, NY: Doubleday, 1974).

17. Ronald H. Spector, *Eagle Against the Sun* (New York: Free Press, 1985), 178.

18. McCarthy and Syron, *Panzerkrieg*, 161.

19. German soldier quoted in Linderman, *The World Within War*, 25.

20. Ellis, *Statistical Analysis*, 302–3.

21. Bill Gunston, *Bombers of World War II* (New York: Arco, 1980), 42–44.

22. Generoso P. Salazar, Fernando R. Reyes, and Leonardo Q. Nuval, *Defense, Defeat, and Defiance: World War II in the Philippines* (Manila: Veterans Federation of the Philippines, 1993), 763–66.

23. Martin K. Sorge, *The Other Price of Hitler's War: German Military and Civilian Losses Resulting from World War II* (New York: Greenwood Press, 1986), 130–31.

24. James F. Dunnigan and Albert A. Nofi, *Dirty Little Secrets of World War II* (New York: Morrow, 1994), 269–70.

25. See also M. J. Whitley, *Cruisers of World War II* (Annapolis: Naval Institute Press, 1996), and idem, *Destroyers of World War II* (Annapolis: Naval Institute Press, 2000).

26. Samuel E. Morison, *The Two-Ocean War* (New York: Ballantine Books, 1963), 17.

27. Spector, *Eagle Against the Sun*, 257.

28. Morison, *The Two-Ocean War*, 165–70, 191–92, 378–79. Description of the Iowa class battleships in Elizabeth-Anne Wheal, Stephen Pope, and James Taylor, *Encyclopedia of the Second World War* (Edison, NJ: Castle Books, 1989), 231.

29. Dear, *Oxford Companion*, 682.

30. Masanobu Tsuji, *Singapore: The Japanese Version* (New York: St. Martin's Press, 1960), 317–18.

31. Roland G. Ruppenthal, *Logistical Support of the Armies*, vol. 1 (Washington D.C.: U.S. Army Center of Military History, 1995), 441; Masanobu, *Singapore*, 338.

32. Bruce F. Johnson, *Japanese Food Management in World War II* (Stanford, CA: Stanford University Press, 1953), 152–53; Ruppenthal, *Logistical Support of the Armies*, 1:255.

33. Dunnigan and Nofi, *Dirty Little Secrets*, 92.

34. Lucas, *Eastern Front*, 56.

35. Ruppenthal, *Logistical Support of the Armies*, 1:225.

36. Les Cleveland, *Dark Laughter: War in Song and Popular Culture* (Westport, CT: Praeger, 1994), 102.

37. Dunnigan and Nofi, *Dirty Little Secrets*, 80–81.

38. Ruppenthal, *Logistical Support of the Armies*, 1:255.

39. Johnson, *Japanese Food Management in World War II*, 152–53.

40. Louis Allen, *Burma: The Longest War, 1941–1945* (London: Dent, 1984), 151–54; Masanobu, *Singapore*, 328; Mary Ellen Condon-Rall and Albert E. Cowdrey, *The Medical Department: Medical Service in the War Against Japan* (Washington, D.C: U.S. Army Center of Military History, 1998), 35.

41. Ruppenthal, *Logistical Support of the Armies*, 1:440.

42. Johnson, *Japanese Food Management in World War II*, 159–60.

43. Peter Schrijvers, *The Crash of Ruin: American Combat Soldiers in*

Europe During World War II (New York: New York University Press, 1998), 166–67.

44. German soldier quoted in Stephen G. Fritz, *Frontsoldaten: The German Soldier in World War II* (Lexington: University Press of Kentucky, 1995), 113.

45. Roger R. Reese, *Stalin's Reluctant Soldiers* (Lawrence: University Press of Kansas, 1996), 183; John Toland, *The Rising Sun* (New York: Random House, 1970), 513; German soldier quoted in Fritz, *Frontsoldaten*, 73.

46. Masanobu, *Singapore*, 325.

47. William Craig, *Enemy at the Gates: The Battle for Stalingrad* (New York: Dutton, 1973), 38.

48. Arthur S. MacNalty and W. Franklin Mellor, eds., *Medical Services in War* (London: Her Majesty's Stationery Office, 1968), 765–67.

49. Alexander Werth, *Russia at War, 1941–1945* (New York: Carroll and Graf, 1964), 260.

50. G. F. Krivosheev, ed., *Soviet Casualties and Combat Losses in the Twentieth Century* (London: Greenhill, 1997), 96; Sorge, *Other Price of Hitler's War*, 62.

51. Linderman, *World Within War*, 1.

52. Ibid., 39; Murray, *Strategy for Defeat*, 303.

53. Krivosheev, ed., *Soviet Casualties and Combat Losses in the Twentieth Century*, 86.

54. Ibid., 86; Rüdiger Overmans, *Deutsche Militärische Verluste im Zweiten Weltkrieg* (Munich: R. Oldenbourg, 2000), 335.

55. Daws, *Prisoners of the Japanese*, 17–18; S. P. MacKenzie, "The Treatment of Prisoners of War in World War II," *Journal of Modern History* (September 1994): 488, 515–16; Charles G. Roland, "Allied POW's, Japanese Captors, and the Geneva Convention," *War and Society* (October 1991): 83–102.

56. MacKenzie, "The Treatment of Prisoners of War in World War II," 511.

57. Ibid., 491–518; Martin K. Sorge, *The Other Price of Hitler's War*, 76.

58. German soldier Erich Dwinger quoted in Lucas, *Eastern Front*, 51.

59. Linderman, *The World Within War*, 148.

60. Ibid., 148–49; Martin K. Sorge, *The Other Price of Hitler's War*, 65.

61. Krivosheev, *Soviet Casualties and Combat Losses in the Twentieth Century*, 88.

62. Ellis, *Statistical Analysis*, 257.

63. Daws, *Prisoners of the Japanese*, 184.

64. Masanobu, *Singapore*, 310.

65. Fritz, *Frontsoldaten*, 23.

66. R. Manning Ancell, *The Biographical Dictionary of World War II Generals and Flag Officers: The U.S. Armed Forces* (Westport, CT: Greenwood Press, 1996), 678–81.

67. Ellis, *Statistical Analysis*, 256; Murray, *Strategy for Defeat*, 183; William L. O'Neill, *A Democracy at War* (New York: Free Press, 1993), 309; Martin K. Sorge, *The Other Price of Hitler's War*, 40.

68. Fritz, *Frontsoldaten*, 110–12.

69. For an account of those abdominally wounded in states of hunger, see Lucas, *Eastern Front*, 51.

70. Craig, *Enemy at the Gates*, 318–19. Major Nishiyama quoted in Richard B. Frank, *Guadalcanal* (New York: Random House, 1990), 500.

71. Norm Davies, *Heart of Europe: A Short History of Poland* (New York: Oxford University Press, 1986), 67.

72. Linderman, *The World Within War*, 221.

73. Omer Bartov, "Germany's Unforgettable War: The Twisted Road from Berlin to Moscow and Back," *Diplomatic History* (Summer 2001): 408.

74. Fritz, *Frontsoldaten*, 93; Douglas Peifer, "Commemoration of Mutiny, Rebellion, and Resistance in Postwar Germany: Public Memory, History, and the Formation of 'Memory Beacons,'"

Journal of Military History (October 2001): 1046–47; Jason Sears, "Discipline in the Royal Navy," *War and Society* (October 1991): 55.

75. William Sargant, "Psychiatry and War," *Atlantic Monthly*, 219 (1967): 102; Paul Wanke, "American Military Psychiatry and Its Role Among Ground Forces in World War II," *Journal of Military History* (January 1999): 131–32.

76. Condon-Rall and Cowdrey, *Medical Department*, 170, 213, 224–25; Toland, *Rising Sun*, 644–45.

77. Bartov, "Germany's Unforgettable War," 405–6.

78. Adolf Hitler, *Mein Kampf* (London: Hurst and Blackett, 1981), 340.

79. Hitler quoted in Norman Rich, *Hitler's War Aims* (New York: Norton, 1973), 159.

80. Murray, *Strategy for Defeat*, 47.

81. See also Richard Hough and Denis Richards, *The Battle of Britain* (New York: Norton, 1989).

82. Hitler quoted in Walter C. Langsam, *Historic Documents of World War II* (Princeton, NJ: Van Nostrand, 1958), 56–59.

83. Hitler quoted in Joseph P. Lash, *Roosevelt and Churchill, 1939–1941* (New York: Norton, 1976), 254, and John Strawson, *Hitler's Battles for Europe* (New York: Scribner, 1971), 132.

84. Overy, *Russia's War*, 152.

85. Antony Beevor, *Stalingrad* (New York: Viking, 1998), 148–50, 157–59.

86. Mikhail Heller and Aleksander M. Nekrich, *Utopia in Power: The History of the Soviet Union from 1917 to the Present* (New York: Summit Books, 1986), 401.

87. Overy, *Russia's War*, 242.

88. David M. Glantz and Jonathan M. House, *The Battle of Kursk* (Lawrence: University Press of Kansas, 1999), 276–77, 336–45.

89. See also David M. Glantz and Harold S. Orenstein, eds., *The*

Battle for Kursk 1943: The Soviet General Staff Study (London: Frank Cass, 1999); Steven H. Newton, *Kursk: The German View* (Cambridge, MA: Da Capo Press, 2002).

90. Werth, *Russia at War*, 964–66.

91. Anthony Beevor, *The Fall of Berlin, 1945* (New York: Viking, 2002), 141–44.

92. Hsi-sheng Ch-I, *Nationalist China at War* (Ann Arbor: University of Michigan Press, 1982), 42–43. Failed Shanghai bombing run described in Jonathan Fenby, *Chiang Kai-Shek* (New York: Carroll and Graf, 2003), 295–96.

93. For the best narrative and evidential account of the attack, see Gordon W. Prange, *At Dawn We Slept* (New York: McGraw-Hill, 1981), 738.

94. Winston Churchill, *The Hinge of Fate* (New York: Bantam Books, 1974), 80. Estimates of POWs taken at Singapore range from 60,000 to 130,000.

95. Headline of Asashi Shimbun in Toland, *Rising Sun*, 346.

96. William Roger Louis, *Imperialism at Bay* (New York: Oxford University Press, 1978), 134–46.

97. Toland, *Rising Sun*, 436.

98. Ibid., 437–50.

99. Frank, *Guadalcanal*, vii, 614.

100. Hsi-sheng, *Nationalist China at War*, 76.

101. Fenby, *Chiang Kai-Shek*, 420.

102. Spector, *Eagle Against the Sun*, 314–17; Toland, *Rising Sun*, 519.

103. Richard F. Newcomb, *Iwo Jima* (New York: Holt, Rinehart and Winston, 1965), 294–306.

104. For U.S. military estimates of invasion of Japan, see John R. Skates, *The Invasion of Japan* (Columbia: University of South Carolina Press, 1994), 78–81, 256–57.

105. Toland, *Rising Sun*, 720–22.

106. Skates, *The Invasion of Japan*, 105–9.

CHAPTER 4: HOME FRONT

1. Bradley F. Smith, *The War's Long Shadow: The Second World War and Its Aftermath* (New York: Simon & Schuster, 1986), 80.

2. John Ellis, *World War II: A Statistical Analysis* (New York: Facts on File, 1993), 253; John L. Hondros, *Occupation and Resistance: The Greek Agony, 1941–1944* (New York: Pella, 1983), 67, 71.

3. Smith, *War's Long Shadow*, 44–45.

4. James M. Burns, *Roosevelt: The Soldier of Freedom* (New York: Harcourt Brace Jovanovich, 1970), 214.

5. Mikhail Keller and Aleksandr M. Nekrich, *Utopia in Power* (New York: Summit Books, 1986), 378–82.

6. James Taylor and Warren Shaw, *A Dictionary of the Third Reich* (London: Grafton, 1987), 89.

7. Craig Nelson, *The First Heroes* (New York: Viking, 2002), 355.

8. Ellis, *Statistical Analysis*, 253.

9. Martin K. Sorge, *The Other Price of Hitler's War: German Military and Civilian Losses Resulting from World War II* (New York: Greenwood Press, 1986), 67.

10. Alfred G. Frei, "'In the End I Just Said O.K.': Political and Moral Dimensions of Escape Aid at the Swiss Border," *Journal of Modern History* (December 1992): S 81.

11. Keller and Nekrich, *Utopia in Power*, 379–82.

12. Peter Calvocoressi, Guy Wint, and John Pritchard, *Total War: Causes and Courses of the Second World War* (New York: Pantheon Books, 1989), 330, 524; S. P. MacKenzie, "The Treatment of Prisoners of War in World War II," *Journal of Modern History* (September 1994): 494. Himmler quoted in Gordon Wright, *Ordeal of Total War* (New York: Harper & Row, 1968), 117.

13. Calvocoressi, Wint, and Pritchard, *Total War*, 523; I. C. B. Dear, ed., *The Oxford Companion to World War II* (New York: Oxford University Press, 1995), 220.

14. James F. Dunnigan and Albert A. Nofi, *Dirty Little Secrets of World War II* (New York: Morrow, 1994), 76.

15. Jane Slaughter, *Women and the Italian Resistance, 1943–1945* (Denver: Arden, 1997), 120–21; Smith, *War's Long Shadow*, 45; Wright, *Ordeal of Total War*, 265.

16. Hondros, *Occupation and Resistance*, 66; Smith, *War's Long Shadow*, 34.

17. Sarah Farmer, *Martyred Village* (Berkeley and Los Angeles: University of California Press, 1999), 1; Jorgen Haestrup, *European Resistance Movements, 1939–1945* (Westport, CT: Meckler, 1981), 449; Ray Mears, *The Real Heroes of Telemark* (London: Hodder and Stoughton, 2003), 248.

18. G. F. Krivosheev, ed., *Soviet Casualties and Combat Losses in the Twentieth Century* (London: Greenhill, 1997), 86; Rüdiger Overmans, *Deutsche Militärische Verluste im Zweiten Weltkrieg* (Munich: R. Oldenbourg, 2000), 335.

19. Smith, *War's Long Shadow*, 39; Arthur Waldron, "China's New Remembering of World War II: The Case of Zhang Zizhong," *Modern Asian Studies* (1996): 971.

20. John A. Armstrong, ed., *Soviet Partisans in World War II* (Madison: University of Wisconsin Press, 1964), 151.

21. Quote of de Gaulle to André Gillois in M. R. D. Foot, *Resistance: European Resistance to Nazism, 1940–1945* (New York: McGraw-Hill, 1977).

22. Haestrup, *European Resistance Movements*, 458.

23. Ibid., 448–49.

24. Norman Polmar and Thomas B. Allen, eds., *World War II: The Encyclopedia of the War Years, 1941–1945* (New York: Random House, 1996), 708.

25. Dear, *Oxford Companion*, 901.

26. Foot, *Resistance*, 43.

27. See Claudia Koonz, "Ethical Dilemmas and Nazi Eugenics:

Single Issue Dissent in Religious Contexts," *Journal of Modern History* (December 1992): S 30.

28. Haestrup, *European Resistance Movements*, 88; Mears, *Real Heroes of Telemark*, 241–42.

29. Haestrup, *European Resistance Movements*, 95–103; Mears, *Real Heroes of Telemark*, 244.

30. Foot, *Resistance*, 24–25; Juliane Furst, "Heroes, Lovers, Victims: Partisan Girls During the Great Fatherland War," *Minerva* (Fall–Winter 2000), 47–50.

31. Bob Moore, *Resistance in Western Europe* (New York: Berg, 2000), 3.

32. Foot, *Resistance*, 23–26; Haestrup, *European Resistance Movements*, 31.

33. Haestrup, *European Resistance Movements*, 90; Gerhard Weinberg, *A World at Arms: A Global History of World War II* (New York: Cambridge University Press, 1994), 473.

34. Foot, *Resistance*, 33.

35. Nicholas Atkin, *The French at War, 1934–1944* (London: Longman, 2001), 83; Haestrup, *European Resistance Movements*, 15.

36. Armstrong, *Soviet Partisans in World War II*, 205, 211, 214; Atkin, *The French at War*, 76.

37. Haestrup, *European Resistance Movements*, 120, 132.

38. Atkin, *The French at War*, 83; Haestrup, *European Resistance Movements*, 76–77; Mears, *The Real Heroes of Telemark*, 245.

39. Haestrup, *European Resistance Movements*, 465.

40. Karl Dietrich Bracher, *The German Dictatorship* (New York: Praeger, 1972), 361; Dear, *Oxford Companion*, 263.

41. Cynthia Eller, *Conscientious Objectors and the Second World War* (New York: Praeger, 1991), 49; Heather T. Frazier and John O'Sullivan, *"We Have Just Begun to Not Fight": An Oral History of Conscientious Objectors in Civilian Public Service During World War II* (New York: Twayne, 1996), vii–xxiv.

42. Peter Brock, "'Excellent in Battle': Conscientious Objectors as Medical Paratroopers, 1943–1946," *War and Society* (May 2004): 41–42, 54.

43. Winston S. Churchill, *The Gathering Storm* (New York: Bantam Books, 1948), viii.

44. For a short description of U.S. adoption of World War II as the official war title, see Walter C. Langsam, *Historic Documents of World War II* (Princeton, NJ: Van Nostrand, 1958).

45. David Reynolds, "The Origins of the Two 'World Wars': Historical Discourse and International Politics," *Journal of Contemporary History* (January 2003): 29–36. It is arguable whether the international turmoil of 1937 to 1945 was just the second "world war" in human history. Among other expansive military affairs, the French and Indian War (a.k.a, the Seven Years' War, the Great War for the Empire, etc.) spawned fighting in the American colonies, Europe, and India. So, too, the Napoleonic Wars scarred three continents. The RUSSIAN CIVIL WAR covered six time zones and involved troops from a score of countries, including Britain, Canada, Finland, Czechoslovakia, France, Poland, Japan, and the United States.

46. Hitler quoted in George H. Stein, ed., *Hitler* (Englewood Cliffs, NJ: Prentice-Hall, 1968), 75.

47. Reynolds, "Origins of the Two 'World Wars,'" 36.

48. Angus Calder, *The People's War: Britain, 1939–1945* (New York: Pantheon, 1969), 38–42; James Chapman, "British Cinema and 'The People's War,'" in *"Millions Like Us?": British Culture in the Second World War*, ed. Nick Hayes and Jeff Hill (Liverpool: Liverpool University Press, 1999), 36; Pat Thane, "Old Age," in *Medicine in the 20th Century*, ed. Roger Cooter and John Pickstone (Amsteldijk, Holland: Harwood, 2000), 621.

49. Calder, *People's War*, JFK quoted in J. Garry Clifford and Samuel R. Spencer Jr., *The First Peacetime Draft* (Lawrence: University Press of Kansas, 1986), 8.

50. Chapman, "British Cinema and 'The People's War,'" 36.

51. John Baxendale, "'You and I—All of Us Ordinary People': Renegotiating 'Britishness' in Wartime," in *"Millions Like Us?": British Culture in the Second World War*, ed. Nick Hayes and Jeff Hill (Liverpool: Liverpool University Press, 1999), 313.

52. Robert G. Menzies, "A Peoples War" (London: Longmans, Green, and Co., 1941), 14; Mikhail N. Narinsky, "The Soviet Union: The Great Patriotic War?" in *Allies at War: The Soviet, American, and British Experience, 1939–1945*, ed. David Reynolds, Warren F. Kimball, and A. O. Chubarian (New York: St. Martin's Press, 1994), 261.

53. John W. Dower, *War Without Mercy: Race and Power in the Pacific War* (New York: Pantheon Books, 1986), 182–90, 234–47.

54. Reynolds, "The Origins of the Two 'World Wars,'" 34.

55. Wright, *Ordeal of Total War*, 256.

56. Alexander Werth, *Russia at War, 1941–1945* (New York: Carroll and Graf, 1964), 324.

57. Churchill, *The Gathering Storm*, vii; see also Maurice Baumont, *Origins of the Second World War* (New Haven, CT: Yale University Press, 1978).

58. For more on the first Thirty Years' War, see C. V. Wedgwood, *The Thirty Years War* (New York: Routledge & Kegan Paul, 1990); Geoff Mortimer, *Eyewitness Accounts of the Thirty Years War, 1618–1648* (New York: Palgrave MacMillan, 2002). For a typical example of Sonderweg historiography, see Bracher, *German Dictatorship*.

59. Ian Buruma, *The Wages of Guilt* (New York: Farrar Straus Giroux, 1994), 223; Saburo Ienaga, *The Pacific War: World War II and the Japanese, 1931–1945* (New York: Pantheon Books, 1978), 247; Dower, *War Without Mercy*, 59.

60. Gerald Astor, *Operation Iceberg* (New York: Dell, 1995), 8.

61. Sebastian Conrad, "Entangled Memories: Versions of the Past in Germany and Japan, 1945–2001," *Journal of Contemporary History* (January 2003): 91–93; Yukiko Koshiro, "Japan's World and World War II," *Diplomatic History* (Summer 2001): 429.

62. Ienaga, *The Pacific War*, 247.

63. Ibid., 248; Koshiro, "Japan's World and World War II," 426.

64. Les Cleveland, *Dark Laughter: War in Song and Popular Culture* (Westport, CT: Praeger, 1994), 11–12; Kathleen E. R. Smith, *God Bless America: Tin Pan Alley Goes to War* (Lexington: University of Kentucky Press, 2003), 144; Alexander Werth, *Russia at War* (New York: Dutton, 1964), 741–42.

65. Adrienne L. Kaeppler and J. W. Love, eds., *The Garland Encyclopedia of World Music* (New York: Garland, 1998), 7:729, 745; Sturmabteilung comments on jazz quoted in Richard Grunberger, *A Social History of the Third Reich* (London: Weidenfeld and Nicolson, 1971), 419; Boris Schwarz, *Music and Musical Life in Soviet Russia, 1917–1970* (London: Barrie and Jenkins, 1972), 176.

66. Russell Sanjek, *Pennies from Heaven: The American Popular Music Business in the Twentieth Century* (New York: Da Capo, 1996), 216.

67. Ben Arnold, *Music and War: A Research and Information Guide* (New York: Garland, 1993), 186.

68. David Ewen, *All the Years of American Popular Music* (Englewood Cliffs, NJ: Prentice-Hall, 1977), 430.

69. Julius Mattfeld, *Variety Music Cavalcade, 1620–1969* (Englewood Cliffs, NJ: Prentice-Hall, 1971), xiii.

70. C. H. Ward-Jackson, ed., *Airmen's Song Book* (London: William Blackwood and Sons, 1967), 222.

71. Calder, *People's War*, 371.

72. Arnold, *Music and War*, 192, 199.

73. Ibid., 189; Roy Blokker, *The Music of Dmitri Shostakovich: The Symphonies* (London: Tantivy Press, 1979), 81.

74. Laurel E. Fay, *Shostakovich: A Life* (New York: Oxford University Press, 2000), 132.

75. Chin-Hsin Yao Chen and Shih-Hsiang Chen, *The Flower Drum and Other Chinese Songs* (New York: John Day, 1943), 47–50; see also Lee PaoCh'en, ed., *Songs of Fighting China* (New York: Chinese News Service, 1944); Smith, *War's Long Shadow*, 30.

76. Carl Hoff and Orrin Tucker song quoted from Smith, *God Bless America*, 13.

77. Sanjek, *Pennies from Heaven*, 216.

78. *Baker's Biographical Dictionary of Musicians, 8th ed.* (New York: Schirmer Books, 1992), 166–67; Ewen, *All the Years of American Popular Music*, 430–31.

79. Archie Satterfield, *The Home Front: An Oral History of the War Years in America: 1941–1945* (New York: PEI Books, 1981), 271.

80. "Anthem for England," *Current History and Forum* (October 22, 1940), 35–36.

81. Baxendale, "'You and I,'" 295.

82. Calder, *People's War*, 371.

83. Louis L. Snyder, *Historical Guide to World War II* (Westport, CT: Greenwood, 1982), 658–59.

84. Michael Burleigh, *The Third Reich: A New History* (New York: Hill and Wang, 2000), 118–20.

85. Horst J. P. Bergmeier and Rainer E. Lotz, *Hitler's Airwaves* (New Haven, CT: Yale University Press, 1997), 136–77.

86. Cleveland, *Dark Laughter*, 9.

87. Smith, *God Bless America*, 111.

88. Gail Braybon and Penny Summerfield, *Out of the Cage: Women's Experiences in Two World Wars* (London: Pandora, 1987), 212–14.

89. Charles Rearick, *The French in Love and War* (New Haven, CT: Yale University Press, 1997), 259.

CHAPTER 5: IN RETROSPECT

1. Lyn Schumaker, "Malaria," in *Medicine in the 20th Century*, eds. Roger Cooter and John Pickstone (Amsteldijk, Holland: Harwood, 2000), 713.

2. Ernest Volkman, *Science Goes to War* (New York: Wiley, 2002), 178. Churchill quoted in Gordon Wright, *The Ordeal of Total War, 1939–1945* (New York: Harper & Row, 1968), 79.

3. James F. Dunnigan and Albert A. Nofi, *Dirty Little Secrets of World War II* (New York: Morrow, 1994), 97–98; Gerhard L. Weinberg, *A World at Arms* (New York: Cambridge University Press, 1994), 539.

4. Daniel R. Headrick, *The Tools of Empire* (New York: Oxford University Press, 1981), 101; Keith Robbins, *The First World War* (New York: Oxford University Press, 1984), 100–101; Daniel Yergin, *The Prize* (New York: Simon & Schuster, 1991), 154–160.

5. Wright, *The Ordeal of Total War*, 84–85.

6. John Campbell, ed., *The Experience of World War II* (New York: Oxford University Press, 1989), 120; Richard Overy, *Why the Allies Won* (New York: Norton, 1995), 50–52.

7. J. Garry Clifford and Samuel R. Spencer Jr., *The First Peacetime Draft* (Lawrence: University Press of Kansas, 1986), 8.

8. Ibid., 10.

9. See also Albert A. Blum, *Drafted or Deferred: Practices Past and Present* (Ann Arbor: University of Michigan Press, 1967).

10. For an in-depth analysis of the 1940 presidential election, see Warren Moscow, *Roosevelt and Willkie* (Englewood Cliffs, NJ: Prentice-Hall, 1968).

11. Michael D. Pearlman, *Warmaking and American Democracy* (Lawrence: University Press of Kansas, 1999), 240.

12. Ronald H. Spector, *Eagle Against the Sun* (New York: Free Press, 1983), 158–63.

13. The first carrier from either side to be sunk in the war was the

British light carrier *Hermes*, sunk April 9, 1942, off of Ceylon by Japanese patrol planes.

14. Edwin P. Hoyt, *Japan's War* (New York: McGraw-Hill, 1986), 281–83; John Toland, *The Rising Sun* (New York: Random House, 1970), 402–5.

15. Jeffrey Ethell and Alfred Price, *World War II Fighting Jets* (Annapolis, MD: Naval Institute Press, 1994), 9–13.

16. Robert Jackson, *Fighter: The Story of Air Combat, 1936–1945* (New York: St. Martin's Press, 1979), 147–57; Williamson Murray, *Strategy for Defeat: The Luftwaffe, 1933–1945* (Maxwell, AL: Air University Press, 1983), 252–53. The four jets that flew in wartime operations were the Me-262, He-162, the German bomber Arado 234 (which functioned better as a reconnaissance plane), and the twin-engine British Gloster Meteor (employed mostly as a V-1 interceptor). The United States produced the Bell XP-59A Comet in 1942, but it never saw action. See Ethell and Price, *World War II Fighting Jets*, 204.

17. Michael J. Neufeld, *The Rocket and the Reich: Peenemünde and the Coming of the Ballistic Missile Era* (New York: Free Press, 1995), 274.

18. For technical specifications on the V-1, see I. C. B. Dear, ed., *The Oxford Companion to World War II* (New York: Oxford University Press, 1995), 1249–50.

19. Winston Churchill, *Triumph and Tragedy* (New York: Bantam Books, 1953), 34.

20. Neufeld, *The Rocket and the Reich*, 274; Albert Speer, *Inside the Third Reich* (New York: Bonanza Books, 1982), 355–56. Account of Hitler's brush with a V-1 in William L. Shirer, *The Rise and Fall of the Third Reich* (New York: Fawcett Crest, 1962), 1350–51.

21. Churchill, *Triumph and Tragedy*, 42–45; Alfred W. Crosby, *Throwing Fire: Projectile Technology Through History* (New York:

Cambridge University Press, 2002), 163–65; Neufeld, *The Rocket and the Reich*, 273–74.

22. Einstein's complete letter in Erik Bruun and Jay Crosby, eds., *Our Nation's Archive* (New York: Black Dog and Leventhal, 1999), 635.

23. Ibid.

24. Volkman, *Science Goes to War*, 139–40. See also David Holloway, *Stalin and the Bomb* (New Haven, CT: Yale University Press, 1994).

25. Crosby, *Throwing Fire*, 171; Julia E. Johnsen, ed., *The Atomic Bomb* (New York: H. W. Wilson, 1946), 65–70; Volkman, *Science Goes to War*, 185.

26. Meyer Friedman and Gerald W. Friedland, *Medicine's Ten Greatest Discoveries* (New Haven, CT: Yale University Press, 1998), 174–79; Charles M. Wiltse, *The Medical Department: Medical Service in the Mediterranean and Minor Theaters* (Washington D.C.: Department of the Army, 1965), 253.

27. Schumaker, "Malaria," 713.

28. Ronald H. Bailey, *Prisoners of War* (Chicago: Time Life Books, 1981), 13.

29. John Erickson and David Dilks, eds., *Barbarossa* (Edinburgh: Edinburgh University Press, 1994), 83; Harrison E. Salisbury, *The 900 Days* (New York: Avon 1969), 396–97.

30. Richard Overy, *Russia's War* (New York: Penguin, 1997), 147.

31. Albert Axell, *Marshal Zhukov: The Man Who Beat Hitler* (London: Pearson Longman, 2003), 113; Igor Vitukin, ed., *Soviet Generals Recall World War II* (New York: Sphinx Press, 1981), 259.

32. Eisenhower quoted in Axell, *Marshal Zhukov*, iii.

33. U.S. Army, *Biennial Reports of the Chief of Staff of the United States Army to the Secretary of War, 1 July 1939–30 June 1945*, (Washington D.C.: U.S. Army Center of Military History, 1996).

34. Barsewisch quoted in Peter McCarthy and Mike Syron, *Panzerkrieg: The Rise and Fall of Hitler's Tank Divisions* (London: Constable, 2002), 107.

35. Ibid., 22–23.

36. Ibid., 27.

37. Ibid., 109.

38. Ibid., 39; Dieter Ose, "Rommel and Rundstedt: The 1944 Panzer Controversy," *Military Affairs* (January 1985): 10.

39. Stephen E. Ambrose, *The Supreme Commander* (Garden City, NY: Doubleday, 1970), 3.

40. Eisenhower quoted in ibid., 535.

41. See also Carlo D'Este, *Eisenhower: A Soldier's Life* (New York: Henry Holt, 2002); Geoffrey Perret, *Eisenhower* (New York: Random House, 1999).

42. David M. Glantz and Jonathan M. House, *The Battle of Kursk* (Lawrence: University Press of Kansas, 1999), 45.

43. Ibid., 46.

44. Walter R. Roberts, *Tito, Mihailovic and the Allies, 1941–1945* (New Brunswick, NJ: Rutgers University Press, 1973), 291, 316–17, 348. See also Milovan Djilas, *Wartime* (New York: Harcourt Brace, 1977).

45. Samuel Eliot Morison, *The Two-Ocean War* (Boston: Little, Brown, 1963), 138–39.

46. E. B. Potter, *Nimitz* (Annapolis, MD: Naval Institute Press, 1976), 3.

47. F. W. von Mellenthin, *German Generals of World War II* (Norman: University of Oklahoma Press, 1956), 30.

48. Correlli Barnett, ed., *Hitler's Generals* (New York: Grove Weidenfeld, 1989), 228.

49. Ibid., 230–31.

50. Carlo D'Este, *Patton: A Genius for War* (New York: HarperCollins, 1997), 4, 575.

51. Russell F. Weigley, *Eisenhower's Lieutenants* (Bloomington: Indiana University Press, 1990), 256.

52. Winston Churchill, *Their Finest Hour* (New York: Bantam, 1974), 87, 94.

53. Gordon A. Harrison, *Cross-Channel Attack* (Washington D.C.: U.S. Army Office of Military History, 1951), 6, 193–94.

54. Shirer, *Rise and Fall*, 1127–37.

55. On Hitler and his ignorance of rocketry, see Neufeld, *The Rocket and the Reich*.

56. John Toland, *Adolf Hitler* (New York: Random House, 1976), 888.

57. Murray, *Strategy for Defeat*, 189.

58. James S. Corum, *The Luftwaffe: Creating the Operational Air War*, 1918–1940 (Lawrence: University Press of Kansas, 1997), 225–28.

59. Shirer, *Rise and Fall*, 690.

60. Dunnigan and Nofi, *Dirty Little Secrets*, 243–47.

61. David T. Zabecki, ed., *World War II in Europe: An Encyclopedia* (New York: Garland, 1999), 571–74.

62. John Erickson, *The Soviet High Command: A Military-Political History, 1918–1941* (New York: St. Martin's Press, 1962), 508, 637; Robert W. Thurston and Bernd Bonwetsch, eds., *The People's War: Responses to World War II in the Soviet Union* (Chicago: University of Illinois Press, 2000), 197. Voroshilov quoted in David Glantz, *Stumbling Colossus: The Red Army on the Eve of the World War* (Lawrence: University Press of Kansas, 1998), 31.

63. Khrushchev quoted in Overy, *Russia's War*, 82.

64. Alexander Werth, *Russia at War* (New York: Dutton, 1964), 306–7.

65. Hsi-sheng Ch-I, *Nationalist China at War* (Ann Arbor: University of Michigan Press, 1982), 42–43.

66. Denis M. Smith, *Mussolini's Roman Empire* (New York: Viking, 1976), 40, 110.

67. Ibid., 223.

68. Nicholas Farrell, *Mussolini: A New Life* (London: Weidenfeld

and Nicolson, 2003), 345. Eden quoted in R. J. B. Bosworth, *Mussolini* (London: Arnold, 2002), 376.

69. Toyoda quoted in John Toland, *Rising Sun*, 498.

70. Hoyt, *Japan's War*, 372.

71. Toland, *Rising Sun*, 690.

72. Hoyt, *Japan's War*, 403.

73. Halder quoted in Dear, *Oxford Companion*, 1269.

74. Earl R. Beck, *Under the Bombs: The German Home Front, 1942–1943* (Lexington: University Press of Kentucky, 1986), 57.

75. Ose, "Rommel and Rundstedt," 8.

76. David Fraser, *Knight's Cross* (New York: HarperCollins, 1993), 537–44; John Keegan, *The Battle for History* (New York: Vintage Books, 1995), 57.

77. Col. Benjamin Dickson quoted in Rick Atkinson, *An Army at Dawn: The War in North Africa, 1942–1943* (New York: Henry Holt, 2002), 123.

78. Ibid., 119–23.

79. Eisenhower quoted in ibid., 123.

80. Shirer, *Rise and Fall*, 1045.

81. Keitel quoted in Robert S. Wistrich, *Who's Who in Nazi Germany* (London: Routledge, 1995), 137.

82. Mutaguchi quoted in Louis Allen, *Burma: The Longest War, 1941–1945* (London: Dent, 1984), 154.

83. Ibid., 151–54.

84. Ibid., 313; Toland, *Rising Sun*, 764.

85. Ose, "Rommel and Rundstedt," 8.

86. Ibid., 8–9.

87. Portions of France were still in German possession on V-E day, such as the ports of St. Nazaire and Lorient. See Steven T. Ross, ed., *U.S. War Plans, 1938–1945* (Boulder, CO: Lynne Rienner, 2002).

88. Conversation between Boldin and Timoshenko in Mikhail Heller and Aleksandr M. Nekrich, *Utopia in Power* (New York: Summit Books, 1986), 370.

89. Alexander Werth, *Russia at War, 1941–1945* (New York: Carroll and Graf, 1964), 40–141.

90. John P. Davies Jr., *Dragon by the Tail* (New York: Norton, 1972), 20–23.

91. Jonathan Fenby, *Chiang Kai-Shek: China's Generalissimo and the Nation He Lost* (Carroll and Graf, 2004), 320–21.

92. Ibid.

93. See also Diana Lary, "Drowned Earth: The Strategic Breaching of the Yellow River Dyke, 1938," *War in History* (2001): 205–7.

94. Hitler quoted in Shirer, *Rise and Fall*, 1215.

95. Yergin, *The Prize*, 326–27.

96. Nimitz quoted in ibid.

97. Ross, *U.S. War Plans*, 247.

98. Ibid., 247–48.

99. See also Charles Whiting, *A Bridge at Arnhem* (New York: Pinnacle Books, 1975).

100. Talbot Charles Imlay, "A Reassessment of Anglo-French Strategy During the Phony War, 1939–1940," *The English Historical Review* (April 2004): 333–72.

101. See John S. D. Eisenhower, *The Bitter Woods* (New York: Putnam, 1969).

102. Winston Churchill, *The Hinge of Fate* (New York: Bantam Books, 1974), 443–45.

103. See also Terence Robertson, *Dieppe: The Shame and the Glory* (Boston: Little, Brown, and Co., 1962).

104. William Manchester, *The Arms of Krupp* (Boston: Little, Brown, and Co., 1968), 416–19.

105. Crosby, *Throwing Fire*, 150–53.

106. Manchester, *The Arms of Krupp*, 419–20.

107. Farrell, *Mussolini*, 342–43; Smith, *Mussolini's Roman Empire*, 232–33.

108. Hitler's suicide lamentation on the Italian failure in Greece in Farrell, *Mussolini*, 343.

109. Susanne Conze and Beate Fieseler, "Soviet Women as Comrades-in-Arms: A Blind Spot in the History of the War," in *The People's War*, ed. Thurston and Bonwetsch, 212, 218.

110. Linda Grant de Pauw, *Battle Cries and Lullabies: Women in War from Prehistory to the Present* (Norman: University of Oklahoma Press, 1998), 236, 239, 248; Shelley Saywell, *Women in War* (New York: Viking, 1985), 103.

111. Claudia Koonz, *Mothers in the Fatherland: Women, the Family, and Nazi Politics* (New York: St. Martin's, 1987), 310; Mark A. Stoler, "The Second World War in U.S. History and Memory," *Diplomatic History* (Summer 2001): 385; Gordon Wright, *Ordeal of Total War* (New York: Harper & Row, 1968), 60.

112. Nicholas Atkin, *The French at War, 1934–1944* (London: Longman, 2001), 85; Conze and Fieseler, "Soviet Women as Comrades-in-Arms," 226; Dunnigan and Nofi, *Dirty Little Secrets*, 102–3; Kirsten Olsen, *Chronology of Women's History* (Westport, CT: Greenwood Press, 1994), 255.

113. Doris Kearns Goodwin, *No Ordinary Time, Franklin and Eleanor Roosevelt: The Home Front on World War II* (New York: Simon & Schuster, 1994), 10.

114. Churchill and Halsey quoted in ibid., 457, 464.

115. Reina Pennington, *Wings, Women, and War: Soviet Airwomen in World War II Combat* (Lawrence: University Press of Kansas, 2001), 1–3.

116. Kazimiera J. Cottam, "Soviet Women Soldiers in World War II: Three Biographical Sketches," *Minerva* (Fall–Winter 2000): 19–25.

117. Pennington, *Wings, Women, and War*, 90–94.

118. Cottam, "Soviet Women Soldiers in World War II," 23, 25.

119. Anne Commire, ed., *Women in World History* (Detroit: Yorkin, 2001), 11:721–24.

120. Israel Gutman, ed., *Encyclopedia of the Holocaust* (New York: MacMillan, 1990), 1059–60.

121. Albert Axell, *Russia's Heroes* (London: Constable, 2001), 107–10.

122. George and Anne Forty, *Women War Heroines* (London: Arms and Armour, 1997), 163–64.

123. Gutman, ed., *Encyclopedia of the Holocaust*, 495–96. See also Joan Campion, *In the Lion's Mouth: Gisi Fleischmann and the Jewish Fight for Survival* (Lanham, MD: University Press of America, 1987).

124. K. Jean Cottam, "Yelena Fedorovna Kolesova: Woman Hero of the Soviet Union," *Minerva* (Summer 1991): 70–71.

125. Ibid., 70–72.

126. George and Anne Forty, *Women War Heroines*, 152–53; de Pauw, *Battle Cries and Lullabies*, 237.

127. Atkin, *The French at War*, 83.

128. Peter Eisner, *The Freedom Line* (New York: HarperCollins, 2004), 301–10; Saywell, *Women in War*, 314.

129. Hitler quoted in Toland, *Adolf Hitler*, 876.

130. Shaaron Cosner and Victoria Cosner, *Women Under the Third Reich: A Biographical Dictionary* (Westport, CT: Greenwood Press, 1998), 125–29.

131. Robert G. Kaufman, *Arms Control During the Pre-Nuclear Era* (New York: Columbia University Press, 1990), 190; Paul Kennedy, *The Rise and Fall of the Great Powers* (New York: Random House, 1987), 352. Göring quoted in Murray, *Strategy for Defeat*, 103.

132. McCarthy and Syron, *Panzerkrieg*, 38–39.

133. Dear, *Oxford Companion*, 1063; Masanobu Tsuji, *Singapore: The Japanese Version* (New York: St. Martin's Press, 1960), 336.

134. Dear, *Oxford Companion*, 1063; Masanobu, *Singapore*, 336.

135. Yergin, *The Prize*, 371.

136. Matthew Cooper, *The German Air Force*, 1933–1945 (London: Jane's, 1981), 270.

137. Yergin, *The Prize*, 347, 361, 366.

138. Guy Hartcup, *The Effects of Science on the Second World War* (New York: Palgrave, 2000), 14–15; Volkman, *Science Goes to War*, 171. See also Leslie E. Simon, *German Research in World War II* (New York: Wiley, 1947).

139. Timothy Mulligan, "The German Navy Evaluates Its Cryptographic Security, October 1941," *Military Affairs* (April 1985): 75.

140. Hartcup, *Effects of Science on the Second World War*, 89; Mulligan, 75–77.

141. Toland, *Rising Sun*, 478.

142. Robert B. Edgerton, *Warriors of the Rising Sun* (New York: Norton, 1997), 294.

143. Louis Morton, *The War in the Pacific—Strategy and Command: The First Two Years* (Washington D.C.: U.S. Army Center of Military History, 2000), 474–75.

CHAPTER 6: PURSUING THE WAR

1. Loyd E. Lee, "We Have Just Begun to Write," *Diplomatic History* (Summer 2001): 367–68.

2. Winston Churchill, *The Hinge of Fate* (New York: Bantam Books, 1974), 80.

3. Winston Churchill, *The Gathering Storm* (New York: Bantam Books, 1974), 4.

4. Gordon Wright, *Ordeal of Total War, 1939–1945* (New York: Harper & Row, 1968), 68.

5. Frank McAdams, *The American War Film* (Westport, CT: Prager, 2002), 47.

6. Russell E. Shain, *An Analysis of Motion Pictures About War*

Released by the American Film Industry, 1930–1976 (New York: Arno Press, 1976), 358–59; Susan Hayward, *French National Cinema* (London: Routledge Press, 1993), 128–30.

7. Between the First and Second World Wars, filmmakers and filmgoers were not eager to cast international hostility in a favorable light. War movies were few and far between. The handful produced usually emphasized the dehumanizing aspects of total war, such as *All Quiet on the Western Front* (UK, 1930), *Grand Illusion* (France, 1938), and *Gone with the Wind* (U.S., 1939).

8. Frederick W. Ott, *The Great German Films* (Secaucus, NJ: Citadel Press, 1986), 297.

9. Ibid., 299.

10. For further detail of German cinema through the ages, see Anton Kaes, *From "Hitler" to "Heimat": The Return of History as Film* (Cambridge, MA: Harvard University Press, 1989); Michael Struebel, ed., *Film und Krieg* (Opladen, Germany: Leske und Budrich, 2002). The story of German-American fights over film rights appears in Ott, *The Great German Films*, 296–97.

11. For details on the film's creation, see Franciszek Palowski, *The Making of Schindler's List* (Secaucus, NJ: Carol Publishing, 1998).

12. Jonathan Rosenbaum, *Movies as Politics* (Berkeley and Los Angeles: University of California Press, 1997), 101.

13. For censorship on *Schindler's List* and other films, see Dawn B. Sova, *Forbidden Films* (New York: Facts on File, 2001), 265–66.

14. See also Emmet Early, *The War Veteran in Film* (Jefferson, NC: McFarland, 2003).

15. Robert Brent Toplin, *History by Hollywood* (Urbana: University of Illinois Press, 1996), 160, 169.

16. Ibid., 156–60.

17. Paul Fussell, "Patton," in *Past Imperfect: History According to the Movies*, ed. Mark C. Carnes (New York: Henry Holt, 1995), 244–45; Toplin, *History by Hollywood*, 170.

18. Akira Iriye, "Tora! Tora! Tora!" in Fussell, *Past Imperfect*, 229.

19. Roger Manvell, *Films and the Second World War* (New York: Barnes, 1974), 333–36; Shain, *An Analysis of Motion Pictures*, 354–55.

20. Lawrence H. Suid, *Guts & Glory: The Making of the American Military Image in Film* (Lexington: University Press of Kentucky, 2002), 631–35.

21. McAdams, *The American War Film*, 266. See also Linda Sunshine, ed., *Saving Private Ryan* (New York: Newmarket Press, 1998).

22. Marek Haltof, *Polish National Cinema* (New York: Berghan Books, 2002), 83–85.

23. Eisenhower's view of *The Story of G.I. Joe* in Brock Garland, *War Movies* (New York: Facts on File, 1987), 188.

24. Carole Cavanaugh, "A Working Ideology for Hiroshima: Imamura Shohei's Black Rain," in *Word and Image in Japanese Cinema*, ed. Dennis Washburn and Carole Cavanaugh (New York: Cambridge University Press, 2001), 250–64. Depiction of confiscated images of atomic blast from Kyoko Hirano, *Mr. Smith Goes to Tokyo: Japanese Cinema Under the American Occupation, 1945–1952* (Washington D.C.: Smithsonian Institute, 1992), 59–66.

25. Phillip Knightly, *The First Casualty* (London: Quartet Books, 1982), 256–58; David McCullough, *Truman* (New York: Simon & Schuster, 1992), 418.

26. Hitler quoted in Albert Speer, *Inside the Third Reich* (New York: Bonanza Books, 1982), 96.

27. Peter Padfield, *Himmler* (London: Macmillan, 1990), 170–74; Bernd Wegner, *The Waffen SS: Organization, Ideology and Function* (Oxford: Basil Blackwood, 1990), 276–77.

28. Hitler quoted in Speer, *Inside the Third Reich*, 94.

29. David Smurthwaite, *The Pacific War Atlas, 1941–1945* (New York: Facts on File, 1995), 24–25.

30. November 27, 1941 War Department communiqué from Gen.

Walter Short's Papers, Hoover Institute Archives, Stanford University.

31. Warnings of attacks on Guam and Philippines came from several U.S. War Department sources, principally the November 24, 1941, message from Assistant Chief of Naval Operations Rear Adm. Royal Ingersoll (National Archives Record Group 80, PEARL HARBOR Liaison Office, Modern Military Records Branch, Archives II). Atlanta Constitution writer Jack Tarver quoted in Gordon W. Prange, *At Dawn We Slept* (New York: McGraw-Hill, 1981), 694–95. Several books and articles contend FDR purposely lured the United States into war with Japan, few of which offer consistent or convincing arguments. Chief among these are Charles A. Beard, *President Roosevelt and the Coming of the War, 1941* (New Haven, CT: Yale University Press, 1948); Robert B. Stinnett, *Day of Deceit: The Truth about FDR and Pearl Harbor* (New York: Free Press, 2000); Vice Adm. Homer N. Wallin, *Pearl Harbor* (Washington D.C.: Naval History Division, U.S. Government Printing Office, 1968).

32. See Talbot Charles Imlay, "A Reassessment of Anglo-French Strategy During the Phony War, 1939–1940," *The English Historical Review* (April 2004): 359, 369; Vivian Rowe, *The Great Wall of France* (New York: Putnam, 1961).

33. William Carr, *Poland to Pearl Harbor* (Baltimore: Edward Arnold, 1985), 67.

34. William J. Fanning Jr., "The Origin of the Term 'Blitzkrieg': Another View," *Journal of Military History* (April 1997): 283–302.

35. Jeffrey Ethell and Alfred Price, *World War II Fighting Jets* (Annapolis, MD: Naval Institute Press, 1994), 9–13.

36. Robert Jackson, *Fighter: The Story of Air Combat, 1936–1945* (New York: St. Martin's Press, 1979), 147–57; Williamson Murray, *Strategy for Defeat: The Luftwaffe, 1933–1945* (Maxwell, AL: Air University Press, 1983), 252–53. The four jets that

flew in operations were the Me-262, He-162, Arado 234, and British Gloster Meteor, which was employed mostly as a V-1 interceptor; see Ethell and Price, *World War II Fighting Jets*, 204.

37. Hitler quoted in Speer, *Inside the Third Reich*, 368.

38. Winston S. Churchill, *Triumph and Tragedy* (New York: Bantam Books, 1953), 42–45; Alfred W. Crosby, *Throwing Fire: Projectile Technology Through History* (New York: Cambridge University Press, 2002), 163–65; Michael J. Neufeld, *The Rocket and the Reich: Peenemünde and the Coming of the Ballistic Missile Era* (New York: Free Press, 1995), 273–74.

39. Neufeld, *The Rocket and the Reich*, 274; Speer, *Inside the Third Reich*, 355–56.

40. The accepted estimate for Jewish victims is 6 million, although the acclaimed authority on the matter, Raul Hilberg, estimates the number to be closer to 5.1 million. See Hilberg, *The Destruction of the European Jews* (New York: Holmes & Meier, 1985).

41. Richard C. Lukas, "The Polish Experience During the Holocaust," in *A Mosaic of Victims: Non-Jews Persecuted and Murdered by the Nazis*, ed. Michael Berenbaum (New York: New York University Press, 1990), 88. Edward T. Linenthal, *Preserving Memory* (New York: Viking, 1995), 240; Wolfgang Sofsky, *The Order of Terror: The Concentration Camp* (Princeton, NJ: Princeton University Press, 1997), 119–21.

42. See Wolfgang Benz, *The Holocaust* (New York: Columbia University Press, 1999); Bodo von Borries, "The Third Reich in German History Textbooks Since 1945," *Journal of Contemporary History* (January 2003); Noam Lupu, "Memory Vanished, Absent, and Confined: The Countermemorial Project in 1980's and 1990's Germany," *History and Memory* (Fall–Winter 2003).

43. For a detailed chronology of Japan's switch from aggressive defense to capitulation, see Herbert Feis, *Japan Subdued: The Atomic Bomb and the End of the War in the Pacific* (Princeton, NJ:

Princeton University Press, 1961). For a balanced historiography of the use of the atomic devices, both for and against, see J. Samuel Walker, *Prompt and Utter Destruction: Truman and the Use of Atomic Bombs Against Japan* (Chapel Hill: University of North Carolina Press, 1997).

44. Robert P. Newman, *Truman and the Hiroshima Cult* (East Lansing: Michigan State University Press, 1995), 2–7; John Toland, *The Rising Sun* (New York: Random House, 1970), 830; Gerald Astor, *Operation Iceberg* (New York: Dell, 1995), 508.

45. Michael Hogan, ed., *Hiroshima in History and Memory* (New York: Cambridge University Press, 1996), 60. War Minister Anami quoted in Robert James Maddox, *Weapons for Victory: The Hiroshima Decision Fifty Years Later* (Columbia: University of Missouri Press, 1995), 148.

46. Richard B. Frank, *Downfall: The End of the Imperial Japanese Empire* (New York: Random House, 1999), 316–20. Several major works contend the atomic bombs were unnecessary for the defeat of Japan. Most argue a Japanese surrender was imminent. Others hypothesize an invasion of the main islands would have been much less costly than projected. See Gar Alperovitz, *The Decision to Use the Atomic Bomb and the Architecture of an American Myth* (New York: Knopf, 1995); Kai Bird and Lawrence Lifschultz, eds., *Hiroshima's Shadow: Writings on the Denial of History and the Smithsonian Controversy* (Stony Creek, CT: The Pamphleteer's Press, 1998); Robert Jay Lifton and Greg Mitchell, *Hiroshima in America: Fifty Years of Denial* (New York: Putnam, 1995).

47. Alan J. Levine, *The Pacific War: Japan Versus the Allies* (Westport, CT: Praeger, 1995), 166.

48. Mark A. Stoler, "The Second World War in U.S. History and Memory," *Diplomatic History* (Summer 2001): 389–92. Truman quoted in McCullough, *Truman*, 458.

49. Patton quoted in Martin Blumenson, *The Patton Papers, 1940–1945* (Boston: Houghton Mifflin, 1957) 698.

50. Walter LeFeber, *America, Russia, and the Cold War, 1945–1971* (New York: Wiley, 1972), 1–2. Stalin quoted in McCullough, *Truman*, 445.

51. A. W. DePorte, *Europe Between the Superpowers* (New Haven, CT: Yale University Press, 1979), 97; Donald E. Shepardson, "The Fall of Berlin and the Rise of a Myth," *Journal of Military History* (January 1998): 139–41.

52. See also John T. Bookman and Stephen T. Powers, *The March to Victory* (Niwot: University Press of Colorado, 1994); Stephen T. Powers, "World War II Battlefields and Museums," in *World War II in Europe, Africa, and the Americas, with General Sources*, ed. Loyd E. Lee (Westport, CT: Greenwood Press, 1997); Chuck Thompson, *The 25 Best World War Two Sites: European Theater* (San Francisco: Greenline Publications, 2004); Chuck Thompson, *The 25 Best World War Two Sites: Pacific Theater* (San Francisco: Greenline Publications, 2002); www.warmuseums.nl; www.afterthebattle.com.

BIBLIOGRAPHY

NEWSPAPERS

Century Sentinel

Des Moines Register

Die Zeit

London Times

New York Times

Omaha World Herald

Pravda

Stars and Stripes

Yank

PERIODICALS

American Journal of Economics and
  Sociology

Atlantic Monthly

Cultures

Current History

Diplomatic History

The Economist

English Historical Review

German History

History and Memory

Journal of Asian History

Journal of Asian Studies

Journal of Contemporary History

Journal of Economic History

Journal of Military History

Journal of Modern History

Minerva

Modern Asian Studies

The Nation (UK)

Der Spiegel

Time (US)

Twentieth-Century China

War and Society

War in History

BOOKS

Adamthwaite, Anthony P. *The Making of the Second World War.* London: Allen & Unwin, 1977.

Allen, Louis. Burma: *The Longest War, 1941–1945.* London: Dent & Sons, 1984.

Ambrose, Stephen E. *The Supreme Commander.* Garden City, NY: Doubleday, 1970.

Ancell, R. Manning. *The Biographical Dictionary of World War II Generals and Flag Officers: The U.S. Armed Forces.* Westport, CT: Greenwood Press, 1996.

Armstrong, John A., ed. *Soviet Partisans in World War II.* Madison: University of Wisconsin Press, 1964.

Arnold, Ben. *Music and War: A Research and Information Guide.* New York: Garland, 1993

Astor, Gerald. *Operation Iceberg.* New York: Dell, 1995.

Atkin, Nicholas. *The French at War, 1934–1944.* London: Longman, 2001.

Atkinson, Rick. *An Army at Dawn: The War in North Africa, 1942–1943.* New York: Henry Holt and Co., 2002.

Axell, Albert. *Marshal Zhukov: The Man Who Beat Hitler.* London: Pearson Longman, 2003.

———. *Russia's Heroes.* London: Constable, 2001.

Bacon, Edwin. *The Gulag at War.* New York: New York University Press, 1994.

Bailey, Ronald H. *Prisoners of War.* Chicago: Time Life Books, 1981.

Barnett, Corelli, ed. *Hitler's Generals.* New York: Grove Weidenfeld, 1989.

Barua, Pradeep. *Gentlemen of the Raj: The Indian Officer Corps, 1817–1949.* Westport, CT: Praeger, 2003.

Bauer, Yeshuda. *The Holocaust in Historical Perspective.* Seattle: University of Washington Press, 1978.

Baumont, Maurice. *The Origins of the Second World War.* Translated by Simone De Couvreur Ferguson. New Haven, CT: Yale University Press, 1978.

Beck, Earl R. *Under the Bombs: The German Home Front, 1942–1943.* Lexington: University Press of Kentucky, 1986.

Beevor, Anthony. *The Fall of Berlin, 1945.* New York: Viking, 2002.

———. Stalingrad. New York: Viking, 1998.

Beidler, Philip. *The Good War's Greatest Hits: World War II and American Remembering.* Athens: University of Georgia Press, 1998.

Benz, Wolfgang. *The Holocaust.* New York: Columbia University Press, 1999.

Berenbaum, Michael, ed. *A Mosaic of Victims: Non-Jews Persecuted and Murdered by the Nazis.* New York: New York University Press, 1990.

Bergmeier, Horst J. P., and Rainer E. Lotz. *Hitler's Airwaves.* New Haven, CT: Yale University Press, 1997.

Bialer, Seweryn, ed. *Stalin and His Generals.* New York: Pegasus, 1969.

Biennial Reports of the Chief of Staff of the United States Army to the Secretary of War, 1 July 1939–30 June 1945. Washington D.C.: U.S. Army Center of Military History, 1996.

Blair, Clay. *Hitler's U-Boat War: The Hunters, 1939–1942.* New York: Random House, 1996.

Blumenson, Martin. *The Patton Papers, 1940–1945.* Boston: Houghton Mifflin, 1957.

Bookman, John T., and Stephen T. Powers. *The March to Victory.* Niwot: University Press of Colorado, 1994.

Bosworth, R. J. B. *Mussolini.* London: Arnold, 2002.

Boyce, Robert, and Esmonde M. Robertson, eds. *Paths to War: New Essays on the Origins of the Second World War.* London: MacMillan Education, 1989.

Bracher, Karl Dietrich. *The German Dictatorship.* New York: Praeger, 1972.

Brackman, Roman. *The Secret File of Joseph Stalin*. London: Frank Cass, 2001.

Braybon, Gail, and Penny Summerfield. *Out of the Cage: Women's Experiences in Two World Wars*. London: Pandora, 1987.

Brendon, Piers. *The Dark Valley*. New York: Knopf, 2000.

Brophy, Leo P., Wyndham D. Miles, and Rexmond C. Cochrane. *The Chemical Warfare Service: From Laboratory to Field*. Washington D.C.: U.S. Army Office of the Chief of Military History, 1959.

Browne, Courtney. *Tojo: The Last Banzai*. New York: Holt, Rinehart and Winston, 1967.

Bullock, Alan. *Hitler and Stalin*. New York: Knopf, 1992.

————. *Hitler: A Study in Tyranny*. New York: Harper & Row, 1964.

Burleigh, Michael. *The Third Reich: A New History*. New York: Hill and Wang, 2000.

Burns, James M. *Roosevelt: The Soldier of Freedom*. New York: Harcourt Brace Jovanovich, 1970.

Buruma, Ian. T*he Wages of Guilt: Memories of War in Germany and Japan*. New York: Farrar Straus Giroux, 1994.

Butler, Ivan. *War Films*. London: Tantivy Press, 1974.

Calder, Angus. *The People's War: Britain, 1939–1945*. New York: Pantheon, 1969.

Calvocoressi, Peter, Guy Wint, and John Pritchard. *Total War: Causes and Courses of the Second World War*. New York: Pantheon Books, 1989.

Campbell, John, ed. *The Experience of World War II*. New York: Oxford University Press, 1989.

Campion, Joan. *In the Lion's Mouth: Gisi Fleischmann and the Jewish Fight for Survival*. Lanham, MD: University Press of America, 1987.

Carnes, Mark C., ed. *Past Imperfect: History According to the Movies*. New York: Henry Holt, 1995.

Carr, William. *Arms, Autarky and Aggression: A Study in German Foreign Policy, 1933–1939*. New York: Norton, 1972.

Carsten, F. L. *The Rise of Fascism*. Berkeley and Los Angeles: University of California Press, 1982.

Casey, Steven. *Cautious Crusade*. Oxford: Oxford University Press, 2001.

———. *Dissent into Cautious Crusade*. New York: Oxford University Press, 2001.

Chadwin, Mark L. *The Hawks of World War II*. Chapel Hill: University of North Carolina Press, 1968.

Chang, Iris. *The Rape of Nanking*. New York: Basic Books, 1997.

Chen, Chin-Hsin Yao, and Shih-Hsiang Chen. *The Flower Drum and Other Chinese Songs*. New York: John Day, 1943.

Churchill, Winston S. *The Gathering Storm*. New York: Bantam Books, 1948.

———. *The Hinge of Fate*. New York: Bantam Books, 1974.

———. *Their Finest Hour*. New York: Bantam Books, 1974.

———. *Triumph and Tragedy*. New York: Bantam Books, 1953.

Cleveland, Les. *Dark Laughter: War in Song and Popular Culture*. Westport, CT: Praeger, 1994.

Clifford, J. Garry, and Samuel R. Spencer Jr. *The First Peacetime Draft*. Lawrence: University Press of Kansas, 1986.

Cole, Wayne S. *America First: The Battle Against Intervention*. Madison: University of Wisconsin Press, 1953.

———. *Charles Lindbergh and the Battle Against American Intervention in World War II*. New York: Harcourt Brace Jovanovich, 1974.

Collier, Richard. *Duce*. New York: Viking, 1971.

Condon-Rall, Mary Ellen, and Albert E. Cowdrey. *The Medical Department: Medical Service in the War Against Japan*. Washington D.C.: U.S. Army Center of Military History, 1998.

Conquest, Robert. *Stalin and the Kirov Murder*. New York: Oxford University Press, 1989.

Cooper, Matthew. *The German Air Force, 1933–1945*. London: Jane's, 1981.

Cooter, Roger, and John Pickstone, eds. *Medicine in the 20th Century*. Amsteldijk, Holland: Harwood, 2000.

Corni, Gustavo, and Horst Gies. *Brot, Butter, Kanonen: Die Ernährungswirtschaft in Deutschland unter der Diktatur Hitlers*. Berlin: Akadamie Verlag, 1997.

Corum, James S. *The Luftwaffe: Creating the Operational Air War, 1918–1940*. Lawrence: University Press of Kansas, 1997.

Cosner, Sharon, and Victoria Cosner. *Women Under the Third Reich: A Biographical Dictionary*. Westport, CT: Greenwood Press, 1998.

Craig, William. *Enemy at the Gates: The Battle for Stalingrad*. New York: E. P. Dutton, 1973.

Crosby, Alfred W. *Throwing Fire: Projectile Technology Through History*. New York: Cambridge University Press, 2002.

Crozier, Andrew J. *The Causes of the Second World War*. Oxford: Blackwell, 1997.

D'Este, Carlo. *Eisenhower: A Soldier's Life*. New York: Henry Holt, 2002.

———. *Patton: A Genius for War*. New York: HarperCollins, 1997.

Davies, John P., Jr. *Dragon by the Tail*. New York: Norton, 1972.

Davies, Norm. *Heart of Europe: A Short History of Poland*. Oxford: Oxford University Press, 1986.

Daws, Gavan. *Prisoners of the Japanese: POW's of World War II in the Pacific*. New York: William and Morrow, 1994.

Dawson, Raymond H. *The Decision to Aid Russia, 1941*. Chapel Hill: University of North Carolina Press, 1959.

Dear, I. C. B., ed. *The Oxford Companion to World War II*. Oxford: Oxford University Press, 1995.

DePorte, A. W. *Europe Between the Superpowers*. New Haven, CT: Yale University Press, 1979.

Deutscher, Isaac. *Stalin: A Political Biography*. New York: Vintage Books, 1960.

Djilas, Milovan. *Wartime*. New York: Harcourt Brace, 1977.

Dod, Karl C. *The Corps of Engineers: The War Against Japan*. Washington D.C.: U.S. Army Office of Military History, 1966.

Doherty, Thomas. *Projections of War: Hollywood, American Culture, and World War II*. New York: Columbia University Press, 1993.

Dower, John W. *War Without Mercy: Race and Power in the Pacific War*. New York: Pantheon Books, 1986.

Dunnigan, James F., and Albert A. Nofi. *Dirty Little Secrets of World War II*. New York: William Morrow and Co., 1994.

Duus, Peter, Raymond H. Myers, and Mark R. Peattie, eds. *The Japanese Informal Empire in China, 1895–1937*. Princeton, NJ: Princeton University Press, 1989.

Early, Emmet. *The War Veteran in Film*. Jefferson, NC: McFarland and Co., 2003.

Edgerton, Robert B. *Warriors of the Rising Sun*. New York: Norton, 1997.

Eisenhower, John S. D. *The Bitter Woods*. New York: Putnam, 1969.

Eller, Cynthia. *Conscientious Objectors and the Second World War*. New York: Praeger, 1991.

Ellis, John. *World War II: A Statistical Analysis*. New York: Facts on File, 1993.

Erickson, John. *The Soviet High Command: A Military-Political History, 1918–1941*. New York: St. Martin's Press, 1962.

Erickson, John, and David Dilks, eds. *Barbarossa*. Edinburgh: Edinburgh University Press, 1994.

Ethell, Jeffrey, and Alfred Price. *World War II Fighting Jets*. Annapolis, MD: Naval Institute Press, 1994.

Eubank, Keith. *Summit at Teheran*. New York: William Murrow, 1985.

———, ed. *World War II: Roots and Causes*. Lexington, MA: D. C. Heath, 1992.

Ewen, David. *All the Years of American Popular Music*. Englewood Cliffs, NJ: Prentice-Hall, 1977.

Farrell, Nicholas. *Mussolini: A New Life*. London: Weidenfeld and Nicolson, 2003.

Fay, Laurel E. *Shostakovich, A Life*. Oxford: Oxford University Press, 2000.

Feis, Herbert. *Japan Subdued: The Atomic Bomb and the End of the War in the Pacific*. Princeton, NJ: Princeton University Press, 1961.

Fenby, Jonathan. *Chiang Kai-Shek*. New York: Carroll and Graf, 2003.

Fest, Joachim. *Hitler*. New York: Harcourt Brace, 1973.

Forty, George, and Anne Forty. *Women War Heroines*. London: Arms and Armour, 1997.

Framer, Sarah. *Martyred Village*. Berkeley and Los Angeles: University of California Press, 1999.

Frank, Richard B. *Downfall: The End of the Imperial Japanese Empire*. New York: Random House, 1999.

———. *Guadalcanal*. New York: Random House, 1990.

Fraser, David. *Knight's Cross*. New York: HarperCollins, 1993.

Frazier, Heather T., and John O'Sullivan. *"We Have Just Begun to Not Fight": An Oral History of Conscientious Objectors in Civilian Public Service During World War II*. New York: Twayne Publishers, 1996.

Freeman, Roger A. *Mustang at War*. Garden City, NY: Doubleday, 1974.

Friedman, Meyer, and Gerald W. Friedland. *Medicine's Ten Greatest Discoveries*. New Haven, CT: Yale University Press, 1998.

Fritz, Stephen G. *Frontsoldaten: The German Soldier in World War II*. Lexington: University Press of Kentucky, 1995.

Garland, Brock. *War Movies*. New York: Facts on File, 1987.

Gilbert, Martin. *The Second World War: A Complete History*. New York: Henry Holt, 1989.

———. *Winston S. Churchill: Finest Hour, 1939–1941*. Boston: Houghton Mifflin, 1983.

Glantz, David. *Stumbling Colossus: The Red Army on the Eve of the World War*. Lawrence: University Press of Kansas, 1998.

Glantz, David M., and Harold S. Orenstein, eds. *The Battle for Kursk 1943: The Soviet General Staff Study*. London: Frank Cass, 1999.

Glantz, David M., and Jonathan M. House. *The Battle of Kursk*. Lawrence: University Press of Kansas, 1999.

Goldstein, Erik. *The First World War Peace Settlements, 1919–1925*. London: Longman, 2002.

———, and John Maurer, eds. *The Washington Conference, 1921–1922*. Essex, UK: Frank Cass, 1994.

Goodhart, Philip. *Fifty Ships That Saved the World*. Garden City, NY: Doubleday, 1965.

Goodwin, Doris Kearns. *No Ordinary Time, Franklin and Eleanor Roosevelt: The Home Front on World War II*. New York: Simon & Schuster, 1994.

Goulding, Daniel J., ed. *Post New Wave Cinema in the Soviet Union and Eastern Europe*. Bloomington: University of Indiana Press, 1989.

Grunberger, Richard. *A Social History of the Third Reich*. London: Weidenfeld and Nicolson, 1971.

Gunston, Bill. *Bombers of World War II*. New York: Arco, 1980.

Gutman, Israel, ed. *Encyclopedia of the Holocaust*. New York: MacMillan, 1990.

Haestrup, Jorgen. *European Resistance Movements, 1939–1945*. Westport, CT: Meckler, 1981.

Hall, Christopher. *Britain, America, and Arms Control, 1921–1937*. London: MacMillan, 1987.

Haltof, Marek. *Polish National Cinema*. New York: Berghan Books, 2002.

Hane, Mikiso. *Modern Japan: A Historical Survey*. Boulder, CO: Westview Press, 1992.

Harrison, Gordon A. *Cross-Channel Attack*. Washington D.C.: U.S. Army Office of Military History, 1951.

Hartcup, Guy. *The Effects of Science on the Second World War*. New York: Palgrave, 2000.

Hayes, Nick, and Jeff Hill. *"Millions Like Us?": British Culture in the Second World War*. Liverpool: Liverpool University Press, 1999.

Hayward, Susan. *French National Cinema*. London: Routledge Press, 1993.

Heiber, Helmut. *Goebbels*. New York: Hawthorn Books, 1972.

Heinrichs, Waldo. *Threshold of War: Franklin D. Roosevelt and American Entry into World War II*. New York: Oxford University Press, 1988.

Heller, Mikhail, and Aleksandr M. Nekrich. *Utopia in Power: The History of the Soviet Union from 1917 to the Present*. New York: Summit Books, 1986.

Hilberg, Raul. *The Destruction of the European Jews*. New York: Holmes & Meier, 1985.

Hirano, Kyoko. *Mr. Smith Goes to Tokyo: Japanese Cinema Under the American Occupation, 1945–1952*. Washington D.C.: Smithsonian Institute, 1992.

Hitler, Adolf. *Mein Kampf*. London: Hurst and Blackett, 1942.

Hogan, Michael, ed. *Hiroshima in History and Memory*. New York: Cambridge University Press, 1996.

Hogg, Ian V. *Encyclopedia of Infantry Weapons of World War II*. New York: Thomas Y. Crowell, 1977.

Holloway, David. *Stalin and the Bomb*. New Haven, CT: Yale University Press, 1994.

Hondros, John L. *Occupation and Resistance: The Greek Agony, 1941–1944*. New York: Pella, 1983.

Hough, Richard, and Denis Richards. *The Battle of Britain*. New York: Norton, 1989.

Hoyt, Edwin P. *Japan's War: The Great Pacific Conflict*. New York: McGraw-Hill, 1986.

———. *Warlord: Tojo Against the World*. Lanham, MD: Scarborough House, 1993.

Hsi-sheng, Ch'I. *Nationalist China at War*. Ann Arbor: University of Michigan Press, 1982.

Hutchings, Graham. *Modern China: A Guide to a Century of Change*. Cambridge, MA: Harvard University Press, 2001.

Ienaga, Saburo. *The Pacific War: World War II and the Japanese, 1931–1945*. New York: Pantheon Books, 1978.

Jackson, Robert. *Fighter: The Story of Air Combat, 1936–1945*. New York: St. Martin's Press, 1979.

Johnsen, Julia E., ed. *The Atomic Bomb*. New York: H. W. Wilson, 1946.

Johnson, Bruce F. *Japanese Food Management in World War II*. Stanford, CA: Stanford University Press, 1953.

Kaes, Anton. *From "Hitler" to "Heimat": The Return of History as Film*. Cambridge, MA: Harvard University Press, 1989.

Kaiser, David E. *Economic Diplomacy and the Origins of the Second World War: Germany, Britain, France, and Eastern Europe, 1930–1939*. Princeton, NJ: Princeton University Press, 1980.

Kaufman, Robert G. *Arms Control During the Pre-Nuclear Era*. New York: Columbia University Press, 1990.

Keegan, John. *The Battle for History*. New York: Vintage Books, 1995.

———. *A History of Warfare*. New York: Knopf, 1994.

Kennedy, Paul. *The Rise and Fall of the Great Powers*. New York: Random House, 1987.

Kershaw, Ian. *Hitler*. London: Longman, 1992.

———. *Hitler 1936–1945: Nemesis*. New York: Norton, 2000.

Kimball, Warren F. *Forged in War: Roosevelt, Churchill, and the Second World War*. New York: William & Morrow, 1997.

———. *The Most Unsordid Act: Lend-Lease, 1939–1941*. Baltimore, MD: Johns Hopkins University Press, 1969.

Kitchen, Martin. *Europe Between the Wars: A Political History*. London: Longman, 1988.

Knightly, Phillip. *The First Casualty*. London: Quartet Books, 1982.

Koenker, Diane P., William G. Rosenberg, and Ronald Grigor Suny, eds. *Party, State, and Society in the Russian Civil War*. Bloomington: Indiana University Press, 1989.

Koonz, Claudia. *Mothers in the Fatherland: Women, the Family, and Nazi Politics*. New York: St. Martin's Press, 1987.

Krivosheev, G. F., ed. *Soviet Casualties and Combat Losses in the Twentieth Century*. London: Greenhill, 1997.

Lacouture, Jean. *De Gaulle: the Rebel, 1890–1944*. New York: Norton, 1990.

Lake, David A., and Donald Rothschild, eds. *The International Spread of Ethnic Conflict*. Princeton, NJ: Princeton University Press, 1998.

Lamb, Margaret, and Nicolas Tarling. *From Versailles to Pearl Harbor*. New York: Palgrave, 2001.

Lamb, Richard. *The Drift to War: 1922–1939*. New York: St. Martin's Press, 1989.

Langsam, Walter Consuelo. *Historic Documents of World War II*. Princeton, NJ: Van Nostrand, 1958.

Laqueur, Walter. *Stalin: The Glasnost Revelations*. New York: Scribner, 1990.

Lash, Joseph P. *Roosevelt and Churchill, 1939–1941*. New York: Norton, 1976.

Lee, Loyd E., ed. *World War II in Europe, Africa, and the Americas, with General Sources*. Westport, CT: Greenwood Press, 1997.

Lee, Marshall, and Wolfgang Michalka. *German Foreign Policy, 1917–1933*. New York: St. Martin's Press, 1987.

Lee, Stephen J. *European Dictatorships, 1918–1945*. London: Routledge, 2000.

Levine, Alan J. *The Pacific War: Japan Versus the Allies*. Westport, CT: Praeger, 1995.

Le Vien, Jack, and John Lord. *Winston Churchill: The Valiant Years*. London: Bernard Geis, 1962.

Linderman, Gerald F. *The World Within War: America's Combat Experience in World War II.* New York: Free Press, 1997.

Linenthal, Edward T. *Preserving Memory.* New York: Viking, 1995.

Lucas, James. *War on the Eastern Front, 1941–1945.* New York: Bonanza Books, 1982.

Lukacs, John. *The Hitler of History.* New York: Knopf, 1997.

MacNalty, Arthur S., and W. Franklin Mellor, eds. *Medical Services in War.* London: HM Stationery Office, 1968.

Maddox, Robert James. *Weapons for Victory: The Hiroshima Decision Fifty Years Later.* Columbia: University of Missouri Press, 1995.

Manchster, William. *The Arms of Krupp.* Boston: Little, Brown, and Co., 1968.

Manvell, Roger. *Films and the Second World War.* New York: Barnes and Co., 1974.

Marshall, Jonathan. *To Have and Have Not: Southeast Asian Raw Materials and the Origins of the Pacific War.* Berkeley and Los Angeles: University of California Press, 1995.

Martel, Gordon, ed. *The Origins of the Second World War Reconsidered.* Boston: Allen & Unwin, 1986.

Masanobu, Tsuji. *Singapore: The Japanese Version.* New York: St. Martin's Press, 1960.

Matsusaka, Yoshihisa Tak. *The Making of Japanese Manchuria, 1904–1932.* Cambridge, MA: Harvard University Press, 2001.

Mawdsley, Evan. *The Russian Civil War.* Boston: Allen & Unwin, 1987.

McAdams, Frank. *The American War Film.* Westport, CT: Praeger, 2002.

McCarthy, Peter, and Mike Syron. *Panzerkrieg: The Rise and Fall of Hitler's Tank Divisions.* London: Constable, 2002.

McCollough, David. *Truman.* New York: Simon & Schuster, 1992.

McManus, John C. *The Deadly Brotherhood: The American Combat Soldier in World War II.* Novato, CA: Presidio Press, 1998.

McNeal, Robert H. *Stalin: Man and Ruler.* New York: New York University Press, 1988.

McNeill, William H. *America, Britain, and Russia: Their Cooperation and Conflict, 1941–1946.* New York: Johnson Reprint, 1970.

Medvedev, Roy. *Let History Judge: The Origins and Consequences of Stalinism.* New York: Columbia University Press, 1989.

Mellen, Joan. *The Waves of Genji's Poor: Japan Through Its Cinema.* New York: Pantheon, 1976.

von Mellenthin, F. W. *German Generals of World War II.* Norman: University of Oklahoma Press, 1956.

Mikesh, Robert C. *Japan's World War II Balloon Bomb Attacks on North America.* Washington D.C.: Smithsonian Institute Press, 1973.

Miller, David H. *The Peace Pact of Paris.* New York: Putnam, 1928.

Mommsen, Wolfgang J., and Lothar Kettenacker, eds. *The Fascist Challenge and the Policy of Appeasement.* London: Allen & Unwin, 1983.

Mommsen, Hans. *The Rise and Fall of the Weimar Republic.* Chapel Hill: University of North Carolina Press, 1996.

Morison, Samuel E. *The Two-Ocean War.* New York: Ballantine Books, 1963.

Morley, James W., ed. *The Final Confrontation: Japan's Negotiations with the United States, 1941.* New York: Columbia University Press, 1994.

Morton, Louis. *The War in the Pacific—Strategy and Command: The First Two Years.* Washington D.C.: U.S. Army Center of Military History, 2000.

Moscow, Warren. *Roosevelt and Willkie.* Englewood Cliffs, NJ: Prentice-Hall, 1968.

Mulay, James J. et al. *War Movies.* Evanston, IL: Cinebooks, 1989.

Murray, Williamson. *Strategy for Defeat: The Luftwaffe, 1933–1945.* Maxwell, AL: Air University Press, 1983.

Naimark, Norman M. *Fires of Hatred: Ethnic Cleansing in Twentieth-Century Europe*. Cambridge, MA: Harvard University Press, 2001.

Neary, Ian. *The State and Politics in Japan*. Cambridge, UK: Polity Press, 2002.

Neufeld, Michael J. *The Rocket and the Reich: Peenemünde and the Coming of the Ballistic Missile Era*. New York: Free Press, 1995.

Newman, Robert P. *Truman and the Hiroshima Cult*. East Lansing: Michigan State University Press, 1995.

Newton, Steven H. *Kursk: The German View*. Cambridge, MA: Da Capo Press, 2002.

Noel-Baker, Philip. *The First World Disarmament Conference, 1932–1933*. Oxford, UK: Pergamon, 1979.

Noggle, Anne. *A Dance with Death: Soviet Airwomen in World War II*. College Station: Texas A&M University Press, 1994.

Oliver, Robert T., and Eugene E. White, eds. *Selected Speeches from American History*. Boston, MA: Allyn & Bacon, 1966.

O'Neill, William L. *A Democracy at War*. New York: Free Press, 1993.

Orseyenko, Anton Antonov. *The Time of Stalin*. New York: Harper & Row, 1980.

Ott, Frederick W. *The Great German Films*. Secaucus, NJ: Citadel Press, 1986.

Overy, Richard. *The Inter-War Crisis, 1919–1939*. London: Longman, 1994.

———. *Russia's War*. New York: Penguin, 1997.

———. *Why the Allies Won*. New York: Norton, 1995.

Padfield, Peter. *Himmler*. London: MacMillan, 1990.

Palowski, Franciszek. *The Making of Schindler's List*. Secaucus, NJ: Carol Publishing, 1998.

Pao-Ch'en, Lee, ed. *Songs of Fighting China*. New York: Chinese News Service, 1944.

Parker, R. A. C. *Struggle for Survival: The History of the Second World War*. Oxford: Oxford University Press, 1989.

de Pauw, Linda Grant. *Battle Cries and Lullabies: Women in War from Prehistory to the Present.* Norman: University of Oklahoma Press, 1998.

Pearlman, Michael D. *Warmaking and American Democracy.* Lawrence: University Press of Kansas, 1999.

Pelz, Stephen. *Race to Pearl Harbor: The Failure of the Second London Naval Conference and the Onset of World War II.* Cambridge, MA: Harvard University Press, 1974.

Pennington, Reina. *Wings, Women, and War: Soviet Airwomen in World War II Combat.* Lawrence: University Press of Kansas, 2001.

Perret, Geoffrey. *Eisenhower.* New York: Random House, 1999.

Polmar, Norman, and Thomas B. Allen. *World War II: The Encyclopedia of the War Years, 1941–1945.* New York: Random House, 1996.

Potter, E. B. *Nimitz.* Annapolis, MD: Naval Institute Press, 1976.

Prange, Gordon W. *At Dawn We Slept.* New York: McGraw-Hill, 1981.

Price, Alfred. *The Luftwaffe Data Book.* Mechanicsburg, PA: Stackpole, 1997.

Radzinsky, Edvard. *Stalin.* New York: Doubleday, 1996.

Read, Anthony, and David Fisher. *The Deadly Embrace: Hitler, Stalin, and the Nazi-Soviet Pact, 1939–1941.* New York: Norton, 1988.

Rearick, Charles. *The French in Love and War.* New Haven, CT: Yale University Press, 1997.

Rees, David. *The Defeat of Japan.* Westport, CT: Praeger, 1997.

Reese, Roger R. *Stalin's Reluctant Soldiers.* Lawrence: University Press of Kansas, 1996.

Reuth, Ralf G. *Goebbels.* New York: Harcourt Brace, 1993.

Reynolds, David, Warren F. Kimball and A. O. Chubarian, eds. *Allies at War: The Soviet, American, and British Experience, 1939–1945.* New York: St. Martin's Press, 1994.

Rich, Norman. *Hitler's War Aims.* New York: Norton, 1973–74.

Richardson, Rosamond. *Stalin's Shadow*. New York: St. Martin's Press, 1993.

Richie, Donald. *A Hundred Years of Japanese Film*. Tokyo: Kondasha International, 2002.

Roberts, Geoffrey. *The Soviet Union and the Origins of the Second World War: Russo-German Relations and the Road to War, 1933–1941*. New York: St. Martin's Press, 1995.

Roberts, Walter R. *Tito, Mihailovic and the Allies, 1941–1945*. New Brunswick, NJ: Rutgers University Press, 1973.

Robertson, Terence. *Dieppe: The Shame and the Glory*. Boston: Little, Brown, and Co., 1962.

Rosenbaum, Jonathan. *Movies as Politics*. Berkeley and Los Angeles: University of California Press, 1997.

Ross, Steven T., ed. *U.S. War Plans, 1938–1945*. Boulder, CO: Lynne Rienner, 2002.

Ross, William F., and Charles F. Romanus. *The Quartermaster Corps: Operations in the War Against Germany*. Washington D.C.: U.S. Army Center of Military History, 2004.

Rothermund, Dietmar. *The Global Impact of the Great Depression, 1929–1939*. London: Routledge, 1996.

Rowe, Vivian. *The Great Wall of France*. New York: Putnam, 1961.

Ruppenthal, Roland, G. *Logistical Support of the Armies, Vol. 1*. Washington D.C.: U.S. Army Center of Military History, 1995.

Safire, William. *Lend Me Your Ears*. New York: Norton, 1992.

Salazar, Generoso P., Fernando R. Reyes, and Leonardo Q. Nuval. *Defense, Defeat, and Defiance: World War II in the Philippines*. Manila: Veterans Federation of the Philippines, 1993.

Salisbury, Harrison E. *The 900 Days*. New York: Avon, 1969.

Sanjek, Russell. *Pennies from Heaven: The American Popular Music Business in the Twentieth Century*. New York: Da Capo, 1996.

Satterfield, Archie. *The Home Front: An Oral History of the War Years in America: 1941–1945*. New York: PEI Books, 1981.

Saywell, Shelley. *Women in War*. New York: Viking, 1985.

Schoenbaum, David. *Hitler's Social Revolution: Class and Status in Nazi Germany, 1933–1939*. New York: Norton, 1980.

Schrijvers, Peter. *The Crash of Ruin: American Combat Soldiers in Europe During World War II*. New York: New York University Press, 1998.

Schwarz, Boris. *Music and Musical Life in Soviet Russia, 1917–1970*. London: Barrie & Jenkins, 1972.

de Senarclens, Pierre. *From Yalta to the Iron Curtain*. Oxford, UK: Berg, 1995.

Shain, Russell E. *An Analysis of Motion Pictures About War Released by the American Film Industry, 1930–1976*. New York: Arno Press, 1976.

Shirer, William L. *The Rise and Fall of the Third Reich*. New York: Fawcett Crest, 1988.

Short, Philip. *Mao: A Life*. New York: Henry Holt, 2000.

Simon, Leslie E. *German Research in World War II*. New York: Wiley, 1947.

Simpson, Elizabeth, ed. *The Spoils of War*. New York: Harry N. Abrams, 1997.

Skates, John R. *The Invasion of Japan*. Columbia: University of South Carolina Press, 1994.

Slaughter, Jane. *Women and the Italian Resistance, 1943–1945*. Denver, CO: Arden, 1997.

Smith, Bradley F. *The War's Long Shadow: The Second World War and Its Aftermath*. New York: Simon & Schuster, 1986.

Smith, Denis M. *Mussolini's Roman Empire*. New York: Viking, 1976.

Smith, Kathleen E. R. *God Bless America: Tin Pan Alley Goes to War*. Lexington: University of Kentucky Press, 2003.

Smurthwaite, David. *The Pacific War Atlas, 1941–1945*. New York: Facts on File, 1995.

Snyder, Louis L. *Historical Guide to World War II*. Westport, CT: Greenwood, 1982.

Sofsky, Wolfgang. *The Order of Terror: The Concentration Camp*. Princeton, NJ: Princeton University Press, 1997.

Sorge, Martin K. *The Other Price of Hitler's War: German Military and Civilian Losses Resulting from World War II*. New York: Greenwood Press, 1986.

Sontag, Raymond J. *A Broken World, 1919–1930*. New York: Harper & Row, 1972.

Sova, Dawn B. *Forbidden Films*. New York: Facts on File, 1997.

Spector, Ronald H. *The Eagle Against the Sun*. New York: Free Press, 1985.

Speer, Albert. *Inside the Third Reich*. New York: Bonanza Books, 1982.

Stein, George H., ed. *Hitler*. Englewood Cliffs, NJ: Prentice-Hall, 1968.

Strawson, John. *Hitler's Battles for Europe*. New York: Scribner, 1971.

Struebel, Michael, ed. *Film und Krieg*. Opladen, Germany: Leske und Budrich, 2002.

Suid, Lawrence H. *Guts & Glory: The Making of the American Military Image in Film*. Lexington: University Press of Kentucky, 2002.

Taylor, A. J. P. *The Origins of the Second World War*. New York: Atheneum, 1961.

Taylor, James, and Warren Shaw. *A Dictionary of the Third Reich*. London: Grafton, 1987.

Terkel, Studs. *"The Good War": An Oral History of World War Two*. New York: Pantheon Books, 1984.

Thompson, Chuck. *The 25 Best World War Two Sites: European Theater*. San Francisco: Greenline Publications, 2004.

———. *The 25 Best World War Two Sites: Pacific Theater*. San Francisco: Greenline Publications, 2002.

Thomson, Harry C., and Lida Mayo. *The Ordnance Department: Procurement and Supply*. Washington D.C.: U.S. Army Office of Military History, 1960.

Thurston, Robert W., and Bernd Bonwetsch, eds. *The People's War: Responses to World War II in the Soviet Union*. Chicago: University of Illinois Press, 2000.

Toland, John. *Adolf Hitler*. Garden City, NY: Doubleday, 1976.

———. *The Rising Sun*. New York: Random House, 1970.

Toplin, Robert Brent. *History by Hollywood*. Urbana: University of Illinois Press, 1996.

Trefousse, H. L. *Germany and American Neutrality*. New York: Octagon Books, 1969.

Vitukin, Igor, ed. *Soviet Generals Recall World War II*. New York: Sphinx Press, 1981.

Volkman, Ernest. *Science Goes to War*. New York: Wiley, 2002.

Walker, J. Samuel. *Prompt and Utter Destruction: Truman and the Use of Atomic Bombs Against Japan*. Chapel Hill: University of North Carolina Press, 1997.

Ward-Jackson, C. H., ed. *Airmen's Song Book*. London: William Blackwood & Sons, 1967.

Washburn, Dennis, and Carole Cavanaugh, eds. *Word and Image in Japanese Cinema*. New York: Cambridge University Press, 2001.

Webber, Eugene. *The Hollow Years: France in the 1930s*. New York: Norton, 1994.

Wegner, Bernd. *The Waffen SS: Organization, Ideology and Function*. Oxford, UK: Basil Blackwood, 1990.

Weigley, Russell F. *Eisenhower's Lieutenants*. Bloomington: Indiana University Press, 1990.

Weinberg L. Gerhard. *A World at Arms: A Global History of World War II*. New York: Cambridge University Press, 1994.

Welch, David. *The Third Reich: Politics and Propaganda*. London: Routledge, 1993.

Werth, Alexander. *Russia at War, 1941–1945*. New York: Carroll & Graf, 1964.

Westwood, J. N. *Russia Against Japan, 1904–1905*. New York: State University of New York Press, 1986.

Wetta, Frank J., and Stephen J. Curley. *Celluloid Wars*. New York: Greenwood Press, 1992.

Wheal, Elizabeth-Anne, Stephen Pope, and James Taylor. *Encyclopedia of the Second World War*. Edison, NJ: Castle Books, 1989.

Whiting, Charles. *A Bridge at Arnhem*. New York: Pinnacle Books, 1975.

Whitley, M. J. *Cruisers of World War II*. Annapolis, MD: Naval Institute Press, 1996.

———. *Destroyers of World War II*. Annapolis, MD: Naval Institute Press, 2000.

Wiltse, Charles M. *The Medical Department: Medical Service in the Mediterranean and Minor Theaters*. Washington D.C.: Department of the Army, 1965.

Wistrich, Robert S. *Who's Who in Nazi Germany*. London: Routledge, 1995.

Wright, Gordon. *The Ordeal of Total War, 1939–1945*. New York: Harper Torchbooks, 1968.

Yergin, Daniel. *The Prize: The Epic Quest for Oil, Money, and Power*. New York: Simon & Schuster, 1991.

Zabecki, David T., ed. *World War II in Europe: An Encyclopedia*. New York: Garland, 1999.

INDEX

U

V

W